FACES ON THE SIDEWALK

SCOTT TEAGUE

ISBN: 149109530X
ISBN 13: 9781491095300

Dedicated to my darling wife, Linda, the most godly person I have ever known. She has walked through life with me, loved me, supported me, and to this day has remained my very best friend.

FOREWORD

You probably cannot understand what I'm about to say unless you've been in my shoes: I believe that preaching on the streets is the highest calling.

The crowd gathers up close, all around me—the rich, the poor, the working class, the uneducated, even a few intellectuals, people of various races, religions, cultures, and world views—and as I look into their thirsty faces, I proclaim the gospel and offer them the Water of Life, who truly satisfies, all the while sensing and feeling the inexplicable presence, power, and pleasure of God. There is absolutely nothing like it!

Scott Teague

CONTENTS

PART THREE: OTHER COUNTRIES

INTRODUCTION

It has been an arduous task trying to compress my life into the pages of this book, and my attempt to share the experiences I have had on the sidewalks of New York City for nearly thirty years has been even more difficult, but I have endeavored to be accurate and factual.

What I have written has been based on years of jotting down quickly what had just transpired and then later describing events thoroughly in my journal. I have snapped pictures, made slides, and taken video for decades. Many conversations that have taken place are verbatim from footage I have saved, especially when I have had encounters with the New York Police Department. God is my witness that I have done my best not to embellish any incident but to tell it like it really was. I have toned down much of the filthy, vulgar language that is so prevalent on the streets, but in order to be realistic, I have retained some offensive words. Also, in the interest of brevity, only excerpts from the preaching are used, not the entire sermons. My prayer is that someone, after reading *Faces on the Sidewalk*, will step back and say, "What a mighty God we serve!"

Preaching on the streets is a forgotten method of spreading the gospel. In our high-tech world, it's been overlooked like tiny blue wild flowers in spring clover. In many people's minds, preaching on the streets is an outmoded means of disseminating the gospel. It is simply out of date, antiquated, obsolete like the Model T Ford; today, in the twenty-first century, we have modern technology with which to proclaim the good news!

So, why did I go to the streets? Did I want to preach the gospel, live, face to face, to devout Muslims? Where else was I going to do it if not on the streets? Did I want to look into the faces of hardened criminals, avowed atheists, hypnotized cult members, ethereal Buddhists, Jewish rabbis, Hindus, and non-church-oriented, self-centered secularists and share with them the claims of Christ? Where else was I going to do it if not on the streets?

There is, of course, mass communication—radio, TV, the Internet, and social media—with which millions can be quickly evangelized. But high-tech methods of communication are not nearly as personal as me looking into the faces of total strangers gathered all around me and sharing, heart to heart, the message of the cross. There is something New Testament about this approach that, I believe, can never be replaced. The gospel is meant to be delivered out of doors, smack dab in the middle of the people. Make no mistake about it!

"No sort of defense is needed for preaching out of doors; but it would need very potent arguments to prove that a man had done his duty who has never preached beyond the walls of his meeting-house. A defense is required rather for services within buildings than for worship outside of them."—Charles Spurgeon

PART ONE:
THE CARNIVAL MINISTRY

CHAPTER 1

LEAVING

As we backed out of my mother and dad's driveway, I saw my dad jump off the side porch and come crawling on his hands and knees and crying. My mother was standing over him with her hand on his shoulder as he slowly moved closer and closer to us. "Son, please don't take those kids up there. Please don't go. Listen to me, son. Don't go up there," he begged, moaning, his face drooping.

When I saw my folks pleading with us not to go to New York, my heart hurt and ached like never before. The day we left Mother and Daddy and drove away to New York City, with Dad on his knees and Mother with a Kleenex in her hand, is a scene indelibly written on my mind. But God had called me to New York. I knew it. He had spoken to me in numerous ways and had confirmed it in scripture. I had to go. I had no choice, really.

Mother, rather short, with a Dolly Parton figure, could not understand our leaving. Months before, when I was watching *All in the Family* with her, I hinted around that I felt the Lord pulling me to New York and that I would one day consider that home. "Scotty, you don't mean that," she said, almost scolding me.

"Yes, Mother, I do," I said, answering her softly. It was hard for Mother to accept that we were going "way up there to New York." She had been making homemade biscuits since she was old enough to stand on a chair and roll them out, and she loved having all of us around her table. We loved being there, too. That would change if we went up north, so I understood how she felt. I wondered if my mother remembered the night many, many years ago at the revival at Waller Church. The evangelist had asked for parents to come forward if they were willing for their children to become missionaries.

My mother, like so many other parents, went forward. I remember the incident. I must have been about eleven.

Dad, six feet two inches, was a John Wayne type—strong willed and independent. A gentle man with few words, he, like Mother, could make no sense out of us going to New York City. One time when I was relatively young, I said, "Dad, you don't really tell us you love us very often." Dad, nodding his head forward and looking over his glasses, said, "Son, I always figured that was understood."

Because his mother died when he was just a boy, Dad dropped out of school in the fifth grade and went to work. Even though he did not have much formal education, he could do anything. A welder by trade, he built our house with his own hands, every inch of it. Dad loved to hunt, was a natural leader, and was the life of the party around the campfire. The stories he told were unique, priceless, and unforgettable.

A month earlier, when I finally got up the nerve to tell Daddy myself that we really were moving to New York, I dropped by the house with great trepidation. As I drove up, I saw Dad sitting in his chair there in the den, looking out of the window. He saw me get out of the car and walk up the steps into the house. This was hard for me. Dad loved me, and I would not say that he was controlling, but he was the kind of man you just didn't go against.

"Daddy, I know you don't understand, but the Lord has called me to New York," I said firmly, but with my voice quivering. At first he sat there quietly with his lips shut, looking down. Mother had already been mentioning our leaving to him, I could tell. Then he said, shaking his head back and forth, "Scotty, God doesn't intend for you to 'purnish' yourself. Think of those kids. Good gracious alive, what do you mean taking Linda and those boys up there in that godforsaken place?"

I had thought much about taking my family up north. Stephen was twelve, and Stewart was seven. I certainly didn't want to take my sons to some housing project with gangs and drugs! Linda really didn't want to go to New York, either, but she was willing to go if I knew for certain that it was God's will. I had always felt my family was my main ministry. Still do. So, I knew in my own mind that I was going to take care of them.

Driving away from Mother and Daddy's a few days later, I didn't look in the mirror. It was just too painful. But I knew that I had somebody else to say good-bye to: my sister, Barbara Ann, "Babs," as I called her. She was working at the Fashion Tree, the dress shop on Benton Road that she and her husband, Marion, owned. With beautiful, thick, brown hair, showing a touch of gray, cut like Geraldine Ferraro, and with a vivacious personality and a huge smile, Babs was a perfect sister. If you wanted to get into trouble, just say something derogatory about Scotty, her "little brother"; she would call your hand quicker than a balloon popping. Babs understood we had to go to New York, but it wasn't easy on her, either. We were tight. Yes, I had to say good-bye to Babs.

Knowing we were coming by, she was waiting on us outside the shop. Driving up, I quickly got out of the car and hugged her. "Hey, Babs," I said, "pray for us. Love you. Tell Marion and the kids bye."

"I will. Be careful. Stay in touch. Love you," she said.

This time I glanced in my mirror as I pulled away and saw her walking with her head down back into the store. She had on a red dress. Leaving Bossier City, Louisiana, I was filled with mixed emotions. Conflicted, I was sad, happy, relieved, nervous, yet I was at peace. I was scared because I knew we were stepping out on sheer faith, but I also felt that I was doing precisely what the Lord had planned for me from the foundation of the world. So I had great anticipation for what lay ahead.

I thought about the many friends that we were leaving, friends like Mary and Richard Johnson, who had given us a going-away party that many other church friends and neighbors attended. I thought about them praying for us. I thought about Linda's sister Shirley and her husband Ronney and their kids, Ronda and Randall. We always had such fun with them eating hamburgers and swimming in their pool at their home near Houston in the "good ol' summertime."

There was one more person we had to say good-bye to—Linda's mother, Memee—and I surely wasn't looking forward to that.

As we drove across Arkansas toward Southaven, Mississippi, a suburb of Memphis, where Memee lived, I saw cotton fields that I knew I would miss. We always looked for that yellow crop duster, flying low over the Mississippi Delta, and there he was, spraying oh-so-close to the ground, and then, at the last second, pulling straight up into the air. I thought about how much I loved Dixie and what a different culture we were going into. But when the idea of preaching on the streets of New York came to mind, my heart raced. Sometimes I got so excited about New York that I could not sleep at night. I was always seeing those faces on the sidewalk.

Pulling up into Memee's driveway, I got out of the car, reluctantly. We were all going to spend the night, so it would be a while before this would be over. I shook hands with Ed, Linda's stepdad. Always cordial, he seemed to sympathize with us, as he smiled and invited us inside. The boys got their usual kisses from Memee, and Linda and I both hugged her mother; but Memee's hug to me was not much of a hug.

"Y'all come on in," she said. "You kids want a Coke?"

"Yes, ma'am!" they said with emphasis, as they began to play with Princess, our little cat.

Memee, a tall, attractive woman, had not had it easy in her life. Having gone through a divorce, she raised her two daughters, Shirley and Linda, by herself. She was very close to them, and they were to her. Memee had remarried and was happy with Ed, a fine gentleman. Her yard was immaculate with colorful flowers and trimmed shrubs, and she loved working in it. I knew that Memee was not pleased with our leaving, and she held it against me. As we talked that evening and even the next morning, Memee told me, straight out, with a frown on her face, "I'll not be coming to New York to see you."

It would have been such a relief if both of our parents had sent us on our way with their blessing, but that was not the case. I began to understand what Jesus meant when he said that a man's enemies

4

will be the members of his own household (Matthew 10:36). It's not that our parents didn't love us. The point is, they did! They just didn't want us way up there in New York, far away from them.

I was thirty-seven and Linda was thirty-six, and we had been on our own for years, but it was the fact that New York City had such a bad reputation—the Mafia, crazies, high crime rate, traffic jams— and we were headed there. And I was going to be preaching on the streets, for heaven's sakes!

We finally said our last good-byes, backed out of the driveway, and were gone. Like her flowers in the August heat, Memee's face fell. My heart broke for Linda because of all that had transpired. Trying to comfort her through her tears, I began to talk once again about our new home. "You'll love it, honey, like I told you; it's two stories, and we have a basement and a big yard, and we are in a great neighborhood," I said.

I had made two previous trips to New York, exhausting trips, just to search for a house. Riding trains, subways, and buses, taking cabs, and getting lost while looking for a home we could afford had been a monumental task; but God had indeed answered our prayers and had led me to a nice home in Smithtown, Long Island. I remembered later that when I was studying the state of New York in Mrs. Fason's fourth-grade class, she had said, "Long Island is the place to live."

Looking in my rearview mirror, I saw both of our sons. How proud we were of them! "Oh, God," I said to myself, "please take care of my boys. I love them so much." It was like the Lord said, "I know about loving a son, Scotty." Stephen had braces and was at that gawky, awkward age. I couldn't believe how fast he had grown. Only yesterday, it seemed, I was asking him when we came home from church, "What did Daddy preach about today?"

"Jesus," he said.

"Good," I said. "What did Jesus do for us?"

"He died on the cross for our sins," he answered.

"Good," I said, and I thought for a three-year-old, he's doing all right. I might have a future Billy Graham here.

"OK, Stephen," I said, "what is sin?" And just as serious as he could be, while hunching his shoulders and opening his hands, he responded, "That's what I dig in, Daddy!" We all got a big laugh at that one, and there was more truth in what he said than he realized!

Several months earlier, when I told Stephen that we were moving to New York, he crawled up under his bed and cried like he did that Sunday when Dallas lost to San Francisco in the Super Bowl. Stephen knew that he would miss his friends and particularly his cousin Grady, my sister's oldest son. He and Grady played ball together, fished and swam together at Cyprus Lake—like brothers, really.

Unlike Stephen, Stewart really didn't mind going to New York as long as he had a nice yard to play in and a big house with a basement, like I promised we would have. But I was certain he would miss his cousins, too. Not so much Grady. Grady was Stephen's age, just a couple of years younger. Stewart would miss my sister's triplets—Bernice, Dancy, and Peyton. They were the same age; well, actually Stewart was two months older.

I'll never forget what happened at my parents' house one day. The triplets began to cry, so Stewart got a bottle out of the diaper bag and stuck it in Peyton's mouth and shut him up; then he pulled the bottle out of Peyton's mouth and stuck it in Dancy's mouth and shut him up; then he pulled the bottle out of Dancy's mouth and stuck it in Bernice's mouth and shut him up; then, Stewart pulled the bottle out of Bernice's mouth and stuck it in his own mouth, took a long, gurgling swig, and said, "Ah!"

It's a long way to New York from Bossier City, Louisiana. We stopped at a number of Cracker Barrels, and at one of them we bought Stephen a coonskin cap and Stewart some candy. We visited the Knoxville Zoo and walked down the steep steps to view the Natural Bridge in Virginia. One evening we parked at a rest area outside of Washington, DC. And as we were walking back to the car, I heard Linda scream, "Scotty!" I turned and saw Linda's face stamped with fear, as she clutched her purse.

"A man tried to snatch my purse," she said.

"Who?" I asked.

"I don't know. Some guy came out of the dark, but I don't know where he went," she answered. Later, as we drove in bumper-to-bumper traffic as far as the eye could see, in front of us and behind us, we knew that we had left the Bible Belt and had driven into spiritual darkness. We could sense it, and we could feel it. Linda was still shaking and talking about the would-be thief. Linda was so sweet and kind, and I knew that in many respects New York was fast and furious and rough and rude.

I thought back to the very first time that I saw Linda. She was standing in a long lunch line at Louisiana Tech. Talking to some friends around her, she said, "My feet hurt!" I couldn't help but overhear her, so I asked, "Who is that girl? Anybody know her?"

"That's Linda Lockard. I went to school with her at Fair Park," said Stanley, sitting across from me.

"Man, would I like to date her," I said, as my eyes popped out!

"You could never get a date with her, Scotty," Stanley quickly retorted. "She's class."

Well, I didn't think I could get a date either, really. But my life was about to change. "Scotty, what about double dating with Snooky and me tonight?" Larry, my roommate asked.

"No," I said. I had recently broken up with a steady girlfriend and wasn't in the mood. But Larry told Snooky to hook me up, anyway. Marti wasn't interested, but Snooky told Marti's roommate, Linda, "Why don't you come with us? Scotty is going to be a Baptist preacher."

"OK," Linda said, jokingly. "I always wanted to marry a Baptist preacher."

And guess what? When I was introduced to Linda, I realized that this was the same girl I had overheard in the lunch line that afternoon, commenting about her feet hurting! No, it was not a coincidence; God's hand was in this. "The steps of a righteous man are ordered by the Lord" (Psalm 37:23).

Sitting in the theater watching *That Touch of Mink*, starring Doris Day and Cary Grant, I could not keep my eyes off of her. I told my best friend, Bill Hill, that very night, "Linda's the girl I'm going to marry!"

This was in October 1962, and the Cuban Missile Crisis was on everybody's mind; for days we were on the brink of nuclear war. But President Kennedy put a ring of ships around Cuba and demanded that the missiles be removed. Nikita Khrushchev of the Soviet Union backed down. The situation cooled off, and everybody relaxed. But during this crisis, Linda and I talked about the end of the world, and we discussed the seriousness of all that was happening. I realized that not only was she gorgeous, but she really loved the Lord, knew what was important, and was a girl of prayer.

We got to know each other more and more and really fell in love. As we walked and talked by moonlight and smooched under those big oak trees beside Lomax Hall, I remember saying, "Linda, I know God could one day call me overseas to Africa or India or someplace I have never heard of."

"Scotty, sweetie," Linda said, looking into my eyes. "I'll go anyplace in the world with you. Oh, I guess the only place I don't ever want to go is New York."

MOTHER

DAD

BARBARA ANN   MEMEE

CHAPTER 2

THE BOW OR THE BIBLE

I have always loved the bow and arrow, and I had a difficult time surrendering to the ministry because I thought my future was in archery, and I sure did not want to give that up to be a preacher!

When I was in diapers, I had a bow in my hands. My folks had a picture to prove it. The first toy I ever remember my dad making me was a bow and arrow. We were at Mama and Papa Scott's grocery store in Lucas, just south of Shreveport, Louisiana. Daddy bent a small limb and attached a string between the two ends. Then, he sliced up the side of an apple crate, rounding off each strip of wood to make me some arrows. Notching them, he tied chicken feathers to them so that they would fly straight. Oh, how I played with that bow and arrow! I was about six years old.

I was born December 21, 1942, in Shreveport, Louisiana, but I was about ten when I really came to know the Lord. Even though my parents took me to Sunday school and church faithfully, I didn't understand very much about what I was doing when I made my decision for Christ. All I knew was that I needed Jesus to be my Lord and Savior. I accepted him and have not been the same since. To this day Christ is closer to me than my very breath.

When I was around twelve, God began to speak to me about being a minister. In Sunday school I learned about the Lord talking to Samuel, and I began to say, as Samuel did, "Speak, for thy servant heareth" (1 Samuel 3:10), and speak God did, not audibly, but I heard him clearly in my heart say, "Scotty, Scotty, I want you to be a preacher." One night I heard him so loudly that I sat up in my bed! But I was not interested. Who wanted to be a preacher and be fat and wear glasses and have soft hands? So I suppressed that voice. Besides, I was really into the bow and arrow.

Dad noticed how serious I was about archery, so he bought me a Bear Kodiak bow, very stout, with a seventy-seven-pound pull! He had paid $59.50 for that bow, and he did not want me to outgrow it. Barely thirteen, I could hardly draw it back; but I got stronger and learned to shoot it. XP 179 was the serial number on that bow, the only serial number I ever memorized. I still have that bow.

Eventually, I got more sensible bows, and I began to compete in tournaments on the local, state, regional, and national level. I even won first place, not in the overall, but in the field round, my specialty, at the National Field Archery Tournament in Grayling, Michigan, in 1958. I was pretty good; no, I *was* good. Practice was never a chore, always a pleasure and a challenge.

Growing up, literally, on the Red River Bowmen archery range and later on the Bossier Bow Hunter's range on Mr. C. K. Britt's property in Fillmore, I began putting on archery demonstrations and continued doing so all through high school. In my teens I was often bothered and troubled by the Lord wanting me to be a minister, but once again I pushed that notion out of my mind and concentrated on my release and follow through. My goal in life was to be the world's greatest archer, and my heroes were Howard Hill, Fred Bear, and Ben Pearson. I wasn't about to give up my dream so I could be a minister!

But God doesn't give up easily, either. He kept at it, disturbing me, quietly and gently calling out to me, and I kept fighting him. As I entered college at Louisiana Tech, I continued shooting and putting on bow and arrow exhibitions, and often I was called Robin Hood by many of my buddies—Bill Hill, Tommy Buford, Marshall Oglesby, Larry Solley, Bill Hughes, and Wiley Richardson. I even got a partial work scholarship at Tech, instructing archery in physical education classes for Coach Bluehog.

However, for the first time in my life, really, I began to realize just how lost the world was, and how much it needed Christ! Many of my professors, classmates, and friends were empty, with no purpose or direction in their lives. Guys were constantly coming to me, of all people, for counsel, and it seemed that every sermon I heard reminded me that God wanted me to be a preacher. The Lord showed me the great need for Christ everywhere I went. Finally, he got me to the place in my life where I had to preach the gospel. I had no choice about it. I realized I could do nothing else and be happy, satisfied, and contented; so I said, "Yes, Lord."

I began to try my hand at preaching, but where could I go where nobody would hear me? There was a railroad track that ran through the Tech campus close to where some of us practiced archery, so I began to slip off by myself, walk down the track, go into the woods, and preach to the stones and trees. One night after I slowly inched my way down and slid through the rocks on the track into the edge of the woods, I began to declare, "What is wrong with the human race? Be sure your sins will find you out. Whatsoever a man soweth, that shall he also reap." Out of nowhere I heard a car engine start up, and I saw two bright lights flash on. No doubt a couple had been in the woods, parking, and my preaching had startled them, and they couldn't get out of there fast enough! In the moonlight I saw the silhouette of a Volkswagen speeding away. Later, the couple must have said, "We heard the voice of God that night!"

I discovered that God had given me the ability to speak, which was surprising, because all through high school I could hardly get in front of my class and say my name without being terrified and turning beet red. So I relinquished the idea of becoming world-famous in archery and surrendered to the ministry. My soul was at rest. I laid my bow down and picked up my Bible, never dreaming that God, one day, would put the two together.

CHAPTER 3

A BRIDE AND A CHURCH

Linda and I were married June 27, 1964, at Morningside Baptist Church in Shreveport, Louisiana, about two years after we met. I had just graduated from Louisiana Tech with a bachelor of arts degree and had recently returned from a mission trip in Phoenix, Arizona. Linda had taken a two-year business administration course, so she was already out of college a year and had been working at Martin Missile Plant in Orlando, Florida.

Oh, what a beautiful bride she was! The Lord was really looking out for me when he gave me Linda. When we were saying our vows, she giggled at the part about obeying her husband. Man, has she milked that for years! Having worked in the summers driving a tractor for Mr. George and the City of Bossier and having worked at Holiday Inn in Ruston, Louisiana, my senior year, I had saved up enough money to pay off Linda's engagement ring, purchase a 1954 Ford station wagon, and still have enough left for a honeymoon. Running to the car together after the wedding reception and dodging rice being thrown at us, we jumped into that Ford and drove away fast, tin cans tied to the bumper, rattling and bouncing. We headed to Silver Dollar City in Branson, Missouri.

After our honeymoon, we saw our folks briefly and then drove west to Southwestern Baptist Theological Seminary in Fort Worth, Texas, with everything we owned packed in that light blue station wagon. I could not wait to begin studying evangelism, preaching, and the Bible; I had had my fill of zoology and French! We rented a small, upstairs apartment in Fort Worth; I enrolled in seminary and got a job stocking groceries at Safeway. Linda applied for a position at Bell Helicopter, and how thrilled and relieved we were when we learned that she had been hired.

15

Returning from Honeymoon

I brought home a stray kitten one day, to the delight of Linda. I never liked cats much, but I loved Tutor Bug, as we called her. I chased both Linda and that kitten around our apartment. It was fun being married! One day as I was seated in a Biblical Backgrounds class, the tall, red-haired guy beside me noticed the scratches on my arm. "How's married life treating you, Scott?" he asked, stuttering a little bit. "Oh, it's great, but there is a period of adjustment," I answered. I never did tell him that the scratches were from my playful cat and not from my playful wife!

I was asked to preach at Grantham Baptist Church in Madill, Oklahoma, 120 miles north of Fort Worth, and I was shocked when they wanted me to be their pastor. I was twenty-one and Linda was twenty, and the idea of pastoring a church scared me, but I said yes. So, along with a new bride, I had a church. Grantham had a membership under one hundred and met in an old, rundown, brick schoolhouse about five miles from Madill. Dusty roads led to it.

My home church, Waller Baptist in Bossier, had already licensed me to preach, and immediately after I accepted the pastorate at Grantham, Waller ordained me. I can honestly say that when the ministers and deacons laid their hands on me, I felt God's anointing in an extremely powerful way.

Something very startling happened the first Sunday that I was Grantham's official pastor. During my sermon a gentleman walked into the church and whispered in a lady's ear. She quietly slipped out of the pew, she and her four children. I learned later that her husband had killed himself. However, for the next three years we got to know that woman, Anita, and her kids very well, often eating Sunday dinner with them. I even had the privilege of officiating her wedding when she later remarried. Anita and Bill have been unbelievable friends for many years.

On Sunday afternoon at the church I often practiced my evening message. My darling wife would be fast asleep on a hard pew with a stack of hymn books for a pillow. She never heard a word even though I often got quite loud! It was not easy commuting 120 miles, one way, from Fort Worth to Madill. We drove in late each Sunday night. There were no seminary classes on Monday, so I could sleep in, but Linda had to rise and shine early in order to get to work on Monday morning. I can still hear her feet now, running across the front porch and down the steps to catch a ride.

Yes, Linda carpooled to and from work, but I recall one particular day when I was supposed to pick her up. It was raining, and my windshield wipers were broken. Well, they would work, sort of. They would go to the right but not back to the left. So, I got the lawn mower cord and tied it to the wiper and ran the cord through the small window on the driver's side, holding the wooden dowel between my fingers. When the wipers went to the right, I pulled them back to the left, so back and forth they went. I just had to be careful driving, because I was constantly having to pull the cord as I went down the road.

Well, it so happened that Linda had already offered to give a friend a ride home. Her name was Sandy. With puffy blond hair, she was a girl who was somewhat sophisticated, or who tried to be, anyway. I pulled up and said, "Hey, y'all, hurry, get in! Hey, babe; hey, Sandy." Man, it was raining. As we drove away, I began to pull the rope up and down in order to make the wipers work, all the time laughing, proud of my ingenuity. Linda was embarrassed, and Sandy was big-eyed and speechless. Linda and I have laughed about that little rainy episode for years, but it was not funny to her at the time!

I was working, attending seminary classes, and pastoring a church. There were always sermons to prepare, associational meetings to attend, Hebrew and Greek lessons to learn in school; and, of course, I was just married! Linda was trying to be the perfect wife and also working full time at Bell. She also did a great deal of typing for me. But we were young and very much in love, so life was good.

Not that it really mattered, but I asked Linda before we were married if she could cook. "I don't know," she replied, grinning, "I've never tried!" One day when I came home, Linda's hands had Band-Aids all over them and even gauze wrapped around a couple of fingers, with blood seeping through. "What happened, honey?" I asked, instantly holding her close, with my arm around her. "Well, those knives are so sharp that I cut myself trying to slice up scalloped potatoes," she said, wincing, as she spread out her fingers. But the meal she had prepared was good, even though she had burned the potatoes a little. "I'll get better," she said. Trust me. She did!

Linda was an unbelievable wife, and I certainly wanted to be a husband worthy of her. One Saturday afternoon as I was watching a college football game, I decided to help Linda by doing our laundry. We did not have a washer and dryer, so at half time, I rushed to the Laundromat around the corner and put our dirty clothes in the washing machine. Then I hurried home to finish watching the game. When the game was over, I returned to the Laundromat. Walking over to the washer where I had left our clothes, I was unable to open the machine because a big, tall, fat woman, smoking a cigarette, had parked her rump on the handle.

"Excuse me, ma'am," I said, "I need to get my clothes."

"I'm not letting you have your clothes until you pay me for my detergent," she said sternly.

"Do what?" I said, "What are you talking about? I need my clothes," I answered, moving toward the washer door. She didn't budge, but continued blowing smoke everywhere.

"You're not getting your clothes until you pay me for my detergent," she said loudly in my face. "You stole my detergent, and you gotta pay me for it," she said, with a firmness in her voice.

"Ma'am," I said, nervously, "I don't know what you're talking about, and I certainly didn't steal your detergent!"

"I sat right over there and saw you take it and walk right outta here," she said, snapping back.

"Look, if I took your detergent, I'm sorry. It was a mistake or something. I need my clothes," I told her, and I was really getting irritated.

"You gotta pay me first!" she snapped.

"Miss, I'm not about to pay you. I'm sorry. Look, I'm a Christian and a Baptist preacher," I said, hoping that would change her mind. It didn't!

"Don't try to hide behind your religion. You gotta pay me!" she said vehemently.

I stepped back, not knowing what do. I waited and waited. I thought about trying to push her away, but she honestly was so huge, I really didn't think I had the strength to do it. Then, I noticed that as she puffed her cigarette, she began looking over my shoulder. I turned my head around, and there was a man standing directly behind me; he was taller and bigger than she was. And he was holding a can of beer!

"Oh, Lord, help me," I said to myself. As I was about to say something, the guy spoke up harshly.

"Give this man his clothes," he ordered, as I walked to the side, away from them.

"Now!" he said, with emphasis. "What do you mean talking to this little guy like this?" he said, taking a swallow of beer.

As the woman started to speak, the man slapped her across the mouth and walked out of the room. The woman began to cry, and she sat down. I then removed my clothes from the washing machine and put them in the dryer. Watching my clothes tumble over and over, I said to myself, "Will that dryer ever stop spinning?" Feeling sorry for the woman, I asked her if she was OK. "I'm all right," she said, as she wiped tears from her face.

A few minutes later I saw her take her clothes to her car. Even though I was anxious to get out of there, a thought crossed my mind—"Maybe I have a Bible or tract that I can give her." When my clothes finally got dry, I found a *Decision* magazine and decided to throw it into her car window, which was rolled down. But I didn't realize that there was an ugly German shepherd lying down in the back seat. Walking by her car, I pitched the magazine through the window, with my hand going well into the car. "Woof! Woof! Woof!" snarled the dog, his teeth showing; he almost bit my arm off! It nearly gave me a heart attack.

Driving away, I noticed the big guy coming out of the bar next door and walking back into the Laundromat, but I wasn't about to say or do anything else. "What took you so long?" asked Linda with a puzzled look when I got back home. "Well, babe, you wouldn't believe it if I told you," I said, sitting down, emotionally spent. To this day I don't know if I accidentally got that woman's detergent or not. I don't know what brand I took into the Laundromat, and I don't know whose detergent I took out!

Seminary was even better than I expected, and I met some other preachers who became my good friends, one of whom was a sharp guy from Savannah, Georgia. Everybody called him Smitty, but Jerome was his name. He helped me make a decent grade in Hebrew because he had a natural ability in linguistics, in which I always struggled. In return, I taught Smitty how to shoot the bow, a fair trade-off in my opinion.

Short, with a flattop haircut, Smitty rode a big Harley-Davidson motorcycle. Sometimes, to the surprise of the other seminary students, some of whom were quite stiff, I might add, I held on tight with an arm full of bows and arrows on the back of that Harley as Smitty whisked us across the campus, with preacher boys' heads turning as I waved, trying hard not to fall off.

Shooting the bow in an open field, we were soon joined by our Greek professor, Dr. Tom Urrey, a long-legged, tall, likable guy from Arkansas, and an archer himself. Throwing a rubber ball into the air and shooting it with Flu Flu arrows was what we all enjoyed. I was the best shot, and I hit the ball the most!

At Grantham, we met an old man named Joe Green. Talking with a thick German accent, Joe was an independent thinker. He also was a marvelous gardener, constantly giving advice to Linda, a gardener herself, about what to plant, when to plant, how to plant. Occasionally, Joe came to church, and often we visited him in his home and ate with him and his wife, Bell, a strong believer who sometimes played the piano at church. Joe was generous, and I could tell he liked us, but he was adamantly opposed to Christ. He refused to make Jesus his Lord. "I'm the boss," he insisted.

Linda and I slept over with them one evening, and their roosters crowed all night. One would crow and then another would crow and then another. Just when we thought, "Surely that's the last one," another rooster would crow. I didn't realize roosters crowed all night, but those Oklahoma roosters did. Daybreak came while we were still awake, and, yes, the roosters were still at it, trying to outcrow each other!

One evening after church, Joe and Bell invited us over for cake and coffee, and, to my surprise, Joe brought up the subject of being saved. "Joe, as I've tried to explain to you before, you must make Jesus your Lord, the boss of your life," I said. "Are you willing to do that?" Pausing, Joe then answered, "Yes, I'll do that." I could not believe it. We bowed down beside the piano, Joe and Bell and Linda and I. And Joe, calling upon Christ to be his Savior and Boss, was gloriously converted. Before I baptized him, Joe said, "I have but one regret: I wish I had done this sooner." Joe was eighty-six.

Several months passed, and one day I got a call that Joe and Bell had been in a terrible car wreck. Joe had been killed, and Bell was unconscious, not expected to live. I preached Joe's funeral, and a couple of weeks later I had Bell's funeral. A number of people shared with me about how much Joe had changed since he had accepted Christ. "He told everybody about the Lord," they said, "the barber, the grocer, the mailman, everybody. He became a different man."

I was blessed and humbled to pastor Grantham Baptist Church in Madill, Oklahoma. Realizing I was in seminary, the church was very understanding and cut me plenty of slack. I was very green and often felt inadequate, but the church loved us, and we loved them.

CHAPTER 4

FIRST STREET PREACHING

Pastoring taught me a great deal, but I knew my heart was in evangelism. In fact, like many other preacher boys, I wanted to be the next Billy Graham. Having heard him preach for years on television, I aspired to be like him when I began preaching. I even memorized, verbatim, two sermons of his: "Why I Believe the Bible is the Word of God" and "Why I Believe Jesus is the Son of God." Then, I had the audacity to preach them at Waller Baptist Church, my home church, as if they were my own sermons!

In high school I had gotten confused about baptism and the plan of salvation while dating a very committed Church of Christ girl. So I decided to go talk to none other than Billy Graham himself. I caught a train to Chicago and attended his 1962 Greater Chicago Crusade at Soldier Field and McCormack Place. Finding out that it was difficult to get an appointment with Billy Graham, I hid behind a water fountain and slipped in among his friends and team members, and I got to meet him. Shaking my hand, he said, "How do you do?" That was it. That was my talk with Billy Graham. I should have known better than to think I would be able to sit down and chat with Billy Graham, given his busy crusade schedule! However, one night I did go forward at one of the services, and I had a very productive and lengthy conversation with a wonderful counselor, who, with the Bible and good reasoning coupled with prayer, was led by the Holy Spirit to really clear up my mind about baptism and salvation. The next morning as I walked among the pedestrians on the busy sidewalks of the Chicago Loop, I felt like a new person. Having these doctrinal issues settled, I was no longer in turmoil, but at peace.

Yes, I knew that pastoring—helping believers grow in Christ, encouraging and discipling others, teaching and preaching the word of God to God's people—was extremely important; but, as I shared with Linda, my main interest was in getting the gospel to the lost, to those who most of the time would not come to church. I began to think, "If I cannot get very many lost people to come to church, why not go to them?" So one afternoon in the driveway of our apartment, I made a light, portable pulpit out of an apple crate, similar to the apple crate out of which my dad made my first arrows years earlier.

I went to downtown Fort Worth, and I saw about a dozen people waiting for the bus. I didn't have the nerve to take my freshly made pulpit with me, but I did walk up to them and begin preaching. These were my very words: "It's been announced in Geneva that the United States now has a bomb so small that you can hide it in a suitcase, yet it's powerful enough to blow up a city the size of Chicago! There is power in the blood of Christ. Christ died for our sins, was buried, and he rose again the third day. He has the power to change your life." And do you know what? To my surprise, those people listened, few though they were. They really did, and I felt very much at home on that street. ' This would work', I said to myself. I imagined that 18th century field preacher George Whitefield must have felt the same way when he preached outside to the

Coal miners at the Bristol coal pits and saw tears "making white channels down their blackened cheeks." He knew he had hit on something, and so had I.

I couldn't wait to get back home and tell Linda. "Honey," I said, "I went to a bus stop, and they didn't turn me off; they really heard what I had to say!" Linda was excited for me, but she must have thought, "My husband, a street preacher?" I could tell that she didn't know where this was going. I didn't either, but I knew that I had to do more. I began reading everything I could about open air preaching. I discovered that there was much outdoor preaching in the Old Testament. Noah, Joshua, Elijah, and Jonah all took their message out of doors to the people. In the New Testament John the Baptist preached in the wilderness of Judea, and, of course, our Lord delivered the Sermon on the Mount outside. The apostle Peter, on the day of Pentecost, preached to the masses in the spacious outdoor temple courtyard, and Paul spoke about the true and living God at Mars Hill.

I read about St. Francis of Assisi and John Wesley and William Booth of the Salvation Army. I read about the Methodist circuit riders and camp meetings and gospel wagons. Yes, open air preaching had a rich history, and God had used this method of evangelism mightily. So I did something that we really could not afford. I bought a flatbed trailer. Mounting an old pulpit that I had obtained from Grantham on the trailer, I strung a large banner overhead that read, "Victory in Jesus," in large, red letters. Buying a public address system and a long extension cord, along with a small generator, I went to Trinity Park. There I ran into some Pentecostals, who asked to join me in my endeavor. "Sure," I said, "I need some help." In a few minutes, however, they took charge and were shouting over my PA. I saw a police car drive by slowly from a distance. My Pentecostal brothers and sisters were sincere and meant well, but I was embarrassed beyond words. Jesus never screamed at people in the streets, and I was not going to do that either.

But I could not forget the faces on the sidewalk at the bus stop. I felt there was still a way to reach lost people with the gospel in the out of doors. I just didn't know how!

CHAPTER 5

"SHOWTIME"

Not long after my first attempt at street preaching, a couple of seminary friends, Lock Mackay and Eldred Hill, invited me to help them do personal evangelism at the Fort Worth Stock Show and Rodeo. "Yeah, I'd love to," I said, and the experience proved to be ministry changing, without a doubt. We rented a booth, passed out "Little Red Bibles" supplied to us by Dale Manos of Sowers of Seed, and talked to those who were interested. Because there were so many people walking up and down the aisles of the exhibit building, a thought occurred to me: "Why not put on a bow and arrow show and draw up a crowd and give your testimony?" I had been performing archery demonstrations all of my life, so maybe, just maybe, it would work. Years earlier, an old archery buddy in Shreveport, Bob House, had said to me when I told him I had pretty much given up archery for the ministry, "Scotty, why don't you put archery and the ministry together?" At the time it did not seem feasible, but now at the stock show, with people walking around, looking, and having time on their hands, I was going to give it a try.

Building a small platform to stand on and setting up a target, I began to shoot stationary balloons and the bull's-eye. The noise from the balloons popping was a natural crowd getter. As onlookers began to walk in my direction, I turned and addressed those who were stopping. "Folks, how are you today? Enjoying the stock show?" I asked. "What I would like to do is see if I can pop that red balloon," I said. After shooting it, I said, "OK, now I'll attempt to shoot five balloons at one time with one arrow." As I started to draw, I paused and said, "I love to shoot the bow, but the biggest thrill in my life is knowing Jesus Christ. Do you know him? We're not here just to put on a show. We hope to gain your attention with an archery exhibition, but our main purpose is to talk to you about the Lord."

Again I mentioned the five balloons. "I'll try to pop all of them with one shot. Next, I'll attempt to shoot out that birthday candle," I said. I then shot five balloons with one arrow. After sharing a Bible verse I tried to extinguish the candle flame. Having quite an array of shots, I attempted to cut a taut thread into with a hunting arrow; I shot at a swinging, suspended Ping-Pong ball. I also popped revolving balloons. I was relatively close to the targets and had been doing this for years, so the shooting was not that difficult. In between shots, I preached truths of the gospel.

"Ladies and gentlemen, Walter Cronkite once said that the greatest news he ever reported was twofold: the landing of man on the moon and the discovery of the polio vaccine. Well, I've got fantastic news for you tonight," I said in a congenial way. I learned to announce the next shot before I mentioned the Lord. This tended to hold the crowd. "You see those two blue balloons, ladies and gentlemen? I'll try to shoot two arrows at one time and pop both of them," I said. "You know, Jesus said there are two roads in life—the broad road and the narrow road. Which road are you on?" I asked. Then, before I shot the two blue balloons, I said, "You know, I don't have to attempt this shot, and you don't have to follow Christ. It's your choice. God loves you, and Christ died for you, was buried, and arose again. He wants to forgive your sins and change your life, but it's up to you." After I spoke a couple of minutes, I tried to hit two blue balloons at one time.

In order to gather a big crowd, I asked for a volunteer to let me shoot an apple off his head. Often, somebody stepped up, and I put the apple on his head and said, "Now, be still. I don't want to miss." People laughed and thought, "Is he really going to do it?" There was an instant rapport between my audience and me. As I started to draw, I said to the crowd that was captured by the suspense, "Now, I would never attempt this because I might shoot somebody. Let's give him a hand anyway." People smiled and clapped. After thanking the guy for volunteering, I reached for a blown-up rubber Bozo, the clown, and said, "Besides, I have another dummy here." Then I shot the apple off of Bozo's head.

When I missed, I usually said, "You know, ladies and gentlemen, one meaning of sin is 'missing the mark.' The picture is actually of an archer who shoots and misses. We have all missed the mark, haven't we? 'All have sinned and come short of the glory of God,' the Bible says. You and I have fallen short of God's standards. We've missed the mark. You have sinned, and I have sinned."

Spectators gathered all around with their eyes fixed on the target. How exciting and fulfilling it was for me to share the gospel. Old and young alike were in my crowd. I could tell that many of my listeners were lost and unchurched; their faces gave them away. The archery demonstration was just a tool to attract and maintain attention while I presented Christ. Did not musicians and chalk artists do the same? On any given day, I put on about ten shows, each lasting approximately twenty minutes. Hundreds of people watched and listened, the average crowd being about forty. Between demonstrations my friends and I talked to various individuals about Christ, and we gave away Christian literature. We then put up a clock announcing the next "Showtime."

This evangelistic approach was, perhaps, strange to a lot of people because it was different and unusual; but for me, it became as natural to put the bow and the Bible together as it was for two rails of a train track to run side by side.

CHAPTER 6

SURVIVING

After pastoring Grantham Baptist Church for three years, I resigned from the church, receiving my bachelor's degree in divinity (equivalent to the master of divinity degree today) from Southwestern in that same year, 1967. I had gained a wealth of experience while pastoring, and we had made some lifelong friends. It was a sad day when we left, but both Linda and I felt that it was time to move on. Because I had such interest in outdoor preaching, I decided to attend seminary awhile longer and study this method of evangelism as I pursued another degree.

Linda was now pregnant with our first child, and we both agreed that she should quit work at Bell Helicopter and be a stay-at-home mom, the hardest job in the world. In order to pay our bills, I worked in package pickup at Montgomery Ward, peddled Bibles door to door, and sold shoes at J. C. Penney at Seminary South, all while studying. That was not easy.

On July 2, 1968, Linda gave birth to a beautiful baby boy, Stephen Scott Teague. Of all the couples in the world who have had children, we were, without doubt, the happiest! Mother and Daddy drove over to Fort Worth from Bossier to see the baby, and what proud grandparents they were!

I didn't realize it, but while I was selling shoes, I was being observed by a pastor search committee from First Baptist Church of Graford, Texas. Looking for a minister, they were checking me out, and after I preached for them one Sunday, the church extended to me a call, and I accepted. They understood that I would be commuting to Southwestern, which was about an hour's drive away. So, here I was—a husband, a proud new father, and a student doing graduate work at seminary—and now a pastor again!

First Baptist Church of Graford was larger than Grantham but still was a small, rural church, so they were only able to give me a modest salary. We lived on the church grounds in an old, rundown adobe parsonage that had a few rats, but no air conditioning. And it got hot in Graford. But the congregation was wonderful to us, especially to our new baby boy. Teenage girls took turns holding Stephen, which made me nervous, and they kissed and pampered him. In a few months, however, as Linda held him in her arms, Stephen was leading the singing, right on beat, his little hands going back and forth in perfect timing.

Attending classes, writing papers, doing research, and endeavoring to be a faithful pastor kept me up late at night. Linda had her hands full, too, being a pastor's wife and taking care of Stephen, who had lots of allergies and who had many doctor's appointments; and, contracting the flu, Stephen really scared us when he had to spend a week in the hospital. Linda's mother, Memee, drove over from Shreveport to see us, and in a sweet letter that she wrote later, she reminded us to "feed Stephen lots of taters!"

We took a group of young people to Glorietta, New Mexico, and one afternoon I carried Stephen for hours on my shoulders with his legs straddling my neck.

After sleeping with that cool mountain air blowing through the window on me all night, I had a crick in my neck like I've never had before or since!

Pastoring brought us great joy, and we felt very much loved, but sometimes sharing the heartaches and burdens of the people was almost more than we could handle. God's grace was sufficient, however. One evening I received a call from a couple whose seventeen-year-old daughter had run away with a thirty-five-year-old man. "The Texas Highway Department has them in custody," the girl's father said to me. "Will you go with us to pick her up?"

I drove the girl's parents to the jail where they were being held, and when we arrived, I noticed the girl's father talking with the man who had apparently "sweet-talked" his daughter into running away with him. Suddenly the man, drinking a Coke, splashed it in the father's face. When he did, that dad slugged the guy, knocking him into the wall hard. Policemen quickly gathered around and got everything in control.

Driving home, I had never seen a man who looked so broken as that girl's father. Sitting in the front seat with his head down, he wept profusely, as the daughter with her mother sat quietly in the back seat, saying nothing. The young lady told me the next morning that she had run away with that guy to "let my parents know that I could do what I wanted."

Not long after that, a very popular young man in high school got accidentally electrocuted while installing a TV antenna, and I officiated at his memorial service. The entire town of Graford was stunned at his untimely death, and many of his classmates, deeply distraught, poured their hearts out to both Linda and me.

One day Bob Hutcherson, a seminary buddy, gave me a call. "Scott, as you know, I'm now director of Camp Lake Forest, in Macon, Mississippi," he said. "What about being camp pastor for our next group of young people? You can bring Linda and your kid. You'll love it; it will be a great vacation." Well, I thought that a few days away from school and the church might do us some good, so I took him up on his offer; and in a few weeks we were on our way.

While driving down a dusty country road and rounding a blind curve, we looked up and saw a teenager on a horse, riding directly toward us in the middle of the road. I hit my brakes, but in a flash we met head on, and the horse's legs broke through our front window, shattering glass all over us. Seatbelts were not required at that time, but Linda somehow managed to grab Stephen, who was about two, and took cover under the dashboard.

Stopping as fast as I could, I shouted, "Are y'all all right, hon?"

"Yeah, we're OK," Linda replied, shaking, as she cradled Stephen even closer in her arms and slowly sat back up.

I saw the horse kicking and bleeding from a gash above the shoulder, but my main concern was the boy. I just knew I had killed him. But walking behind the car, I saw him dusting the gravel from his bare stomach. "You all right, son?" I asked, nervous yet relieved.

"Yes, sir, I'm OK. I guess I flipped over your car. My horse, what about my horse?" he said anxiously. His horse had managed to get up and was blowing air through its nostrils and moving its legs. Linda, Stephen, and I were fine; the young man was all right, and the vet sewed up the horse, so it was going to fully recover. Our car was towed, but our insurance covered the damages, and it was repaired by the time we headed back to Graford. Thank God for his protection!

Camp Lake Forest was more than we expected, extremely beautiful, with great accommodations and superb meals. The recreation including skiing, fishing, and swimming, and of course I enjoyed shooting my bow. Preaching evangelistic messages was my main responsibility, and dozens came to know Christ in a personal way, and many more, I believe, began to develop a closer walk with the Lord.

One night after the final service, Bob said, "Scott, y'all come on over, and we will throw some burgers on the grill and play dominoes or something." That sounded like a winner, so we began to get ready. All of us had been in the pool that afternoon, so Linda, not having time to fix her hair, slipped on a wig, which she had never done before. We had a good time with Bob and his family, eating, laughing, joking, and rehashing the horse incident. As I got up to leave, I reached over and lifted Linda's wig off. "Hey, Bob, how do you like my wife now?" I asked, laughing.

Linda looked like a "skint" monkey with bobby pins and Scotch tape holding her hair down. When she looked at me, I knew my playfulness had gone too far. I had embarrassed her, and she felt very humiliated. What did she say to me? Nothing, then. But when we got back to our cabin, the most godly woman I've ever known told me how she felt about what I had done. The tornado hit! Linda has never worn a wig since, and I certainly have never done the likes of that again!

Soon, we were back at Graford, but our trip to Camp Lake Forest was refreshing, despite the collision with the horse and the wig fiasco!

While pastoring and attending seminary, I continued preaching at the Fort Worth Stock Show and Rodeo, always held in January. Astronaut Frank Borman of Apollo 8, that Christmas Eve, 1968, had just transmitted a broadcast back to the United States as he and the rest of the crew successfully orbited the moon. He read several verses from Genesis chapter 1 and wished everybody a Merry Christmas.

At the stock show a couple of my professors from seminary walked up as I was shooting the bow, heard me preach a few seconds, then turned around quickly and left. That really hurt me because I wanted their acceptance and approval very much. Were they embarrassed? Afraid to be seen with me? I felt I was being sane and sensible, and people were listening, so I did not understand their reaction. But another professor, Dr. Roy Fish, my evangelism professor, always encouraged me. He even invited me to accompany him on several revivals. Before the service I put on an archery show to help pull in the youth. It was Dr. Fish who told me about the Open Air Campaigners, a group that ministered on the streets of major cities throughout the world.

Learning OAC was conducting a seminar at Moody Bible Institute in Chicago, I felt I really needed to attend. My thesis at seminary was on outdoor preaching, and, no doubt, I would gain valuable information. But we were barely able to pay our bills—surviving, that was about it. In order to bring in additional income, I had been assisting one of my deacons, Bill Alcorn, in building his new home. We had just finished roofing when I mentioned the OAC seminar to him. Bill cracked his big smile and explained, "Go ahead, Scott. Have a good time. I'll get somebody else to help me." So, I was off to Moody. It was July 1969.

At the seminar I discovered how OAC effectively evangelized the unconverted on the street. Using a few sleight-of-hand tricks, they got people's attention first; then, they illustrated the gospel, using brushes and tempera paints on a sketch board. For three weeks we conducted numerous adult, teen, and children's meetings throughout Chicago. Large crowds listened to the good news. No sound system was employed; instead, the audience was asked to move in close where the preacher used conversational speech. Teamwork was stressed, and being at the right place at the right time was emphasized. Up to this point, I had been using the bow and arrow to draw up a crowd and then present the claims of Christ at public events; but at the OAC seminar, I found out that there were other creative ways to capture and hold people's attention. I also learned that I could successfully preach the gospel on busy city sidewalks! So now I was not limited to using the bow and preaching at carnivals and fairs. What an eye opener that was!

And something happened at Moody that I'll never forget. Some of us attending the seminar were anxiously watching television, waiting for the moon landing. Just as we were about to see Neil Armstrong put his foot on the powdery surface of the moon (July 20,1969), a woman, shabbily dressed, with dark brown hair, walked in from the street and into the big TV room. Obviously emotionally disturbed, she asked to talk to somebody because she had a heavy heart. Several of us, including me, looked at her, then at each other, but none of us left our seats to help the woman. Instead, we all turned back and watched television. How many times does a person get to see a man walking on the moon, live? The poor woman, with a blank, unbelieving stare on her face, strolled out of the room and back onto the street. I wondered later what ever became of her.

We made many friends at Graford. Sam and Dortha Ford were especially close. Sam, very soft spoken, was a deacon and a pillar in the church. His advice, wisdom, and encouragement gave me confidence as I sought to lead the church. Also the school principal, Sam wore glasses, had a big smile, drove a Ford pickup, and had a positive outlook on life. Dortha, his wife, was always praising Linda and offering her support. She seemed to understand the pressure that a pastor's wife was under. Our church pianist, Dortha had a touch like Roger Williams, only she was anointed. I don't believe she ever hit one bad note, ever!

Bill Alcorn, whom I had worked with a little pounding a few nails, had a hand the size of Texas. He and his wife Doris often sang "He Touched Me." What a fine Christian couple they were! Claude and Hatti often had us over for fried chicken. Hatti chased the chicken down herself, wrung its neck, and fried it up tender and brown, with just enough batter. Claude listened to Lester Rolloff on the radio, and he literally had his bags packed, anticipating the rapture! "Claude, you don't need a suitcase, brother," I said, jokingly.

Bobbi and Vicki Manley had a little boy, Randy, who was Stephen's age. Vicki, Miss Possum Kingdom a few years earlier, dressed like a movie star, but little Randy always had his diapers full and about to fall off! Bobby pitched for his local softball team, but I would not catch for him because he threw the ball so danged hard. We spent many fun days together, talking Dallas Cowboys football.

Then I got a phone call. It was the cavalry. No, it was my sister Barbara Ann. "Scotty," she said, "how would you like to come back home and teach school?" I guess she sensed that we were struggling financially and having a hard time. "Babs," I answered, "I'm a preacher, not a schoolteacher."

"I know, Scotty, but you could get on your feet, and as many people as we all know here in Bossier, probably a church will soon open up," she said, with excitement in her voice.

Well, the more I thought about it, the better that sounded. Since my postgraduate seminary classes were almost over, I knew I could finish my thesis in Shreveport. Linda and I began to talk about it and pray about it. We came up with the conclusion that, considering everything, it was time for us to leave. After two years, I resigned from the church at Graford. It was another sad day for us, but we felt we were in God's will.

Mother and Dad came over and helped us move back home in a U-Haul truck. Storing our furniture in Dad's garage, we stayed with Linda's mother, who was living in Shreveport at the time.

CHAPTER 7

TEACHING AND PREACHING

Before I resigned at First Baptist Church of Graford, Texas, my sister, Barbara Ann, had talked with Mr. McConathy of the Bossier School Board, so I had a teaching position lined up when I got back to Bossier. I was to teach eighth-grade English, and later eleventh-grade English in Haughton, Louisiana, forty-five minutes south of Bossier City.

Teaching school was a new experience for me. On the first day, two big black guys got in a fight in the schoolyard. A crowd gathered, and as the dust flew, the students began yelling at me to "Break it up! Break it up!" But I wasn't about to jump in between those guys. "Call Mr. Harlan, the principal," I said in my defense. As the fight continued, I didn't think that the principal would ever show up. But at last I saw a gentleman walking fast across the school grounds in my direction. I knew it was Mr. Harlan. "All right, fellas, that's enough; break it up," he said, stepping between the two sweaty, bloody teenagers.

"Man, am I glad to see you," I said, "I didn't know what to do."

Smiling at me, Mr. Harlan said to the unruly crowd in a calm, yet authoritative voice, "Everybody back to class. Fun's over."

Teaching school was a lot more stressful than I thought it would be. It was an entirely different world from eight o'clock to three o'clock each day. Lesson plans, grading tests, and trying to maintain order in the classroom stared me in the face constantly. Having a double major in English and speech from Louisiana Tech, I enjoyed teaching English. And there was a large percentage of blacks in my classes, so I got a quick dose of black culture. In the past I had worked with blacks, and I certainly had some black friends, but being in class day after day with black students, listening to them and learning their values, likes, and dislikes, was extremely enlightening.

I knew that my first responsibility was to teach English, and that's what I endeavored to do. But I had complete freedom in the classroom to share the Lord, if the subject came up, and all of my students knew that I was a minister.

"Mr. Teague, what's your position on the tribulation in the book of Revelation?" Bill Britt, one of my students, asked one day. I knew what he was doing—diverting my attention from the grammar lesson. I knew Bill and his entire family very well. His father owned the acreage in Fillmore where our archery range was located and upon which I literally grew up, so I knew the Britts. Bill was a B student in the accelerated classes and could have easily been an A student if he had applied himself a little more. Today, he is a dynamic evangelist who travels the globe, preaching the gospel.

"Well, Bill, before we go over that list of prepositions," I replied, "I'll give you my opinion about the tribulation, but I am certainly no authority on Revelation." The class then discussed the concept of heaven and hell for a few minutes. Eventually, we got back to the prepositions. So I was in a good situation, being able to make a decent living, doing something I enjoyed, but I longed to do more open air evangelism, or at least preach.

One afternoon Craig Barnett, one of my students, asked, "Mr. Teague, do you have a church?"

"No," I answered, "but I've got my eye open for one."

"My church, Koran Baptist Church, is looking for a pastor," he quickly replied.

Driving by the church, I saw that it was a Southern Baptist Church, red brick, with a nice parsonage. Soon the church contacted me, and I could see the hand of God at work, and just like that, I was the new pastor at Koran Baptist Church. The name of the church had nothing to do with Islam, of course; Koran was the name of the rural community.

Linda, Stephen, and I were excited to move into a pretty, three-bedroom parsonage with a double carport. We were much closer to the school than we were from Memee's home in Shreveport, and my drive to the school took just a few minutes. Linda's mother had been gracious to allow us to live with her, and although it was just for a few weeks, we were very appreciative.

The people at Koran were fine, God-fearing folks; and could those women in the church cook or what! Chicken and dumplings, fresh tomatoes, peas and squash and corn, tender roast and gravy, homemade buttered rolls, topped off with mouth-watering peach cobbler with ice cream—all of this, and more, when we had "dinner on the ground."

Soon after becoming pastor at Koran, I finished my thesis, "Open Air Preaching: Effective Method of Evangelism for Today," and in January 1970, I returned to Southwestern to receive my master of theology degree. I was elated finally to graduate for the last time. Six years of seminary after four years of college were enough!

Koran had a membership of about two hundred, so there were always hospital visits to make, sermons to prepare, funerals and weddings to attend, plus constant counseling. In addition, I was teaching rowdy eighth-graders Monday through Friday.

Mother and Daddy drove out to see us quite often, many times bringing Grady, Babs's son, to play with Stephen. Daddy chased the geese around the pond, and the geese chased him, pecking him in the behind, as the boys laughed in the swing. Memee visited us when she could, and always she and Linda talked about the flowers and the garden. One Sunday evening after church, she rode with us in the church bus as we dropped off kids around Lake Bistineau, all the while singing "I've Got Peace Like a River."

One old gentleman in the church whom everybody dearly loved was Mr. Tom Holstun. He was the best fisherman in those parts, although Thelma Tooke took a close second. One day I said, "Mr. Tom, how old do you have to be before you stop looking at pretty girls?" Drinking a Coke, as he always did, and smiling, he replied, "I don't know, preacher, but it's older than ninety-two!"

Mrs. Brunner was a smart, pleasant, elderly woman at Koran who lived in a beautiful old home up on a hill. A dumpy lady with thin lips and glasses, she was fun to be around. The massive oak tree in her front yard, she told me, was the second largest tree in Louisiana. She probably was correct, because with my arms spread wide open, I could not come close to halfway reaching around that tree. Visiting her one afternoon on her long front porch, I noticed a small goat just a few weeks old, skipping around. "I would love for Stephen to play with that goat," I said to her as I sipped a glass of iced tea.

"Take him. He's yours," she replied, chuckling.

So, I picked up the tiny goat, held him in my arm, and put him, knobby knees kicking, in the front seat of my car and drove home with him as I waved good-bye to Mrs. Brunner.

"What on earth do you have?" Linda asked, with an astonishing look, when I returned home. And before I could answer, she said, "Scotty, we have a dog. Oh, we don't need a goat!"

"Well, this may be the only chance my little boy can ever have a goat. Stephen will love him," I said, grinning. And Stephen, age four at the time, did love him, running and playing with him and feeding him milk in a baby bottle. The goat followed him everywhere, even into the house. "No, son, he's got to stay outside," I said. But when that goat started through the door, we could not keep him out! He was determined to get in, in spite of me pushing him back with my hands, knees, and legs and calling Linda to help me!

Then, it started happening. Early, very early in the morning, the goat wanted to be fed. "Bah, bah, bah," it bawled, over and over. What a nerve-racking sound! "Scotty, I got up with Stephen, but I'm not getting up to feed that blame goat," Linda exclaimed, sleepy eyed, as she turned over in bed. So, each morning, I grabbed a baby bottle of milk; no, I didn't warm it, I just poked it in his starving-goat mouth to shut him up. And it did. Instantly. This went on for weeks. I tried to wean him, but it was no use. Morning after morning the goat started begging for that bottle, "Bah, bah, bah." When I gave it to him, he shut up.

Then, a couple of men who lived on the United Gas plant yard adjacent to the parsonage came over and said in desperation, "Preacher, you're going to have to do something with that goat. It's keeping us up. We're losing sleep, and we've got to get up and go to work." Yes, they were laughing somewhat, but I knew that they were serious and meant what they said. But I was ready to get rid of that stupid goat, because we were losing sleep, too. So, even though we had some explaining to do to Stephen, I carried it back to Mrs. Brunner. She was smiling at me when I drove away. I think she knew that I would not keep that little goat very long!

We made lifelong friends at Koran Baptist Church. Tom Holmes, our minister of music, and his wife, Carrie, along with their three fine sons, were very supportive and extremely faithful. Tom, however, was tone deaf and was always singing off key; but he was a dedicated music man. Often Mr. and Mrs. Biggers had us over for strong coffee and dessert after the Sunday evening service. Mrs. Biggers laughed loudly at all of my jokes, and with his deep voice, Mr. Biggers gave me wise counsel.

Nina and Wayne Adams lived next door to us and were great neighbors. Wayne, always with twinkling eyes and a wide smile, tilled our garden with his tractor, his belly up tight against the steering wheel; he could not help us enough. Nina stood up for me in business meetings and was highly respected, and everybody valued her opinion. Their three children, Jackie, Rusty, and Darrell, took time with Stephen, walking him all over their pasture. Linda taught Darrell in Sunday school, and he was just like his daddy, full of mischief. Today Darrell is a godly man with a godly family. The Lord blessed us when we were at Koran Baptist Church. Many people were saved and baptized. In fact, we had such growth that we had to build a new educational building.

Teaching school was not easy, especially since I was pastoring at the same time. But I was glad that I had the opportunity to see education from the teacher's point of view. But I began to get restless, and Linda sensed it. And I think my congregation did, too. Knowing that my heart had always been in evangelism, I could not wait to get back to the Fort Worth Stock Show and Rodeo each year and preach to those lost crowds that were walking around the exhibit halls and fairgrounds.

So, I could restrain myself no longer. One Sunday morning I said to the church, "If I were going to pastor the rest of my life, I would be completely satisfied to pastor Koran Baptist Church. But I know God has called me into evangelism." With those words, I resigned from the church and went into a carnival and fair ministry full time. Leaving Koran was not an easy decision because we loved the people very much, and we knew that they loved us.

CHAPTER 8

FUN HOUSES AND SUPER LOOPS

After leaving Koran Baptist Church to go into a carnival ministry full time, we moved into a small house in Sun City in south Bossier. We began to live strictly by faith. I had a few revivals lined up as well as some youth camps, but my heart was in the carnivals and fairs. The polka music from the carousel, with brightly painted horses rising up and down, the smell of cotton candy and corn dogs, the long, green and yellow fluorescent lights on the Ferris wheel, the screams and laughter coming from the roller coaster, and even the smell of sawdust on a muddy midway made my heart race. My passion was taking the gospel to those curious crowds meandering everywhere.

Once again I used archery to capture and hold people's attention as I declared the good news. I also incorporated into my preaching much of what I had learned at the OAC seminar in Chicago—the use of the sketch board and a few sleight-of-hand tricks.

At the Louisiana State Fair one year, I preached outside on the midway. Sharing a big, flatbed eighteen wheeler with several singing groups, I realized that I had more freedom and room outside instead of inside the exhibit buildings where, up until now, I had always ministered. I could also gather larger crowds outside, and it was safer than being inside with people breathing down my neck.

Once, when I was inside, an arrow went through the target and penetrated the tin building. In a couple of minutes an angry rancher charged up to me and yelled, "Stop shooting that thing. I've got a prize bull behind the wall!" Before shooting again, I stretched a piece of burlap behind my target, thinking that would solve the problem. However, when I released an arrow, it bounced hard and fast out of the target, hitting a tall cowboy on the wrist. "Oh," he cried, flinching and holding his hand. He was not hurt much, but, pretending everything was OK, I quickly repaired the target. I had insurance, but this incident scared me. So, after the Louisiana State Fair, whenever possible, I set up out of doors, which allowed me more room and was safer. Besides, usually the carnival owner gave me a spot outside free of charge!

My dad, a welder by trade, made me a small, metal trailer that I used. The top slid back and became a platform upon which I had a large, wooden cross. My target folded out, as did my revolving balloon machine. The trailer had lights and a nylon safety net to catch my arrows as I shot at Ping-Pong balls and weighted balloons that I threw up into the air. This little trailer was extremely practical and functional. It was very light, so after I unhitched it, I could easily push and maneuver it around the carnival midway. Once again, I ministered at the Fort Worth Stock Show. Eldred Hill, whom I had met in seminary and who worked with me along with Locke McKay the first time I preached at the stock show, always opened his home to me when I was in the area. What great hospitality Eldred and his wife, Bernice, showed me for years. Their four children, Leslie, Faith, Ruth, and David, were always willing to give up their rooms for me, and they let me have my pick.

The year was 1973, and the Vietnam War was still being fought; soldiers and civilians were dying. One night a hippie standing in the crowd raised his hand. He had long, shabby hair and was dirty looking, but I sensed that he was not trying to disrupt and was sincere with this question.

"Tell me," he said, "if God is a God of love, why is there so much pain in the world—the war and all?"

Well, I didn't know how to answer him, but the Lord gave me the words. "Well, let me ask you a question," I said. "If you were God, how would you have made the world?"

"I would have made the world perfect," he answered.

"That's what God did," I said. "He made the world perfect in the beginning."

"He did?" he said.

"Yeah, now if you were God, and you made the world perfect, how would you have made man?" I asked.

"I would have made him perfect, too."

"Well, that's what God did. He made man perfect."

"He did?"

"Yes, in the beginning, God made the world perfect, and he made man perfect," I said.

The carnival crowd was growing in numbers, and they were really into our dialogue.

47

"OK," I asked the guy, "if you had made man perfect, would you have given him freedom?"

"Yeah, sure," the hippie said to me.

"Freedom even to do wrong?" I said.

"Yeah, I would, even to do wrong."

"OK, that's exactly what God did; he gave us freedom even to do wrong, to hurt and kill, and to do bad things," I said.

"Then why doesn't God get rid of all the bad people in the world?" he asked.

"He would have to get rid of you and me, then, brother," I answered.

The people crowded up closer as the hippie and I continued. Then the young man, as he looked around at the people staring at him, threw his head back, swinging his hair, and said, "Why doesn't God do something about the bad in the world?"

All eyes shifted to me. The hippie, sincere and well mannered, really thought he had stumped me. But the Lord gave me the answer. "Young man, that's what God was doing when he sent Christ to die on the cross. When Christ died, he was doing something about the sin, the bad in the world," I exclaimed. With that answer, the hippie nodded his approval, seemed to be satisfied, and walked away. For the next fifteen minutes I elaborated on the cross and its meaning. Many people seemed to be reassured in their faith.

I got to know a number of carnival owners as I went from fair to fair. One owner was particularly kind to me. Always treating me with respect, he gave me a spot every year on his midway. One morning he asked me to ride around the fairgrounds with him on his golf cart. As we rode and talked, he introduced me to many of his employees, "carnies," as they called themselves. Obviously, this opened up opportunities for me to share Christ with them from time to time. One day this gentleman asked me to drop by his office. As I sat across his desk, he began writing. Then, with tears streaming down his face, he handed me a note, which read: "My child recently died of a heart attack on the playground at school.

Since that time, I have been unable to cope with it. Do you have any advice?"

I sat there, numb, not knowing what to say, and quickly, silently, asking God to help me. "Sir," I replied, "I'm sorry, and I don't have all the answers, and I know I can't feel what you are feeling. I want to help you, but I'm not sure I can." I told him that God knows how he feels and that God does not directly cause everything, even though he does allow things to happen. I shared the gospel with him and tried to explain that the Lord would bear his burden if he would let Christ take it. But I felt so inadequate. After I prayed, he said that he felt better and that he had been helped. I'll never forget how he looked, and I'll never forget that conversation with him.

One afternoon at the Houston Stock Show and Rodeo, I walked around and talked to the carnies in their joints. Seeing a carny leaning out of the "glass pitch," I introduced myself, said I was a Baptist preacher, and asked him if he knew the Lord. "I'm an atheist," he quickly replied. After a few words with him I went to the next tent, with baseballs and milk bottles. "Do you know the Lord?" I said to a carny who had that hard, weather-beaten look. "I'm an atheist," he answered. I talked to probably ten different men, and each one gave me the exact same answer—"I'm an atheist!" It was as though they had all taken the same course, "How to Get Rid of a Baptist Preacher." Just say, "I'm an atheist." It was like a virus had spread from joint to joint, causing all of them to claim to be atheists. Without arguing, I attempted to give some evidence that God exists, but I think they all had their minds made up.

That same year in Houston, Buster Brown, the carnival owner, gave me a place on the midway to set up my trailer, but it was on the loudest part of the midway where the noisy, heavy rides were. I really needed to be in a relatively quiet place with few distractions and gobs of people, but this unusually loud spot was all I could get, so I took it!

Across from me "Una Paloma Blanca" blared as the Himalaya circled around and around on a slant. On one side of me was a large, brown, metal fun house with loudspeakers, horns, flashing lights, and whistles. Couples laughed and girls squealed. On the other side of me was the Super Loop, which made an annoying, grinding noise, back and forth on a track. In the middle of all these distractions and deafening noises, I was shooting the bow and arrow and trying to preach the gospel. If I had not had a strong PA system that cut through the racket, nobody could have heard me at all.

But with God nothing is impossible. Two nuns walked up and listened, causing others to pay attention to me. And crowds gathered all around me, watching me shoot at Ping-Pong balls that I threw into the air. Billfolds, spare change, car keys, cigarette lighters, and glass cases were hitting the ground beside my trailer, all of them coming from the people being turned upside down while riding the Super Loop next to me. Those nuns stood there for at least forty-five minutes amid that awful noise. Thanking me when they left, they said they would be praying for me. Then a small group of young people from First Baptist Church of Houston were captivated by my evangelistic approach and told me that they were thrilled to see me there.

James, a young, dark-skinned Mexican who operated the Himalaya ride, heard me preach the gospel many, many times, and one day during a slow period at the carnival, he actually came over and talked with me a long time about the Lord Jesus Christ. Whatever happened to James, only God knows.

I commuted back and forth from Bossier to the Four States Fair in Texarkana. Since some of my equipment had recently been stolen at another carnival, I asked a carny next to me if my rig would be safe while I went to get a hamburger. "There used to be honor among us thieves," he said, like a sly fox, "but due to the moral decline of our country, we will rip you off anytime we get a chance!" And he was looking at my trailer when he said it! During this fair I stayed one night in an old navy exhibition trailer that was parked on the fairgrounds, and the glassblower next to me paid a fifty-dollar deposit on my spot for the next year.

Supporting my family was top priority, yet the carnival ministry that I felt so strongly about was not self-sustaining. I knew that I had to have outside financial support. Dennis Mote, a deacon of mine at Koran Baptist Church, had once mentioned his employer to me. "Scott," he said, "you should go talk to him. He's a fine Christian man; hey, he owns a lot of big trucks. He might help you out. You never know. Tell him I sent you."

Well, I went to see the gentleman. Introducing myself, I mentioned that Dennis Mote referred me to him and that I was formally pastor of Koran Baptist Church. He was cordial and asked me to sit down. "Well, Dennis is a good man. What can I do for you?" he asked.

"Sir," I explained, "I go to carnivals and fairs and preach the gospel, and I believe the Lord told me to come and talk to you about one of your trucks. Maybe you could donate one to the ministry?" (Talk about "zeal without knowledge"—I was young and didn't know any better!)

This man looked at me, turned his head a little, like a curious dog, and had an "I can't believe what I just heard" look on his face. Pointing to his chest, he replied, "Young man, when the Lord tells me to give you a truck, that's when I'll do it." I told him I appreciated his time and that I would be praying that the Lord would bless him, and I left.

Next, I went to see Mrs. R. G. Latourneau in Longview, Texas. I understood that she was a wealthy businesswoman. Several months earlier I had put on a bow and arrow demonstration at the Latourneau Chapel and had preached to the Letourneau plant employees, at their request. Mrs. Latourneau was pleasant enough, but after listening to me a few minutes, she politely told me that I needed to help myself. I explained to her that the type of ministry that God had called me to required financial backers from believers. "Mrs. Latourneau," I said, "I can't take up offerings at carnivals, or I would lose what little credibility I have." We then had prayer, and she wished me well.

The Bible in 3 John mentions brothers going out for the sake of the Name and receiving no help from the pagans. John was commending Christians for supporting them financially, so I knew that I was biblical in my attempts to have Christian men and women stand behind me.

Having heard Billy Graham say one time that the bulk of his financial support came not from a few big donors but from many ordinary Christians who gave faithfully, I stopped going to wealthy individuals for potential financial backing and turned my attention to local Southern Baptist churches.

As a former Southern Baptist pastor, I realized that it would be difficult to get financial backing from local Southern Baptist churches. Members tithed to their own local church, and they supported missions through the Cooperative Program. Often churches struggled to meet their budget, and many times members were already committed to a building fund. In addition, some members already gave to Billy Graham and other Christian organizations, as well as to their local church. For someone like me, with a rather unusual ministry at carnivals, to expect immediate financial support from them was unrealistic.

However, I did talk to a few pastor friends in the area. A couple of them designated a small amount for me in their budget, and some others took up an offering for me and added me to their prayer list. They did not have to do that, so I was very appreciative.

Various Christian friends said, "Scotty, why can't you get some funding from the Home Mission Board (NAMB today)?" I contacted the Home Mission Board and was told that no money was available for this type of ministry. If I had been a church planter, I probably would have been able to get financial backing from the board, for a while, anyway; but what I wanted to do, what I was called to do, was to use the bow and arrow and preach at carnivals and fairs. Try to convince others that this was worthwhile! I knew that I was pushing the bounds of credibility. Ministering outside the walls of the church made follow-up difficult, and results were hard to measure.

So, what was I to do? I knew that it would not be right for me to go gallivanting around the country and neglect my family, and I certainly wasn't going to do that. When I was growing up at Waller Baptist Church, we sang, "Everybody Ought to Know Who Jesus Is," and it was ingrained in my mind that all the world needed Christ! Mrs. Kirby Wilson, our Sunday school director, inspired us with her devotionals. She brought to life missionaries in faraway places. Somehow, I had picked up the idea that the person who was in God's will and who trusted in the Lord—that person God would provide for.

We had noticed God's miraculous provision already. Invariably, when we were close to running out of money, I was asked to hold a revival or be a camp pastor or fill the pulpit for a friend. By God's grace, we always had plenty to eat, good clothes to wear, and money to pay our bills. Jesus said, "Seek ye first the kingdom of God, and his righteousness; and all these things shall be added unto you" (Matthew 6:33). Linda and I resolved to trust God's word, knowing that the Lord was our source.

CHAPTER 9

EXPERIENCE AND FRIENDS

First Baptist, Bossier, asked me to be camp pastor at their youth camp in Lone Star, Texas. A number of young people rededicated their lives to Christ, and I spent a lot of time in prayer, by myself, seeking God's perfect will for my life. The Lord God did a work in my heart that week.

Then the church asked me to help with their vacation Bible school, the largest in Louisiana, and to spearhead Backyard Bible Clubs, using several teens in the church. The Holy Spirit moved in a mighty way, and many boys and girls were converted. To God be the glory!

A few days later I got a phone call one morning. "I don't know who this is, but Linda and I are sure having fun!" I said, thinking that it was my sister, Babs.

"Hello, is this Scotty?" came a voice that I instantly recognized, and it wasn't my sister's! "This is Damon." It was Dr. Damon Vaughn, pastor of First Baptist Church, Bossier!

"Yes, sir, Dr. Vaughn, I didn't know it was you," I replied. "We were just laughing and joking," I explained.

"Scotty, I'd like you to be my minister of youth. Will you?" he asked.

"Dr. Vaughn, you know I'm preaching at carnivals and fairs now," I said.

"Well, think about it, and I would like you to preach for me Sunday and give me an answer," he said.

Stunned, I hung up the phone and said to Linda, "That was Dr. Vaughn. He asked me to be his minister of youth, and he wants me to preach for him Sunday!" We chuckled a little bit about what I said when I answered the phone, but then we got serious. Linda and I really didn't know what to do. I was scared of Dr. Vaughn anyway. Me? Minister of youth? At that big church? I felt at peace preaching at the carnivals, and I didn't want to give that up.

"Lord, what are you up to?" I kept asking. At the youth camp I had earnestly prayed for God's will to be done in my life. Was this God's perfect will for me? What about the outdoor evangelism at the carnivals and fairs? My darling wife, Linda, was expecting our second child at the time, and for months she had been sick, extremely nauseated. I could tell that she was miserable. Maybe this was the hand of God. I wasn't sure.

Later, as I shared my heart with Dr. Vaughn about my carnival ministry, he told me that if I came on staff as his youth minister, I could be gone three months out of the year for my fair ministry, and the church would pay me for twelve months. So, considering our circumstances, I sensed that the Lord was at work; and, realizing I would not have to relinquish my fair ministry, I said "Yes" to Dr. Vaughn. I was age thirty.

Soon I went to work at First Baptist. Boy, did I ever! I found myself in charge of the youth but also leading the bus ministry and children's church. We opened a new gymnasium, and I was asked to help organize the roller skating schedule as well as enlist scorekeepers and referees for the basketball games. Then Dr. Vaughn requested that I speak on Wednesday nights in addition to being in charge of prospect visitation and house-to-house evangelism. As one of Dr. Vaughn's assistants, I conducted funerals and weddings, made hospital calls, and had to be ready at a moment's notice to preach for him when he was out of the pulpit. Dana Howard, my secretary, was invaluable to me and helped me wonderfully; otherwise, I would not have been able to keep up with all of my responsibilities. I was coming and going like a dog chasing his tail! Eventually, an outstanding gentleman who oozed love for others, Charlie Barnett, lifted a lot of weight off of my shoulder in the bus ministry, and Willard Cagle, who related well with teens, began working with the youth.

After watching Marcus Welby on TV, I followed the example of his sidekick, Steve Kiley, and bought me a motorcycle; well, a Honda motorbike, really, and I made my hospital rounds on it. I was scooting around everywhere trying to cover all the bases. Amid all of this responsibility I was going to various outdoor events, a few carnivals, revivals, youth camps, youth rallies, bow and arrow exhibitions, and then it was back to the church!

But then another glorious event happened on July 21, 1973. Linda gave birth to our second son, Stewart Paul Teague. Once again we were superproud parents! We thought we might have a little girl, but once Stewart got here, it did not matter. He was a big, fine, healthy baby boy, and we thanked God!

One Saturday, our older son, Stephen, and I were getting ready to walk around the pasture behind our house. Stephen had his Red Ryder BB gun loaded, the BBs rolling up and down the barrel as he raised and lowered the gun. Then I got a call to make a visit to a prospective church member. Instead of taking Stephen to the field, I made the visit. It broke my son's heart. I promised myself that I would never do that again. Unless it was extremely urgent, that church visit could wait. I had read about preachers getting so involved in their ministry that they neglected their family. I did not want to be guilty of that, and, looking at Linda with our new baby boy one night, I said to myself that I had to get my priorities straight. From then on, I resolved to do just that!

A few months after Stewart was born, Linda and I both noticed that Stephen, almost six, was asking a lot of questions about God. One Sunday night after church, we all headed home. I was riding my Honda, and Linda had Stewart and Stephen with her in the car. At a red light she pulled up beside me and said anxiously, "You need to talk to Stephen; he wants to accept Christ."

"Pull over up here," I said. Parking in front of Pizza Inn on Barksdale Boulevard, I set Stephen on the back of the car.

"Stephen, son," I said gently, "what do you want to do?"

"Daddy, I want to ask Jesus to come into my heart," he answered.

"Son, do you know what you're doing? You must accept him as your Lord and Savior. You have to really mean it," I said.

"Yes, Daddy," he said, "God has been talking to me. I'm ready."

Well, I went over a few verses of scripture with him, explaining to him what it meant to invite Christ into his heart. Then I had the great privilege of leading my older son in prayer to receive the Lord Jesus Christ into his life. I knew Stephen was young, but he had grown up in church, and, being a very precocious child, he had a good knowledge of God's word. Without doubt, the Holy Spirit had been dealing with him. How happy Linda and I were, and Stephen has never been the same since.

After a two-year stint at First Baptist, Bossier, I found myself less and less involved in outdoor evangelism, and that was where my heart was; and, once again, a restlessness set in. So, believing I was following the Lord's leading, and taking a deep breath, I resigned my position at First Baptist and went back into full-time evangelism.

I realized that God had placed me under Dr. Vaughn so that I could learn valuable lessons. I had watched him delegate, reason with committees, pray with his deacons. Extremely organized, he planned a year ahead on his church calendar. Dr. Vaughn had given me more than I thought I could handle, stretching me to the limit; but I learned that I was capable of doing what he asked, and that gave me confidence. But most of all Dr. Vaughn was an excellent preacher who had no rivals. His preparation was thorough, and his delivery was flawless. He did it right, and his example, I believe, improved my preaching. I thank God for my time with Dr. Vaughn at First Baptist Church of Bossier.

Having been there for a couple of years, I met some fantastic Christians who, now that they knew me, had caught a glimpse of my heart and of open air preaching. Several began accompanying me to a number of carnivals and fairs, including Mrs. Lillian Scott, Patti Sherrod, Cliff McArdle, Tim Stinnett, and Al and Doris Bohl. Others at the church stood behind us in prayer and some of them, in addition to supporting their church, began helping us financially. I gained much experience and made lifelong friends at First Baptist, Bossier.

CHAPTER 10

"THE WAR-HORSE"

Mrs. Lillian Scott, whom I met at First Baptist, Bossier, was quite a lady. Because she was so spirited and was such a hard worker, unselfish and committed to Christ, I called her "the War-Horse." Talk, talk, talk. She was always laughing and talking. Wearing an infectious smile, her signature comment was "Have mercy." It was from Mrs. Scott that I really learned the lesson of "Quit trying and start trusting," as she put it. And she reminded me not to pay attention to praise. "Have mercy, we really rurn (ruin) preachers by bragging on them," she preached.

When Mrs. Scott was just a small child, her father was crossing a barbed wire fence, and his gun accidentally discharged, killing him. Mrs. Scott and her husband, who died years earlier and whom I never met, were obviously happily married by the way she talked about him, but they were unable to have children of their own. But Mrs. Scott had many other children. There was always some lady that she was mentoring or some child that she was visiting on her bus route. Dr. Vaughn, pastor of First Baptist, Bossier, had a son, Philip, who was mentally challenged and who lived at the Northwest Louisiana State School. The person who picked him up and brought him to Wednesday night supper and prayer meeting was Mrs. Scott. She dearly loved Philip, and Philip dearly loved her.

Patti Sherrod, whom I also met at First Baptist, Bossier, thought of Mrs. Scott like a second mother. They were very close and often visited Linda and me; and from time to time they joined me as I ministered at the carnivals. Mrs. Scott counseled and gave her testimony. Patti sang, God having blessed her with a beautiful voice. Mrs. Scott could not sing a lick; in fact, I cannot think of anybody who sang worse than Mrs. Lillian Scott!

Kin to well-known Texas evangelist Manley Beasley, Mrs. Scott had evangelistic blood in her veins. In addition to being related to the Beasleys, her niece was Donni Gilchrist, who was married to Mike Gilchrist, an outstanding evangelist in Shreveport. Mrs. Scott's family tree was littered with pastors and youth directors and evangelists.

One year Mrs. Scott went with me to the San Antonio Fiesta, and we stayed with Manley and his wife, Marthy. I never traveled with just a woman, but Mrs. Scott was the same age as my mother, and since we were staying with the Beasleys, I figured her going was acceptable. What a blessing it was to be around Manley, Marthy, and Mrs. Scott in San Antonio. They were so deep in the Lord that I just sat back, listened, and soaked it all in. One afternoon at the Fiesta several of us got caught in a downpour, including Mrs. Scott. Her hair was drenched. She looked pitiful, like a dog who just had a bath. We were running late for prayer meeting, so Mrs. Scott, a natural brunette, grabbed a blond wig from Marthy as we headed to church. Our entire group sat on one pew up front, close to the preacher. About the time the service started, a frail little old lady with a cane slowly worked her way down the aisle and sat down on my right.

The church was large and was packed. In the middle of the Bible study I glanced to my left and saw Mrs. Scott's blond wig on, crooked. I tried not to laugh, but holding it in made the pew shake. Then, the little old lady with the cane burped. I couldn't contain my laughter any longer. Looking at Mrs. Scott's wig and hearing that woman burp, simultaneously, caused me to laugh out loud, uncontrollably! Everybody on the pew by now was laughing and bending over trying not to disturb the service. But it was too late. Loud, hilarious laughter erupted, causing our pew to vibrate from one end to the other! The preacher was extremely understanding, which was amazing, but when he finally said "Amen," the lady who burped practically ran down the aisle with the cane in her hand and out the front door!

Once, Linda and I took Mrs. Scott and a few other friends to hear Corrie ten Boom in Waco, Texas. How inspired we were just being in the presence of Corrie ten Boom, but, you know, Mrs. Scott was every bit as close to the Lord as Corrie ten Boom. I'm not taking anything away from Corrie; I just knew what a godly woman Mrs. Scott was.

The last time I saw Mrs. Scott was in an assisted living complex. Still upbeat, she introduced Linda and me to a gentleman in a wheelchair, and we could tell that she had built many meaningful relationships and was witnessing to everybody. She looked like she was practically running the place.

I used to joke with her, saying, "Mrs. Scott, when they bury you, even if I don't know where your grave is, if they will point me in the right direction, I'll be able to find your grave. The earth will be quivering because your tongue will still be going full speed!" Just smiling and laughing, she would say, "Have mercy, Scotty." Mrs. Scott—"the War-Horse"!

Chapter 11

PEANUT BUTTER COOKIES

In 1975 I left the staff position at First Baptist Church, Bossier, and went back into full-time evangelism. It was not a revival ministry, so I was not receiving love offerings. Most of the time I was preaching at places where I acquired no money—stock shows, rodeos, carnivals, fairs, city streets, and housing projects. In fact, I had to pay my own expenses.

When I left Koran Baptist Church, a couple of years earlier to go into this same type of ministry, I was not as prepared, financially, as I should have been. We made ends meet by God's grace, and then I went on staff at First Baptist, Bossier, which kept us afloat. This time I wanted to be wiser than before and better prepared moneywise. Dr. Vaughn, pastor of First Baptist, Bossier, tried to elicit backing for me from the Home Mission Board but was told that no funds were designated in their budget for ministries such as this one. I had heard that before!

After much soul searching and prayer, I made a list of people with whom I had made contact over the years—friends in churches that I had pastored, buddies that I had attended school with, acquaintances that I had made during college and seminary days. I then wrote to a number of them and visited in person many more, sharing my heart, my vision, the call of God on my life. "All I'm asking is that you pray about standing behind us," I said, as sincerely as I could. "The Lord will reveal to you if you are supposed to help us." Then I kissed Linda, Stephen, and Stewart good-bye and headed to Austin, Texas, to preach the gospel, trusting that the Lord would provide.

In Austin, I set up my trailer in front of an oval tin building where Johnny Rodriguez was performing. As people walked to and from the entrance, I endeavored to snag them. "Folks," I said, "I'd like to see if I can shoot out that birthday candle. Just gather in close. I don't want your money. I'm here talking about the Lord. If you've ever shot a bow, you know why the Indians got whipped," I said, evoking a few laughs. Taking careful aim at the tiny flame, I shot. "Oh, I missed. Give me another shot. If I were really good, folks, I'd be on TV," I said; a few more laughs followed. I was amazed at how many people stood, watched me shoot, and listened to the gospel.

"You see this arrow? It's twenty-eight inches long, made of aluminum. It has three feathers on it. And it has a certain stiffness. This arrow is made for this bow, a forty-pound pull. My friends, hear me a minute. You and I are made for God; God created us in his own image so that we might know him," I declared.

One night a young man, tall and wearing a big white cowboy hat and sharp-looking boots, began to talk to me and help me pull arrows from the target. He hung around for a couple of hours. Then, all of a sudden, he burst out, "Man, I need to be saved. What do I do?" Having no idea that God was dealing with him, I saw then that he was really under conviction. "Well, like I've been preaching, turn from your sin, ask Christ to come into your life, and rely just on him to be your Lord and Savior. Don't depend upon your church to save you or anything else. Just trust Christ and what he did for you on the cross," I said, pointing to the cross that was mounted on my trailer.

It was beginning to rain, but right there that young man called on the Lord to save him. "Man, I feel great. Let me take you out to dinner. You like steak? Let me buy you a steak," he said, smiling. I had been staying at the Salvation Army and eating cold oatmeal, so I gladly took him up on his offer, and off we went for a big, juicy, Texas-sized steak!

I was convinced that the young man had truly been converted. He was happy. He had a serenity on his face that had not been there before. After our meal, I returned to preach awhile longer. The crowds were surprisingly good even though it was still lightly raining. Later, as I put up my equipment, an older couple walked over to me and introduced themselves as Bea and Charles Lorain. "We've been observing you, and you have a unique approach in presenting the gospel," they said in a very encouraging way, "and we would like to invite you to breakfast in the morning."

"Great!" I said. "That would be great!" They gave me directions to their mobile home, and I was so high that I called Linda and told her what had transpired.

"Well, Scotty, I have some good news for you, too," she said, with excitement in her voice. "You know Joe and Jeanette Spears at church?"

"Yeah," I answered.

"Well, they gave me a car," she said, and in my mind I could see Linda smiling.

"A car?" I replied.

"Yes, a white Pontiac. It's old and has lots of miles on it, but it runs real good," she said.

This was an answer to prayer because we just had the one car, and Linda had to take the kids to Dr. Kelly sometimes, and she had to get groceries and run other errands. So, now, when I was away with the car, she wouldn't have to depend upon anyone to carry her around, not even to church.

We had very little money, and we both had agreed that I would wait for some funds to come in before I wrote a check on our account. "Babe, I've not written that check yet," I said, "but I think I'm going to write one for one hundred dollars and get a motel room. It's rough staying at The Salvation Army." I told her that a guy woke me up the other night and asked, "Got a woman?"

"No, I'm married, a Baptist preacher," I said.

"What are you doing here?" he questioned.

I explained that I was preaching the gospel at the fair. "Why doesn't your church or denomination support you?" he asked, his brow wrinkling.

"The Lord takes care of me," I answered.

After Linda and I had talked a little bit more on the phone, she said, "Yeah, go ahead and write a check, Scotty. Some money has come in. We're all right." So I got a decent room and slept well that night.

The next morning I located the home of Mr. and Mrs. Lorain. "Come on in," they said, opening the door, "and have a seat." I sat down to the biggest breakfast I have ever had in my entire life. Mrs. Lorain had cooked everything—scrambled eggs, fried eggs, pancakes, toast, French toast, biscuits, cinnamon rolls, hash brown potatoes, grits, bacon and sausage, cereal with fresh strawberries, and orange juice, coffee, and milk. I ate until I could eat no more. King Solomon never ate so well! What a fantastic Christian couple Bea and Charles Lorain were!

That afternoon in my motel room, as I was rehearsing a sermon, I turned on the black and white TV. A peanut butter cookie commercial caught my attention. "Man, do those look good. I would love to have some of those," I said out loud. After that huge steak with all of the trimmings the night before and after that feast for breakfast, here I was, craving those peanut butter cookies! I reached down and turned the TV off and lay back on the bed. About that time somebody knocked on my door. "Who could that be?" I thought. I opened the door, and there stood Mr. Lorain.

"Mr. Lorain, how did you know I was here?" I asked.

"Well, I have my ways of finding out," he said, laughing.

"Come on in," I said. He stepped inside, and I noticed that he had one arm behind him. He pulled a dish covered with foil from behind his back, and said, "Bea made these and asked me to take them to you."

I pulled the foil away, and there were at least three dozen peanut butter cookies!

CHAPTER 12

THE HAND OF GOD

I certainly had seen the hand of God when Mr. Lorain brought me those peanut butter cookies. God was showing me that he was quite capable of providing in miraculous ways, a lesson that I needed to be reminded of. I began to see the hand of God in all sorts of ways. Not only did the Lord supply our every need, but he led and directed, opening doors of opportunity for me to preach the gospel.

In August 1975, about three months after the fall of Saigon, several friends from First Baptist Church, Bossier, accompanied Linda and me to an Open Air Campaigner's staff conference in Chicago. While having a marvelous time, we learned a great deal and were inspired by the preaching, awed by their use of the sketch board, and impressed with their specially equipped vans that were designed for outdoor preaching.

I had previously met several OAC evangelists at an OAC seminar in Chicago in 1969, but I met others at this staff conference, including George Naggy and Jim Vine. Several weeks after we returned from Chicago, Jim gave me a call, inviting me to meet him in Fort Smith, Arkansas. "OAC has an opportunity to preach to the Vietnamese refugees at Fort Chaffee. How about working with me?" he asked.

"You bet I will," I quickly answered. The thought of sharing the gospel with all of those Vietnamese, who had little or no knowledge of Christ and who, instead, worshiped rocks, wooden idols, and the spirits of their ancestors was a chance I could not pass up.

Setting up outside, close to the barracks, and using interpreters, we took turns presenting the claims of Christ. I used the bow and arrow, which they seemed to enjoy, and Jim employed the sketch board, effectively communicating the gospel. One afternoon as

I preached, a siren went off, and the refugees began to scatter—jumping under cars, our trailer, the barracks—thinking that the siren was an air raid signal. Servicemen drove around in jeeps and announced with bullhorns, "This is just a drill. Do not be afraid." Slowly, the refugees crawled out from under their cover and gathered back around us, so I began preaching where I had left off.

This was my first experience using an interpreter, but it was not as difficult as I thought it would be. I had seen Billy Graham preach with an interpreter, and he used short, succinct sentences. Following his example, I found this technique worked well.

Our stay at Fort Chaffee was extremely gratifying because hundreds of lost Vietnamese heard the gospel for the very first time, and I truly believe many were genuinely saved. As we were leaving, one refugee, with tears in his eyes, told us he didn't think he would ever see his children again. "They were with me in Saigon at the airport," he said, crying, "I was holding their hands, and then they were gone. They hurried us into the helicopter and wouldn't let me look for them. I'll never see them again." Jim and I prayed for him and told him that maybe they would show up with another group, but I never found out what happened.

A. J. Semira, whom I had met while on staff at First Baptist, Bossier, had roots in New Orleans, so he and I spent several days ministering on the streets of the Big Easy. On the corner of Saint Charles and Canal we met a tall, black junkie named Percy. Wearing a black motorcycle jacket and a silver chain and medallion around his neck, he lived on the streets of New Orleans. A likable guy, Percy knew everybody. Constantly, he slapped hands with this brother and that brother. A Vietnam vet, he believed that hell was in this life; and, without doubt, being addicted to drugs and living a life apart from God, Percy was living in a sort of hell on earth. For a number of days, A. J. and I tried to win him to the Lord, reminding him that Jesus talked about hell being a place of everlasting punishment (Matthew 25:46), but we had no success in persuading Percy to repent and accept Christ.

However, while preaching in front of Walgreens at a bus stop, I saw a thin, elderly, gray-haired man who was really paying attention. When I challenged the small group to come to Christ, he stepped forward. We learned that his name was Mr. Tisch and that he was Jewish. I had been emphasizing the resurrection of Christ, and I'm sure the Holy Spirit used that great, historical event to draw him to Jesus. God opened the heart of Mr. Tisch and removed his spiritual blindness, and he accepted Christ. Oh, how thrilled and relieved he was! Once again I saw the hand of God at work.

Before A. J. and I left New Orleans, I asked the crowd one day, "What is your biggest need?" A wiry black dude wearing a colorful cap came shuffling through my crowd, and without even stopping he answered my question by saying, "Unemployment, man, that's why you out here on the streets, 'cause you can't get a church!" As he strutted away, what he said was like an arrow shot through my heart. I knew that I was a street evangelist because of the call of God, not because I could not get a church. But I also knew that that's what many people thought, even though they did not voice it. Preaching in the open air, particularly on a street corner, was a forgotten ministry. Because it had been so poorly done, many people didn't like to be associated with it. The stereotype of a guy, with his hair blowing in the wind, holding up a big Bible and condemning everybody in an attacking mode, was downright embarrassing. Even though that was not my approach, I knew that I was viewed this way, as a crackpot who was on the street corner because no church would have him. I would carry the stigma connected to street preaching for the rest of my life.

The most difficult aspect of the carnival ministry was the fact that I had to be away from Linda, Stephen, and Stewart a great deal of the time. It helped knowing that we lived in Bossier close to my parents, my sister, and Linda's mother. They were available when Linda needed them and company for her and the boys. Most fairs lasted ten days, but counting travel time, I usually was away about two weeks, home awhile, then on the road again. Knowing that Linda had a hot cup of coffee and lemon icebox pie waiting on me made me drive a little faster when I headed home. And Stephen and Stewart were always excited, too, wondering what I had brought them. What a time we had, playing football, shooting the bow, and tumbling with our little dog, Jack.

One afternoon when I was home, Linda was running an errand, and Stephen was in school. I was painting my carnival trailer and watching Stewart while I did it. As I painted, Stewart was walking around between my legs and crawling under the trailer, just looking to see what he could get into. I noticed that Stewart, about age two, had a touch of paint in his blond hair. "Come here, son, you've got paint on you," I said. I had paint on my hands, of course, so within a minute or two, as I tried to remove the paint, I got more and more paint in his hair; so much blue paint that his blond hair began to turn green! I knew that I had to act fast. Grabbing some turpentine, I hurried to the bathtub and turned on warm water. I held Stewart under my arm like a squirming little pig. Placing him in the tub, I said, "Stew, you've got to trust me; you got to trust Daddy. Lean your head back under the water and let me wash the paint out." As I poured turpentine on his head, he began to say, "Ting, Daddy, ting!" Stewart didn't cry, but he almost did. After washing the paint and turpentine out of his hair, his hair looked clean and blond again. But I washed it some more just to be sure. Drying him off, I felt I had averted a lengthy explanation to Linda about what had happened. I just prayed that Stewart wouldn't be bald! Once again, I saw the hand of God.

Richard Johnson and I went to school together, beginning in the first grade and going all through high school. We played on the Waller Wildcat football team in grade school, so we had been friends forever. We had even worked together in the bus ministry at First Baptist, Bossier. One day Richard called me and said, "Scotty, I am selling a rental house. Help me paint it, and whatever profit I make, I'll donate to you." Immediately, I started helping Richard paint that house and even recruited my dad to give us a hand.

Several weeks later when I was visiting Mother and Daddy, Linda called me and said, "Scotty, you got a letter from Richard today. I didn't open it, but I can tell there is a check inside. I've got to run to the store; I'll leave it on the kitchen table." Hurrying home as fast as I could, I jumped out of the car and ran to the front door, but for some reason I did not have my house key, so I could not get in! I went around back, looked through the window, and saw the letter lying on the kitchen table. Locked out, I put my back to the door and slid down slowly, sitting on the patio. "I cannot believe this," I said, huffing. I waited. And waited. Wondering how much the check was, I didn't think Linda would ever return home. Finally, I heard her drive up. "I forgot my house key," I told her, as she got out of the car. Entering the front door, we opened the letter together, and there was a check for seven thousand dollars, an unbelievable amount of money. Once again, I saw the hand of God.

I knew instantly what I was going to do with the money, because I had thought about it for weeks. Remembering the OAC vans at the staff conference in Chicago, I had to have one just like them. So, with part of the money, I made a huge down payment on a Chevrolet van, buying it from K. D. Phillips at Red River Chevrolet in Bossier. The rest of the money we put in the bank and saved.

Richard also asked me to do a spot on the radio, sponsored by Johnson Furniture Company. It would be advertising his business, and I would get to preach on the radio. The program was called "Moments of Gold." Each spot was just sixty seconds, so I had to be brief, concise, and to the point. I deemed it an honor to do the radio program for Richard, and I got experience over the air.

Not long after I began preaching on the radio, I drove to Elizabeth, New Jersey, and had my brand-new van equipped like the vans used by the Open Air Campaigners. A steel platform slid out of the side door. On top of the van, there was an aluminum, overhead canopy equipped with lights and a sketch board. Across the Hudson River from Elizabeth were the bright lights of New York City, and before leaving New Jersey, I drove all around Manhattan on the

FDR; but I never dreamed that one day New York City would be the very place I would preach the gospel thousands of times.

Mr. Chester Edwards, whom I also met in the bus ministry at First Baptist, Bossier, wore a big straw cowboy hat and rattlesnake-skin cowboy boots. He spoke with a husky voice, almost like something was stuck in his throat. Fair skinned, he always looked blistered. A gentleman in his late fifties, he was known as "the Pottery Man." He often drove to Mexico and picked up clay pots; then, returning to Shreveport-Bossier, he delivered the pottery to various outlets. One day while he was visiting his bus route, he dropped by. "Scott," he said, "if you'll help me go pick up a load of pottery, I'll give you my step van. Maybe you can use it some way in your ministry."

"All right," I said. So, off we went to Mexico.

I cannot believe how many clay pots we put in that truck! Pottery of all sizes and shapes and colors—yellow, red, black, blue, green, white, orange. Then, after roping down wrought iron patio furniture on top of the truck, we headed home. "If you're ever back down here," Mr. Edward said to me on our trip back to Bossier, "you ought to look up a missionary friend of mine. Roland is his name. He lives in Laredo and has a great ministry across the border."

When we unloaded everything in his front yard, with pottery stacked everywhere, Mr. Edwards wiped sweat off his brow and, with a big smile, said, "There it is, Scott; it's yours."

The truck was old and had a lot of miles on it, but it ran great. I was very happy to get it. Dad and I converted it into a motor home. A fine, Christian businessman at Fore Travel in East Texas sold me motor home parts at cost, and Dad and I worked for weeks, installing a full kitchen, a bedroom, and a bathroom. When Dad connected and clamped all the hoses in the shower, he said, "Turn the water on, son; let's see how it does." I turned on the water, and the shower looked like a Christmas tree, spraying water in all directions. We both got soaked! "Turn it off! Turn the water off," Dad shouted, laughing at the same time. "We've got to tighten everything up!"

The hand of God was in the generosity of Mr. Chester Edwards, "the pottery man." It was very expensive staying in motels at the fairs and carnivals. So that big, brown step van that we made into a motor home really helped me to defray traveling expenses. The old truck wasn't pretty, but it was functional, and I used it for years.

Not long after that, I went to Laredo to minister on the streets. One afternoon as I preached in the town square to a small Mexican crowd, an elderly gringo walked up and began to listen. When I finished and began folding up my sketch board, this old guy complimented me and told me he was a missionary himself. "I own a curio shop on San Bernardo here in Laredo, and I go back and forth across the border and try to reach the people," he said.

"Is that right?" I replied. "I was supposed to contact a missionary if I ever came back down here, but I can't remember his name. A Mr. Edwards told me about him."

"Chester Edwards? The pottery man?" he asked. "I know him."

"You do? What's your name?" I asked.

"Roland," he said.

"Roland, yeah, that's the name. You're the missionary Mr. Edwards told me to look up. I couldn't remember your name," I said.

Wasn't that something? At the exact moment that I was preaching, the very person I was to contact was in my meeting. The hand of God was at work again! We rode through the streets of Nuevo, Laredo, and passed out hundreds of tracts and Spanish Bibles. Hungry for the word of God, Mexicans hurried out of their little shacks to grab them. Gracias, gracias" they said over and over, as they examined them carefully.

Mr. Roland was a great man of God. At age sixty-nine, he shook so much that he could hardly drink a cup of coffee without spilling it. He had awesome faith, and he knew what it meant to work. His name was never up in lights, but his zeal put many of us to shame. While committees planned evangelism, and many well-known evangelists got glory for it, he was just faithfully sowing gospel seed, losing his life for Christ.

At the New Mexico State Fair I was sponsored by the First Baptist Church of Albuquerque. Two months before the fair, I held a revival at the church and trained counselors to do personal evangelism and follow up when the fair came to town. When the State Fair was held, hardly any of those whom I had trained actually showed up. This was very disappointing, but the Lord worked mightily anyway; hundreds of people heard the gospel, and many were converted.

I distinctly remember seeing a man who appeared very lonely standing in the crowd one evening. He was a little brown-faced, humble-looking Mexican who seemed extremely interested in the message. When I invited people to receive Christ, he raised his hand. As some of us talked with him, he bowed his head and removed his hat, placing it over his heart. As he prayed to accept Christ, tears of repentance, as well as tears of joy, streamed down his face. His name was Manual, and he was overcome by the love and grace of God. "I'm age forty-five," Manual told us. "I'm an entertainer and owner of a music store in Santa Rosa. I've searched for this all of my life."

A young man in Bossier kept wanting to go with me to the fiesta. "It's not easy, Jeff. I spend long hours on those fairgrounds, and I never know what might happen," I said, warning him. But he insisted on going with me to San Antonio. When we arrived and were in the process of positioning my equipment, a teenager walked by and grabbed an arrow from my quiver. "Whoa!" I said. "Put that back, young man!" Without even looking, the kid threw the arrow, point first, over his shoulder, and it hit Jeff right between the eyes. Blood trickled down his face. And within five minutes as Jeff talked to a drunk, the drunk pulled a knife on him! Jeff was ready to go home right then. "Jeff," I said, "we've come a long way; we are not leaving yet." But I could tell that Jeff was miserable, so after just a few days, we left for Bossier before the fiesta was over.

I was driving the step van that Dad and I had converted into a motor home, and I was pulling my Chevrolet van behind it with a tow bar. Just as I made a right turn at Keachi, the ball on the trailer hitch broke loose. Looking into my mirror, I saw the van that I was towing rolling by itself down the road and heading directly into a Texaco station. "Lord, have mercy!" I cried out.

The van hit the gas pump and knocked it over, spilling large amounts of gasoline in all directions. The hand of God was in control, however, and nobody was injured. A state trooper soon arrived, and without thinking he pulled out a cigarette and started to light it. "Officer, don't. Man, the gas!" I exclaimed in horror. The state trooper about choked on that cigarette and dropped his lighter. My insurance covered all damages, but Jeff never asked to go with me again.

CHAPTER 13

Not All Cookies and Cream

At the carnivals and fairs I was able to preach to hundreds and hundreds of lost and unchurched people. Also, I was able to present Christ one on one to many who were very difficult to reach. This was extremely gratifying. I was doing what I really enjoyed and what I felt called to do. I loved it like a dog loves a bone!

However, I encountered many obstacles, and I had to overcome unforeseen problems. There were a few heartaches, too, along the way. In other words, it was not always cookies and cream. Sometimes, I experienced castor oil! Shakespeare said it this way: "The web of our life is of mingled yarn—good and ill together."

A pastor friend told me one day that he knew about the glory of evangelism "Being able to travel around and soak in the accolades from people would be nice," he said. He was speaking from a pastor's perspective, and, having been a pastor myself, I knew that being a pastor was an extremely difficult task and that much of what a pastor did was unappreciated. But if my friend had followed me around from carnival to carnival, I feel certain he would have changed his mind about me experiencing "the glory of evangelism." What I did was taxing work and was considered by many to be the lowest rung on the ministry ladder! I had about as much chance of receiving praise from preaching at the carnivals as a Brahma bull had of getting killed in Kerala, India!

As I was driving to a carnival one afternoon, my van began to go slower and slower, finally coming to a complete stop. Looking under my vehicle, I noticed some plastic that was wrapped around my driveshaft. I then remembered driving over a large sheet of plastic a few miles back. That was, no doubt, what had wound itself up under my van. I must have worked for at least an hour, cutting and pulling and tearing off that plastic. At last I was rid of it, and with bloody knuckles and greasy hands, I drove on to the carnival. Any glory in that?

Another time as I was driving into Dallas early one morning, I ran out of gas. Nobody's fault but my own. I was within sight of the service station, too. But while I was walking to get gas, I tripped over a taut chain about two feet high that was stretched across the sidewalk. Feeling like a dunce, I quickly jumped to my feet, suffering only scraped elbows; somehow, I had escaped without a scratch on my face. It was not quite daylight, so I didn't think anybody saw me.

On my way to a carnival in Decatur, Texas, I had several friends with me in my vehicle, and I was pulling an extra heavy load on my trailer. Five minutes from Boyd, where we would be staying with Eldred Hill and his family, I came to a red light. When I stopped, the load shifted forward on my trailer, causing my trailer hitch to drag the pavement. Two buddies that were with me, Cliff and Tim, said, "We'll hop on the back, Scotty, and our weight will lift up the trailer hitch."

"Well, I'll drive slow. I sure hope a state trooper doesn't see us. Be careful," I replied. There was no traffic, so we headed down the highway; but when I looked in my rearview mirror and saw those two young men sitting high on that trailer, I shouted out the window, "You guys look like Tarzan and Cheetah!" By this time all of us were laughing and praying at the same time, but we made it to Eldred's. However, we got snowed out at the carnival, and it was April in north Texas!

Bad weather was always possible. Often I had to work in frigid temperatures, and many times I had to quickly fold up everything when it began to rain. At one fair my PA system got stolen. On another occasion my car got sideswiped. A number of times I had to practically beg the fair manager to allow me to preach. Sometimes I had to talk my way in through the gate because I was not given any vehicle passes.

Once I allowed a band to share my spot. We took turns. I shot the bow and preached, and then they played and sang. But the band began to take longer and longer to finish their music. I was hardly getting to preach at all. Talking to the leader, I said with as much diplomacy as I could, "Brother, you're taking up too much time. This is not working out. Cut it back a little, OK?" But the band ignored me, including the leader. I had not asked them to shut down, only not to hog the time. Finally, I lost my patience, and I had to do something. I threatened to report them to the fair manager if they didn't leave. Huffing and puffing, they loaded up their drums, slammed their guitar cases together, and left, accusing me of being selfish! So it was not always fun and games when I ministered at the carnivals.

He had long hair, pulled back with a rubber band tied around it, forming a pigtail. A young man, his face was chapped from the cold wind. With his faded jeans and dirty shirt, he fit the stereotype for someone who worked in carnivals, and he was an electrician for the carnival. As he connected my extension cord to the electrical box, he stuck the naked wires inside the box using small sticks, like pickup sticks. Trying to start a conversation with him, I said, "Man, that looks dangerous."

"Well, it is, and I'm real careful," he replied, not taking his eyes off of the wires.

I thanked him for his work, and then I said, "My friend, I'm a preacher, and I'm preaching over here." I motioned with my head back to my right. "It's the bow and arrow show. Drop by sometime. We're just talking about the Lord. Do you know the Lord?" I asked.

"Yeah," he said, "and sometimes I just hate him."

"I know what you mean," I replied.

Turning his head, he looked at me, grimaced, and said, "No, you don't. You don't know anything about me. You don't know what I've been going through, so don't tell me that you know what I mean."

As our eyes met, his pent-up bitterness struck at me like a cobra. "You know, you're right. I don't know what you're dealing with, but if I can be a friend, I want to be," I said with as much empathy as possible. That guy taught me a lesson: if you haven't walked in somebody's shoes, don't act like you have. I talked to that young man several times and learned that his name was Jack. He never did divulge to me why he was so mad at God.

Leaning up against my trailer was a four-foot-by-four-foot plyboard sign that read "Free Bow and Arrow Show." One evening as I was preaching, I noticed out of the corner of my eye, a man dressed in slouchy clothing, bumping through my crowd. Standing and looking at my sign, he mumbled something; then he walked away. About an hour later, as I was again preaching, I saw that the same man had returned and was painting over my sign with long, broad strokes, back and forth, covering it with white paint! I stopped shooting and talking to the crowd and said, "Hey, mister, what are you doing? That's my sign!"

"I heard you preaching; I want to paint you a real sign," he replied, slurring his speech because he was about half drunk. So, without even asking me if he could do it or not, he picked up my plyboard sign and walked away with it, caring it off into the night. I couldn't believe it. No longer did I have my sign, which informed fairgoers about what I was doing.

The next evening the guy returned, carrying a sign depicting a picture of Jesus. Proudly, he showed it to me, pointing at it, as he stepped back admiring his work. "That's a beautiful picture, and I appreciate what you're trying to do," I said, "but I need a sign that reads 'Free Bow and Arrow Show.'"

"You do?" he said, obviously still drinking.

"Yeah," I said, "it lets people know what we're doing."

"OK, I'll take care of it," he answered as he walked away, dizzy-like, carrying the sign on his back.

In a couple of hours, he returned with a fantastic sign. He had painted on the plyboard "Free Bow and Arrow Show" in big red letters against a bright yellow background with silver sparkles all around the edges, just exactly what I needed! He had turned my "sow's ear" sign into a "silk purse" sign!

Over a period of about a week, I got to know this man. His name was A. J., and he was a professional painter. Fragile looking and very thin, A. J. had a problem with booze, and he had lost his family because of his drinking. Realizing that he was in the grip of alcoholism, I spent quality time with him. One night he did pray to receive Christ, and he told some friends who were with me, "I would gladly lay down my life for that guy, Scott."

Several friends accompanied me to the fair in Longview, Texas, but I was embarrassed at what took place. My trailer was not far from the dunking booth, sponsored by the Jaycees. Their loudspeakers were, unintentionally, pointed directly at me and were extremely annoying. To the crowds it was just plain fun to watch people fall into the water, so I had great difficulty competing with the Jaycees. I would gather up a small group of people, but when they heard the water splashing, along with the roaring laughter, off they went to the dunking booth. "Scotty," a friend said to me one night, "after you shot those balloons and turned to address the crowd but found absolutely nobody standing there, you should have seen the look on your face!" We all joked about it, but I really felt like a failure in Longview.

I looked up one day, and there was Lenny. "Lenny, my friend, what are you doing here? Do you have a joint?" (Not marijuana, but a game he managed. In his case, people tried to throw three baseballs into a bushel basket in order to win a prize.)

"Yeah," he answered, "on the independent midway."

I had met Lenny at another fair. Jewish and from the Bronx, he was bald, chubby, but had a sharp mind. I was surprised at how well read he was. Many who worked the carnivals had police records; others were hiding, but more than a few were world travelers and very intelligent. By his vocabulary I could tell Lenny had an extremely high IQ. Not allowing me to talk to him one on one, he did slip up, from time to time, and listen to me preach, sitting way back in the shadows. Lenny told me that he was staying in a campground not far from the carnival. One night it rained a deluge, and he felt like he had gotten flooded out. He was about to take a cab to the campground to check everything over when I said, "Lenny, I'll give you a ride to the trailer park if you let me talk to you about the Lord. Save you a few bucks. How 'bout it?" I asked. He agreed.

His small trailer was not flooded, so he asked me in, and for over an hour we talked and argued and discussed and debated the Bible, who Jesus was, and the resurrection. Then I made a terrible blunder. Frustrated with him, I blurted out, "Come on, Jew. (I honestly meant to say, Lenny.) You know I'm right." Well, that did it. Very much offended, he replied, "Yeah, it would be a feather in your cap if I, a Jew, got converted. Well, no thanks!"

I apologized, but the damage had been done. I left and never saw Lenny again, but for years, at every carnival I attended, I looked for him.

At one particular fair, an old carnival owner was heartless, refusing to give me a spot on the midway even though I had offered to pay him a good price. Finally, he conceded, but after I had set everything up, which took about two hours, he made me move to another location. But once again when I got all of my equipment in place and hooked up to electricity, he told me to move to another place. I was hot and sweaty and didn't know what to do, but I went to him and tried to return good for evil, telling him how much God loved him and that Jesus Christ died for him. Looking stunned, this old, white-haired man began to cry and, taking a handkerchief from his back pocket, he began to wipe tears that were flowing down his red, sunburned cheeks; then he awarded me with a good spot, free of charge, and never gave me any more trouble.

From time to time, my good friend Al Bohl joined me at the fairs, carnivals, and rodeos. An anointed singer, Al was also a gifted artist and compelling preacher, just a multitalented guy. Sometimes at fairs we worked from a big white concession trailer that I had purchased from Wells Cargo. (My old brown step van that I had converted into a motor home finally played out.) Everything was already set up inside this big concession trailer—PA system, lights, target, and sketch board. The entire right side of the trailer swung open and became an awning.

Once, at a particular carnival, I received permission to park my concession trailer at a specific location. Having ministered there for a couple of days, I was shocked when I discovered one morning that it was not at the site where I had left it. Had it been stolen? Moved? We didn't know what had become of my trailer. When we talked to the carnies in the joints around us, one of them said that the police had impounded it. "We had permission to be there! What do they mean?" I said, in disgust.

Al and I went to the police station, but the cops gave us no explanation; instead they charged us fifty dollars to get my concession trailer back. What was so ironic about all of this was that two days earlier, the police had asked us themselves to come to the jail and put on an archery exhibition, preach, and sing. This we did that very afternoon. But how strange it was having my trailer impounded by the very police who had us minister in their jail a couple of days before! By the way, we never were reimbursed our fifty bucks.

His name was Ace, and his girlfriend's name was Shepherd. They ran the toboggan ride. As I looked around the midway, I saw them huddled against a tent. Quivering and shaking, they both were mainliners, addicted to heroin. I had never seen a couple so filthy. Covered with oil, grease, dirt, sweat, and smoke, they reeked with the smell of beer and urine. Their faces were dark with soot. Mrs. Lillian Scott, Patti Sherrod, and I engaged them in a conversation, offering them hope and freedom in Christ. They seemed untouched by what we said. I knew that only the Holy Spirit could break their chains and salvage their lives. Ace and Shepherd have been in my prayers for years.

No, it was not always easy preaching at the carnivals and fairs. I had my problems and setbacks and disappointments, but doesn't everybody? But I was so greatly blessed while preaching at them that I felt like Father Abraham, whom God had so richly blessed in the past!

One evening a group of Christians stopped and watched and listened to me preach the gospel. They said they were from Victory Temple, not far from the fair. Bubbling with joy and enthusiasm, they obviously loved the Lord very much. After telling me where their church was located, they invited me to visit sometime, had prayer for me, and went on their way, rejoicing.

The next day I noticed a guy sleeping on a piece of cardboard under a big eighteen wheeler. I eased up under the trailer, made a little noise on purpose, and he woke up. Introducing myself, I began to talk with him about his relationship with God. A Chippewa Indian, he was unbelievably receptive to the gospel, and he received Christ right there under that old truck. Guess where I took him? Right! Victory Temple.

When we walked into the storefront church, we found ourselves in the middle of singing—loud and strong singing. The music, "I'm so glad Jesus lifted me, I'm so glad Jesus lifted me," resonated with great conviction throughout the building. Here, gathered in Victory Temple, were ex-cons, former drug addicts, former alcoholics, as well as a few former prostitutes. Talk about praise! All were singing with gusto, swaying from side to side and clapping. They welcomed us with big smiles. What a place to take a newborn Christian! We felt totally accepted and wanted.

At the Louisiana State Fair in Shreveport, a young man saw what we were doing and began talking with my friends and me. His name was David Reed, and he was a high-wire artist, performing the high-wire act thirty-three feet in the air at the grandstand. A dedicated Christian, David gave his testimony from our platform. I asked him in front of the crowd how he came to know Christ. "I was up on the wire," he replied, "and the thought occurred to me that if I fell, I was not prepared to meet God. I couldn't get down fast enough. I soon came to know Christ as my Lord and Savior."

Meeting Christians like David Reed at the fairs taught me that God has his people in all walks of life. And I can truthfully say that as I traveled from place to place, I met some of the most talented, interesting people, I believe, in all the world.

I ministered at the Fort Worth Stock Show for fourteen straight years. Year after year an attractive, smiling lady wearing glasses would push her son, who was in a wheelchair, up close to watch me shoot the bow. I always tried my best when they were present, but I had tears in my heart, looking at that kid in the wheelchair. After the exhibition, that mother would release the brake and roll her son away. "See you next year," they would say, smiling and waving.

Often, I shot a balloon attached to a sign which unrolled and read "Christ Died for Our Sins." Then I popped another balloon attached to another sign, which unrolled and read "He Arose Again the Third Day!" One afternoon as I was standing around waiting for the next "Showtime," a man with a teenage boy walked up and said to me, "You don't know me, but I've been bringing my son by here for years. And I want you to know that for at least ten years I've seen those signs unroll. I've seen them when I drive; I've seen them in my sleep; at work, all over the place. Recently, I was converted at a James Robison Crusade, but I want you to know that God really used those signs to get me to Christ."

When that gentleman revealed his story to me, I was super high! Does not the Bible teach in 1 Corinthians 3:6–9 that somebody sows, another waters, but it is God that gives the increase?

Coming back from a carnival in south Texas, I noticed the beautiful Texas bluebonnets and orange-red Indian paintbrushes along the highway. Knowing how much Linda loved flowers, I decided to pick a few of them, even though it was against the law, I had been told. A few months earlier Linda and I had passed a Volkswagen parked beside the highway, and we noticed a fellow obviously picking flowers for his girlfriend. "Scotty," Linda said, "why don't you ever do anything like that for me? You used to before we were married."

So, thinking about that incident, I decided to take her some flowers. Not having a vase, I looked around for a container, and I spotted a plastic Clorox bottle floating in the ditch. Cutting the bottle in two, about halfway down, I dipped it in the ditch and filled it up with brown, muddy water. Waiting for all the traffic to get out of sight, I quickly picked as many bluebonnets and paintbrushes as I could stuff into that plastic bottle. Then, I gently rearranged the flowers, making what I thought was a pretty good bouquet. Trust me. I did a balancing act all the way home to keep them from spilling.

But did it work or what! When I got home and gave Linda those flowers, you would have thought I had given her two dozen long-stemmed red roses! She couldn't hug me enough! For days she kept them over the sink until they finally were so wilted that she had to throw them out.

PART TWO:
NEW YORK CITY

CHAPTER 14

THINKING ABOUT THE BIG APPLE

On August 16, 1977, Elvis Presley died. That date sticks in my mind because when I heard about his death, I was with George Naggy of the Open Air Campaigners, and we were preaching at Times Square. I first met George in 1975 in Chicago at the OAC staff conference. At the time, I was very much involved in carnival evangelism, but George said to me, "Scotty, if you want to preach to a lot of unconverted people, you need to come to New York City. It's the greatest city in the world for outdoor preaching."

I had visited New York City when I was in high school as a member of the Bossier High School Band, and I had driven to New York a couple of years earlier in order to get my van equipped like the OAC vans, so I was somewhat familiar with the Big Apple.

I was having more and more difficulty getting a spot at the carnivals. They were being inundated with the cults. Many fair boards were refusing admittance to anybody, even legitimate ministries, in order to keep out the Moonies, Hare Krishnas, and other similar groups. So, I began to think seriously about George's invitation for me to come to New York.

"Lord, I am not asking to be famous or world renowned, but I am asking you, Lord, to let me preach the gospel to tons of lost people," I had said to God many years earlier. The Lord had been answering my prayer by opening doors of opportunity for me to preach at the fairs, so I was grateful; however, George's words about my being able to preach to so many unconverted on the streets of New York kept coming to mind. So I decided to check New York City out for myself.

"George," I said over the phone, "I'd like to come to New York and work with you a few days. Any place I can stay?"

"Yeah, Scotty," answered George, "you can stay with Betty and me or even at the church." So off I went. I had grown up with the opinion that practically everybody in New York was a mugger, a con artist, or a drug dealer, so, the first time I opened my van door in Hicksville, where George lived, I stepped out with clenched fists, thinking that at any moment somebody was going to jump me! Well, I learned that that simply was not the case. Hicksville, a city out on Long Island, was very much like Shreveport-Bossier, with beautiful red and pink azaleas and yellow forsythia growing everywhere. I was in a somewhat different culture, but the people were nice, not at all threatening or abrasive; direct, to be sure, but friendly, once they got to know you. I stayed at the church, Hicksville Baptist Church, sleeping in the nursery on a pallet, but I slept comfortably and had my privacy.

One morning George picked up a kid named Bruce Hoppe from his church, and the three of us headed to the city. I realized quickly that driving from Hicksville to Manhattan was a nightmare. The Long Island Expressway was jammed. The Northern State Parkway was jammed. Sunrise Highway was jammed. Bruce suggested the Southern State Parkway, but it, too, was bumper to bumper. I had never seen such traffic in my entire life, and I had visited many major cities.

My jaw flung open when George did a U-turn directly in front of the New York Stock Exchange "Gotta grab that parking place," George exclaimed. Our very first open air service was a noon hour meeting on Wall Street, and I was intimidated by the business suits and huge, monstrous stone buildings. Before he preached, George did a couple of sleight-of-hand tricks that I had learned years earlier at my first OAC seminar and had been using at the carnivals; quickly, to my astonishment, a standing crowd of professional men and women gathered all around us.

Later, it was my turn to preach. Accustomed to using a bow and arrow demonstration to gather a crowd, I was uncomfortable standing on the van platform and using just the sketch board. But by doing the same "magic tricks," I soon had an attentive crowd, to my surprise. I didn't need the bow and arrow in New York City; besides, I might accidentally shoot somebody! I think my thick, Southern accent actually helped me draw a crowd. Once, however, a guy walked by and said to me, "You talk like you are from the 1890s." But by and large, my accent was an asset, not a liability.

Seeing the faces on the sidewalk began to haunt me. I had been preaching in the Bible Belt to a lot of lost people at the carnivals, but, still, most of them were church oriented, had a fair knowledge of the Bible, were somewhat familiar with the facts of the gospel, and had a biblical world view. But here on the streets of New York were people of every race and culture and religion in the world, with philosophies, ideas, beliefs, opinions, and views that I had never heard before. What a place for the gospel of Christ! During my visit in 1977 to New York, the Lord God opened my eyes to the needs of New York City, and I could not keep from thinking about the Big Apple.

A few days after I returned from New York, Ken Norris, pastor of Baptist Church of America, asked me to take a load of food, candy, and medicine to Old Mexico, which I was glad to do. When I arrived, a man named Francisco, with his wife and little baby girl, saw aspirin, milk of magnesia, and other medicines that I had with me. How elated and relieved they were when I gave them all I could. Those few supplies meant the difference between life and death for their baby.

I worked with Bob Smith, a missionary and founder of a Bible school in Matamoros, Mexico. What a tremendous job he was doing, training young ministers to preach the gospel and plant churches. One afternoon Bob asked me to start shooting the bow and arrow as he announced over a loudspeaker in Spanish that we were holding a street meeting. Small Mexican boys and girls looked wide eyed at the balloons and crept up closer for a better view. Teenagers watched from a distance. Eventually, many Mexicans, young and old alike, gathered around us and listened to the music and testimonies.

Bob and I both preached; he, of course, was my interpreter. When the invitation was given, four elderly women came forward. One old woman was on a cane, and I had to help her up a muddy embankment. Bob asked them several questions and led them in prayer. When those four old Mexican women looked up, they were glowing like I pictured Moses's face when he came down from Mount Sinai! It was a beautiful sight to behold. Later, we distributed lots of candy to the children; but as we drove away, I saw tiny kids blowing up bubbles in the pieces of balloons that they had found. Some sat in raw sewage.

Bob drove me around and showed me the needs of his area. I could tell by the way that he talked how much he cared about the people. God had called him to Mexico. But I was inexplicably drawn to New York, and I could not quit thinking about it. So, Linda and I, along with several of our close friends, Mrs. Lillian Scott, Eldred Hill, and Doris and Al Bohl, flew to New York in early August 1979. George and his wife, Betty, made us feel very welcome, and their church allowed us to stay in the missionary house, which had not been occupied for quite some time. Actually, Linda and I slept in a van. Eldred got the big bed, and the others had good sleeping quarters, too. I complained about it to everybody, but nobody paid any attention to me!

George gave us a tour of the Big Apple, and I was once again proud of being an American as I gazed on the Statue of Liberty, but was a little disappointed with Coney Island. We had many successful outdoor meetings from Harlem to Chinatown, from Bedford Stuyvesant to the South Bronx. Linda didn't like the city. She agreed with those who said "New York is a nice place to visit, but I wouldn't want to live there."

After returning from New York, Al and I were invited by Fred and Claudine Embry of Mena, Arkansas, to the Polk County Fair. The Embrys ran a grocery store outside of Mena and lived in a pretty, A-framed house. Al and I had great accommodations and were treated like kings. What committed Christians Fred and Claudine were!

At the Polk County Fair there were lots of folks walking around the midway, but they were very laid-back and polite, wonderful people, really. As we ministered, we noticed how quiet the midway was. Then Al and I both began to chuckle. We realized that we had just returned from preaching on the streets of New York City. Compared to that place, Mena, Arkansas, was like a graveyard!

Even though New York was very much on my mind, during the next year I continued ministering at the carnivals and fairs. I even tried my hand at preaching on the streets of Houston and Dallas. But cities such as these were not very conducive to street preaching; there were not enough pedestrians on the sidewalks, and only in a few places could I gather a significant crowd. New York was unique. Great hordes of people filled up the sidewalks throughout its five boroughs. Many nights, as I dropped off to sleep, thoughts of the Big Apple rushed through my brain.

CHAPTER 15

THE CALL TO NEW YORK CITY

I had visited New York a number of times, and in early August 1979, I had taken Linda with me; but, later that same month, I went back to New York because I could not get it out of my system. Once again, I ministered with George Naggy on the streets. But Art Williams in Plainfield, New Jersey, the head of OAC, invited us to go with him and Jack Kreidler to Atlantic City to preach on the Boardwalk. George could not make it, but I went, anxious to see the Boardwalk that I had run up and down on as a member of the Bossier High School Band back in 1959.

Art had been an atheist but was converted to Christ at Purdue University. A thin man who wore glasses, he now was a very mature, committed Christian. Extremely proficient on the sketch board, he was quite an artist and had a deep understanding of God's word. It was an honor for me to accompany him, and I tried to learn all that I could from him, just as I had sought to learn from George.

Jack was an Italian who ministered in Rome. He looked Italian with his thick, black, wavy hair, chiseled features, and streetwise charm. Before he was converted, he was involved in what he labeled as the "Italian Mafia." One day Jack shared his testimony with me. "I had everything I wanted, but I was miserable, and my mother could see that," he said. "Why don't you try God?" his mother asked. "Five little words," Jack said, as he held up his fingers and pointed to each one of them. "I had religion but not Christ. The Lord saved me, and I've been preaching ever since," he said with a broad smile. He then folded his arms behind his head and leaned back in his chair.

Art, Jack, and I stayed in a little bungalow on the beach, and we had some marvelous outdoor meetings on the Boardwalk. We also spent a lot of time in prayer on our knees. Art said to me one afternoon, "Scotty, I believe God is calling you to New York City." Jack agreed.

"I don't know," I replied. "That's a big step, coming way up here with my family." Tossing and turning that night, I couldn't sleep and was restless and confused. "Lord," I said, "do you want me up here? I'll come, but I've got to know for sure." God began to show me for certain that he had indeed called me to the streets of New York City!

I returned from New York, and not long after that, the Louisiana State Fair opened in Shreveport. That was a special fair, not only because it was in my hometown of Shreveport-Bossier, but because that's where I had given Linda an engagement ring and had asked her to marry me. The State Fair game was between Louisiana Tech and Northwestern, fierce rivals at that time. I don't remember who won, but I do remember that Linda said, "Yes."

It was also at the Louisiana State Fair that I had begun preaching outside for the first time at carnivals, several years earlier. Previously, I had ministered from booths, inside, at the carnivals and fairs; but there was no space available for me one year at Shreveport, so I preached from a big, eighteen-wheel, flatbed truck that I shared with other groups. It was also interesting to me that Billy Graham first began holding his crusades outside at Shreveport, back in 1950. Because the Municipal Auditorium could not accommodate his crowds, he elected to move to State Fair Stadium. Attendance tripled. I was present at that crusade.

One night at the fair my revolving balloon machine got stolen, and shooting at moving balloons really attracted people, so I was sick about it. But whoever took it must have had a guilty conscience, because he brought it back. One afternoon I looked, and there the machine was, sitting beside the truck. Yes, the Louisiana State Fair was a special fair in my eyes.

This particular year (October 1979) was no exception. The weather was perfect, with the crispness of fall in the air. The crowds were good; there were many decisions for Christ. One evening as I was shooting the bow and preaching, a young man walked up and observed what was happening. Later, he introduced himself and said that he was going to New York. "Is that right?" I asked. "I just came back from New York and Atlantic City a few weeks ago. I've been praying about moving to New York."

"Well, I'm going up there to see about becoming a youth minister. I've got a good friend there, and they need a youth guy, so I'm going to check it out," he replied. We talked awhile, and then he disappeared into the crowd on the midway.

About two weeks later I got a phone call. "Remember me? I'm Alan. I met you at the fair," he said. "I'm the guy from Arizona. I heard you preaching, and we talked. I was heading to New York."

"Yeah, I remember you now," I answered.

"Listen, I've got something to tell you. Can I meet you somewhere?" he asked. He sounded urgent, and I felt he was legit; so we decided to meet at the Shreve City Bowling Alley. I walked in, and we recognized each other.

"What's going on?" I asked as we sat down at a table.

"Well, let me ask you a question. How many people do you know in New York?" he asked.

"Well, I know George Naggy and his family," I answered.

"Do you know anybody in New Jersey?" he asked.

"Yeah," I said, "I know…"

He then interrupted me. "Don't tell me. I think I can tell you who you know up there," he said, smiling. "Art Williams. Is that right?"

"Yeah, how did you know that?" I asked.

"As I told you on the fairgrounds a couple of weeks ago, I was headed to New York—well, actually, New Jersey, to check out a position on staff—and the guy who is the pastor, Charlie Horton, is a close friend of Art Williams. And one night Charles said that he was going with Art to hold a street meeting. He asked me to join them. So I went, but it was chilly and windy, so we didn't have much of a meeting; maybe two or three people listened a little bit. Later, we went and got a cup of coffee and began to talk," he said.

"Where you from?" Art asked.

"Arizona," Alan replied.

"How did you get up here? Drive?" Art asked.

"Yeah," Alan said, "and it's a long way to New Jersey."

"Well, I've got a friend down in Shreveport," Art said.

"I came through there," Alan told him.

"This guy shoots bows and arrows and preaches," Art said to Alan.

"I met him!" Alan said.

"You did?" replied Art.

"Yeah, at the fair. He was shooting that bow," said Alan.

"Was his name Scotty?" Art asked.

"Yeah, Scotty, that was it. I don't recall his last name," Alan said.

"Scotty Teague," answered Art.

Art then asked Alan if he was going back through Shreveport, and Alan said that he was. "Well, be sure and give him this message. Tell him that Art Williams believes that the Lord has called him to New York and to get himself up here," Art said, with emphasis.

"I'll tell him," Alan replied.

"So, here I am," he said, smiling.

I sat there in the bowling alley in disbelief. I had heard Tom Brokaw say on the news that there were twenty-five million people living within fifty miles of the Empire State Building, and the only person I really knew in New Jersey, this guy had run into! The odds of that happening were mind-boggling! I could see the hand of the Lord in this, and I could see his hand very clearly.

I was excited about maybe moving to New York, but I loved Dixie and didn't want to leave the South. Most of all, I did not want my family to be hurt. Linda and I had often talked about New York, and it was always upsetting to her when we did. Late one night I happened to be watching the movie *Midnight Cowboy* on television. The sight of New York City made my heart beat faster. Listening to the soundtrack, "Everybody's Talking," and seeing a limping Dustin

Hoffman slap that taxi as he walked across the street touched me emotionally. I wanted to be there, in that rat race, with all of that noise and confusion and rudeness and blatant directness. New York was calling!

I had been to New York enough to know that the cost of living was astronomical and that housing was difficult to find and extremely expensive. So one day I said to the Lord, "Lord, I do believe you are steering me to New York, but, Lord, you know I've got to be sure. I don't want to make a mistake." I then put out a fleece, not the mark of a mature Christian, perhaps, but that's what I did anyway. "God," I said, "if you really want me to move to New York, provide housing for me, free." "There," I said to myself, "that ought to do it." Then I went about my business of trying to be a good husband and father and ministering every chance I got.

One evening the unexpected happened. I got a call from George, my OAC buddy who lived in Hicksville out on Long Island. "Scotty, this is George," he said.

"Hey, George, what's up?" I asked.

"Scotty," George continued, "you remember that missionary house on the church grounds?"

"Yeah, George, the one all of us stayed in, back in August?" I answered.

"Well," George said, "I know how you've been wanting to come up here, so I brought it up at the business meeting at our church. No missionary family is living there now, and our church discussed it, and it was unanimous! You and Linda and your boys can live in that missionary house, rent free, for one year."

I about dropped the phone. "Are you serious, George?" I asked.

"Yeah," he replied, "so come on up."

When I got off the phone and reminded Linda of the fleece that I had put out about free housing, and then told her what George said, that the missionary house was available to us for one year without costing us a single penny, my head was spinning! It sure looked like God was trying to tell me something. I had not been able to erase New York from my mind. And then there was the young man I met at the Louisiana State Fair. When he returned from New Jersey with words from Art Williams, the only person I knew in that state—that was almost eerie. The way that scenario played out was no coincidence. And now the missionary house was available, fulfilling the very sign I had requested from God. Talking to friends and fellow ministers, I got the same message—"Scott, it looks like God is calling you to New York City."

Without telling anybody but Linda, I checked into the Mason Motel on Barksdale Boulevard and prayed and fasted, seeking God's face. This was all new to me. Honestly, I had never fasted before, but this was something that I had to do, now. I took a little fruit with me, and my Bible. That was it. Day and night I prayed and searched the scriptures. "Lord, not my will but your will be done," I prayed over and over. "Father God, I will do anything," I said, "just please give me scripture to validate all that has happened, pointing me to New York."

And God began to do just that! The Holy Spirit spoke to me in verse after verse. "For a great door and effectual is opened unto me, and there are many adversaries" (1 Corinthians 16:9). "I have set before thee an open door, and no man can shut it" (Revelation 3:8). "For thou art not sent to a people of a foreign language" (Ezekiel 3:5). "We were willing to have imparted unto you not only the gospel of God only, but also our own souls" (1 Thessalonians 2:8). There were scores of other verses also—at least two pages—that God used to confirm my call to New York. When I left that motel, I knew that God had called me to the streets of New York City to preach the gospel. No doubt about it. The Holy Spirit had spoken through the Bible to me.

As I drove home, I rounded the curve on Orbit Street, a block from my house. I saw that man again. Many times I had passed him and had been impressed to give him a visit, but I had neglected to do it. God spoke to my heart. "You are thinking about going to New York, and you haven't even talked to your neighbor down the street." I pulled over and stopped. "Hey, my friend. How are you doing today?" I asked, addressing the gentleman in the chair.

"Good, have a seat," he said politely.

We talked awhile, and I learned that he had terminal cancer. Presenting the gospel to him, I then had prayer. We shook hands, and he told me that he really appreciated my talking to him. As I drove on home, "the peace that passes understanding" came over me—great, assuring peace, perfect peace, the peace of God.

Seeing my face when I walked into our home, Linda knew that we were going to New York. As I hugged her, I remembered the words that she had said to me under those oak trees before we were married: "I'll go anywhere with you, Scotty. Oh, the only place I don't want to go is New York."

CHAPTER 16

MONEY MATTERS

The decision had been made. We were moving to New York in August 1980. I talked to Stan Palmer, who not only was a trusted friend but who also was in the real estate business. "Are you sure you want to sell your house, Scotty?" Stan asked. "Your monthly payment here is very low; you'll never again have a house note as cheap as this."

Pausing a little, I replied, "I'm sure. I just hope and pray that we can get what we're asking for it." So, we put our house in Bossier up for sale.

We had been living by faith for years as I had ministered at the carnivals. A number of people had backed us faithfully, unbelievably so. But I knew that since I was moving to New York, I needed to increase our base of support. It was going to take more money to live and preach in New York than it did to live down south and minister at the carnivals and fairs. I certainly didn't have a "Daddy" Warbucks!

I called Brother Stogner, who had been my pastor at Waller and who now was director of missions of the Northwest Louisiana Baptist Association. Asking him if I could speak to the association about my ministry in New York, I was told, "Sure, Scotty, I'll put you on the program."

Soon the day came for me to address the association. The meeting was packed. Dr. Bailey Smith was the guest speaker, so there were probably one hundred pastors present. Dr. Bailey Smith gave an inspirational message, which we all enjoyed, but he went over his allotted time. I was left out. But just as Brother Stogner was about to dismiss the meeting, I stood to my feet. "Brother Stogner," I said, "I won't take but a few minutes, but let me say a few words about New York, OK?" Before he could answer, I began passing out pictures of me preaching on the streets of New York City, along with a brief biological sketch. Then, for the next five minutes, I poured my heart out about God calling me to New York. I asked for their prayer support and, if possible, for a little financial help.

Many of the pastors that were present knew me. I had preached in their churches, put on bow and arrow exhibitions at their sweetheart banquets, been camp pastor at their youth camps, spoken at their vacation Bible schools. They knew I had grown up at Waller under Brother Stogner, had pastored Koran Baptist Church, and had been on staff under Dr. Vaughn at First Baptist, Bossier. Yet none of them offered to give me any support. I got a few "amens" and "God bless yous" and "We'll be praying for yous." That was it. (Several churches in the association later began helping me.)

As I gathered up some of my materials that were left on tables, Brother Step Martin, pastor of Calvary Baptist Church in Shreveport, came up to me and said, "Scotty, we're going to put you in our budget for fifty dollars a month. I was blessed by what you said." A few weeks later, Billy Crosby, a close friend of Brother Step, asked me to speak at his church in Houston. It was a Wednesday evening service. Using the sketch board, I preached a brief message and asked the church to pray for my family and me as we headed to New York. Brother Billy then took up an offering, and it was an absolutely fantastic amount.

Years earlier, I had endeavored to gain some financial backing from the Home Mission Board when I was engaged in the carnival ministry, but to no avail. Perhaps they would help me with a ministry in New York. So I gave them a call and asked to address the board and share my heart about the New York street ministry. I was told, "Scott, our executive board meeting is coming up soon. You may talk to them then." The gentleman gave me a date. "Well, sir, thank you. I'll be there, the Lord willing," I replied.

Soon I caught a plane to Atlanta, walked into the Home Mission Board, and knocked on the door of the executive director. "Come on in," he said, "what can I do for you?" he asked.

"Sir, I'm Scotty Teague. I talked to you on the phone the other day about my speaking to the executive board concerning the ministry in New York," I said.

"Well, Scotty, that meeting was held yesterday," he nonchalantly said to me. "I'm sorry."

"Yesterday! Sir, you told me the date. I wrote it down. I've flown all the way from Shreveport at my own expense. Is there another time I can speak to them?" I said, totally frustrated.

"Well, no, the meeting took place yesterday," he said.

I paused, and then looked at him straight in the eyes. "God bless you, sir," I said. I didn't say anything else. I walked to the elevator and caught a taxi to the airport. I couldn't help but spill my guts to the cab driver, and when he dropped me off at the airport, he said, "No charge. This one's on me." I flew home feeling betrayed. I felt like the sheriff (Gary Cooper) in the classic movie *High Noon*. Wanting him to leave, the town folks would not help him. After the sheriff took care of the bad guys, he set his jaw, stared at every body with a disgusted expression on his face, took off his tin star, and without even looking down, he threw it in the dirt. Then, he and his new bride (Grace Kelly) rode away in the wagon and never looked back.

Returning from Atlanta with a bad taste in my mouth, I met with my close friend Al Bohl, and we talked about all that had transpired. "Scotty," Al said, "you'll probably thank the Lord one day that they did not support you. You would've had many forms and reports to fill out constantly. You would've had to fit into their mold. You would've had to do it their way and not your way."

I've never forgotten Al's words, and I have thanked God numerous times that the Home Mission Board did not undergird my ministry. As Al reminded me, if they had, I would have been chained to their structured approach and would not have been free to minister as the Lord led me. Also, I would've never known the sheer joy of living by faith and watching God provide in miraculous ways, being accountable only to him and to those who chose to help us.

One of my favorite professors at Southwestern was Dr. Ken Chafin. He taught evangelism and was fun to listen to. Before heading to New York, I decided to seek his counsel. Dr. Chafin was then pastor of South Main Baptist Church in Houston. A friend of mine, Ken Hansen, whom I had met at First Baptist, Bossier, was now living in Houston, and he asked to go with me to see Dr. Chafin. "Yeah, Ken, come on," I said.

Now, Ken was an unusual young man. Very thin and wearing glasses, Ken was as dry as West Texas dust in a drought, but he was always trying to promote me. He wrote letters, made phone calls, and earnestly tried to gain financial help for my ministry, most of the time without my knowledge! But we were friends, and he meant well. I understood him, but, man, was he bulldog persistent or what!

Dr. Chafin's secretary told us that he was busy and unavailable, but Ken and I waited in the hall of the church and spotted him going into a room. Knocking gently on his door, I stood there with Ken. Both of us were nervous. When Dr. Chafin opened the door, I said quickly, "Dr. Chafin, I'm Scotty Teague, and I had you for Evangelism at Southwestern. This is my friend, Ken. We know you're busy, but Dr. Chafin, I need to talk to you for ten minutes."

"Come on in, Scotty; you guys sit down," he said, politely. Dr. Chafin sat on a couch, and Ken and I sat across from him. "Now, what can I do for you, Scotty?" he asked.

Speaking very fast, too fast, really, I began: "Dr. Chafin, the Lord has called me to New York City. I do a lot of preaching on the streets, but it's not what you might think. I use a sketch board, and I don't employ a PA. I get the crowd up real close. I'm not preaching to a parade of people walking. People really listen. I've preached at carnivals for years, too."

"OK," he said, a little perplexed.

"Well," I continued, "I'm having difficulty getting financial help, and I wonder if you have any pull with the Home Mission Board."

"How much do you think it will take a year?" he asked. "You probably have a family."

"Yes, sir," I said, "a wife and two sons, and I think it will take about twenty to twenty-five thousand a year."

"I think it will take more than that," Dr. Chafin replied. "It's expensive to live in New York." We talked a few minutes, and Dr. Chafin reminded me that in church, people were at least interested or they would not be there.

"I know, sir, that's just it. I want to reach those who are not interested and who are not in church," I answered. Then I said, "Well, Ken, we better go. Dr. Chafin, I just wanted to know if there was anything you could do. My ten minutes are up."

As I got up, Dr. Chafin asked me to sit back down, and the three of us continued talking. I shared with him about the carnival ministry that I had been in for years and that now the Lord was leading me to New York. Then, my friend Ken stood up and began to speak and, walking over to the couch, he continued to talk, telling Dr. Chafin all about my ministry. I was embarrassed, but there was little I could do. Ken sat down and, in his monotone, never stopped speaking. Then, still talking, Ken pulled his legs up under himself on the couch. He inched closer and closer to Dr. Chafin, still talking and bragging on me.

"Ken," I said, "we probably need to go." But then Ken got right up in Dr. Chafin's face and pointed his finger at him and asked, "Why doesn't the Home Mission Board support Scotty?"

Dr. Chafin was very courteous and patient while this was happening. He did not appear to be embarrassed at all. He told us that he would like to help but that he had no input into the Home Mission Board budget.

"Dr. Chafin," I said, "we did not mean to be pushy. Please forgive us." We had prayer and, with a firm handshake, he said very graciously that he would be praying for me and to keep him informed. Ken and I left not knowing what to do next. (I realize that many godly men and women are associated with and are supported by the North American Mission Board, formerly the Home Mission Board.)

Years earlier, while attending Southwestern Seminary Chapel, I heard Gil Strickland preach. He had been Billy Graham's press secretary. The Lord brought him to mind, so I went to see him. What a man of God he was, too, very open and transparent and sympathetic to my ministry in New York. After talking and praying together, Gil said, "Scott, it boils down to this. If God has called you to the sidewalks of New York City, God will provide."

I had done everything I knew to do to raise funds for the New York ministry. "Lord," I prayed, "I'm going to New York City. I'm trusting you to provide, and I'm never looking back."

CHAPTER 17

ARRIVING

My family and I arrived in New York on Labor Day weekend 1980. I was thirty-seven and Linda was thirty-six. I could not wait to show Linda and the boys our new home in Smithtown, Long Island. As we wound around the crooked road leading into Smithtown, I noticed that Linda was looking at the neighborhoods, the houses, the yards. You would have thought we were in a nice suburb of Shreveport-Bossier. Pulling into the driveway at Rotundi Court, I blurted out to Linda and the kids, "Here it is; how do you like it?"

The house was more than we could have ever dreamed of—big, spacious, a two-story colonial with a large basement, and a big yard on a cul-de-sac in a very good area. We were able to assume the previous owner's loan, and the money that was required was about what we had to put down. (Even though the missionary house in Hicksville was available, we never actually lived there.)Praise the Lord! Linda, who is easy to please, was smiling, and I could that tell she approved of the house, especially after I gave everybody a tour. I had warned her about the living room carpet, a bright, Arnold Palmer golf course green that hit you in the face when you first saw it. "You're right, Scotty, that's a loud color," Linda exclaimed, "but I love the house!"

During a previous trip house hunting in New York, I had opened a bank account and purchased a post office box. When our bank transferred our money from Bossier to Smithtown, we learned that the money was not going to clear and be available for a few more days, and the moving company would not unload our furniture until they got their money. Realizing that we were in a bind, the Smithtown bank manager took money from her own account and said, "Use this to pay Mayflower; you can reimburse me when your money clears." We couldn't believe it. We were total strangers to her, and she was a New Yorker. New Yorkers were supposed to be uncaring and untrustworthy. This generous gesture on her part caused me to begin dropping my prejudices against Yankees, and I was reminded once again that people are pretty much the same everywhere.

Settling in was not easy. First, we were alarmed when our lawyer did not show up at closing. Some guy eventually appeared and finished the deal. "I come here with egg on my face," he said, apologizing. Then, the house required much more repairing than we had realized. Not being accustomed to water-based heating, one night we heard water gurgle and other strange noises. I just knew our basement was flooded, or there was a burglar in the house. Trying to locate the light switch in the dark, with a pillow in my hand, I walked down the steps into the basement, lifting my feet real high, up and down, like a cat with socks on, thinking that at any minute I would be in water knee deep. Thankfully, there was neither flooding nor a thief, just the bubbling from the water-based heating. But as I walked back upstairs, the smoke detector went off directly above my head, scaring me so much that I shouted and threw the pillow up into the air. Linda, sitting up in bed, screamed, "Scotty, is that you?"

"Yeah, babe, it's me," I said, and I explained what had happened. We laughed ourselves to sleep, but we had a good sleep in our new home.

While contemplating New York, Linda and I certainly didn't want to put our sons in some inner-city, drug-infested, dangerous school, so, I had already inquired into the schools in Smithtown and felt that they were excellent. The next day we enrolled our kids in school, Stephen in the seventh and Stewart in the second grade.

Soon I was headed to the post office to see if we had received any mail, meaning financial help from back home. Richard and Mary Johnson, two of our best friends in Bossier, had given us a going- away party, and many people attended, assuring us that they would pray for us and stand behind us. Letters of encouragement and checks came in, and have to this very day.

My family and I began attending Grace Baptist Church in Lake Grove, a small, Southern Baptist Church not far from Smithtown. Bob Books was pastor, and he and his wife, Mary, as well as the rest of the church, welcomed us with open arms. It was good to be with God's people. Another church relatively close to us, North Shore Baptist Church, was without a pastor, so I preached for them several weeks. They asked me if I was interested in becoming their pastor. They were wonderful people, but I told them no because God had called me to the streets. Soon we were regular attenders back at Grace Baptist and began making terrific friends. Two people that we met and came to know were Burris and Jana Jenkins.

I had met Burris when I was house hunting out on Long Island a few weeks back. Working in real estate part time, he tried to help me relocate. Burris, a portly, bald man who always had his glasses hanging around his neck and a book in his hand, fit the typical stereotype of a New Yorker—blunt, rude, arrogant, with a superior know-it-all attitude. Not only did he constantly interrupt me—I couldn't even complete a sentence before he would take over the conversation—he talked to me in a very condescending way. No, I did not like him at all. And here he was at Grace Baptist Church, he and his wife, Jana.

"That guy Burris is the jerk I met in real estate," I whispered to Linda in church. We learned later that Burris had told Jana, "That fellow Scott is the Southerner who has come up here trying to teach us how to evangelize. He's the guy I met in the real estate office. He was inquiring about schools in the area. A redneck, if you ask me." So, neither of us liked each other when we first met.

But Burris Jenkins became my best friend. A Baptist minister himself, he was one of the most well-read, articulate, intelligent men that I had ever met. His father had been a famous political cartoonist, and his grandfather had been the pastor of a large, prestigious church in Saint Louis. Having been in the navy and coast guard, and having been a former TWA pilot, now retired, Burris had traveled all over the world. He loved sailing and had an old, antique-looking wooden sailboat named *Ararat*. My, how he adored that old boat.

"Scott, come with us to Greenport. We'll sail *Ararat* around the island and then back into Port Jefferson. It'll take just a few hours; you'll have a ball," Burris said to me one day. P. T. Barnum, who was actually born in Port Jefferson, said, "A sucker is born every minute." And when I took Burris up on his offer, I proved P. T. Barnum correct and myself to be a sucker! It took us two days to get back! Burris and his cronies relished every second, but I was miserable. I didn't get seasick, but I nearly froze to death. Burris put me in a tiny hole that he called a bunk bed, and when I finally dropped off to sleep, he shook me and woke me up. Handing me a cup of chicken soup, he said, "Come with me. I want to show you something." Crawling out of that so-called bed, I reluctantly followed him up top. "Look at that moon, Scott. Notice how it sparkles on that water. Have you ever seen anything so gorgeous in all your life?" said Burris, with a huge smile.

"Burris, you got me up for this?" I said, shaking my head. "Yes, it's gorgeous, Burris, but I'm going back to bed," I mumbled, as I poured the soup into the ocean. It was lukewarm anyway!

Arriving back home, I was red-faced; my hands were like ice, and I was wet and cold, shivering like a dog drying himself. I never went on another boat ride with Burris.

Jana, Burris' wife, had her own story, and what a story it was. An attractive woman who was several years younger than Burris, she resembled Mariel Hemingway. She seldom wore dresses, taught PE in school, and was an excellent swimmer. Extremely bright, she passed the test to become a certified public accountant the first time that she took it. Even though Jana was born and raised in Czechoslovakia, she spoke excellent English, although she still had quite the foreign accent. We often laughed when she pronounced ridiculous, "ridiculous," and Valley Stream, "Wally Stream."

Growing up under communism, she did not believe in God and, of course, had limited freedom. During the Prague Spring of 1968, a Russian tank was pointed directly at her children's school. That did it! Determined that her kids would not grow up under communism, she would leave her beloved country, now the Czech Republic, and her relatives, and escape to freedom. Planning for two years by forging passports and various other documents and obtaining the required papers, Jana, with her three small children, John, Eva, and Peter, boarded a train to West Germany on June 19, 1970. She told a friend, "If I make it, I'll start believing in God." Armed soldiers walked up and down the aisle of the train. Nervously they rode, her children thinking that they were all just going to visit their aunt. It was too dangerous to reveal to her own children that they would not be returning.

If she were caught, she could be shot or go to prison for at least ten years for attempting to kidnap her children from the State. But she and her kids made it. Coming to America, she eventually met Burris and was converted to Christ. Her life was radically changed. Later, she and Burris married.

Like Burris, Jana was openly opinionated, painfully so! She would set a person straight, fast. And she would tell a minister, quickly, that his sermon was off target. But also like her husband, Jana had a warm and tender side. If she was your friend, you had a friend for life who would defend you to the death if necessary.

Even though we were from different backgrounds and were from entirely different cultures, the four of us—Linda and I and Burris and Jana—became the closest of friends, complementing each other like sunshine and shade.

Before we knew it, winter had come, and my family I were not prepared for the cold weather in New York. We loved the snow, but we eventually got tired of it, like everyone else. Well, Stephen and Stewart didn't get tired of the snow; in fact, they enjoyed shoveling it, which was great from my point of view. We bought heavy coats at Macy's, and I learned real fast to zip up my coat and wrap a scarf around my neck before I stepped out into the frigid temperatures.

One afternoon I walked up to a saleslady at Penney's and asked, "Where are your muffins?"

"Muffins?" she said, with a puzzled look on her face.

"Yeah, for your ears—ear muffins," I replied, pointing to my ears.

"Oh, you mean ear muffs," she answered, sort of chuckling and smiling. "They are over here." I couldn't believe I had said "ear muffins"! Hearing that in my Southern accent, she gave me that look people give you when they think you're a little backward and uneducated. Leaving the store laughing and somewhat embarrassed, I had verified what that New Yorker probably already thought about people from below the Mason Dixon—are they stupid or what?

CHAPTER 18

THE BIGGEST CIRCUS IN THE WORLD

I had pastored churches and had been on staff at a rather large church; and since seminary days, I had had a tremendous interest in outdoor preaching. Consequently, I had, for years, ministered at carnivals and fairs and on the streets of several major cities. Without doubt, God had been preparing me for the biggest circus in the world—New York City!

Having moved into our home in Smithtown and having moved our letter to Grace Baptist Church, soon I was on the sidewalks of New York City. One day as I was preaching to a sun-drenched crowd who had gathered around me on Fourteenth Street, I noticed that faces were turning and looking down the sidewalk. Hearing snickering and a little laughter, I myself looked, and I was shocked, unprepared for what I was seeing. A chubby Hispanic man in his thirties, wearing only diapers, was rolling a tire and guzzling a can of beer. Stopping, he laid the tire down on the sidewalk and sat down in it about six feet from where I was preaching. He set a Styrofoam coffee cup in front of him and stuck a pacifier in his mouth. Only in New York!

About that time a tall, skinny woman, dressed in a flowing, green, sheer dress, began to dance around, spreading her long, spiderlike arms and pointing to the paper cup and asking for change. Obviously, the two were working together. By this time my street meeting had fallen apart, but after watching the show a few minutes like everybody else, I tried to talk to the guy in diapers. He was stoned, so I could not get through to him very much. I then had a conversation with the woman who was dancing beside him; she told me that her name was Cynthia, and she revealed to me that she had been born a boy, but that her father wanted a girl and had never accepted

" him," so he had made himself into a girl, having had all of the operations and having taken hormones. It was a very sad story, but that's what she told me. After talking with her awhile, I had a prayer with her. She strolled on down the sidewalk with the guy in diapers following. He still had that pacifier in his mouth.

Up and down the sidewalk con artists played three-card monte, luring spectators to bet on a certain card, letting them win for a few minutes, but actually setting them up to lose big money. I started preaching on "The Ultimate Set-Up," emphasizing that Satan lets us believe we're doing well, but actually he's deceiving us, scamming us, and pulling us into hell.

As I finished a meeting, a young man walked up and began talking to me about my sketch. "I am an artist myself," he said to me.

"Well, I'm not an artist," I replied, laughing a little, "but I illustrate the gospel with these paints." After I demonstrated block lettering, I presented the gospel to him on the sketch board. At first he didn't get it, but I continued, and he began to understand. Then he started crying. In a few minutes the young man prayed and invited Christ into his life. He wept like I had never seen anyone weep before. He was sniffling and wiping his nose, with tears going everywhere. "I am going to tell my mother today that I am saved," he said, hugging me. I had seen "break dancing" in various parts of the city. Large crowds surrounded young, athletic guys, clapping for them as they performed energetic dance steps and moves. But in heaven, there was greater joy in the presence of the angels of God when that young man, crying so profusely, got saved than there could ever be from New Yorkers being entertained on the street!

I cannot possibly explain how I felt as I preached on the sidewalks of New York. It was like "for this cause I was born." Completely satisfied and fulfilled, I gazed into people's eyes and shared the gospel of Christ. It made my heart sing! I thought of whales swimming in the ocean, spraying water everywhere as they loudly pounded the surface of the sea. Obviously having great fun, they were doing exactly what God created them to do. That's how I felt on the streets. God had given me birth for this reason: to proclaim the Lord Jesus Christ on the sidewalks of New York City. I knew that this was where I was supposed to be, with shish kebab smoke in my eyes and the smell of mustard and hot dogs lingering in the air, car horns honking, the shuffling of feet, and hearing laughter, anger, arguments, and profanity—all at the same time.

And there were those faces that had haunted me for years and had prevented me from enjoying a good night's sleep—depressed and empty faces, glad and happy faces, young faces, old, tired, hopeless faces, twisted and distraught. There were faces of scorn and bewildered faces; and, thankfully, many, many listening faces—people waiting to be fed with the word of God like little baby birds stretching their necks, with beaks wide open. And there I was, surrounded by all of those races and religions and cultures and belief systems and world views and diverse languages so prevalent in New

119

York. But I was loaded with the gospel, knowing that God's truth impacted and changed lives. Man, there was nothing like it!

I was not preaching to a parade of people who shunned me. No, I had stationery, listening crowds, most people standing there until I finished. I did have individuals coming and going during my street meetings, but I had experienced a little of this with my audiences at the carnivals. As various people left my meetings from time to time, I knew that they were not really rejecting me or my message. They simply had other business to attend to; sometimes they even told me so. Some just had to return to work; others had to pick up their kids at school; some had other appointments to keep.

I think that some of my friends thought that I was either standing on the street corner, shouting into thin air to nobody, or receiving tongue lashings or being pelted by stones or being bombarded with threats, and that many people were voicing their complaints. That was not the case at all. The truth of the matter was that some people stopped and listened; others didn't. I was similar to an ice cream cone. Some people wanted one. Others didn't. No big deal. I didn't expect all of New York to welcome me with open arms. Like a light pole, I was impervious to many people on the sidewalks; but that was OK. I loved being on the street.

I'm not saying that it was easy, because it wasn't. Even while using several sleight-of-hand tricks, I often had great difficulty getting a sizable listening audience; but once they stopped and got up close and heard me say that I didn't want anybody's money and that they were valuable and Jesus loved them, most stayed and listened, and I received very little flak.

Did I ever feel rejected? Sometimes, but that was mainly because of the "offense of the gospel" that the apostle Paul mentioned (Galatians 5:11). As soon as I declared that Christ was the only way to be saved, I knew that some people would label me as intolerant and then would walk away. When I preached, "Your own righteousness, according to the Bible, is not sufficient to merit God's favor," I could count on a few people turning me off. But there was nothing

I could do about that. I certainly was not going to change my message in order to hold my crowd. However, during most of my meetings on the sidewalks of New York City, I had very little repudiation from anybody.

Preaching, talking and listening to people, and ministering on the sidewalks of New York City was an education like I had gotten nowhere else. I'll have to admit that when I got to New York, I probably had too harsh of an attitude about people with problems. I believed that whatever trouble you had, it was your own fault. You were just reaping what you sowed. You should have thought of the consequences of your actions. But working the streets of New York changed my mind drastically. I came to realize that while it was true that many people "hung" themselves with bad choices, there were many other people who were ruined and devastated by circumstances beyond their control.

My heart broke for the lady on Thirty-Fourth Street, whose husband was blind and who had no arms or legs; then, there was Jeff, a Jewish atheist who had a horrible-looking, ugly, red birthmark on his face and who blamed God for it. This seemed strange for someone who denied the very existence of God. And what would I have done in Willis's shoes? He was a sincere, devout Muslim who was open to the gospel but who said with tears, "Put yourself in my place. All of my family are Muslim. Do you know what would happen to me if I became Christian?"

I met a fellow named Jerry, who was a stamp collector with an office on the corner of Forty-Second Street and Broadway. "I'm forty-three years old, never been married, so I have no wife, no children. Both of my parents are dead. I have no brothers or sisters. I am totally alone." And one day I saw a man walking barefooted, and all that he had on was his jockey shorts. Red paint covered his entire body. His hair, head, chest, arms, stomach, torso, legs, and feet were solid red. Most of the paint was dry, but it was wet enough around his face that he had trouble blinking his eyes. He disappeared around the corner.

One afternoon as I loaded my equipment into the van, I heard from a distance, "Mama, Mama, Mama." It was a heart-wrenching cry. Then, as I glanced across the street, I saw where the cries were coming from. A man was walking, and his whining—"Mama, Mama, Mama"—got louder and louder the closer that he came to me. Then, as he got further away, his cries got softer and weaker, until all I heard was a faint "Mama."

I thought of those little babies who, when they took their first breath, were already addicted to drugs. Whose fault was that? Not theirs. Many children were born with HIV, infected with the AIDS virus. What if I lived in a roach-infested apartment? What if my father had abused me? I might have dropped out of school, too. I might have turned to gangs, drugs, or committed suicide. What if, when a child, I had played next to garbage while crack dealers fired pistols near my swing?

A fine Christian woman said to me one day, "My six-year-old daughter died on my shoulder, and my other daughter, who is sixteen, is terminally ill." What would I be like if that were me? I talked to one woman who had been evicted from her apartment and had been living on the street for the past seven years. Covering her body, she had dress on top of dress on top of dress.

Seeing firsthand the poverty, the confusion, the lack of job opportunities, the crime, and the hopelessness made me loosen up a bit and caused me to rethink my position that only reckless and irresponsible decisions tore people's lives apart. Day after day on the streets I talked with wounded people who unloaded their burdens and complaints on me. I came to realize that many times people were indeed victims and that what was happening to them was not much, if any, fault of their own. Digesting this fact altered my preaching. Instead of being judgmental and indicting, I think I became more compassionate and understanding; at least I hoped I did.

Preaching on the sidewalks of New York City was exciting and challenging but also very frustrating because the city was so big.

Even though I had marvelous crowds many times, in comparison to the millions of people in the city, I was hardly touching New York. I felt like a small electric heater out in a snowstorm; better yet, out in a blizzard!

Coming from a small town down south, I experienced huge culture shock. I could not believe the filthy language that I heard all around me, day after day, from people of all ages on the streets—language which cannot be repeated. I had heard God's name taken in vain and the *F* word, of course, in the Bible Belt; but not on such a large scale as this. "Get used to it," I told myself. "You are not in the sanctity of the church; you're on the devil's turf, for crying out loud!"

There was such violence—cruel, open, daring violence—and it appeared that people expected it. Nobody seemed shocked when something egregious took place. One afternoon as I preached in front of Macy's on Thirty-Fourth Street, a guy snatched a purse from a woman in my audience. (My friend George told me that he saw a thief steal two purses during the same meeting.) Another day, as I was driving through Central Park, I saw a thief slowly sneaking a purse from a woman sitting on a park bench. She was totally unaware of what was happening, and before I could warn her, he was gone with her "pocketbook," as they say in New York.

You could expect terrible crimes to take place after dark in the projects, but I witnessed meanness in broad daylight. One day directly across from where I was preaching, I saw several guys crash in a couple of TV trays that were covered with costume jewelry. They grabbed the stuff and dashed away. The Japanese ladies who were selling the jewelry looked on in horror. But in a matter of seconds everything was back to normal. They were selling more jewelry, and I began preaching again. Every few days I heard heated arguments, and I always hoped that these verbal bashings would not turn into fist fights. Some guys were very crude. One day two men urinated on the wheel of my van directly in front of my audience as I preached the good news of the Lord Jesus Christ, and from time to time, somebody would push through my crowd, hear me speaking about the Lord and yell, "*F—*Jesus!" and keep on walking. I generally ignored disparaging remarks, but sometimes, in order to retain my crowd, I did retaliate by saying, "By thy words thou shalt be justified, and by thy words thou shalt be condemned" (Matthew 12:37).

I was amazed and appalled at the spiritual darkness on the sidewalks of New York City; other than the obvious Christians that sprinkled my crowds, I hardly ever talked to anyone who had a biblical world view. The screwed-up concepts about God, the ideas that people had conjured up in their minds, and the distorted views of the Bible were unreal! Sometimes I spent close to an hour explaining the basics of Christianity to someone, but regardless of how much truth I shared with him, he walked away more blind than when we began our conversation. Like shining a light on an owl—the more light you shined on it, the more blind it got.

New Yorkers were bombarded from every direction. The Mormons in their white shirts and ID badges were bearing witness to the *Book of Mormon.* The Jehovah's Witnesses, whose world headquarters is in Brooklyn, were holding up "Awake" and "The Watchtower" and doing a pretty good job of convincing people that Jesus was not God and that there is no hell. The Black Israelites were a racist sect, full of hate, and were preaching that Christianity was a white man's religion and that the original Jews were black. The Muslims were saying that Allah did not have a son and that Jesus was just a prophet. The Hare Krishnas, singing and chanting in their orange, pajama-looking clothes, were pounding their drums, shaking their tambourines, and declaring "spiritual enlightenment." The Moonies, with glassy, artificial expressions, were selling their roses and promoting their leader, Sun Myung Moon, as the true Messiah because Jesus had failed, having been crucified.

Fortunetellers promised instant knowledge of the future, for the right price. New Age books lined the shelves of all major bookstores and were sold on card tables that were set up on the sidewalks. *Star Trek* and Stephen Spielberg movies speculating about aliens and UFOs influenced the thinking of biblically ignorant youth. The Bible was no longer even brought up in school, of course, and in many universities a number of professors discredited the Bible, casting doubt on the authenticity of the word of God. Often, I heard words such as this: "There is no God. Evolution has proved that. Everything is God. I am God."

I did meet many Christians in every borough, and there were churches and ministries throughout the city who were faithfully fulfilling the great commission. However, the vast majority of individuals that I talked with daily had a smattering of God's truth, but did not have a clue about what it took to be made right with God.

Many people were into voodoo, ancestor worship, self-flagellation. Others were taught that "Saturday is the Sabbath; don't worship on Sunday." Many were taught to eat kosher foods only, from the cradle to the grave. Once, a thin-faced woman in her late twenties, as she smoked a cigarette, said to me, "My husband is from Uranus. By the way, Jesus is not real." I met a guy who had hanging around his neck a cross, a crescent moon, a Star of David, a Hindu idol, and a crystal. "I want to be covered," he said.

But what an environment to preach the gospel of our Lord Jesus Christ. Let the light shine in the darkness!

Driving in the traffic was mentally exhausting. When I had visited my friend George Naggy in New York, I had accompanied him, and he drove. Now I was on my own. Often I met George and others in the city, but, still, I had to drive in and out of the city myself, learning my way around. Smithtown was just thirty miles from New York City, but usually it took me an hour and a half to get there. Sighing when I saw red brake lights come on became an everyday occurrence. Changing lanes became as common as breathing. New York driving was give and take, mostly take! By the time I got to the city, drove around looking for a parking place, located what I thought was a good preaching spot, and set up my equipment, I was worn to a frazzle, and I had not even begun ministering yet. After conducting four or five adult meetings, and, perhaps, a children's meeting or two, and after conversing with numerous people on the sidewalks, I was almost a basket case. Then, I had at least a two-hour drive back home, even longer when there were wrecks and inclement weather; and there was always worrisome construction as I drove through Lefrak City in Queens!

Easy? No way. But what I had waiting on me back in Smithtown was a big hug from Linda plus some tasty Southern cooking, and, of course, Stephen and Stewart, who usually met me at the door, always wanting to wrestle with me on that putrid-looking green living room carpet.

CHAPTER 19

SOUTHERN COMFORT

I had not been ministering on the streets very long before a friend of mine, Andy Anderson of Bossier City, showed up. He was in New York on business, and he paid us a visit. How good it was to hear a Southern accent! Having learned my way around a little, I gave Andy a tour of the city, going from Queens to Brooklyn into Manhattan and over into the Bronx. I had practiced my route, but I was still praying that I would not get lost. On Friday evening Andy accompanied me to Times Square. Having never been in a street meeting, he did not know what to expect. I tried not to act nervous, but I was, because sometimes the meetings went well, and sometimes they didn't.

Before we got started, I said, "Andy, stay with my sketch board while I run to the restroom. I'll be right back." When I returned, I could tell that he had been worried. "Man, am I glad to see you," he said. "I was sweating it." Looking back on it, I had left him alone at Times Square on a Friday night with hordes of people everywhere. He didn't know what to do or where to go or exactly where I was or when I would be back. Being at Times Square was becoming commonplace to me but was frightfully new to Andy.

After a couple of relatively good street meetings with many people huddled up around us and responding well to the gospel, three fine young men walked over to us. They introduced themselves and said that they were believers from Texas. They hung around and helped us attract the next crowd. Several Muslims walked into the meeting and stood real close to me. Then it happened! Challenging what I was saying, one of them kicked my paint box. At this time I was using Gerber baby food jars to hold my tempera paints, so when they kicked my paint box, glass,

127

brushes, and paint went flying everywhere, all over the sketch board and the sidewalk. Thankfully, nobody was hurt, and to my amazement, nobody much left, except the cap-covered Muslims, who jolted down the sidewalk.

"You want us to whup them fellers? We can catch 'em. Just say the word. Really, we'll git 'em!" the three Texans said to me.

"Naw, they're gone. We'll be OK. Thanks, though," I replied, laughing inside because a few minutes earlier they were talking about the Lord, and now they wanted to go "whup" those Muslims. They meant well, however, and I appreciated their willingness to defend us.

I explained to Andy that that had never happened before, and he did not seem too upset. He bought my dinner at Courtney's restaurant that evening, and we rehashed all that had happened that night.

"Tell everybody hello," I said to him as he headed back to Louisiana.

It was a real treat when friends came up from down south to work with us. "Southern Comfort" was what we called it. No, not the whiskey—the friendship. Linda really enjoyed having them, too, although it was extra work on her because the vast majority of times they stayed with us and she cooked all of our main meals. Stephen and Stewart were privileged to be around many men and women of God when they visited our home, and our boys joked and clowned around with them and made us proud.

Not long after Andy left, Al and Doris Bohl came to New York. They had accompanied me at a number of carnivals and fairs, and we had become good friends. When living in Bossier, I often listened to Al's radio program, *The Solid Rock*. Doris worked right along beside him and was a smart counselor who could defend and share her faith as well. One day on Fourteenth Street, while holding a portable radio that was playing background music, Al sang, "He died of a broken heart." The crowd was noticeably moved, and many folks waited around, asking question after question. Later, when Al preached, he quoted Hebrews 12:3 about people not being wearied, and then he quoted Hebrews 4:5 about Christ, our high priest, being able to understand our infirmities. The word of God says, "How beautiful are the feet of them that preach the gospel of peace, and bring glad tidings of good things" (Romans 10:15). Trust me. The feet of Al Bohl were beautiful that day.

AL BOHL

As Al and I worked together, not everybody was receptive to the gospel; no, far from it. Many people were rebelling against God, and upon hearing the name of Jesus, they were off and running. Jesus said, "Men loved darkness rather than light, because their deeds were evil. Neither cometh to the light, lest their deeds should be reproved" (John 3:19–20). One evening we talked to a young Jewish man. With an angry face, he said, "I hate the name of Jesus, and I wish someone would kill Moshe Rosen!" (the leader of Jews for Jesus). The Bible says, "For we are to God the aroma of Christ among those who are being saved and those who are perishing. To the one we are the smell of death: to the other, the fragrance of life" (2 Corinthians 2:16).

One afternoon in Harlem a lady accused us of preaching a "white Jesus" to "her kids." We stood our ground and tried to really demonstrate the love of God to her. The situation cooled down, and many children as well as teens accepted Christ. We even had prayer with this woman and were able to share the gospel with her, and, as we were leaving, Al won a drug addict to Christ. Praise the Lord!

One evening at Times Square, Al, Doris, and I worked with Art Williams, head of OAC in New York. The Lord had used Art to get me to New York, and I always learned a great deal from him every time we ministered together. After Al and I had each preached, Art prepared the sketch board and was just beginning to speak when Gabe began to cause trouble. Gabe, a professing Christian, was an insidious troublemaker. Searching out ministries with the express purpose of wrecking them, Gabe, I believe, felt that he was doing God a service by trying to straighten out everybody. As I stood in the crowd, I spotted him easily because of his unkempt gray beard. He had a guy with him, and they "snaked" their way through the attentive audience, saying very loudly, "These men are not telling you the truth. Don't listen to them." As they passed out their negative tracts, I attempted to run them off. "It's serious in the eyes of God to interfere with the preaching of the gospel," I warned firmly. But that tactic did not work.

"Gabe, hear me a minute," I said, but he persisted in saying, "These guys are false prophets." He and his protégé were obnoxious, and they claimed to be brothers in Christ! Because many people wanted to hear Art's message, I tried every ploy I knew to get them to leave. But I had no success. Gabe would not quit criticizing and accusing us. Art finally stopped preaching. There was nothing else he could do. When the crowd scattered, Gabe and his friend, having disrupted us, were nowhere to be seen. That really irritated me—someone interfering with the proclamation of the gospel when others were trying to listen.

One day at a children's meeting, Al and I mentioned that the first kid on the van platform would receive the picture that Al just drew. Instantly, about thirty children swarmed all over us, knocking the sketch board down, spilling red, black, blue, yellow, and green paint all over us. Later, as we cleaned up as best we could with wet wipes, Al, Doris, and I cracked up and said to each other, "How could we have been so stupid?"

One evening we took my son Stephen with us to Times Square. Stephen was about thirteen and, thinking that he might be a little uptight, I assured him that we seldom had any problem. But wouldn't you know it! As soon as we parked, we spotted a big pool of blood on the sidewalk. And as we began ministering on the street, a drunk fell across our platform and into our van. Somebody said, facetiously, "You saved one soul tonight, brother." This frightened Stephen so much that he got in the back of the van, and I had to coax him to come out. A while later, two street gangs got in a fight on the sidewalk, and a fellow got beat up with a chain and was kicked unconscious. This incident had nothing to do with our street meetings, but it happened just a few feet from us; so, quickly, I turned out my sketch board lights, closed my overhead canopy, and slid my platform inside the van. I did not want the cops to connect the fight with our meeting. Trying to act calm in the face of all that had happened, I said, "Everything is OK, son," but I could tell Stephen was still upset. So was I.

One evening in front of the *New York Times* building, a man touched my arm while Al was preaching. "Can I talk to you a minute?" he asked.

"Sure, but let's step back here where we won't interfere with the meeting," I suggested.

We stood against the building and introduced ourselves to each other. "I'm homosexual," Eddie said to me, "I feel like I've always been this way. I don't believe that it's wrong. My priest told me it was OK."

"Eddie," I said as tactfully as I could, "I don't have all of the answers. But the Bible teaches that homosexuality is wrong, just like adultery is wrong." I could tell that he was extremely distraught. Emphasizing that he was valuable and that God loved him and that all of us were sinners, I shared the gospel with him. With the bright lights of Broadway shining and blinking from all directions, that young man received Christ right then. "Eddie," I said, "you may always have a struggle with this, but don't give up. If you fall, confess it to God. He will forgive you. The Lord will work with you. He knows our weaknesses, and when we are tempted, the Bible teaches that God will give us a way of escape." He smiled, and we shook hands. As he was walking away, I said, "Eddie, be sure and get into a good church; rely on Christ's strength. And stay in God's word." He nodded and strolled on down Broadway.

Al, by this time, had finished preaching, and he told me that he had been sharing the love of God with a teenager who called himself "Guarantee."

"The young man had been hanging around in the back of our meeting," Al said, "hoping to get picked up for sex." Many young people with big dreams came to New York, but when their plans fell through, they often ended up on the street. Chasing pretty rainbows led many to a life of drugs or prostitution or suicide.

As we were packing up and leaving Times Square, we attempted to talk to a couple of Moonies, members of the Unification Church. They had been selling roses not far from where we had been preaching. The couple would not listen, however. Instead, the young man said with a twinkle of conviction in his eyes, "Sun Myung Moon is my Lord!" Hearing those words devastated us. That couple was so brainwashed. Satan had blinded their minds so that they could not see the Light (2 Corinthians 4:4).

"I'll go get the van and pick y'all up," I said to Al and Doris. "Stay with our stuff, OK?"

"Scotty!" Doris exclaimed. "You don't need to go by yourself."

"Doris," I answered, "I'm by myself lots of times. I'll be OK."

"Oh, yeah, I forgot that you don't always have someone with you," she said, laughing and smiling.

It was an honor to work with Al and Doris Bohl.

Two older women from Bossier came through to see us in New York on their way to Israel: Mrs. Sarah Lawrence and Mrs. Lillian Scott, "the War-Horse," as I called her. Both were quite loquacious, and that was an understatement. When Mrs. Scott was with Linda and me, she would say, "That Sarah just doesn't know when to shut up!" And when Mrs. Lawrence was with us, she would say, "That Lillian just doesn't know when to shut up." Linda and I were thinking, "Neither of you knows when to shut up!" Oh, we loved them, but, man, could they talk!

They were godly women, however, and went to the street with me. Both had big hearts and were not intimidated by anyone. Mrs. Lawrence, Pennsylvania Dutch, knew her Bible very well, and one day she stood on the platform, gave her testimony, and almost preached. She shook her finger at that crowd, and they listened, too, as she told about how she came to know Christ.

Mrs. Scott, having worked with me in the carnival ministry for several years, was never ashamed to share her faith in Christ and was extremely bold. What a Spirit-filled woman she was! One night as I preached at Forty-Third and Broadway, a prostitute walked into my listening audience and stood beside Mrs. Scott, not realizing that Mrs. Scott was with me, of course. When the hooker heard me speaking about the Lord Jesus Christ, she began to shout with a very shrill voice, "Shut up! Shut up! I don't want to hear that! Shut up!" Hearing that prostitute, Mrs. Scott's eyes just danced! Grabbing that woman by her arm, she replied harshly, "No, you shut up!" That woman looked at Mrs. Scott in surprise and quickly darted away!

As we conducted a children's meeting in Harlem, twenty-five or thirty children were sitting on a canvas in front of my sketch board.

Standing in the back of the crowd were a few adults and a number of tall black teenagers. Mrs. Scott was also in the back of the meeting. Those teenagers began playing a loud boom box, making it extremely difficult for any of us to hear. Walking over to them, Mrs. Scott said, "Now, boys, turn that radio off right now. Can't you see that they can't hear him? Now turn it off, and you need to hear this, too." Here we were in Harlem, and Mrs. Scott, an old white woman, was telling, not asking, this group of tall blacks to turn their radio off and to listen. They looked at each other as if to say, "Who is this?" But then they turned their radio off, stood there, and quietly listened. I believe those guys knew that this woman cared. She was firm yet kind. Her age, plus experience from working with children, compelled those young men to do what she said.

There were many others from Dixie who, at their own expense, came to New York to minister with me on the sidewalks. Always, they reminded us of the warmth and friendliness of the South—Southern Comfort, in other words. As we dropped off our guests from the South at LaGuardia for their flight home, there was always sadness in our hearts.

CHAPTER 20

NOT YOUR ORDINARY DAY AT THE OFFICE

George Naggy and I held teenage meetings a block from Newtown High School in Queens, and many students were hanging out, smoking pot, but a great number of them listened to the gospel. Faced with peer pressure, several students still raised their hands, indicating that they were interested. Then counseling took place. What was exciting to me was that a friend of George's, Paul McArdle, was starting a new church in Queens, and he and his son, Tim, were going to be following up those who made decisions for Christ.

Mike was one of those students we met at Newtown. As I talked with him about Jesus, he kept bringing up the subject of hypocrites. "Mike, Jesus said that the wheat and the tares will grow together. There will always be hypocrites, man." Dressed in dirty, faded blue jeans, unshaven, with greasy black hair, he lived on the streets. "I live under the stairs," he said, pointing to a small dark hole. Mike told me that he was twenty-five and was not married. "But I have a kid, four years old," he said, bragging, obviously proud of his child; and then he showed me a picture of him.

Mike said that he did not believe in hell. "Christ said there is a hell, Mike, and he warned us not to go there. It's foolish not to believe the words of Jesus," I replied. "Well, when I'm in hell, God will say that I was just a fool!" he answered, smirking. There was no fear of God in Mike's eyes. I left some "Smiles" on the steps, but I don't know if he ever picked one up. It was tragic because he had such potential and yet was wasting his life away. I do know that every time I saw Mike after that, he had on the same worn-out, dingy clothes.

One night when I arrived back home and walked in the front door, Linda said, "Somebody shot John Lennon. It's all over the news." John Lennon of the Beatles, shot to death outside his West-side, Manhattan apartment (December 8, 1980). Just forty years old. The news reported that Mark David Chapman, age twenty-five, had shot Lennon five times in the back with a .38. Chapman had been reading *Catcher in the Rye* and had gotten Lennon's autograph a few hours earlier. I didn't sleep well that night. Lennon's death reminded me of how fragile life was. "Man, that's young; just forty. I'll be thirty-eight in a few days. I must remember to mention him the next time I preach," I said to myself, as I finally fell asleep.

I began helping to train and disciple students from Word of Life Bible College in upstate New York. Every few months the school sent twenty-four students, male and female, to New York City. Even though I was not "officially" an Open Air Campaigner, I worked with OAC quite often. We all had the privilege of pouring our lives into these young people. Many of the students would become pastors, evangelists, teachers, church planters, and missionaries and would scatter all over the world in the years to come. Hopefully, our training in sidewalk evangelism would enable them to have a greater impact for Christ.

The young people were taught personal witnessing, counseling, how to conduct adult, teen, and children's meetings, and follow-up. After lectures, we took them to the street and demonstrated on the sidewalks what we had just taught them in the classroom. Gradually, we gave them assignments and let them assist us. At the end of two weeks the students were doing everything. The young men were preaching, and the young ladies were counseling, giving their testimonies, and sharing Bible stories. Both men and women were taught how to use the sketch board to illustrate the gospel.

I told the students one afternoon, "My wife is a great Southern cook, and she makes a fantastic coconut pie—with a rich, creamy filling and homemade crust that's flaky and just melts in your mouth. Now, let's say that I want you to have a piece of pie. I don't shove it in your face and force you to eat it. No, I know how good it is, but I offer it to you. Young people, that's how we should evangelize.

Christ is wonderful. We offer him to others. We don't shove him in people's faces. The Bible says, 'O taste and see that the Lord is good' " (Psalm 34:8).

Many children in the projects were starved for love. And there were so many of them. In one little corner of Brooklyn called Starrett City there were forty-six high-rise apartments. Kids filled the playgrounds and were unchurched and unreached with the gospel. Most did not know and had never heard of John 3:16.

One beautiful, sunny day I took four students from Word of Life with me, and we went to the Fort Green Project in Brooklyn, not far from where Nikki Cruise had grown up, in order to conduct a children's meeting. I had learned that it was always wise to have both men and women on my team when I held children's meetings. It looked wholesome and more appropriate than just having two or three guys working alone around all of those children. Setting up the sketch board and spreading a canvas, we invited the children to be seated on it. About forty kids sat down, joined us in a couple of songs, and began listening to a Bible story. Suddenly, a glass bottle hit the pavement. It shattered not far from us.

"Up there! Up there!" shouted the children as they pointed up. When I looked, I saw three teenagers on top of an apartment building several stories up, waving and cursing, and they threw other bottles, and rocks, too. Realizing that somebody could get hurt, I moved my team and the kids to another location about one hundred feet away. When we set the sketch board up and spread the canvas, the kids sat down once again. Then bottles started coming from another building. One bottle exploded about six feet from us with a pop, and tiny white pieces of glass of all sizes splattered everywhere.

"Let's go, kids! We gotta go. Hurry up," I said. "This is dangerous." The Word of Life students were visibly shaken, and I knew that they were looking to me to tell them what to do next.

"Don't go," the children pleaded, "they are only trying to scare us. Go over there to the basketball court. They can't hit us over there."

Well, I wasn't sure if we should do that; but I decided to give it a try. So, we gathered everything up and moved to the court, far from the apartment building. I prayed that we would be safe there as I finished telling the children about blind Bartimaeus. The Spirit of the Lord really moved. Many of those children accepted Christ, and we enrolled them in the Mailbox Club—a Bible correspondence course. God had turned defeat into victory.

Ministering on the sidewalks of New York City was not your ordinary day at the office, to be sure! Walking through Greenwich Village, I saw two students proudly waving the communist red flag and distributing revolutionary literature. "Guys, the only way we are going to change society is to change the hearts of people; only the Lord Jesus Christ can do that," I said, throwing out a challenge. One of them shouted back at me, "Jesus! He died two thousand years ago!" How thrilling it was for me to be able to say, "Yes, he died, and he rose again! And the whole world is going to be celebrating his resurrection Easter Sunday morning!"

I asked a good crowd one afternoon, "Have you seen the little rope trick? It's called the professor's nightmare. I have a short piece of rope, a medium-size rope, and a long rope. What I'd like to do is try to make all these ropes the same size. Now, some people have a short list of sins, like this little rope. Some of us have some good, some bad, like this medium-size rope. Some people have a long, long list of sins like this long rope. (I then made the ropes appear to be all the same size.) But you know, folks, when God looks at us, he sees all of us pretty much the same. We are all sinners. God loves all of us. Christ died for all of us. And we all have to be born again in order to go to heaven."

Later, after I had finished preaching and was packing up and getting ready to leave, a young woman, wearing glasses and dressed in a white blouse approached me and reprimanded me, "You shouldn't mix magic with preaching. God is against magic," she said.

"Miss, what I do is not really magic," I said. "It's just sleight-of-hand."

"I saw you," she replied.

"Here, let me show you," I said. I opened up my hand and showed her the ropes. "All I'm doing is doubling the rope. It's just an illusion."

"Well, the Bible is against magic," she insisted.

"Miss," I said, "I agree with you; but when the Bible talks about magic, it's referring to a person calling upon the forces of evil and trying to connect to Satan and his power. I'm not doing that. I'm totally against actual magic, just as you are. That's wrong. Fortune telling, seances, psychics, trying to tap into the forces of evil—I'm opposed to that. I would never do that."

"OK," she said. "I was just wondering."

"Miss, what's your name?" I asked.

"Carolyn," she said.

"Carolyn, Jesus said that we are to be 'wise as serpents and as harmless as doves' (Matthew 10:16). All I'm doing with these little sleight-of-hand tricks is just getting people's attention. They help me get a crowd, and from the very start, I tell the people that I'm talking about the Lord," I replied.

As the woman began walking away, I said, "Thank you for being concerned. Hey, you're my sister in Christ. Pray for me. God bless you."

"God bless you, too," she answered, smiling and waving.

One day George called and asked me to meet him and Art Williams in the Far Rockaways. "We're going to have a couple of kids' meetings," he said. I had been to the Far Rockaways one previous time, and I was not that familiar with it, but I did manage to hook up with George and Art, who had brought along a couple of his kids. The children's meetings were well attended, with lots of children paying close attention, but I could hardly believe what I was hearing. As much as George and Art had preached in New York, even they were shocked. When I asked what happened to Jesus Christ on the third day, none of them knew about the resurrection! I repeated the question, thinking that they misunderstood.

"Jesus—he died; then on the third day, he came back alive, right?" I asked.

The children began looking at each other, puzzled. Then one little boy answered, "He's dead, like my grandmother."

Most of the children that I had dealt with in the projects and on the streets in New York knew a little bit about Jesus. But these kids were shockingly ignorant of the basic facts about Christ. Billy Graham was correct when he once said, "Every generation must be evangelized."

When all of us returned to our vans, George's windshield had been smashed. "Can you believe it?" sighed George, knowing that he would never find the culprit. The windshield was somehow holding together, although it was shattered in a thousand pieces. Art and his kids headed back to New Jersey, but George followed me home as I drove my van slowly in front of him, hoping that it would somehow block the wind. Eventually, we made it back to his home in Hicksville, his windshield partially intact. When I walked through my front door in Smithtown, Linda, preparing supper, said, "How did it go?"

"Well, honey," I answered, "it was not your ordinary day in the office."

One evening a bitter black militant disrupted my meeting and actually threatened to shoot me. "You better shut up!" he shouted. Several Christians from Brazil with whom I had been talking took up for me. "That's OK, thank you, though. Everything will be all right." But I was a little nervous because the guy, spewing anger, was enraged and wanted trouble. A Moonie had been selling roses next to me, even hitting on some people in my crowd. I had asked him a couple of times to move on down away from us, because I didn't want people to think I was a Moonie. But he would not leave. So what happened? The angry black militant continued cursing and telling me that he was going to shoot me.

About that time, the Moonie with his roses walked up to him. "Get outta my face! Get outta my face!" the militant screamed. Then he smacked the Moonie right in the face, knocking him to the pavement and leaving him with a bloody nose. I felt sorry for the Moonie; really, I did. But he got up and walked off, holding his nose, flowers and all, and the black militant quickly fled the scene. The angels of God were looking out for me, no doubt! My Brazilian friends observed what had happened, and they didn't know what to say. Neither did I. Preaching on the sidewalks of New York was not your ordinary day in the office. That's for sure!

Looking into faces that I had never seen before at Times Square, I asked the question, "Have you ever felt like something is missing in your life? That runner in *Chariots of Fire* said, 'I am forever in pursuit of something. I just don't know what it is.' Ever feel that way? You want something, but you don't know what?"

As I finished preaching that evening, I stepped down from the van platform and began talking to various people. A well-dressed, sophisticated young lady walked over to me and said, "I'm a professional singer, and I sing on Broadway. Would you mind if I sing?" Normally, I didn't allow that, because I never knew if somebody was a crackpot or not, but in this case I gladly said, "Yes, you're welcome, Miss."

It was a typical night at Times Square. Junkies, perverts, hookers, drunks, hecklers, cults, gays, and out of towners were milling around. I offered the young woman a hand, and she stepped up on the platform; and as her long, brown hair blew in the wind, and with the noise of cabs and buses behind her, she began to sing "I'd Rather Have Jesus." What a beautiful voice she had, and so strong! I could tell immediately that she was a pro. At first, a few people, without even stopping, joked and laughed a little. But as she sang the chorus, her voice got louder and tears, filling her eyes, started slowly running down her cheeks. People started standing still and began listening. The crowd grew, and people stepped in closer to hear. Then a quiet hush came over everybody. When she finished, people began whistling and clapping!

The lady stepped down, shook my hand, and said, "Thank you."

"Thank you!" I replied. "That was of the Lord."

She walked into the crowd, and I never saw her again. I never even got her name.

CHAPTER 21

MINISTRY CHANGERS

In June 1981, we were excited about being able to go back home to Louisiana for a visit. My mother and dad's golden wedding anniversary was June 27; I remembered the date because Linda and I were married on that same date in 1964. Seeing my relatives and friends, we had a great time at my parents' reception. After eating a little cake, Dad leaned over and kissed my mother. We have a picture of that kiss in our bedroom. I asked my dad what was the biggest lesson that he had learned from living with my mother. "To know when to keep my mouth shut," he replied. Then, he continued, "I don't believe you've learned that lesson yet, son." Everybody laughed, and he was, no doubt, correct!

Mother and Daddy flew back to New York with us, visiting ten days. Remembering how much it hurt all of us when we left a year earlier, I knew that they felt better about our being in New York after seeing where we lived, Linda's garden, and attending our church and meeting many of our friends. They enjoyed their stay in New York, but I could tell that they were ready to get back home. On our way to LaGuardia for them to catch their flight, Mother touched my arm and said, very sweetly, "Son, we love y'all, but I'll be glad to get back to Bossier. This city is too big for me—whew, all this traffic!" Before their plane got out of sight, we began missing them.

Burris Jenkins had major medical problems with his back and heart, and he took far too much medication; but he began to accompany me to the city. Even though he had been a pastor, Burris was an evangelist at heart. In the past he had used his sailboat, *Ararat*, in various evangelistic endeavors. It wasn't long before he, too, was preaching on the street.

Because Burris had graduated from Union Theological Seminary in New York, we were always discussing the Bible, world religions, and all sorts of political, philosophical, and theological issues as we drove in and out of the city. It's often difficult for preachers to have someone in whom they can trust and confide, but I found out quickly that I could trust Burris explicitly. Sharing my heart, I knew he would never betray my confidence. He was completely genuine and sincere. What a friend Burris Jenkins became! But at times, Burris could still be unbearable, extremely blunt, and haughty. And I would tell him so. Burris would just chuckle. What a magnanimous spirit he had! He was never offended, and he never held a grudge. Always, he forgave.

There was an attractive couple at Grace Baptist by the name of Tom and Phyllis Krilovich. Tom, with thick, white hair, and Phyllis, fashionably dressed, always entered the church smiling. But they had suffered much pain in their lives, having lost a teenage daughter due to kidney failure. Phyllis had donated one of her own kidneys in an attempt to save her, but still the Lord took her home. Their eyes always sparkled when someone mentioned that they would one day see their precious daughter in heaven.

Of Russian descent, Tom had a very deep voice that a Broadway actor, radio announcer, or preacher would covet—a low, soothing, resonant voice that you just enjoyed listening to. Exceptionally generous, he always insisted on picking up the tab when we all went out to dinner. Growing up in an orphanage, Tom had a huge heart, always overlooking people's faults, loving people, period. Phyllis was an exceptionally talented artist. Her paintings were so beautiful and pleasing to look at, you thought they belonged in the Louvre. Tom and Phyllis Krilovich became close friends.

One morning Burris, Tom, and I drove to the city in order to have some street meetings. Tom kept mentioning "tube steaks." "I don't have a clue what you are talking about, Tom," I said.

"Hot dogs, pal. New York hot dogs, right off the street vendor," Tom replied, smacking his lips.

"Well, let's have a couple of meetings first. Then we'll eat hot dogs, OK?" I said.

Pulling into a parking place where there were tons of shoppers walking around in all directions, I raised my van canopy, slid the platform out, set up my sketch board, and began stirring my paints. Burris, using a sleight-of-hand trick, quickly gathered a nice crowd. Tom knelt down in front so that people standing behind him could see. Filling in the block lettering, I began preaching a sermon entitled "Four Lies of the Devil."

"Ladies and gentlemen, let me tell you one of the biggest lies of the devil. The devil says, first of all, that there is no such thing as Satan, and he says that there is no hell. Secondly, Satan says our good works can save us. That's another lie. Third, Satan says that there are many ways to God, not just one way. Fourth, Satan says that you have plenty of time to come to Christ. 'Do it later, not today,' the devil says."

I preached too hard and too loud, but this was Tom's first street meeting, so I was trying to impress him. However, in spite of me, the Lord's power was evident, and a number of people indicated that they were interested in becoming a Christian. The three of us spent quality time with several inquirers. Tom, as always, was very complimentary of my street preaching. Soon Tom reminded us that it was time for some "tube steaks!" So, we devoured a number of hot dogs, bragging about them as we ate. I got extra mustard, like always. Linda, I believe, would just as soon have a hot dog with pickle relish as a steak at Outback. "I could eat hot dogs seven days a week!" she says, and she's serious!

After holding another street meeting, Burris, Tom, and I fought traffic all the way back to the Smithtown Bull, the huge, bronze statue at the edge of town.

A few days before Christmas, the three of us held a noon hour meeting on Wall Street. While Christmas carols echoed from a distance through the canyons in the financial district, businessmen and women stood on the steps of Federal Hall and politely listened to the good news. I asked Tom to step up on the platform and say a few words, which he was glad to do. Once again, I envied his deep voice.

"Tom," I asked, "when your daughter died, did your faith in Christ help you cope?"

Shaking his head and tearing up, he answered, "No, not really; maybe a little."

His answer was so real that many in the crowd empathized with him, and he gained credibility, reminding our listeners that Christians go through difficult times, too, just like everybody else.

One day as Burris and I were driving into the city, we both saw a big chain lying in the road, in the middle of the Brooklyn Queens Expressway. "Pull over! Quick, I'll grab it," Burris exclaimed.

BURRIS JENKINS

The traffic was at a crawl, so, glancing in my mirror, I slowed down to a gradual stop, and Burris picked it up—a long, heavy black chain—and he threw it in the van. We both began to use that chain in our street meetings. Often, Burris hung the chain around his neck, gave his testimony, and then dropped it on the steel platform upon which he was standing. "Kaboom," went the sound, resonating up and down the block. "I used to be a big shot…When I found the Lord, a huge weight came off of my shoulders," he declared.

For years as I used the sketch board, I had a cloth to wipe my brushes on and to remove some of the tempera paints from my hands; it became a dirty rag fast. I had a reputation for being messy with the paints, and usually I had red, yellow, blue, black, and green paint covering my fingers and brush handles. Often, in order to illustrate that "our righteousness was like a filthy rag" (Isaiah 64:6), I held up that dirty cloth, which was saturated with smeared paint. One day I used a clean, white cloth to illustrate the purity of Christ. But I did not use that white cloth a half dozen times before some blacks in my audience took offense. "You sayin' that white is clean and pure? Man, I guess that makes us bad, dirty" were words that I heard.

So I started using a red cloth to represent the blood of Christ and his righteousness. As I preached, I covered the dirty rag with the red cloth, not a white cloth; after that, I never got one complaint.

As I searched the scriptures, the Lord gave me many ideas for other object lessons:

A railroad spike and a hand-sized rock to strike it with whenever I mentioned the death of Christ on the cross.

A string of pearls and a huge pearl to illustrate the Pearl of Great Price.

A gift to represent eternal life, which is a gift of God.

Soap bubbles to illustrate that our life is brief, like a vapor.

When I was a pastor in Graford, Texas, back in the sixties, I found an old, unfinished, steel knife that looked like a small Roman sword. I used that knife when I quoted Jesus: "I came not to send peace, but a sword" (Matthew 10:34).

A ragdoll—I put a blindfold on it, stuck a Velcro wicked heart on it, and put an American flag in its pocket and a "Little Red Bible" in its hand. This was a picture of a person with outward religion. Then, I stuck a Velcro new, red heart on the doll, illustrating that when you are born again, God gives you a new heart; you are changed from within.

A set of weigh scales from Chinatown was great to demonstrate good deeds versus bad deeds.

When preaching on money, I used a bag of coins, rocks, costume jewelry, and beads that my mother got at Mardi Gras in New Orleans. Pouring them into a tin pan grabbed people's attention.

Matrouska dolls—I called them Russian dolls—were marvelous to illustrate that God sees through all of the barriers and walls that we put up around ourselves.

Through the years, I employed many other props.

One day after standing in my crowd and observing me preach, Linda said, "Scotty, every time you turn your back to put something on the sketch board, somebody walks away."

"I know, Hon," I replied, "I try not to completely turn my back to the people, but I know that that happens." I began to notice that when I used the visual aids and faced my audience, hardly anybody walked out of my meetings. So I started demonstrating my messages with them more and more. Sometimes I used these object lessons in conjunction with my sketch board; other times, I used them by themselves.

There was nothing "high tech" about them, but these visual aids changed my ministry! They worked. They were easy to use by anybody and were great for capturing and holding people's attention. They made crystal clear the truths of the gospel. Ministry changers!

Phil Foglia of the Open Air Campaigners often ministered with me on the streets.

He grew up in Brooklyn and was co-pastor of Anchor Baptist Church in Starrett City. Phil often preached on John 3:16. I joked with him about his Brooklyn accent, especially when he said "earl" for oil. One day he shared with me that a family had joined their church after listening to us in an open air meeting. I preached at Phil's church not long after that, and I met them. That did my heart a world of good!

One night, when Phil and I were at Times Square, I noticed a man hanging around during a couple of our meetings. Overweight and with no front teeth, he had on a flannel coat and part of his belt hung down on his pants, which were street dirty. We talked a little, and I learned that his name was Joseph.

"I wish I had a watch," he said, as he looked at my watch.

"You don't have a watch?" I asked.

"I can't afford one," he replied.

Well, I had a brand-new watch on, a Timex, but I liked it and was proud of it. Feeling sorry for Joseph, I pulled my watch off and said, "Joseph, my wife just gave me just watch, but I'm going to give it to you in Jesus's name, OK?"

"Oh, thank you," he said, and he walked away looking at the watch I had just given him.

But a few minutes later, as I stood in the crowd, I overheard Joseph say to Phil, "I wish I had a watch."

"Joseph!" I cried in disgust, "I just gave you a watch!"

He smiled real big and pulled his coat sleeves up, revealing several watches on each arm. Instantly, he ran into the crowd, and I have never seen him or my watch again.

Phil taught me two valuable lessons. The first lesson concerned my driving. "Scott," he instructed me one evening as we drove up Eighth Avenue, "when you drive in the city, try to stay in the middle lane. The cabbies are stopping and cars are turning left and right. The traffic moves better in the middle lane." I took his advice, and from then on I endeavored to stay in the middle lane as much as possible.

The second lesson concerned my preaching. One night a very well-dressed woman scolded me for being too harsh when I preached. "You're doing this and that (she frowned and gestured with her arms). You mean well, but you are coming across too uncaring," she said, without apology; then she walked on down the sidewalk.

Later, in the van, Phil said with his deep voice and that Brooklyn accent, "Scott, that lady was right. If you are going to reach this city, you have got to do it with love. New Yorkers will respond to love. You can't come on with a take-it-or-leave-it attitude. Preach with love."

I thought I had been preaching with love, but obviously I was not communicating very much love. From then on, I sought to preach with great love and compassion, and I tried to understand people from their point of view. This also, like the visual aids, changed my ministry.

Jesus taught that if you're not received, go somewhere else where you will be received (Matthew 10:14). Sometimes that's what I had to do. One afternoon a couple of friends and I approached a group of men sitting on an old, rain-soaked couch. When I mentioned the Lord, they told me to get the hell out of there. So we left.

Walking about a block, we saw a large contingent of guys playing basketball. When they took a break, we began giving them "Smiles" and said that we would like to share some good news with them. Man, were they receptive! They listened, asked questions, and asked us to return. Many of those guys, I believe, were saved. A fine Christian teenage girl told me later, "I've been praying that somebody would come give them the gospel. Those guys really needed it."

From time to time, I preached on the wedding supper and told my audience, "If you don't want what God offers you, he'll offer it to somebody else" (Luke 14:16–24). So, when rebuffed, I took my message to someone who would receive it.

Calvary Baptist Church of Shreveport, Louisiana, sent seven people to work with us: Carl and Carolyn Carrigan, plus five students—Tina Martin, Bill Martin, Dana Ulmer, Michelle Gould, and Todd Thrower. Two of those students, Tina and Bill, were kids of Brother Step Martin, the pastor at Calvary who, back in 1980 at an associational meeting, had taken a stance to support my ministry.

We were honored to have the Calvary group in our home. Carl and Carolyn were fantastic with the students; they had great faith and were marvelous examples to them. One morning on our way to the city there was an unusually long delay on the Long Island Expressway. Cars were backed up in front of us and behind us as far as we could see.

"Can we pass out tracts?" the young people asked.

"Go ahead, but get back in here if these cars start moving," Carl ordered.

So, up and down the LIE went those kids, passing out "Smiles" and talking to people in their vehicles. One truck driver was leaning out of his window listening to Tina when the traffic began to move. Quickly, they all piled back into the van, laughing. "That was fun!" someone said. Those students were not trying to show off; they had a burden for people and wanted to win others to Christ.

Having worked in vacation Bible school and in the bus ministry at Calvary, the students were proficient at relating to the children in the projects. At one kids' meeting when the students sang and acted out "Father Abraham," more than one hundred children got into it, laughing and turning around and around. After a Bible story, we passed out New Testaments and visited with the children and some parents. As we were leaving, three ladies reprimanded us in a very warm, touching, sweet way. "When you comin' back? Our kids need this: Why haven't you been here sooner? Why didn't you stay longer?" they said, smiling and praising God. I tried to explain to them that there were hundreds of places in New York City just like this one and that everywhere we went, folks wanted us to come back.

Once I told a very receptive group of adults, teens, and children that I would be back the very next day. When I returned, they were waiting for me to show up, sitting around in lawn chairs, many of them. What if something had prevented me from coming back that day; I would have greatly disappointed that group. From then on, I began telling people that we would come back as soon as possible.

Oswald J. Smith, the famous pastor of the People's Church of Toronto, once said, "Nobody has the right to hear the gospel twice until everybody has heard it once."

Should I go where they had not heard the gospel? Should I go back to an area where I had already been? The decision was not an easy one.

One day we worked on Wall Street, and later that night we were at Times Square, ministering in the very heart of Manhattan. What a beautiful sight it was seeing those fine, clean-cut young people sing on Broadway, "I just feel like something good is about to happen." They radiated Christ, and their music in the middle of all of that noise was soothing and refreshing.

When we returned to Smithtown, we were exhausted, but my darling wife, Linda, had a hot, scrumptious meal waiting on us. Walking through the front door, we could all smell Southern cooking. I believe that the group from Calvary had a memorable time on the sidewalks of New York City. I know I did.

One afternoon I was struggling, trying desperately to get a crowd. The wind was blowing hard, and that was a deterrent. Two or three people stopped, then walked away; a few others hesitated but, after hearing me mention Christ, they quickly scampered away. By myself, I began folding up my sketch board. A gentleman in a dark suit walked up to me and said that he was a Harvard professor. He began to berate what I was doing. "I have been watching you," he said, "and what you're doing is a useless waste of time."

Feeling defeated already, I really was distressed by his words. "Sir, it is not always like this. The wind is strong. Lots of times, I have good, listening crowds; I'm working by myself," I responded.

"Well, if I were you, I'd use my talents elsewhere," he answered, as he walked away.

When I got home, Linda could tell I was distraught. "How'd it go?" she asked.

"Oh, baby," I said, "I wanted to just quit today. It was windy; nobody was stopping. And this guy who claimed to be a professor from Harvard really discouraged me, told me that I was wasting my time. Maybe he was right."

Linda and I talked awhile, and then I asked, "Any mail today?"

"Yeah, you got a letter from the Bronx," she said.

"The Bronx? Let me see it," I said.

The letter was from Margaret Bishop and Mary Cassulis. I remembered them. They were two young ladies in their midtwenties who, weeks earlier, had accepted Christ at an open air meeting in the Bronx that Phil Foglia and I conducted. Overwhelmed by the love of God, both of them wept openly, black mascara running down their cheeks. We directed them to Manhattan Bible Church, and they met us a few days later at Times Square and gave their testimonies.

Here is a portion of their letter:

> We've just written a letter to a girlfriend of ours from high school telling her of our salvation. She had been trying to tell us the gospel for four years. Now

her prayers have been answered. Praise God. We are both receiving Open Air Campaigners' home Bible study course. We are happy at the church, Manhattan Bible. We both were baptized on the same day, Easter Sunday, April 11, 1982, by Pastor Tom Maharis. Margaret's boyfriend, Charlie, and the lady I live with, Linda, were baptized last night, June 13, 1982. Linda's son Chris and a lot of his friends were saved last week. Luke 2:1.

Love you all,

Margaret Bishop and Mary Cassulis

What an encouragement their letter was! It came just at the right time. God reminded me that he was at work in people's lives and that I should not give up.

One day as I drove into Manhattan, I prayed, as I usually did, for Linda, Stephen, and Stewart. Linda had made friends with one of our neighbors named Rose Lee, a staunch Catholic, and had presented the gospel to her. "Lord, help Linda reach her," I prayed, "and God, take care of my boys. Help them to make friends and do well."

Stephen and Stewart were now enrolled at Smithtown Christian School. They had been attending public schools, but we felt that they would be better off in a Christian environment. The school gave us a break with tuition because I was a Baptist minister, and Linda and I once again felt that the Lord was providing for us in a remarkable way.

Much around me in the city disturbed me, however. The communists were selling their newspapers all over the city, and I was shocked at the number of communist posters in some areas. Violence on the street, always crouching beneath the surface, broke out from time to time. One day, standing beside my sketch board, I happened to be looking directly at a hot dog street vendor on the corner of Sixth Avenue and Fourteenth Street. Out of nowhere two guys attacked her. One hit her in the face with his fists, knocking her down. The other grabbed her apron, which held her money. Then the two thieves bolted down the subway steps and onto the train, just as the doors shut, their crime planned with perfect timing. I felt sorry for the street vendor; I had seen her there in her spot many times. She was very hardworking and was crippled. Banged up and bruised from the mugging, she was there selling hot dogs again the next day.

Linda's father passed away, and we returned to Shreveport for his funeral. Even though Mr. Lockard was an alcoholic, he was a good man and came to know Christ as his Lord and Savior, which relieved him of much guilt over the loss of his family—Linda, Shirley, and his wife. One day we will be reunited with him, so we did not weep "as those who have no hope."

After listening to the gospel in Queens one day, a Jewish woman said, "Oh, I wish I could leave Judaism for Christianity!"

"You can; you can!" I exclaimed. "The Lord Jesus Christ, the Messiah, was a Jew. The gospel is for the Jew first. We love Jews!"

She allowed me to present the gospel to her in depth; then she was gone. A minister with me said, "Man, I have a special Jewish booklet that I wish you could have given her."

"Me, too, but we will probably never see her again," I answered. But about fifteen minutes later, that Jewish woman walked up to me and offered me a dollar.

"Thank you, ma'am, but we don't take money," I said. Then I thought about the Jewish booklet. "But just a second," I said, "Here's a booklet just for you,"

"Oh, thank you," she said smiling, as she gladly took it.

That kind woman thought she was coming back to give me a dollar, but I believe the Spirit of God led her back to us so that we could give her that booklet written especially for Jews. We could see in this incident both the free will of man and the sovereignty of God working together.

A couple of days later Jim Krause, a friend from our church, went with me to the streets of Harlem and was just amazed at the response. "I had no idea those men would listen like they did and then beg us to come back," he said.

CHAPTER 22

BLINDSIDED!

Sometimes a quarterback gets hit hard by a fast, mean linebacker coming from the direction he was not expecting. Being blindsided, we call it. The painful tackle often makes a quarterback skittish and jumpy; and, because he's thinking about the possibility that he might get brutally hit again, he becomes less effective.

One afternoon I was blindsided by the cops. Their threats and intimidation caught me off guard. I certainly was not expecting the policeman to give me a hard time as I preached the gospel. Were they not supposed to serve and protect?

George Naggy, Bruce Hoppe, and I were on Fulton Street in Brooklyn at a place we had ministered many times before. George had gone to the restroom, so Bruce and I set up the sketch board. I had just started preaching when a cop drove up behind me and called for me. Telling my crowd, "Stay here; I'll be right back," I walked over to the police car, and the officer said, "Stop, you can't preach here!"

I remembered the first time I heard a policeman tell George to stop preaching, and George replied, "I will not, Officer. I am preaching the gospel!" I could not conceive of talking to a policeman that bluntly; later, I questioned George about his response to the cop. "Scotty," he said, "I've learned that here in New York you've got to hold your ground and stand up for your rights, or they will run you over." So I thought I would use this same approach with this policeman. When he told me to stop and that I could not preach there, I replied, "Officer, yes, I can. I'm not hurting anything."

He replied, "I said you can't preach here. You can't have a stand." He was equating my sketch board on a tripod with a street vendor's stand.

"Officer," I said, "I'm not selling anything; I'm not a peddler. I'm not trying to rip people off. I'm just telling people they are valuable, and Jesus loves them."

"You're not going to do it here," barked the officer. Nobody had complained. In fact, the crowd was on my side.

"Go catch the crooks and leave him alone!" someone said. "Yeah, yeah," others said.

I said, "Look, Officer, the people want me here. I'm on your side."

Questioning me, he replied "Are you going to stop?"

"I am not going to stop," I answered, "I'm not doing anything wrong."

The policeman exclaimed, "If you don't stop, you're going with us."

I returned to my sketch board and said, "People, I'm not selling anything. American boys have died for our freedom of speech and freedom of religion and freedom of assembly. I have a right to be here."

About that time the policeman grabbed my arm and said in an extremely obnoxious manner, "Come on, let's go."

"What for, Officer?" Then I said to everybody standing there, "People, this isn't Russia. We're not in a communist country."

"All right, that's enough," the cop said to me, and then he put me in the car.

"When is it wrong to stand on the corner and tell people that they are valuable and they have worth? Why don't you catch the pushers and those hustling, the pimps and prostitutes and drug addicts and thieves?" I asked.

The crowd agreed. (Bruce shared with me later that after I left, the people were very upset.)

"Bruce, come with me," I shouted from the police car.

"No, he's not coming with you," said the cop. As we were about to drive away, I heard "Eighty-Fourth Precinct" coming from somewhere, and then Bruce shouted, "The car keys."

Throwing the keys out of the window, I said, "They're taking me to the Eighty-Fourth Precinct." As I looked back from the police car, I saw George walking up. The officer called the station. "I've got a peddler. We're bringing him in," he said over the radio.

"Sir, I'm not a peddler," I exclaimed, "I'm a Baptist minister, and I wasn't doing anything wrong." (I later learned to use the term "illegal"—a term the police were more afraid of.) "I work with the Open Air Campaigners. They've been here twenty years. The last three years I've been right here." (Beginning in 1977, I had made several trips to New York and had preached at Fulton Mall many times with no interference from the police whatsoever.)

When we arrived at the station, the officer said rudely, "Get out!" We walked into the station, and as I tried to say something, the cop interrupted me. "Sit down over there!" he ordered. So I sat down.

"He was out there shouting, 'Jesus, Jesus,' and a big crowd had gathered; and he had a stand," the policeman said to several other cops.

"I wasn't acting like that, and I didn't have a stand. I wasn't selling anything," I said in my defense. Two or three cops told me to be quiet.

"Hear my side," I said.

"Sit down over there, and shut up!" they said.

"When is it wrong to preach the gospel?" I answered.

The officers got together and mumbled to each other and whispered, and I got up and asked, "Can I say anything?"

One cop said, "After they hear him, we'll listen to you." But they never did.

Finally, several cops reprimanded the officer that brought me in. Looking at me, the officer said, "The man abused me, saying, 'This is America.'"

The police seemed to realize that I had done nothing wrong, but one said, "Write him a summons."

"Summons for what?" I asked.

One of them said, "You violated the administrative code."

"What? What does that mean? The administrative code?" I said, perplexed.

Then the officer that brought me into the precinct walked over to me and said, "Let me have your license. You got any identification?" I gave him my New York driver's license. As he started filling out a summons, I said, "Officer, this is wrong. Summons for what? Are you running from Jesus?"

"I'm a 'Nam vet; I ain't running from anybody. You in the service?" he asked.

"No," I said.

"Don't talk to me about America—boys dying; I was there!" he said to me forcefully.

"We're supposed to have freedom of speech in this country," I said. "Sir, the Lord will take care of you."

"Don't try to make it sound like I'm fighting Jesus," he replied.

"You are! You have interfered with the preaching of the gospel. I'd hate to be in your shoes," I answered.

About that time a guy brought over a white sheet of paper. He handed it to me. It was the summons.

"Officer," I said, "I'm going to fight this, if I have to go all the way to the Supreme Court. You're in for the fight of your life. Will anybody hear my side of it?" I asked, desperately. Nobody paid any attention to me. The officer wrote some numbers down, but that law applied to peddlers and obstruction.

Everybody began to leave. "Well, I'll see all of you," I said, "I'm going right back there and preach."

One officer replied, "Nobody will bother you."

"When do I go before the judge?" I asked.

"August 3; he'll decide if you were right or wrong. You're not supposed to have a stand," he said.

"Will anybody give me a ride?" I asked.

"Walk," a policeman said.

I walked back to the place where I had left Bruce and George, but they showed up at the precinct immediately after I left. At first, nobody acknowledged that I had even been there. Finally, one man in plain clothes told Bruce and George that I was there. They then returned to Fulton Street and found me at the spot where I had been preaching.

I had always heard that if a horse bucks you off, you need to climb right back into the saddle, or your fear may prevent you from ever riding again. In the same way, I knew that after this altercation with the cops, I had to go right back to the same location and preach. If I had not done so, I would have been reluctant to ever preach there again. So, going back to Fulton Street, I preached with George and Bruce for a couple of more hours.

This was just an attempt by Satan to prevent me from preaching at Fulton Mall. Over the years I've probably preached in that area more than in any other area, and, I believe, I've had the best results there, too.

As I look back on the incident, I realized that I was young, inexperienced, naïve, and too zealous while talking with the cops. But I was scared, and I was trying to exercise my First Amendment rights; however, I went about it the wrong way. I should have obeyed the officer and stopped preaching. Then I should have gone to see the captain.

My parents had taught me to always respect the police. I grew up believing that if you got in trouble with the cops, you were at fault. You were either speeding or you were illegally parked or maybe you were shoplifting; but obviously you had broken the law. I discovered that in New York City, the cops could and would bust me for doing absolutely nothing wrong or illegal.

If I preached employing a public address system, the law required that I obtain a permit; but I useded no PA. The cops had no legal right to stop me from preaching. As an American citizen, I had rights. However, that made no difference. If an officer decided to shut me down or make me move, there was absolutely nothing that I could do about it.

I knew that the NYPD had an unbelievably difficult job, and my friends and I constantly prayed for them, and I had met many terrific New York policeman who watched out for me. They were respectful of what I was doing and nodded their approval. But others, completely in the wrong, would threaten me with summonses and arrests if I did not cease and desist. My greatest fear as I preached on the sidewalks of New York City became possible confrontations with the New York City cops.

Having been summoned to appear in court in Brooklyn, I really did not know what to expect. My good friend Burris Jenkins supported me and went with me, however, which made me less anxious. We were told to sit down and wait for my name to be called, which we did. After about thirty minutes the judge started reciting names. People began standing up and walking up in front of the judge: pimps, prostitutes, drug pushers, child abusers, peddlers, and thieves. And then my name was called.

Burris and I joined the group. There we were, standing in the middle of that riffraff. I felt a little humiliated, but I knew I was there because I had been preaching the gospel, so that gave me solace. When the judge got to me, he asked me why I was there. He had been hearing people answer "Stealing," "Dealing," "Domestic abuse," "Soliciting." I looked at the judge and said, "I was preaching the gospel, your Honor."

Instantly, the judge sounded his gavel and said, "Case dismissed! Next."

Well, Burris and I left relieved that that ordeal was over, and we thanked God for the outcome. But little did I know that many more clashes between the NYPD and me lay ahead.

CHAPTER 23

PLANES, TRAINS, AND AUTOMOBILES

Renting a motor home, Barbara Ann, Marion, their four sons, and Mother and Daddy drove up to visit us in New York one summer. "Take the Northern State Parkway," I said, forgetting that the parkways don't allow motor homes because the overpasses are too low. Arriving, all of them were laughing. "Gosh, we barely made it under those bridges," said Marion, exhausted after a long drive.

"Man, that's right!" I replied. "I forgot that trucks and motor homes are prohibited on Northern State. My fault, Marion!"

Giving them a tour of the Big Apple, I dropped them off at Macy's. Sure enough, Babs ran into somebody she knew. She couldn't go anywhere in Shreveport-Bossier without that happening. But Manhattan? You gotta be kiddin'!

After Christmas one year Linda's sister Shirley, who lived in Houston, called and said she and Ronda and Randall were coming up to visit us. We were excited, and, as always, Linda began baking cookies and doing a little extra housecleaning as we prepared for their visit. When the day of their arrival came, Stephen and I headed to Kennedy with a light snow beginning to fall. Halfway to the airport it became a blizzard!

Shirley's flight was canceled, but we didn't know it; so Stephen and I drove on to Kennedy. When we got there, nothing was stirring, "not even a mouse." With no planes arriving or departing, we turned around and carefully drove back to Smithtown, sliding as we went. Thousands of cars were stranded in the snow and ice on the Southern State Parkway. The only reason that we didn't get stuck was because Stephen jumped out of the van and ran along beside it as I drove very slowly and cleaned the ice from my windshield wipers. This kept me from having to stop, for if I had, we, too, would have bogged down in the snow and ice. Uptight, I was sweating it, too, but Stephen was having the time of his life, eating the snow as it fell in his face, laughing and thoroughly enjoying himself as only a fifteen-year-old could!

Normally, for me to drive to Kennedy and back home took approximately two hours. But because of the "blizzard of '83," Stephen and I drove up the steep, slick hill of our subdivision and back into our driveway a little over eight hours from the time we had left our house in Smithtown. By the grace of God we made it!

The cold weather was a major hindrance when it came to holding successful street meetings. More than once I had to break the ice of my tempura color paints before I could put the yellow and black border around my sketch board. Snow, sleet, ice, and particularly the cold wind caused people to walk briskly down the sidewalk, so it was very difficult to get them to stop and listen to some preacher out in that inclement weather.

However, when winter finally set in and people were used to bundling up, if an icy wind was not blowing, I could set up in a sunny spot and have excellent sidewalk crowds. Group after group would huddle up close, shivering a little and breathing warm air, and listen to the old, old story of Jesus and his love.

Eventually, the cold got unbearable and became so miserable that I had to go underground in the subway to minister. It was frightening for me even to walk down the subway steps. Train after train loudly rumbled down the tracks. Screeching brakes and blaring train whistles, along with hordes of riders darting in all directions, were nerve-racking. My friends George Naggy, Phil Foglia, and others were accustomed to the subway, but I was not. Despite signs and numbers and directions everywhere, I had to ask, "Which train is coming?" and "Where is that train going?"

How did we minister in the subway? Well, we boarded a train and walked up and down the aisle and passed out tracts, "Smiles," and "Little Red Bibles." As the train made a curve, more than once I had to grab a strap in order to keep from falling into somebody's

lap! Most people were extremely appreciative and took our literature; others just shook their heads "No" or ignored us, perhaps
continuing to read the *Daily News*. But it was a glorious sight to see
people on each side of the train—people of all races, color, religions, and ethnic backgrounds—sitting there reading a little Bible
while the train hurried to the next stop.

After handing out Christian literature in the trains, my friends
and I went to a platform where people were waiting for their train,
and, in a nonthreatening way, we presented the claims of Christ.
Union Square was a favorite place of mine in spite of the noise
that developed as hundreds of people feverishly stormed in and out
of the trains and then went in all directions—upstairs, downstairs,
transferring to other trains and walking up numerous steps to the
street. Then, all was church-mouse quiet. And slowly people began
trickling onto the platform. Then, they waited patiently for their
train to arrive.

When it was my turn to preach, I stood with my back against a
steel support for safety reasons. From time to time someone got
shoved in front of an oncoming train, and I didn't want to be next!

"Folks, hear me a minute," I said. "We are Christians, and we
don't want your money. When the weather is bad, we come down
here and talk about the Lord. I've got some fantastic news that
could change your life. In *Les Miserables,* Jean Valjean asks the question: 'Who am I?' Let me ask you, 'Who are you, anyway? Why are
you here? Where are you going?'"

Depending upon the time of day and the train schedule, we
normally had about ten minutes to share the Lord. Often, the train
was late, giving us extra time, sometimes fifteen or twenty minutes.
When we all heard the train coming and saw its bright light beaming
toward us, whoever was speaking quickly challenged those listening
to come to Christ. The rest of us began passing out literature to as
many people as we could, some people getting off the train when
it stopped, others getting on the train. As the doors closed and the
train slowly began creaking away, we could see people sitting and

reading the literature; others held on and swayed with the train, discussing what had just transpired with other passengers.

One evening I had the opportunity to address over forty Guardian Angels, a crime-fighting group composed mostly of young men and women in their late teens and early twenties. They cooperate with the police and stand guard on the trains. If someone needs them, they are there. Wearing their red berets, they swarmed all around me, anxiously listening as I told about the rich, young ruler and then explained John 3:16. Eagerly, they took literature, and several of them indicated they had just accepted Christ.

One day seven of us preachers spent five hours on three different levels under May's Department Store. The people were extremely attentive on the platforms. Between trains, we spent quality time with various individuals, answering questions and presenting the good news.

As I talked to a Jewish woman, she said to me in a very blunt way, "Jesus is not my Messiah!" A Jewish rabbi told me that Jesus's bones just decayed. Still another man claimed to be the Messiah himself!

"Racist, sexist, antigay! Cops and Koch, go away!" Over and over this catchy statement was chanted in rhythm as hundreds and hundreds of homosexuals marched at Times Square.

At the St. Patrick's Day parade days earlier, many gays had picketed in front of St. Patrick's Cathedral on Fifth Avenue, protesting the Roman Catholic Church's position on homosexuality. Mayor Koch on the evening news had said, "If they don't like their religion, why don't they pick out one that they do like?"

On this particular night at Times Square, the police had blocked all traffic, but Burris, Phil, and I had already parked my van on Broadway, so there we were, stuck right in the middle of this loud demonstration, confined until it was over. Many of the gay activists were seething with bitterness, anger, and hate. Some were lewdly dressed and carried filthy signs. We saw a few children, too. Hostility and fierceness could be seen in their eyes, for they obviously felt their rights had been violated. Fear was palpable.

We knew that in this environment we had to be cautious and sensitive, "swift to hear, slow to speak, slow to wrath" (James 1:19). Those that were marching were people that our Lord died for, and without condoning their behavior or lifestyle, my heart was heavy, and I grieved for them. Praying that the Holy Spirit would communicate God's love through us, we shared the truth of God's word.

Compared to the army of demonstrators, our crowds were sparse; yet the cops themselves noticed the difference between the cursing, discord, and shouting of the protesters and the peace and serenity of our sidewalk meetings. Praise the Lord. Instead of giving headaches to the police and clashing with them, our groups displayed order and calmness.

Most of the protesters did not even see us and were unaware of our sidewalk gospel meetings; however, a number of gays and lesbians gathered around us and listened. Several of them met with us one on one, poured their hearts out, and asked us to pray for them.

Trying to preach with understanding, compassion, and great diplomacy, I declared, "No matter what you've done, God loves you. Christ died on the cross for all of us. We're all sinners. He arose from the dead. He will forgive you and change your life if you'll let him." We shared what the Bible teaches about homosexuality but made it a point not to argue. Many tears were shed by those trapped in this sinful, depraved lifestyle. We had sought to hold up God's standard of holiness and not compromise the Bible and had endeavored to speak the truth in love. And I believe the Lord God was glorified.

Before long Carl and Carolyn Carrigan brought another group from Calvary Baptist Church in Shreveport to minister on the streets—Gene, Michelle, Melody, and Terry. Outstanding, all of them! In the past, Carl had given his testimony and counseled, but on this trip to New York, he began preaching on the streets. He was a natural—funny, instructive, entertaining, biblical. Carl had a way with people on the sidewalks! His first sketch board sermon had four points: Dead, Depraved, Doomed, and Delivered. Many people accepted Christ as a result of that sermon, and Carl has been a fantastic preacher on the streets ever since.

CARL CARRIGAN

One day Gene talked to a murderer by the name of Charles who had been paroled but who just could not forgive himself. But after he accepted Christ, he was relieved, and his guilt was gone. Now forgiven, he was unbelievably thankful. Charles hugged all of us, and we felt his gratitude.

Carolyn spoke to a woman named Rose Mary. In her early forties, she appeared desperate and without hope. As it began to rain, Carolyn asked her to step over against the building to get out of the rain. An alcoholic on her way to get another bottle, Rose Mary accepted Christ.

"I feel so new, so new," she explained, almost beside herself, "I can't wait to tell my two daughters at home."

Once, when flying to New York, I had an interesting conversation with a businessman who was seated beside me. "Tell me," I asked, "how do I reach men like you with the gospel?"

"Well, don't always be talking about the afterlife. Show us how Jesus relates today," he replied.

One afternoon the young people from Calvary sang in front of Federal Hall in the financial district. Scores of professional men and women gathered in close, and we had a nice audience. Remembering what that guy on the plane had said to me, I preached on "The Bottom Line," and I asked my crowd many questions: How do you handle your guilt? What's the purpose of life? Why are you here? Are you prepared to meet God? When I was finished, I talked with a very well-educated woman who was fashionably dressed and who seemed very perplexed at what she had heard. I briefly shared the gospel with her again, and she accepted Christ. Before she left, she confessed, "You know, I never stop at meetings like this, but something held me today, and I began to try to answer those questions." No doubt, the Spirit of God was at work in her life.

At Washington Square we had the privilege of ministering to a large group of New York University students. They were rowdy and cynical, and a few bearded intellectuals interrupted somewhat as I spoke on "What is Truth?" The young ladies of Calvary Baptist began singing, however, and God used their singing to soften the hearts of many of the students.

Refusing to quarrel, we had a number of the students who spilled their guts. A pretty teenage girl, half stoned, with stringy, disheveled, dirty blond hair, told me, "My parents are in Europe. They don't give a F#*'^ what I do or where I go." I could tell that she felt unloved, unwanted, thrown away. Several talked with us for a long time about having a personal relationship with the Lord Jesus Christ.

Many said that they had religion but not a personal walk with Jesus.

One day as I was counseling, someone behind me said rather loudly, "Scott Teague!" Startled that anyone would call out my name, I turned around and I saw Jeff walking toward me.

"Jeff, my man!" I replied. Jeff was the Jewish guy with a big, red birthmark on his face that Phil Foglia and I had spoken with over a year ago. Jeff still had not accepted Christ, but he talked with our group for over an hour, took a New Testament, and promised us he would read it and give God a chance.

I received a letter from a young person who said there were tons of lost people in Bossier City, so why did I go to New York? Well, I tried to explain why I was in New York. First of all, God had called me up there. Secondly, I knew there were untold numbers of unconverted people in Bossier, but there were also numerous churches and many radio and TV programs reaching out to them. In New York there were relatively few evangelical churches and very little radio and television exposure to the gospel.

In a few days, the group from Calvary returned to Shreveport. The Holy Spirit had led in every way imaginable—providing parking places, showing us where to attract good, listening crowds, and giving us the very words we needed as we talked to various individuals. All of us sensed the anointing of the Holy Spirit in our street meetings. To God be the glory!

CHAPTER 24

MOVING BACK TO BOSSIER

Invited to attend the Billy Graham Conference for Itinerant Evangelists in Amsterdam, I immediately accepted and began making plans to attend. As I did, I started thinking about moving back to Bossier City, Louisiana. Why? I don't know. I even shocked myself! I knew God had called me to those dirty sidewalks, yet here I was contemplating going back to the South. It made no sense whatsoever. Was the Lord speaking to me? I was not sure.

I think I got scared. We were living from month to month on donations from faithful friends, and I wondered just how long they would continue to back us. Also, I missed Dixie, and I knew my family did, too. They had accepted our moving to New York, and Linda had made our house a home, but I knew it would please her beyond words to raise our kids down south. My dad was sick, too; no doubt, my mother needed me. Barbara Ann, my sister, was looking after them by herself.

It occurred to me that I could make my headquarters in Bossier, expand my ministry overseas from the contacts I would make at the Billy Graham conference, and commute to New York City in the months suited for street work. When I shared my thoughts with Linda, she did not know what to think. "Scotty, you know God called us up here," she said.

"I know, babe, but I think the Lord is telling me to move back home down south," I replied; but I had a "check" in my spirit when I said that.

"Well, I just want you to be sure," Linda said.

We had been in New York for just three years. What would people think? We prayed about it, and we sought advice from our friends back home in Bossier and in New York. We did not mention our possible move to Stephen and Stewart at first. However, we eventually discussed the matter with them, and, just as we expected, they were elated! After weeks of very little sleep as I struggled with this decision, I came to the conclusion that it would be wise for me to move my family back home to Louisiana.

So back home we went. Our house in Smithtown, Long Island, sold fast, and in a matter of weeks we had purchased a home in north Bossier, at 206 Kensington, and our boys were enrolled in school.

Linda's mother was very happy that we were back in Louisiana, and my parents had told us that if we ever moved back down south, they would buy us a piano. We reminded them of their promise, and soon a brand new piano was in our dining room. Playing by ear, I entertained my folks. My dear mother thought I was Van Cliburn, but I knew better! They, too, were overjoyed that we were back in Bossier. Once again I experienced culture shock. I had grown accustomed to people not speaking much in New York. If they did, I thought like a typical New Yorker. What's he up to? Is he dealing drugs? What's his angle? In "good ol' Dixie" people spoke and smiled, and often they did it first. It took some getting used to.

Al Bohl and I flew to the Billy Graham conference in Amsterdam together. My luggage did not show up for three days, but I wore some of Al's shirts. They were tight, but I was glad to get them.

The conference was truly inspirational, more than I ever imagined. I'll never forget the opening ceremonies when five thousand evangelists from 134 countries paraded in, dressed in clothing representative of each country. Many from Africa wore headdresses and feathers and carried drums, animal skin shields, and spears.

What preaching! What singing! What praise! With all of us singing in unison, "Freely, freely you have received, freely, freely give," I stood with my hands lifted toward heaven and cried. So did practically everybody else. Billy Graham preached many times, and you could tell this conference was a dream of his fulfilled. Pat Robertson of the 700 Club and Bill Bright of Campus Crusade spoke, as well as Robert Schuller of the Crystal Cathedral. E. V. Hill preached to standing ovations, and Anne Graham Lotz challenged us to greater commitment to Christ. Many other outstanding preachers, unknown but filled with the Spirit of God, lifted us to higher ground!

We had daily workshops on evangelism, follow-up, church planting, and discipleship. And I observed that the Third World evangelists packed the seminars and workshops that taught open air preaching.

At the conference I met many men of God from all over the world, a number of them from Africa and Asia; and, I was invited by several of them to come to their countries and preach the gospel to those who had never heard the name of Christ and to help train Christian leaders in outdoor evangelism. This excited me beyond words!

But soon after returning from the conference, I kissed Linda and the boys and left for New York City.

CHAPTER 25

COMMUTING

Our friends Jerry and Darlene Langston, whom we had met at Grace Baptist Church, had insisted that when I came back to New York I should stay with them, which was exactly what I did. They were about our age, and we had developed a strong friendship. Jerry was a country boy from North Carolina and was just plain fun to be around. Darlene looked like Roseanne on television, and she laughed very loudly like Roseanne, too, only Darlene had a strong, very obvious Long Island accent. When I walked into their house, she gave me a big hug and asked, "How are you?" which sounded like "Hawaii?" Before I could answer, she and Jerry both said, "We miss Linda and the kids."

"I do, too," I replied. "I'm sure they'll be back to visit."

I was anxious to see Burris and Jana, two other friends on Long Island. When we had left New York to move back to Bossier City, Burris noticed that I was leaving a large metal desk. "Scott, I'd like that desk if you're not going to take it," he said to me one afternoon.

"It's yours, my friend," I said. So Burris drove his automobile to our house and turned that huge table upside down and placed it on top of his car, which, by the way, was very small; then he drove away with it, without tying it down.

"It'll be OK," he said to me, chuckling, "I just have a block to go."

Soon Burris and Jana had me over to eat. Jana's meals always had that Czechoslovakian flavor and tasted delightfully different but lip-smacking delicious!

"I guess you made it home with that desk?" I asked, as we finished dinner.

"No problem," Burris answered with that New York moxie of his, as Jana cackled out loud!

175

Calvary Baptist Church of Shreveport, Louisiana, sent another group of young people to New York, led by Carl and Carolyn Carrigan once again, all of us staying with Jerry and Darlene.

The team from Calvary worked with me for a few days on the streets, and, oh, how God blessed! Nearly three hundred decisions for Christ were made. Follow-up material and lists of churches were sent to each person, and fifty-eight of those making decisions for Christ were personally counseled and given New Testaments. The group worked tirelessly, Carolyn collecting the decision cards and Carl giving his testimony and preaching.

Terry Martin, the daughter of Brother Step, the pastor at Calvary, was one of the young people who came up, as well as Melody, the daughter of Price Harris, the music minister at Calvary. Both girls, just teens at the time, answered questions from people and shared their faith as they sat on benches at Albee Square in Brooklyn.

One event with the Calvary group stood out above all others. After we had conducted a well-attended children's meeting not far from the Williamsburg Bridge, we headed uptown on Sixth Avenue to minister at Times Square. On our way, I spotted about twenty-five punk rockers in a vacant lot. Dressed weirdly and sporting mohawks, clad in black leather, silver chains, feathers, and painted purple, they probably needed Jesus, we felt. When I pulled over, we introduced ourselves and began talking with them.

"What about me preaching the gospel to you guys? Will you listen?" I asked. They looked at each other, mumbled, and then said, "Yeah, go ahead." The young people from Calvary stepped up on the van platform and began to sing. Then, out of the blue, all hell broke loose. We had been set up!

The punk rockers cursed, pounded hard on trash cans, screamed, and shouted obscenities. "F.*^# you! What kind of s#.*^ is this?" they yelled.

Normally, when blatant, vicious rejection like this occurred, I left, because our Lord taught us not to cast pearls before swine. But in this case the Spirit of the Lord said to me, "Continue. I'm in control."

As the roars and filthy language increased to a fever pitch, the girls in the singing group began to cry—tears of pity and compassion—but they continued to sing. All of us were cold-blooded afraid because we did not know what might happen. I knew I was responsible for the group, but just about the time I felt we should shut down and leave, something marvelous took place. When the punkers saw those young men and women singing in the face of adversity, God broke their hearts. They stopped jeering, and as I stepped up on the platform and began preaching, they stood quietly, not saying a word.

"God loves you, young people. But God is holy, too. He hates our sin. That's why he sent his Son, the Lord Jesus Christ, to die for our sin. Christ paid the penalty for your sin and my sin on that cross," I declared, as boldly as I could.

When I was finished, the punk rockers mixed and mingled with us, conversed with us, asked questions, expressed their views. There was a mutual sharing of ideas between us and the rock group. Many hearts were deeply and profoundly moved on both sides.

Later that evening we drove to Times Square, and I'll never forget the smiles and the glow that those kids from Calvary had on their faces as they sang "Beulah Land."

"When thou walkest through the fire, thou shalt not be burned; neither shall the flame kindle upon thee" (Isaiah 43:2).

The Calvary group had experienced some trying, spiritual battles and had come through them unscathed. I thanked God for the leading of the Holy Spirit and for answering prayer.

A few days later after the group from Calvary Baptist Church returned to Shreveport, Jerry and I were driving across the Lower East Side when we saw some Hells Angels sitting on a stoop. Apparently, they had rented an apartment.

"Hey, Jerry," I said, "why don't we give these guys some New Testaments?"

"Well, I don't know, Scotty," replied Jerry.

"Come on. We will be OK," I said.

Loading up our bags with New Testaments, we walked up and I said to one of the gang members, "My friend, we're giving away these New Testaments, and we would like to leave a few with y'all." The guy didn't say anything, but, reluctantly, he did take a Testament. We set a stack of about fifteen more New Testaments beside him, and I said, "Take care." And we left.

After grabbing a bite to eat, we decided to drive back around to where we had seen the Hells Angels. Approaching their apartment, we noticed that nobody was on the stoop, but that all of the New Testaments had been thrown away into the big steel trash can.

"Man, they threw them away!" I exclaimed. "Let's go get 'em. If they don't want 'em, we'll give 'em to somebody else."

"Scotty," Jerry said quickly, "I'm not going back. That guy was very unfriendly. You know what those guys might do."

"Well, I can't stand to see the Bibles in the trash, so I'm going to go get 'em. I'll be careful," I said.

I knew that the Hells Angels were outwardly very macho, but I felt that probably many of them were desperate, lonely, and scared. Some were getting old, and they knew it. I nervously walked up to the trash can, and I began to gather them into my arms one at a time, all the while praying that I would not have a confrontation with the Hells Angels. Nobody came out, but I could feel the tension as I stuffed my bag with the New Testaments.

Knowing their reputation, I was relieved when I got back to the van and drove away. "Nothin' to it!" I said to Jerry.

"Yeah, but you're glad it's over!" Jerry answered, laughing out loud.

Anxious to see Linda and the boys, I returned to Shreveport, and soon Linda had cataract surgery on one of her eyes. The surgery was successful, and we thanked God. Linda was just thirty-nine years of age (at age forty-three, she had surgery on her other eye), but I guess she took after her father, who had cataract surgery at a very early age, too. Her mother, however, did not wear glasses and could read the smallest of print.

While in Shreveport, I preached at the Louisiana State Fair one night in conjunction with Summer Grove Baptist Church. It felt good to preach to a fair crowd, which I had done so much in the past, but what a difference the Bible Belt was from New York City! Soon I was back on the streets of the Big Apple.

When I was growing up, I knew absolutely nothing about drugs. I still know very little, but what an education I got on the sidewalks of New York. One afternoon a junkie said to me, "We will sell our babies for crack cocaine." The more I preached on the streets, the more my eyes began to detect pills being passed out, even in our street meetings from time to time.

I knew instinctively not to act like I had been on drugs. If I did, the users would see right through me. A fake is detected quickly on the streets. I just had to be myself. Often, when addressing a bunch of drug addicts, I said to them that I had never even smoked a cigarette, much less smoked pot or used hard drugs, and that I didn't know what they were going through. I sensed that they respected me for being up front with them.

I learned that if I came across as real and spoke like a man and never had a condescending manner, I did not have to dress, talk, or act like them in order to reach them for Christ. I could simply preach the gospel, and more often than not, they would listen.

Why God chose me, someone from a small town down south, and someone relatively sheltered from the awful, dark, soul-gripping world of drugs, I'll never understand. Oh, I knew I wasn't perfect and had done my share of sinning, but drugs? No. Yet God in his sovereignty put me in the drug-infested areas of New York to preach God's word to those who had incurred irreparable wounds.

One afternoon on the Lower East Side of Manhattan, Jerry, Darlene, and I had the privilege of speaking to a hundred or more junkies, many of them mainliners with tormented, ruined lives. As I looked into eyes whose clearness had long since been replaced by dreary, shadowy hopelessness, I felt so powerless to help them.

179

Strutted fingers—swollen, crusty, and bloody—openly dealt heroine, crack cocaine, needles, and pot.

Stepping into the middle of them, I said, "Hey, fellas, let me show you this newspaper trick. I'm going to tear this newspaper up and make it come back. I'm a preacher man; I don't want your money. Get in a little closer, OK? We won't be here long." As the crowd, made up mostly of men, moved in, I tore up the newspaper and said, "Do you ever feel like your life is all torn up?" Heads began nodding up and down.

"Yeah, man, my life's over, man," I heard somebody say in the crowd, but I didn't know who it was because many of them were talking.

"Do you ever feel like a thrown-away shoe?" I asked.

"Come on, now; all right now," two or three answered.

"The devil will tear your life apart. You know what I'm talking about," I said, praying that I was getting through to them.

"We hear you. We hear you," many said.

As I mashed the newspaper together, I stomped on a Coke can. "That is what the devil will do to our lives. He hates you. He wants to kick your head in," I exclaimed. The crowd thickened all around me. In my mind I was thinking, "Oh, God, I can't change these men; they are so messed up, so far gone, beyond help."

"But God can take a life," I said, as I put the paper back together, "and can put it back on the right road."

"Whoo," the guys said, as they clapped and slapped each other's hands together.

"How did you do that?" someone asked.

"I can't tell you my tricks, but I've got some fantastic news to tell you. Listen up, OK?" I said.

Grabbing my set of weigh scales, I began, "Some people think that every time you do something good, you get a point (I dropped a coin on one side of the scales), and every time you do something bad, you get a point (I dropped a coin on the other side of the scales). If you do more good than bad (I dropped lots of coins), you get to go to heaven; but if you have more bad than good (I dropped many coins), you go to hell. Many people believe that. But hear me, guys; that's not true. No matter how much good you do, and God wants you to do right—it'll keep you out of jail—no matter how much good you do, all of our goodness is like a filthy rag (I held up a dirty rag) compared to God. He is so holy!

"You know, when you step in dog poop, it doesn't take much, man. It stinks! Well, just a little sin is a stench in the nostrils of God. God is so holy! You and I, guys, have offended a holy God. You might as well try to climb to heaven on a rope of sand as try to get to heaven based on your good deeds! Your good works can never earn your way to heaven (Ephesians 2:8-9), but Christ took our sins on the cross (I held up the dirty rag and motioned like I was laying it on a cross). When you accept Christ, God clothes you in the righteousness of Christ (Romans 4:7)! Now, your sins are covered by the blood of Christ (I covered the dirty rag with a red cloth) and you get to walk right straight into heaven. That's the love and mercy of God. Now, we're still sinners, but God no longer credits you with sin.

"You say, 'If I believed that, I would get my sins covered, and then I would live any way I wanted to.' No, a thousand times, no! When you accept Christ, you repent; you're willing to turn from your sin, and Christ becomes Lord in your life. He changes you from within. You become a different person. Now, with Christ living in you, you want to do what is right. And now you have the power to do it! That is the wonderful, thrilling good news!"

I shared the gospel as best I could for about a half hour. Tears streamed down their dirty, grimy faces as I said, "God hates your sin, but he loves you very much, so much that Christ died on the cross for you and took the rap for your crimes…He can set you free today."

Many, many of those men prayed out loud to receive Christ. As Jerry, Darlene, and I passed out New Testaments and business reply cards so that they could enroll in a Bible correspondence course, we met a guy who called himself "Frogie." A thirty-three-year-old gang leader who looked fifty, Frogie said to me, "God shot my heart today, man." He told us that he had just been released from prison, having spent eight years behind bars. Openly weeping, he thanked us for coming to them, where they were.

"I didn't think I had feelings for anybody anymore. Thank you for giving me my feelings back," Frogie said. Of course, that was the Spirit of God, not me, who had reached inside his soul and had embraced his heart!

One Friday evening Jerry, Darlene, and I went underground because it was just too cold to minister effectively outside. Everywhere in the subway were posters of the man who had shoved a lady under the train the day before. As I briefly shared a word about Jesus, the crowd was nervous, and so were we. Yet God blessed, and many people were genuinely interested, and a number of them accepted Christ.

Then, a tall, well-educated, well-dressed Muslim stepped forward on the subway platform, and in front of everybody boldly declared, "Jesus is not God. Moses did miracles, too!"

But he was too late; many had just received Jesus and would never be the same. Shaking his head in disgust, the Muslim walked away, defeated.

After a couple of more meetings in the subway, a mean-spirited guy walked up and told us out of the blue that he hated Jerry Falwell. A lady with a troubled face peered through the staircase railings, waiting to see our reaction. We tried to speak to the guy, but he would not listen and walked on down the platform. Leaving the subway, I saw a sharply dressed airline attendant who obviously was polished and fashion-conscious. "Miss," I said with a little timidity, "You're valuable, and Jesus loves you." Sneering at me, she boarded the train. Her total disdain not only for me but for the Lord was chilling.

CHAPTER 26

ALMOST A RIOT

Setting up in front of A&S, one of my favorite preaching stations, I had just written in block lettering on my sketch board "Five Things God Does Not Know" and had gathered a small crowd up close when a Black Israelite walked into my meeting. (The Black Israelites are a racist group that teaches hate. They claim to be the original Jews.) In his forties with a dark beard and dressed in a long-sleeved, navy-blue shirt rolled up to his elbows, with a matching skullcap and carrying a leather bag on his shoulder, he looked over the situation and then began to disrupt. As I said, "God does not know a sinner he does not love," he began speaking with a loud, penetrating voice, "That man don't know nothin', Israel. He can't teach you nothin'." Several people turned and looked at him.

"Do he look like you? Do he look like you?" he asked the predominately black crowd in downtown Brooklyn. "That white man came teach you nothin'," he said.

Attempting to hold on to my crowd, I replied, "Ladies and gentlemen, we're not here to argue, and God looks on the heart, not the outward appearance; you're valuable, and Jesus loves you." This made the guy get louder, and he began to scold the blacks in the audience. When I mentioned that Christ died on the cross for our sins, he replied, "He didn't die on no cross." Walking in closer and leaning over into the crowd with his long arm pointing to an elderly black woman, he said, "And that woman (referring to the Virgin Mary) didn't have no baby, neither. Don't listen to that lie. No woman can have a baby without sex; that's Greek mythology. Don't listen to that." The old, white-haired black woman just looked up at him through her glasses and didn't say a word—then.

"God does not know a sin he does not hate," I said, and began quoting the Ten Commandments and checking them off on my sketch board. But he continued disputing everything I said; it was very hard to talk over him.

"We hear you," a lady said in the crowd, letting me know that they were with me. The audience was getting thicker and swelling by the minute. Shaking his hand in my face, he exclaimed, "You are Satan, the devil." Ignoring him, I said, "The Lord God of Israel is the true God, and he gave us these commandments. He hates our sin, but he loves the sinner."

"That cracker don't know nothin', Israel. That cracker don't know nothin', Israel," he blared.

"Young man, listen to me," I said. "With all the love that is within me, one thing I do know, ladies and gentlemen, is that Jesus Christ is alive. He changed my heart!" I heard applause. It was extremely upsetting to me that he was interfering with the preaching of the gospel. I did not think that he was dangerous, but I really did not know what he might do.

"I am from the South," I said, "You know I'm from the South, but you see this lady?" I reached and put my hand on the shoulder of a black woman who had been "amening" me and sort of turned her to the crowd and said, "You see this lady? She's black, and I'm white, but we're brothers and sisters in Christ, 'cause Jesus makes us that way." (For every one black that bothered me, ten thousand blacks were for me, respected me, defended me, and often listened to me.)

The crowd noise got louder, many agreeing but others disagreeing, apparently on the side of the Black Israelite. Louder and louder it got, with people shouting for me and against me. "Hate is of the devil; hate is of the devil," I said as loudly as I could, "but Jesus is love!" Desperately trying to continue my message, I declared, "God does not know a worse place than the place called hell."

A blue-and-white police van drove by slowly! No doubt the cops were observing and thinking that this was a borderline riot. I was praying that the police would not stop us, because I felt the Holy Spirit was speaking to lots of folks. Continuing to preach, I said, "God does not know a better place than the place called heaven," and I began to quote John 3:16, and said, "Join me," and many people in the crowd, young and old alike, quoted this verse with me. It was at that moment that I felt a special anointing of the Holy Spirit. God gave me an unusual unction and authority.

"You are a lying jackal! You're a lying jackal!" shouted the guy, obviously a tool of the devil. His long arm bending back and forth and his big hand moving around looked like a king cobra about to strike!

"They put his body in the grave, but he rose again the third day," I exclaimed, experiencing the power of God on me. I had absolutely no fear whatsoever. I knew God was in control, and he gave me great peace. I felt compelled to preach on. Many people were wanting to hear what I had to say despite the Black Israelite's hateful words. I believe the Christians in the crowd knew that this was a battle between good and evil, between God and Satan, and they wanted to see how it was going to come out.

"I know some of you may not have work, but in heaven there will be no unemployment. There will be no crime and no hate," I said. Because this was a massive crowd in front of the main entrance into A&S, I was hoping that the manager would not ask us to leave. He didn't.

"Explain what is sin. Explain what is sin," said a man, joining the heckler.

Ignoring him, I said, "God does not know a better time than now to accept the Lord."

"You're of the devil! You're of the devil!" said the Black Israelite.

"I'm not of the devil! I'm not of the devil!" I said with great emphasis, defending myself, hopefully with righteous indignation.

"Jesus is the truth. Jesus said, 'I am the way, the truth, and the life. No man cometh unto the father except by me' " (John 14:6). I said that as forcefully as I could.

"Everything we have is free. We don't want nobody's money," I said, as I held up "Little Red Bibles." Hands from every direction grabbed them.

"Don't listen to him," he shouted.

Some people began to move on down the sidewalk, but most stayed. One young man was eating a hot dog, another was sipping a soda with a straw. A Muslim who had on a long white robe had stayed the entire meeting. I thought, "What a place for the gospel!"

The Black Israelite continued, "That's Satan, the devil. Four hundred years of slavery all over the world. Slaves, slaves to this man right here."

"I love you, young man, and Jesus loves you," I said.

"You don't love me," he answered, turning his head away from me.

"Yes, I do," I replied. "Folks, we're not here to argue," I said as I passed out more Bibles.

"Let me have another one," somebody said.

"Don't be stupid!" said the heckler.

"Folks, you are valuable, and Jesus loves you. These are all free," I said as I passed out more Christian literature. "He died for us and shed his blood for us. You're valuable, and Jesus loves you. No matter what you have done, he loves to forgive. Anybody else? Yes, these are free," I repeated.

"God bless you," somebody said softly.

"Folks, listen to me. Let me tell you the biggest lie of the devil," I said as I sought to present the gospel another way. I then tore the used newsprint from the sketch board. But before I could continue, a slim black lady whose hair was held back with hair combs, maybe in her thirties, and wearing glasses, walked up to me. "Can I say something?" she asked. I had noticed her standing up close to me and praying.

"Yeah, go ahead," I said.

Addressing the crowd, I said, "This is a black sister that knows the Lord; hear her, please."

"Let me say one thing," she said, but the Black Israelite kept shouting at her. "Respect the lady," I said.

"Get away from that snake! Get away from that snake!" the guy screamed, leaning into her.

"Will you listen to me?" the young woman said, sort of pleading with him. But the guy would not let her speak. "Get away from that snake!" he screamed again.

"Respect the lady!" I said, strongly.

"I ain't gonna listen to that lie; I ain't gonna let her tell no lie," he said angrily.

"You know what? I can't talk over his screaming. I can't talk over his screaming," the lady said, obviously frustrated. The guy was so loud that she could not make herself be heard.

"That white man is Satan, the devil," the heckler said even louder.

"Could you just hear me out?" the woman asked. The crowd was getting bigger and bigger.

"Hear you out? Lie you gone tell?" he said.

The young woman said, "I can't talk too loud because he's screaming over me, but I want you to hear one thing." Gesturing toward me, she said, "He's not out here to convince you of something, but he's out here…"

But the Black Israelite interrupted her and shouted her down. Then the lady, now with a strong, mighty, God-anointed voice, exclaimed, "Wait a minute. If you are so much of God, you'll hold your peace, brother!"

The crowd noise was deafening. The girl turned and prayed, "Lord, bind that spirit."

"In Jesus's name," I added.

"Lord, I bind that spirit. I bind that spirit," she said again.

"Go ahead, young lady," I said.

"You better shut up! You better shut up!" the Israelite warned.

Again the woman tried to talk to the crowd. "I want to say one thing; I want you to hear what I'm saying," she said. We both bowed our heads and prayed that God would intervene.

"Go ahead," I said, nodding at her. Everybody was talking and expressing his or her own opinion—men, women, kids, teens, blacks, and even a few whites, young and old, some for us and some against us. And it was loud.

"How many of you want to hear the lady?" I shouted above the confusion as I lifted up my hand. Hands went up all around us that made up most of the crowd.

"We plead the blood of Jesus. We bind the power of Satan. In Jesus's name. We plead his precious blood. You are Lord, Jesus," I prayed, as the young lady cleared her throat and got ready to address the people again.

The Black Israelite's arm was in her face, but she started speaking, and it was powerful.

"I've got news for you," she declared, her voice going up a notch in intensity, "Jesus is Savior! Jesus is God!" People everywhere began to shout, "Jesus, Jesus, Jesus!" Momentum swung our way! Hands went up. People stood and prayed. "If you want to know the truth," she said with unction, "the Bible says you shall know the truth and the truth shall set you free (John 8:32)! You don't have to argue about the word of God. The word of God can fend for itself," she exclaimed, as she lifted a Bible high in the air.

Many "amens" were heard, and many people began to clap. "Praise the Lord; praise the Lord!" the people shouted.

"Let me tell you something else, people. When God begins to move, the devil gets mad, hallelujah!" the young woman said, stepping back into the crowd.

The Black Israelite would not give up. He stormed back and said, "This man had us in slavery four hundred years. Our forefathers, this man right here. Don't be so ignorant, stupid. When you gonna wake up, Israel?"

"Jesus loves everybody. Jesus loves everybody," I said, trying to defuse any bad vibes.

"Jesus is Lord!" I heard somebody say.

"I tried to warn you," the Israelite said.

A man touched my arm and said to me, "Somebody stole your bag, but I ran after him and brought it back."

"Thank you, sir," I said.

Then, something beautiful happened. The crowd, total strangers teeming around me, spontaneously began singing, "He is Lord. He is Lord. He is risen from the dead, and He is Lord. Every knee shall bow, every tongue confess, that Jesus Christ is Lord." Over and over the crowd sang as hands of praise went up. Christians that I didn't even know had turned a volatile situation into a revival meeting! Satan was defeated. The Black Israelite turned and shook his head and walked away. A massive crowd kept singing, "He is Lord" in the heart of downtown Brooklyn. People stood on benches. Many people shook my hand. Many people hugged each other.

"God bless you, ladies," I said. "Greater is he that is in you than he that is in the world."

"The devil is a liar," said the old, white-haired, black woman that the Israelite had scolded earlier. "I'm not ashamed of Jesus," she said, smiling big. She had stood there the entire meeting, a very long time for a woman her age to stand on her feet.

I wrote on the sketch board "Jesus is coming!" and there were shouts of joy and tremendous applause. The man who had retrieved my bag stood up on a bench and said, "Hang around. We're talking about Jesus," then, he began passing out tracts.

I preached another message, feeling unction from the mighty God, and I had no interruptions. Many, many people accepted Christ. I told a lady, "God bless you. I'll see you in heaven by God's grace."

After it was all over, I was emotionally and spiritually drained, yet I was ecstatic. The Black Israelite was an unreasonable man whom I could not handle, but, to use the words of the apostle Paul, "I was delivered out of the mouth of the lion" (2 Timothy 4:17).

Chapter 27

BACK TO THE BIG APPLE

Now living in Bossier City, my hometown, I was commuting to New York, having made several trips, and preaching on the sidewalks. For a while everything was kosher, but not for long. I began to feel out of place in Bossier, unneeded; then, I began to be uncertain about our move back south. I experienced mental anguish, and I had no peace.

Linda knew that I was miserable, too, and my folks sensed that something was wrong with me. So did my sister and her husband. We had been with our loved ones and friends, and that had been great; but I could not get New York out of my system. Had I made a mistake? Hadn't the Lord promised in his word that he would direct our path if we trusted him and acknowledged him?

After an intense study of the Bible and much prayer, I came to the conclusion that I had gotten off track a little, but, based on Romans 8:28, I knew that somehow the Lord would work all things together for my good and use my mistakes to help conform me to the image of his Son.

"Man's goings are of the Lord; how can a man then understand his own way?" (Proverbs 20:24).

How would I break the news to my wife and kids? I had always felt that my family was more important than my ministry; yet I realized that I had been double-minded. I had treated them unfairly by following my elusive dreams. I had not meant to hurt them, but I had. Linda, Stephen, and Stewart had moved to New York, stayed there three years, moved back to Bossier for a year, and now I would be asking them to move back to New York. It was almost too much to ask!

"Linda," I said one day, "I believe we should move back to New York." I think she saw it coming, but she was still extremely upset. She was not thinking so much about herself. She was thinking about our boys. Stephen was fifteen and had lots of friends at Airline High School. Many of them played basketball with him in our driveway. What would Stephen think about our moving back to New York? Stewart was ten, had lots of buddies, and rode his bike all over our neighborhood. What would his reaction be? Both of our sons were very content in Bossier.

Linda and I talked with them about our going back to New York, and it was traumatic for us to do it. They didn't like it, but what else could they do?

Linda, Stephen, and Stewart had always been very supportive of me, but when the decision was made for us to move back to New York, it was a monumental sacrifice on their part. Having lived back down south for just a year, we put our house up for sale in Bossier, and in August 1984 we headed back to New York.

I had butterflies in my stomach when I drove up in front of the home of Burris and Jana. It was late, after ten at night, but I figured Burris would be up. Sure enough, the light was on, and the blinds were open as usual, and there he was at his desk.

Quietly, I got out of my van and walked through the garage. I knew their door would be unlocked. It always was, day and night. "We can't even locate our house keys," Burris once told me. Lightly knocking, I opened the door and walked into his room. He heard me and, looking up through his glasses, Burris said, "Scotty, I've been expecting you. Have a seat. I read in your newsletter that you guys were moving back up here. When will it be?" Before I could answer, Burris continued, "Gosh, it's good to see you. When will you be moving back?" Typical Burris. I could not get a word in, as always.

"Now! We are here now! Staying at Darlene and Jerry's," I answered.

"Great! Linda and the boys with you?" he questioned.

"We're all here," I said, "I'm still looking for a house." Burris knew that I had been keeping an eye open for a house lately, while commuting to New York.

"Well, let's see what's for sale around here," he said.

"Burris, it's late. We'll wake Jana," I replied.

"No, come on!" he said.

We had lived just a block from Burris and Jana previously, so we started looking there in our old neighborhood in Smithtown. After driving around awhile and house hunting, we called it a night, but it was good to see Burris.

For the next few days Linda and I drove all over the area, and we realized soon that the prices of houses had skyrocketed on Long Island and that there was no way we could now afford a home. I didn't want to do it, but we had to rent. We were accustomed to having our own home and yard, so I knew it would be a change. We found an affordable upstairs apartment not far from our friends Jerry and Darlene in Ronkonkoma. A Jewish woman named Arlene, single, with a small daughter, lived downstairs, and they seemed nice enough.

One Saturday afternoon as I cleaned out the garage, I had an interesting talk with Arlene about the Lord. "To tell you the truth, I never believed in God. I didn't know Jews were supposed to believe in God," she said outright.

"Arlene, what's your purpose in life?" I asked.

"Life has no meaning at all to me," she answered.

That night Linda and I once again prayed for her that she might come to know Christ as her Lord and Savior. Maybe God had us in that apartment so that we could share the Christian life with her.

Smithtown Christian only went to the eighth grade, and Stephen was in high school now, but he got a scholarship to attend Stony Brook School, one of the top prep schools in the nation. Because I was a Baptist preacher, Stewart got a break on the tuition and enrolled once again at Smithtown Christian School. All of us praised the Lord!

Life on Long Island was good. Burris and Jana had a beautiful swimming pool and often invited us over to swim and eat Jana's flavorful Czechoslovakian food. Their sons, Mike and Peter, played "Marco Polo" in the pool with our boys, and sometimes Jerry and Darlene—with their three children, Lisa, Lila, and Keith—joined us. What fun all of us had! We still missed our family down south, but Long Island was really becoming home to us now.

The sandy beaches on Long Island's South Shore were breathtaking. We enjoyed the rolling waves although the water was always cold for us, even in July and August. We were told not to go past the lighthouse because that was where the nude beaches were. Bagels with cream cheese became a staple. At the diners we specified "iced tea"; otherwise, we were served hot tea. But there was never enough ice in the glass, and the tea was not sweet like good ol' Southern iced tea!

From our apartment in Ronkonkoma I had to drive a little farther to the city than when we lived in Smithtown; but, as usual, autumn on Long Island was spectacular with red, orange, and yellow colors splashed all over the shrubs and trees. So the drive into the city was pleasant except for that horrid traffic.

Soon I was back out on the sidewalks, where I knew in my heart that I belonged. How and why I had moved back south was still a mystery to me, but I was glad to be living in New York now.

One day as a friend of mine and I held a meeting in front of May's Department Store, I noticed a young man straddling his bike in the back of the crowd. When I finished preaching, he motioned for me to come over to him. As I walked toward him, I saw red and purple marks of various shapes all over his face and neck.

"As you can tell, I am dying with AIDS," he said, with despair in his voice. "Would you please pray for me? I heard you speak. Everybody has rejected me. I need your prayer." Thinking about Jesus touching the leper, I grabbed his hand and said, "Young man, I'll be glad to pray for you." After I prayed, he smiled and told me he felt the prayer. Emphasizing that he was valuable and Jesus loved

195

him, I shared the gospel with him. Nodding, he slowly pedaled away, and I never saw him again; but I've often wondered about the guy who had contracted that dreaded, terminal disease, standing there, straddling that bicycle.

With turmoil taking place in India even as I spoke, three Hindu women listened curiously as I proclaimed the gospel. "Christ is alive! He arose from the dead! I'm not talking about religion. I'm talking about knowing Christ personally. I know about President Bush, but I don't know President Bush personally. A lot of people know about God. God wants us to know him personally." I prayed that they would not walk away. But a man was shouting at me from the back of the crowd,

"Liar! Liar!" Because of his shouting I didn't know what the Hindu women would do.

They had dark eyes and red dots on their foreheads. Leaning toward me and straining to hear above the shouting, they really seemed captivated as I preached about the empty tomb of our Lord. As I concluded, I noticed the three Hindu women had left, but inwardly thanked God for giving me such a great opportunity to preach Christ to so many people of other religions who probably had never been inside a church.

As my buddy and I folded up my sketch board, a pitiful-looking, bald-headed man was collecting cans and putting them in his bicycle basket; but the dirty, filthy, ragged man who had been following us around and shouting "Liar, liar! These men are liars" was gone.

"Just about everybody I talk to says he believes in Jesus," I said to a number of shoppers as I preached in front of Macy's in Brooklyn. "But what does it mean to believe in Jesus? What does the Bible mean when it says, 'Believe on the Lord Jesus Christ and thou shalt be saved' (Acts 16:31)? That's what it says, doesn't it?"

"Sure do," said a rather large black woman.

"Let me illustrate. You know that if you want to go to the seventh floor there in Macy's, you've got to take the elevator; the steps just go to the third floor. Isn't that right?" I asked.

"That's right," people mumbled.

"So you get on the elevator and you push the button and you just stand there. You rely on that elevator to get you to where you want to go. You just trust it. You put your faith in it. You believe in it. You rely on it. That's what it means to believe in Jesus. You just put your faith in him as your Lord and Savior. You just rely upon him to save you. He did everything necessary for you to be saved when he died on the cross. All you have to do is rely upon him and what he did for you at the cross. That's what it means to believe in Jesus," I said. Wow! What a response I had. It seemed that my entire crowd said the sinner's prayer.

One noon hour I preached on "Drugs, Suicide, or Jesus." A young man spoke up and asked, "Are you saying that Christians never commit suicide?"

"No," I replied, "but I am saying that many people who do kill themselves might not if they knew the Lord."

The young man said that he was Jewish and that his name was Marty. He began asking us question after question about the Christian message and lifestyle. More and more people stopped, gathering around. God gave Burris and me answers, and a very civil dialogue took place between the guy and us. There was no arguing, and we sensed the Holy Spirit was moving in that crowd. Sure enough, he was! Over three hundred pieces of literature were distributed!

Later, before Marty went on his way, the three of us shook hands, and we felt mutual respect. From time to time this type of give-and-take street service took place, a spontaneous, impromptu scenario that you couldn't plan.

As Burris and I were leaving, a man seated on a bench across the street motioned to us to come over. "My three sons have become

Christians," he said, confiding in us. "I'm close. I'm close." Burris asked him if he would commit himself to Christ right then and there. He hesitated, then bowed his head and prayed to receive Christ. He did it in a very quiet and meaningful way. Praise God.

CHAPTER 28

THE QUARTER IN THE STUMP

Not liking our apartment very much, we later rented from an elderly woman named Mrs. Wojtech, a godly woman who was a member of our church, Grace Baptist. Small and frail in stature with solid white hair, she reminded me of my dear mother. Mrs. Wojtech lived above us and was a sheer delight to be around, unbelievably sweet, and, my, what a prayer warrior she was!

"I prayed for my husband to be saved for years and years, and finally he came to know the Lord," she said one day, with a broad smile and a twinkle in her eye. We loved Mrs. Wojtech, and she loved us. Living downstairs in her home presented no problems, but we really wanted our own home. (Soon after we moved in with Mrs. Wojtech, the space shuttle *Challenger* exploded during liftoff, killing all seven aboard, including New Hampshire schoolteacher Christa McAuliffe, on January 28, 1986). Not only did we desire our own place, but Stephen and Stewart also wanted a dog. We had a frisky white cat named Snowball, but we had always had dogs, and the boys wanted another one. So did I. Soon we got a beautiful little golden retriever puppy that we named Cody.

Cody had the most adorable baby face of any dog I had ever seen. Smart, too. When Stew got in from school, we often took Cody for a romp in the woods nearby. Stephen went sometimes, but mostly it was just Stewart, Cody, and I. One afternoon as we walked the trail and Stew played hide and seek with Cody, we rested beside an old stump. Stewart began asking, as he and Stephen did quite often, "Dad, when are we going to get our own house?"

"I don't know, son," I answered, "but you know we are praying about it." I knew it would take a miracle for us to be able to get into our own home again. Sometimes I could have kicked myself for selling that beautiful home in Smithtown, moving back to Bossier, buying another home in Bossier, and then putting it up for sale. I probably was getting what I deserved—having to rent!

We needed a large down payment, which we did not have. Banks were reluctant to give a "street preacher" a loan, someone like me who lived strictly by faith and who had no other source of income. I knew the Lord God would have to intervene.

As Stewart, Cody, and I rested by that old stump, I took a quarter out of my pocket and said, "Son, we need about twenty-five thousand dollars for a down payment. You see this quarter? It's twenty-five cents, as you know. I'm going to put it in this old stump, and every time we come by here, this quarter will be a reminder for us to pray for money to get a house." I placed the quarter down inside the stump where it could not be easily spotted, and we bowed together and prayed, right then.

Day after day, week after week, and month after month we walked by and prayed by that quarter in the stump. "It's still here!" Stewart often shouted as he looked inside the stump. Then he and Cody would run and play in the woods. " Lord, if it's your will," I prayed, "somehow, please provide for us to get into or own home." Then, one day as Stew peered into that stump, he exclaimed, "Dad, It's not here! It's not here!"

"Are you sure?" I asked, as we both looked deeply into the stump, our hands feeling around everywhere. "Well, you are right, Stew, it's gone. Somebody must have discovered it," I said. "We can still pray," and we did. Then one day,several months after leaving the quarter in the stump, I got a letter in the mail from a wonderful Christian couple who believed in our ministry and enclosed was a check for twenty-five thousand dollars! It was the largest single amount I had ever received. "There is our down payment," I immediately thought.

Stewart has never forgotten that quarter in the stump, and neither have I.

CHAPTER 29

IF I'M LYING, I'M FLYING

Bob Brooks, our pastor at Grace Baptist, told us about her. "She's in the hospital, Scotty; I'm sure she would appreciate a visit."

The woman Linda and I visited was Janet Raines. In her thirties, a little pudgy, with short, brown hair and small, beady, dark eyes, Janet had undergone another surgery, one of many. Smiling big with an absolutely great sense of humor, Janet grabbed our hearts. We had a good time visiting her, which was unusual for me, because I never liked visiting hospitals. We became the best of friends, but we soon learned that Janet had megaproblems.

Spots on her legs would fester into abscesses, requiring surgery to drain and remove them, leaving big, X-looking scars all over her legs. Janet was in and out of the hospital constantly.

Janet shared with everybody her story, a sad one. "My father abused me and was partial to my sister. I got married but didn't stay married because my husband was gay. We had a baby, a little girl, but she died, and my husband was decapitated in a car accident. And then I'm sick all the time," she said.

The more Janet talked to us the more our hearts broke for her. She was so likable but had such pain in her life. Even though she suffered immensely, she was warm and friendly. You could not help but like Janet Raines. "If I'm lying, I'm flying" was one of her favorite sayings. She was transparent, direct, and honest. At least that's what everybody thought.

Then, doctors discovered needles that were taped under her cabinet drawers in her hospital room. They realized that Janet had hidden them and was injecting herself with toxic chemicals—lighter fluid, Raid bug killer, whatever she could obtain. The poisonous material was causing the abscesses. Her sores were self-induced!

Janet had obviously wanted and needed attention so desperately that she had gone to that extreme to get it.

"Janet, we love you. God loves you. Why, Janet? Don't you know you don't have to harm yourself?" all of her friends said to her, including us. Eventually, however, many people began to see her as a hopeless case and dropped her. A few of us didn't, including Linda and me.

Janet had severe mental and psychological issues and became a regular patient at Kings Park Mental Institution. Extremely intelligent and witty, she could fool the psychiatrists and then laugh and tell a joke about it. She was diagnosed as being manic-depressive, a compulsive liar, and mentally unstable. One doctor told Linda and me that nobody could ever do enough for Janet. "No matter how much love and attention she receives, it will never be sufficient," he said with regret.

But Linda and I never gave up on her; neither did Burris and Jana Jenkins nor our pastor, Bob Brooks.

We often had Janet over for meals, especially during the holidays. Her laughter and cleverness alleviated our loneliness which was the result of our being separated from our friends and relatives back down south. Jokingly, she would say, "Archie Bunker, he's my kind of guy!" Then she would say, "Somebody's gotta sit in the back of the bus, and it sure ain't gonna be me." Or "It's ten o'clock; do you care where your children are?" On and on she would draw comical lines from her razor-sharp mind, keeping us loose and causing us to laugh hilariously.

We knew that Janet could not be trusted. She lied about everything, and we caught her at it. To this day we're not even sure if she was ever married or if she ever had a child. Fantasy and reality blended together like sugar and salt to Janet. She could not tell the difference.

Telling several pastors that she owned property in the Hamptons and that because she was terminally ill, she wanted to donate the property to them, Janet had them drive her around and buy her expensive meals. Eventually, realizing they had been duped, they shunned her.

Addicted to prescription drugs, Janet connived, deceived, and fooled anybody she could. Walking out of the hospital one night in only a gown, she had a taxi driver take her to the trailer park. As she quickly jumped out of the taxi, the cabbie shouted "Hey, my money!"

"Sue me," she hollered, walking barefoot into her trailer only to get stoned later.

Linda and I tried every approach we could in order to help her. We hugged and loved her. We scolded her, shamed her. "You are responsible, Janet, for what happens to you," we warned, hoping that she would straighten up. We never gave her money. "We'll buy your lunch, Janet, but we're not going to buy you any cigarettes," we told her emphatically.

Often we hid her drugs to prevent her from overdosing, but she always was able to get some kind of pill from somebody, somewhere. As you can imagine, dealing with Janet took its toll on Linda and me. But we continued loving and befriending her. Visiting her, we knew she could turn on us at any time.

"She's using you!" we were told by a number of people, but we felt that the Lord wanted us to minister to her. Time after time when we believed that Janet was better, she overdosed and ended up in Kings Park. We then kept her cat, fed Peewee, her dachshund, cleaned up the filth in her trailer, and, using Janet's money, Linda paid her bills.

Soon Janet would be back home, only to roll down the hill again, draining us emotionally. I came in from the city many a day, only to learn that we needed to do something for Janet.

One day Janet told us that her parents' house was up for sale. "We're looking for a house!" I exclaimed.

"I know. I know," she said with excitement. "It needs a lot of work, but check it out."

The house was in Bay Shore, a lot closer to the city than where we were presently living. It was a split level, with a basement and a large, deep backyard which was great for our kids and also for Linda, who could now have a big garden. We could tell that the house needed an unbelievable amount of repair, but since we had recently received that large monetary gift of twenty-five thousand dollars, we were able to make a large down payment, qualifying us for a loan, and we bought Janet's parents' house. I thought about the quarter in the stump.

We finally had our own home again, but before we moved out of Mrs. Wojtech's apartment, the arduous work of renovating the house had to be done. All of the carpets were pulled up. The entire house had to be painted inside. The basement had to be refinished, and the downstairs bathroom needed a makeover starting with the plumbing; yet we were overflowing with joy.

Not long after we began working on our home in Bay Shore, Carl and Carolyn Carrigan, our close friends from Louisiana, visited us. They brought hundreds of New Testaments from Milldale Baptist Church in Zachary, Louisiana.

For years I had used my specially equipped van with its platform and overhead canopy. But in doing so, I was restricted to preaching only where I could find a suitable parking place. So I had begun having more "walk-in" meetings, using just my sketch board. But the New Testaments were difficult to transport into a walk-in meeting, so Carl and I devised a rig upon which I could mount my sketch board and which could also be used to carry boxes of Bibles and many visual aids. The rig, equipped with lights, ran on a twelve-volt battery, had wheels, and could easily be pushed down the sidewalk. I eventually used it almost exclusively. Carl called the rig "the bag lady."

While Carl and Carolyn were with us, several other friends from down south joined them—Bill Britt, Frank DeLoach, Ray Wilson, and Bo and Dewayne. They were God sent! All were young and strong and knew how to work, just what we needed to move from Mrs. Wojtech's apartment into our home in Bay Shore. The sovereignty and providence of God!

And work they did! It took all of us to pick up our piano and lift it over the stairs to the second floor, but we did it. We also ministered on the sidewalks of New York City, spending long hours driving in and out, preaching and counseling with the unthinkable and unbearable sometimes, as we stood on hard, concrete pavement hour after hour.

With part of the money that Janet made from the sale of the house, she bought herself a brand new Hyundai, standard shift. Attempting to teach her to drive, I held my breath as she took corners too fast, ran stop signs, and ignored red lights, all the while drinking her coffee, smoking a cigarette, and grinding gears!

"Use the clutch, Janet!" I pleaded.

"It's too much trouble," she yelled back, laughing, with coffee spilling all over her dress. I'm telling you, she was a "pip," to use her own word.

Janet finally learned to drive, but she refused to shift gears.

"You're going to tear up the transmission," I explained as I shook my head.

"It's under warranty; they'll give me a new one!" she quipped, lighting another cigarette.

"This is a small car. Don't have a wreck, Janet," I warned.

"Oh, God ain't proud. He'll kill you in a big car just like a small one," she answered, giggling.

CHAPTER 30

THE TURKEY LEG

It was fairly cold and windy as I sat inside my van, parked on Seventh Avenue at seven thirty in the evening, the time I started unloading my equipment for ministry at Times Square. Looking directly out of my front windshield, I was shocked at what I saw. A haggard man, wearing an old brown coat, apparently homeless, was chewing on a large turkey leg. He then laid it on a newspaper rack, wiped his mouth on his sleeve, and walked across the street when the light changed. In just a few minutes another man, who also looked homeless, meandered up and began eating on that same turkey leg. After he ate several bites, he laid the turkey leg back down and disappeared into the night.

Homeless, emaciated men and women were all over the city. In the coldest of weather they were lying around outside, wrapped up in plastic, and sleeping on subway grates, in cardboard dumps, beneath park benches, or huddled up in alleys.

Wrapping torn, tattered old clothes around themselves, they sometimes went to shelters, but many of them didn't like the shelters because their stuff got stolen. Some slept in the Port Authority, or tried to, because the cops constantly chased them away. Others dozed on trains or shook off doldrums as they sat by themselves. I saw many a drunk sprawled out on the sidewalk, looking dead, as passersby glanced at them and then went on their way. Some sipped coffee, trying to sober up. There were hordes of homeless men and women who actually lived in tunnels under the subway, deep beneath the city—"moles," they were called.

My team and I often ate at the Apollo Diner after we had finished our work at Times Square. Many nights as we parked, we saw a derelict couple sitting in the exact same place. We learned that

207

their names were Alice and Joe. In their seventies, with no place to go, they began recognizing us and waving, being very appreciative of anything we gave them. Even when it was blistering cold, we saw them there, close together, bundled up, red faced.

One evening as my friends and I unloaded our equipment, we saw a man unfolding a cardboard box in front of the bank. He obviously was getting ready to bed down for the night. We introduced ourselves and gave him a few dollars and a New Testament. We learned that his name was Alfie.

"I'm a Christian, too," he said, smiling. "Thank you very much."

For several weeks when we parked on that same block, we saw Alfie. He was a friendly man, in his forties, maybe, who had an ordinary face, the kind that you don't particularly notice and that blended in with the crowd. He always came over to us, apparently wanting a handout, but he never asked. He told us that he had a hernia that caused him severe pain in his side. "I need an operation," he said, and asked us to pray for him, which we did.

One night as we drove up, Alfie came running over to us, excited and cheerful. "Guess what?" he said, "Times Square Church paid for my operation. I feel great! I also went on a picnic with the church!"

Times Square Church on Fifty-First and Broadway, started by David Wilkerson, had a great ministry in the city. We often referred people who made decisions in our street meetings to that church. Obviously, they had taken Alfie under their wing and had ministered to his physical needs. After Alfie shared what the church did for him, we never saw him again. I often wondered whatever became of Alfie.

One cold, wintry day I was not having much success drawing up a crowd on Fourteenth Street. Up walked Mayor Koch, I thought. The man wasn't the mayor after all, but he looked exactly like him. Wearing a gray coat and a red ski cap, he had a white beard and a remarkable resemblance to Mayor Koch. Shaking a small bell that made a faint ring, he leaned toward me and recited these words: "It seems to be my fate, to trip from place to place, worse than gypsies, I am alone, with no place to rest my weary hemorrhoids."

"Hey, a poet! You have more?" I asked, but in a flash he was gone.

I was hungry, and I had a five-dollar bill; that was it. I rushed to McDonald's for a Big Mac, fries, and a Coke. I could taste it. As I walked toward the front door, I noticed a pitiful-looking man, obviously homeless, who apparently needed something to eat. I didn't have enough money to buy both of us a meal; and, besides, I was starved, and my mouth had been watering for that Big Mac. While standing in line, 1 thought, "What should I do, Lord? I worked hard today, and I'm famished!" But I felt guilty about that guy not having anything to eat.

"All right," I said to myself, "if that man is still out there when I get my order, I'll give him my lunch." In a couple of minutes I grabbed my McDonald's paper bag, some ketchup, a straw, and some extra napkins and headed out the door to my van. I looked, and he wasn't there! He wasn't there! But rounding the corner, I saw him. He was sitting there alone, of course; so, remembering what I had told myself about giving him my lunch if he was still out there, I handed him my Big Mac and said, "Here you go, my friend. Jesus loves you."

"Thank you!" he replied, smiling and looking into the bag.

Still hungry, I started home. I could wait. Linda always had a big supper. I said, "Lord, forgive me for being selfish. As fat as I am, it would do me good to miss a few meals."

One afternoon I saw a man sitting on the sidewalk in the warmth of the bright sun; his head was bent over a little, and he had downcast eyes. Wearing worn-out jeans and an old, faded blue shirt that somebody had probably discarded, he was leaning up against the side of the building. As I looked at him, I thought of the song sung by Johnny Cash, "Sunday Morning Coming Down."

Buying both of us a cup of coffee, I sat down beside him. "Here you are, my friend," I said, handing him a cup. Surprised, he thanked me. We talked awhile, and I told him I preached on the sidewalks, and he shared with me that he had fallen on hard times. But I could tell that already. He looked like he was sixty, but he, no doubt, was in his forties. "I lost my family. I don't have nothin' left," he said, with a furrowed brow and regret in his voice.

Giving him a "Smile," I reminded him that he was valuable and that the Lord had not forgotten him. But I knew that that was easy for me to say. I gave him a dollar, and as I handed it to him, he said, "Look, I need your prayers more than I need your money."

"Well, take this," I said, "and I'll be praying for you, too."

"Let's do this," he replied, as he tore the dollar bill in half, giving me one part. "Every time I see my half, I'll pray for you; and every time you see your half, you pray for me."

"Sounds like a winner to me," I answered.

I've carried my half of the dollar bill with me for years and years. When I change wallets, or when I'm looking through my wallet to find, perhaps, a picture or an insurance card, I often run across that half dollar bill. Immediately I think of that man, and I pray for him. I suspect he does the same for me.

One day when it was bitter cold outside, Burris suggested that we preach at Grand Central Station. Usually, a number of homeless could be found there in a couple of big rooms off to the side of the main area. "I'm tired of the subway; let's give it a try," he said.

I didn't want to do it. "Burris, security is going to come down on us," I replied.

"Oh, come on. All they can do is stop us," Burris said, laughing.

We took turns speaking. Burris did a rope trick, and I tore up the newspaper to get their attention, and as I did, many of them set up from the pewlike benches that they were lying on.

"God knows your name; he has not forgotten you," I said quietly, my voice echoing and bouncing off the old brown marble walls and ceiling. Continuing, I said, "Jesus taught that a sparrow does not fall to the ground without the Lord knowing it. Men, don't give up. Christ died for you. He arose and can salvage your life." Tired, crusty, old-looking faces stared back at me, faces that had nothing left to give in them. Some men listened with wine bottles in their hands. They sat there alone, penniless, overlooked. Unwise decisions haunted them. I thought of the scripture "the way of the transgressor is hard" (Proverbs 13:15).

When Burris spoke, he asked the question, "Is it true? What we're saying—is it true? Well, all I can tell you is that the Lord changed my life. I was a big shot, an airline pilot, flew a big plane for TWA. I had to have proof…"

A few lifeless eyes sparkled and several of the guys took literature and thanked us. As we were leaving, a young man with watery eyes came up to us and, almost begging, said, "I'm hooked on drugs. Can you help me?"

He was not old like many of the others, and we spent extra time with him. We prayed with him, giving him, first of all, the gospel, then a list of soup kitchens and missions, then a Bible. We knew it was just a start. Only God knew where that "prodigal son" went after we left.

CHAPTER 31

A FIERCE ADVERSARY

On Sunday, May 25, 1986, millions of people joined hands, beginning at Battery Park in New York City and stretching across America to California, in a project called "Hands Across America," which raised millions of dollars to fight famine in Africa and homelessness in the United States. Those holding hands included President Ronald Regan, many rich and famous movie stars, and millions of ordinary Americans. The unity was clearly evident.

But less than a month later, I was being verbally attacked in New York by a fierce adversary! As I prepared for Times Square one night (June 20, 1986), the Lord gave me a verse of scripture to direct me. "Make no friendship with an angry man; and with a furious man thou shalt not go" (Proverbs 22:24). I did not understand at the time why that particular verse spoke to my heart, but I understood later.

Two young women sent to New York by the Home Mission Board, Sheri and Liz, accompanied Burris and me, so I really prayed that everything would go well.

In the heart of New York City I preached on "Private Pain," and we had a wonderful crowd. I asked Sheri to say a word, catching her off guard, but she gave an excellent testimony. Liz also spoke and did well. Both young ladies handed out many "Little Red Bibles," and Liz witnessed to Joseph of the Islamic faith. Our entire team began to share the gospel with him, but I guess we scared the fish off because he said he had to go and quickly left.

As I later preached on "The Ten Commandments," I noticed a white-robed Muslim standing in the crowd, but I did not realize that he was Madsu, an enemy of the cross and a formidable foe. (Most Muslims were indifferent and passive; but others could be extremely hostile toward me as I preached Christ.) Just as I finished asking people to accept Christ, this Muslim spoke very loudly to the crowd, saying, "I've been listening to this man, and I can't believe that for twenty minutes none of you have asked him one question. He doesn't even have a Bible. How could you be so stupid to let him talk to you and you never ask a question?"

At this point I recognized him as Madsu, the guy who had wrecked many of my street meetings in the past; I always dreaded having him anywhere near! With his booming voice, Madsu quickly had everybody's attention. I wrote on the sketch board "Jesus arose from the dead" and I told the crowd, "We're not to argue."

Madsu kept saying, "We're not to worship idols, and Jesus was a man!" How bitter and angry he was. Livid would be a better word to describe him. A young man in the crowd began to answer Madsu. He was small, but he had a lot of courage, and he said that he was a Christian. I switched off the canopy lights and let them go at it. In past altercations with Madsu I had attempted to deal with him by asking him questions and quoting scripture. But this night I felt that the Lord wanted me to be silent. I told Sheri and Liz, "Don't worry. This happens once in a while. We're not to 'cast pearls before swine'; Jesus did not quarrel in the streets, and we're not going to, either." Both young ladies understood.

Burris mounted the platform, turned the lights back on, and wrote on the sketch board "Who is the Word?" Madsu shouted, "The Word is Allah. He is the true God. It's not Jesus."

Madsu had been standing in the crowd, facing us. Now he got in front of the platform and addressed the people. Some of Madsu's friends had joined in and, pointing to Madsu, they hollered out, "Let him on the platform. Let him talk! Let him talk!"

There was no way I was going to allow him on the platform, not if I could help it.

"Why don't you let me up there? He is afraid of me!" exclaimed Madsu to the people. Madsu then chested me, trying to push me out of the way; but, standing my ground, I pushed back.

"Don't shove me!" Madsu cried out loudly so the people could hear him. He was about six foot two, built like an oak tree, had very broad shoulders, and was also a boxer.

Another young man said to me, "I'm a Christian. Can I say something?"

"Sure, go ahead," I answered. He jumped up on the platform.

"You let him up there. Why not me?" said Madsu.

Then, the young man on the platform gave a marvelous testimony about how God had changed him. "I used to be a homosexual, but Jesus Christ saved me. Now I'm engaged to be married to a fine Christian girl. I used to be in this trash down here having sex with those of the same sex as me. But Jesus saved me and delivered me," he declared, and the people listened.

Madsu shouted, "You're a liar, a liar!"

The young man asked Madsu, "Do you know God? Has he changed your heart?"

"Too many questions," answered Madsu. Then, standing on the sidewalk, Madsu spoke directly to the crowd, most of whom were black, and with great volume said, "You are listening to the same people who brought you over here and put you in chains."

Burris tried to speak, but now Madsu's friends made up the majority of the crowd, and they rebuked him.

Then, out of nowhere, a group that was carrying very tall banners positioned themselves all around us. The banners read "Repent" and "Jesus is Lord." With bullhorns they quoted verses of scripture and began arguing with Madsu and his cohorts.

We closed everything down, waved good-bye to the group with the banners, and left.

Sheri said that she was impressed that we did not argue.

"Well, the Lord told me in his word not to make friends with an angry man. I now understand what that meant." Liz said she had never seen anything like that before. We had prayer and stopped at Howard Johnson's on the way home.

About a year later at Times Square I could not believe my eyes. There was Madsu, the mean-spirited, argumentative Muslim, standing in my crowd and listening without uttering a word as I preached the gospel! Usually, he disrupted and caused trouble like he did that night with Burris, Sheri, Liz, and me, often ruining our street meetings. But this night he did nothing.

Carl Carrigan, who was with me, had been disrupted by Madsu also; but he and I spent forty-five minutes in a controlled dialogue with Madsu. Asking question after question, he was extremely open, very polite, actually. In fact, I felt we made a friend that night with the one man who had caused me more trouble than any other ten men combined!

After Madsu left, Carl and I prayed that God would save him. With his charisma and thundering John Wesley voice, what an evangelist he would make!

"Either save him, Lord, or kill him," we both said, chuckling, yet we were a little bit serious.

I never saw Madsu again.

CHAPTER 32

FAMILY AND FRIENDS

I had read that missionaries often got very lonely, and now we understood completely. We missed our family and friends very much. Linda, Stephen, Stewart, and I were tight, but Stephen was no longer in New York very often because he was now attending the University of Arkansas. Stewart, an eighth grader who was forever combing his hair and eyeing the girls, was growing up fast, and we knew that soon he would be away in college, too.

"Linda," I said from time to time, "one day when we have grandkids, I believe the Lord will let us live close to them." I didn't know if my darling wife believed that or not, but I knew that she was praying for that to happen.

In September 1986, my father, who was eighty, had a massive stroke. We happened to be visiting in Louisiana, so I was thankful to be there when this occurred. To see Daddy in this condition was heart-wrenching for all of us, especially my mother. I thanked God that we had spent a great deal of time with him the year that we had moved back to Bossier. Perhaps, in the providence of God, the Lord had permitted me to return to Bossier so that I could be with my dad the last year he was in relatively good health, before he had that stroke. In October of that same year my dad passed away. Two friends from Bossier, Frank and Fern Page, were visiting us in New York at that time and were a real comfort to me. We flew back to Louisiana in order for me to conduct Daddy's funeral. God gave me a verse of Scripture that I held onto: "Precious in the sight of the Lord is the death of his saints (Psalm 116:15)." I got through the service, but my pastor, Brother Stogner, was on the podium beside me, and I was glad he was present.

When autumn leaves drifted by my window, I usually thought of my father. Daddy love to hunt, and in the fall he got his bow and arrows ready so that he could go bow hunting. I went with him as a youngster, but I never was much of a hunter. He would do anything for Barbara Ann and me, and mother, too. There was no telling how many pounds of pecans that he picked up and then shelled for her. He also made by hand nine tables out of solid oak, one for mother, one for me, one for Babs, and one for each of his six grandchildren.

Sometimes in New York City I would see a man walking, slumped over a little, and he would remind me of my dad, especially if he had gray hair like Daddy. I must have contributed to his gray hair that morning years ago when, as a happy-go-lucky kid, I hopped on the front right fender of Dad's '48 Chevrolet. We had replaced some target faces, and Daddy was driving back through the pine trees to target number one at the archery range. Before he came to a complete stop, I nonchalantly slipped off the bumper and began walking. Dad, looking back to his left, didn't know that I had stepped off the car, and he turned into me, knocking me to the ground. Both front and back right wheels ran over my ankles. Realizing what had just happened, Dad quickly slammed on the brakes, bolted out of the car, and in a panic mode ran around to the front of the vehicle, shouting, "Scotty, Scotty!" About that time I jumped up, laughing. "I'm OK, Daddy," I exclaimed. "I saw the wheels run over both of my legs." The ground was soft, and I had on boots. And being young, age fourteen, I was not seriously injured, just a bit sore.

Daddy thought for certain that he had killed me, so he was shook up. No doubt, another gray hair or two sprouted up on his head. Thank God I was all right. Arriving back home, I told Mother as she opened the screen door and stepped onto the porch, "Daddy ran over me, but I'm fine."

"Oh, my Lord, Scotty. What do you mean?" she asked, looking like she was in shock. We told her about it, and she had to sit down, realizing that I could have been badly hurt.

Yes, my heart ached for Daddy. Did I tell him how much he meant to me? Did he know how much I loved him? Oh, how it must have grieved him when we left for New York. I could not ever forget seeing him on his knees, begging us not to go.

Always, my daddy cleaned up his shop when he finished working. "Dad," I used to say when I was a kid, "we're going to be back in here tomorrow. Let's just leave everything out, and we will be ready to go to work in the morning."

"Son," Dad instructed, "put all the tools up. We can get them back out. Something may come up, and we might not get back in here tomorrow." So I had to roll up the extension cords, put the saw and the drill away, and sweep up the sawdust.

I should have followed his example as I got older, but I didn't. For you see, it took a lot of time and effort for me to prepare to minister in the city, and often I did not clean up my shop. Each day I had to measure and cut newsprint, redo my tempera paints, fold several newspaper tricks, gather up my follow-up material and New Testaments, make sure my video camera was charged and ready to go, and then I had to load everything into my van. Finally, after rushing at Road Runner speed, I was ready.

Well, one day, I was late getting off to New York City, so I hurried downstairs. "Man, what a mess!" I thought, looking at my shop. My paints and brushes had dried up, and newspaper was everywhere. I couldn't find the glue. Where were the scissors? My friends were counting on me to use my equipment. Then it hit me. Dad, you were so right. I should have cleaned up my shop like you did!

Not only did I miss my daddy, I missed my dear mother's touch and sweet kiss. I loved to pick at her and make her laugh, and more than once I heard her tell this story: Mother said that when I was born, her breasts were impacted, so her milk was not flowing normally. In order to open up the obstructions, she let a small puppy nurse from her breasts. Finally, her breast milk ran naturally, so then I, as an infant, was able to nurse.

Once, when Mother was talking about this, I jokingly replied, "Well, that's the reason I scratch for fleas like a dog and lift my leg every time I pass a tree!"

"Oh, Scotty, you are terrible!" said mother, roaring with laughter. Then, I began tickling her under her neck. "Stop, stop," she screamed, "somebody come help me! Somebody come help me!"

One day, as I drove into the city, I heard on the radio "The Homecoming," one of my sister's favorite songs. Memories of Babs flooded my heart.

I thought about the time that Barbara Ann comforted me when I was in the first grade, walking around the monkey bars, homesick, crying.

"What's the matter, Scotty?" asked Babs, coming out of nowhere.

"My eye hurts," I answered, bawling and rubbing my eye. Then she hugged me and said, "It'll be all right."

I thought about the time I pitched the softball to her. She batted it hard, and the ball struck me squarely between the eyes, knocking me flat on my back! I never liked pitching after that. I thought about all of those times when she called me home for supper. "Scotty, come eat!" she yelled, throwing her voice. Usually, I was behind the church practicing with my bow when I heard her loud mouth! I began missing my sister so much that day as I drove into the city that I picked up my phone and gave her a call about the time I crossed into Queens.

"Hello," she said.

"Babs, how you doin'?" I asked. "This is Scotty."

"Scotty, where are you?" she asked.

"I'm in New York, Barbara Ann, and I heard 'The Homecoming' on the radio—you know, the piano song that you like so much."

"Yeah," she said, laughing.

"So I thought of you and decided to call you," I replied.

We talked for several minutes, just the two of us, brother and sister. And it felt good. But when I hung up, I missed her even more, and I felt sure that she missed me a lot, too.

Arriving back home, I told Linda about my conversation with Babs. They were close, too, and I knew Linda longed to see her about as much as I did. Linda accompanied me to the streets occasionally, counseled, and shared her testimony. She was good at it, too, because she was genuine and related to people extremely well. However, she felt more comfortable behind the scenes—helping with follow-up, typing newsletters, guiding the household, and keeping the home fires burning.

And Linda was incredible when it came to hospitality. My, how she worked, preparing meals, washing clothes, and making our guests feel welcomed—because they were! A number of friends visited us through the years—Price and Ann Harris, Carl and Carolyn Carrigan, Dr. Cky Carrigan, their son, Linda and Bill Fleischaker, Richard and Mary Johnson, Howard Greer, Ken and Gail Hansen, Ray and Judy Wilson, and many others. Sometimes large groups of people came up to New York to work with us. Once we had a team of sixteen; on another occasion, we had a group of twenty-two.

Richard and Mary Johnson spent several days with us in New York. Through the years they had hosted parties for us when we visited Bossier in the summer, inviting many supporters of my ministry. Mary was anxious to see the Statue of Liberty, so off we went to Liberty Island. Arriving, we saw that the lines were unusually long, and, it being July, New York was hot! We decided not to go. With tears in her eyes Mary said, "But that's all I wanted to see."

"OK, let's go," replied Linda.

Richard and I visited the New York Stock Exchange, but Linda and Mary stood in line for five hours in that scorching heat in order to see the Statue of Liberty! When all of us met back together, Mary was smiling big and was, as we say down south, "as happy as a pig in mud!"

Linda's parents visited us again. The beautiful flowers on Long Island surprised Memee, and the apple tree in our backyard, which was loaded down with apples, caught her eye, too. I gave Ed a tour of the Meadowlands, and we all enjoyed *Cats* on Broadway, even though Ed nearly got hit walking across the street by a bus.

"The bus would have hit him if he hadn't tucked in his behind," said Memee, laughing.

Both Ed and Memee were amazed at how mature Stephen was, back home from college for the summer, and how tall Stewart had grown.

Stephen and Stewart had learned to ski while on school trips and had convinced Linda and me to give it a try. Well, I had many a wipeout in the snow, and so did Linda; but, after taking lessons, we eventually learned to wedge and began skiing the green slopes. We shared our experience with Barbara Ann, and the next winter the entire Pace tribe came up to go skiing, bringing my mother with them.

All eleven of us—Linda and I, Babs and Marion, Mother, Stephen, Stewart, Grady, Dancy, Bernice, and Peyton—plus our skis, boots, poles, groceries, and luggage squeezed into my van, and we drove to Killington, Vermont. One of the triplets got sick and began throwing up. We pulled over and threw his clothes out of the window onto the snow and ice and kept driving!

Peyton, as athletic as any of his brothers, if not more so, had the most difficulty trying to ski, and we could not understand why. Then we realized that he had skied the entire first day with his boots on the wrong feet! Marion stood all day in the snow with his boots on, but never dared to ski. Babs got stuck on a mountain and had to be carried down in a snowmobile. Grady, swinging his ski poles around with his long arms, nearly beheaded another skier, making the guy angry. Mother got sick and vomited in the ski lodge, all over the dining room table.

I drove home cautiously over the icy roads and thick, falling snow. When we finally walked in the front door, we discovered that we had no heat and that our dryer was not working. Yes, we froze our buns off that night!

Years later, Barbara Ann and Marion, who now was terminally ill, came back to New York. We toured upstate New York, which was absolutely gorgeous. Visiting the Baseball Hall of Fame in Cooperstown, Marion was elated. Not long after that, Marion went on to be with the Lord. I miss him to this day. Years later, my sister married another fine Christian gentleman named Homer Jones. Every time I see them they are 'bubbling" and holding hands!

One afternoon I noticed Linda staring at a picture on our dresser of her sister Shirley with her husband, Ronney, and their two children, Ronda and Randall. She didn't talk much about it, but Linda missed all of them. So did I. Walking up behind her, I said, "Hon, remember how excited our boys used to get when we got close to their house?"

RONNEY AND SHIRLEY

"I sure do," Linda replied, smiling. "They couldn't wait to go swimming."

Yes, when our sons, Stephen and Stewart, both small boys at the time, saw the Porter exit off Highway 59 South to Houston, they quickly started stripping in our van and began slipping frantically into their swimming trunks so they would be ready to hit the pool when we arrived. What great memories we had!

A few years later all of us were taking turns riding Ronney's three wheeler, going down in a ditch and then jumping into the air while on the vehicle. "Lean forward when you come out of the ditch," shouted Ronney, but instead of leaning forward, I pulled back on the handlebars which instantly flipped me on my back, three wheeler and all!

"You all right?" everybody asked, as they came running over to me.

"Yeah, I'm OK!" I answered, but, man, was I embarrassed.

Yes, our hearts ached to see Shirley, Ronney, and their kids. We always got pumped when we visited them.

Chapter 33

RATS ON THE TRACKS

The gray, dirty subway train, draped in red and blue meaningless graffiti, pulled away with a roar and a loud electric rumble. It was filled with standing people who gazed but did not see, their thoughts elsewhere. However, many other people were still on the platform.

Realizing that we had just several minutes to preach before the next train came, I began: "Ladies and gentlemen, how about a little good news? We don't want to be pushy, but we would appreciate it if you would hear us. Did you see *The Mission* with Robert De Niro? It's been nominated for several Academy Awards. In this movie a mercenary kills his brother. Trying to relieve his guilt, he ties heavy metal armor on his back and attempts to climb hill after hill as a form of penance. Is there something that you've done that brings such guilt that you cannot sleep at night? Christ died on that cross and took our guilt. He took my guilt. He took your guilt. He was buried and arose again. When you ask him into your life, my friend, he takes the guilt away…"

As I spoke, I was amazed at how open the people were to the gospel, and I prayed, "Oh, God, don't let the train come yet." When I invited people to accept Christ, many all around me on the platform stepped forward and took literature and decision cards. "Thank you! Thank you!" several people said, but others stood there, cold, hard, indifferent, glad that we were finished.

The subway ministry was not easy even though group after group listened to the gospel as they waited on the platform for their train. Sometimes I was stared at like I was the village idiot. I absorbed pathetic looks from hurried yuppies with briefcases and appointments to keep. High-society-minded businesswomen, decked out in

225

the latest coat and sweater conglomerations, yet wearing sneakers, never even looked my way. I was sometimes mistaken for a Jehovah's Witness.

The train was now coming. It got louder and louder and finally stopped with a screech. The doors opened, and, like ants, people quickly rushed and bumped into each other as they went on their way. A few minutes later, I talked to a clarinet player named Joe who was panhandling. "I am a Buddhist," he said, and I could tell that he had never heard the gospel. He seemed interested enough, but I had the feeling that he did not understand the urgency of the matter. Then I saw the same Muslim selling perfume on the same folding card table at his same spot. Although he had been somewhat friendly before, when I endeavored to talk to him today about the Lord, he went into a frenzy, full of hostility. Looking at the Muslim, I said, "You don't even know me, yet you hate me." He bitterly replied, "I hate what you represent!" Ken Fisher, my buddy, reminded me quietly under his breath not to cast pearls before swine. Ken was right, but I thought, "Maybe I can take that Muslim a cup of coffee sometime, because it gets cold down here."

We met three Christians from Guyana who said that they would be praying for us; then, a woman asked me what the next stop was.

"Sixth Avenue, ma'am," I replied, and even though I had been in New York for a number of years, I could not believe I was actually giving directions in the subway!

As Ken and I bought hot dogs, we learned that the cashier was a Hindu and did not see why he needed Jesus because he had his own religion.

Later, as I was about to speak, three very important-looking, well-dressed men stood directly in front of me. I was scared to start preaching, and I thought of what God told Jeremiah: "Be not afraid of their faces: for I am with thee to deliver thee, saith the Lord" (Jeremiah 1:8). But I was afraid. Seeing their glasses and briefcases, I thought, "These guys are intellectuals," so I waited until they left before I began preaching.

In the middle of the next message a gentleman whom I had never met but who was a distinguished-looking member of the Salvation Army asked to say something. "Of course," I replied, stepping to the side and fastening my eyes upon him.

"I've known Jesus for many years. He saved me when I was very young. What this man is telling you is true," he said without apology and as tears filled his eyes. When he got on his train, he waved good-bye to me and turned and began to talk to a young man who had just accepted Christ on the platform. I thanked God for putting those two together.

Then Steve, a pastor from Queens, joined us. His congregation had several converts from our street meetings. Steve preached on the second coming of Christ. How capable he was! And to have a pastor evangelize alongside me felt good.

We had had a long, tiring day, yet a very rewarding day, but we were all ready to go home. After having a quick prayer off to the side, I said, "See you guys later! Praise the Lord!" Then I waved to them on their train as I waited for mine.

As the bright headlight of my train reflected off the wall when it came around the curve, I saw tiny rats scurrying across the tracks and through little puddles of muddy water. I had seen small mice quite often before, but now I noticed a huge rat. It was enormous, and I watched his long tail slowly disappear into a black hole.

Stepping onto my train, I held to the greasy metal strap. I thanked God for protecting me from all kinds of germs and diseases. I guess I had built up an immunity. Drug addicts, prostitutes, and openly gay individuals were all around me daily. AIDS came to mind, even though I knew I could not contract it casually.

As the train pulled out of Union Square, I was surprised that I had learned to spread my legs in order to keep my balance. Finally, I got a seat and noticed a lady mumbling to herself. I gave her a few dollars, and she was very grateful. A guy wearing torn jeans with Clorox spots all over them and who had on a headset was leaning against the subway door, which read "Do not lean on door."

Then a bullhorn interrupted. Two Hare Krishnas came through the train collecting money in coffee cans. I thought of the two Krishnas who a while back had told me to go "bathe in the blood." An Orthodox Jew sitting beside me said, "There are all kinds of religious crackpots in the city." He took a "Little Red Bible" from me, and we talked about the resurrection as the train picked up speed. Getting off at Lorimer, he gave me a fleeting glance. Chances are I would never see him again.

In a few minutes, I struck up a conversation with another very old Hasidic Jew. His eyes were so sad. He was dressed in black with a hat and beard. His walk was slow, his shoulders slumped and heavy.

"Sir," I said as politely as I could, "please let me talk to you for just a few minutes." He stopped. No one else was around.

"Sir, I am a Christian, but the gospel is for the Jew first," I said, hoping that he would not turn me off.

Of Russian descent, he asked question after question. Then I explained to him from the Christian perspective the meaning of Isaiah 53, the resurrection, the new birth. He seemed to respect me for talking to him, laid his hand on my shoulder, looked deeply into my eyes, smiled ever so slightly, and slowly walked away.

As I walked up the subway steps, it seemed unusually quiet. Then I realized as I stepped outside what had taken place. A huge snow had fallen. When I had gone down into the subway earlier, it was about noon, cold with bright sunshine. Now, it was five in the afternoon, dark, and the ground was covered with fresh snow.

I always had an eerie feeling when this happened. Steam rose up from manhole covers into the air as a bus with lights blinking drove by slinging mud and water up on the sidewalk.

"I guess the traffic really will be congested now," I thought.

Chapter 34

TOXIC WASTE

We were living in a deep freeze. Day after day the temperature was so cold that I could hardly stand it, and there was no end in sight. As I drove over the Throgs Neck Bridge into the Bronx, the cars ahead of me were hardly moving, the smoke from their tailpipes drifting up into the bleak, grayish skyline to my left. Red lights flashed like a digital clock as drivers hit their brakes in an endless stop and go.

As snow flurries darted and glided in the wind, I frantically searched for a parking place, and I had to go to the bathroom badly—like now! I noticed scarves, chapped faces, and pedestrians with their hands in their pockets as they walked briskly down cluttered sidewalks on which trash cans had blown over. Hot dog wrappers and napkins were stuck against light poles and parking meters, held there by the brutal wind. I heard tin cans rolling around, and shoppers' breaths of steam went up like dragons.

Man, did I need to pee! I was in pain, but I could not find a place to park, even though I had looked in block after block. Desperate, I drove to a secluded area, opened my van door, and peed. Finishing, I saw a guy in a brown uniform get out of his vehicle and walk my way.

"Just a minute, Officer," I said. "Man, I had to pee!"

He had folded his pad back and was writing. "What's the matter, sir?" I asked. He then handed me a ticket. "What's this for?" I said.

"Read it. Disposing of toxic waste," he replied.

"Toxic waste! What do you mean? Sir, I had to go. What was I to do?" I asked. "Fifty dollars! I'm not paying this. That's ridiculous!"

Talking to me in a very condescending manner, he drove off with me standing there holding the ticket. I tried to forget it and drove around until I found a parking place.

It was cold and getting colder. I knew I had to be careful and not to park on ice because I was alone and would have a rough time of it if I got stuck. Finally parking and stepping out of my van, I mashed my boot down into a foot of soft, mushy, dirty snow and ice in order to keep myself from slipping.

I saw a man quickly stripping the inside of a car door as a woman in a coat with the collar turned up watched in all directions.

On the card in my hand was the name of a couple who had recently accepted Christ in one of my street meetings and had requested a visit from a minister. An hour later, I was still looking for their apartment. A man in his twenties told me that he had been living in an abandoned automobile and then pointed to it. As I gave him a few dollars, a list of food pantries, job programs, soup kitchens, missions, and shelters, he told me he had spent two years in jail for dealing drugs to an undercover cop. Was he conning me? I didn't think so.

There it was. The house number I was looking for, but the house was vacant. White skeleton bones were scrawled all over the metal door. Discouraged, I left Bibles and follow-up material with neighbors.

Later, while looking for a guy named Carlos, I entered government housing. I found that the elevator did not work, so I walked up five flights of stairs, observing terrible living conditions on each floor. The cutting wind whipped around plyboard that was nailed over a gaping hole in the outside wall, revealing light and the street below. Four-letter words were scribbled on the walls of the staircase, and the smell of urine was everywhere; because light bulbs were either broken or not there, the corridors and halls were dark. Nobody admitted that they knew Carlos. I think they suspected that I was a narcotics agent. After finding his apartment, I knocked on his door. "Carlos. Carlos. This is Scott, the preacher on the street," I said.

"Carlos is not here," came a voice from behind the door.

"I've got some things for him," I answered.

"Slide it under the door. I'll give it to him," the voice said back. So I slid the follow-up materials under the door.

"Thank you," I said. There was no sound. I left.

Yes, locating someone who made a decision for Christ on the streets of New York City was a wearisome task. Often, the person was not at home or had moved out or I could not read the address on the card or the phone number was incorrect.

The devil sometimes whispered, "You are wasting your time. They didn't mean it. You're doing no good. Quit!"

However, I was able to make connections with some people. One day, several floors up an apartment building, while wild, screaming kids, loaded down with books, horsed around, I found Vera in apartment A. Reluctant at first to open her door, she recognized my voice and unlocked several door chains and gladly took follow-up literature and a Bible storybook for her young son. Vera told me that she had indeed accepted Christ and was now in church. Hearing her words made it all worthwhile.

At times I was unwise and placed myself in precarious situations, but people were no doubt praying for me, and God watched over me.

Driving back home that night I wondered how Linda had made out that day with Janet Raines, who seemed bent on committing suicide.

I had not been home long when I told Linda about the ticket I got for disposing of toxic waste. "You're joking," she replied.

"No, it happened, but I'm not paying it," I answered.

I knew that I had done nothing wrong or illegal, so when the notices came in concerning the ticket, I ignored them. Eventually, the fine skyrocketed to three hundred dollars. So I went to court. The fine was given to me in the Bronx, but I had to go to the Environmental Control Board in Brooklyn.

The judge reduced the ticket back to fifty dollars. "It's the law," he explained.

"What was I to do, Your Honor?" I asked.

His exact words were: "Well, paying fifty dollars beats pissing in the van. It's nothing to be ashamed of."

"I know. Natural bodily function," I replied. I paid the fifty dollars and left, disgusted.

The news broke about Jimmy Swaggart's scandal (allegedly, he had solicited prostitutes) On February 22, 1988, and after I had finished preaching one day on the subject "The Day the Bad Guy Got Saved," a gentleman walked up to me and said sarcastically, "Still out here? Seems like you guys would be embarrassed over Swaggart and not be out here preaching."

Looking at him in the eyes, I replied, "Well, I really regret what happened, but Jimmy Swaggart has admitted his sin and has confessed it publicly, and, I believe, has repented of it. But he's still human and my brother in Christ."

As I continued, I said emphatically, "My friend, when you find something wrong with Jesus, that's when I won't be out here!"

One day a Hispanic pastor heard me preach and invited me to come and speak at his church. "I'm not far from here. Follow me, and I'll show you my church." he said.

So I loaded everything into my van and pulled out into the traffic directly behind him. While driving, I heard an unusually large number of car horns, but I didn't think much about it. When I began parking next to his church, the pastor pointed at the top of my van. "Wait! Wait! You didn't put it down," he said, shaking his hands. Jumping out of my van, I saw what he was so upset about. In my haste not to lose him, I forgot to lower my overhead canopy! That's what all of the honking was about. People were trying to alert me.

I had driven through traffic for at least a mile and a half, making a couple of turns, with buses, automobiles, and trucks all around me, and with that huge aluminum overhead canopy wide open! Fastened on the top of my van, it extended several feet into the air when it was opened up.

"I can't believe I did that!" I exclaimed to the pastor. We joked and laughed about it then, but I knew I could have struck other vehicles or posts are signs. God was surely looking after me.

One day after putting money in my meter, I saw a young lady standing motionless with a blank stare on her face. When I began to talk to her, she said, "Look around." And she pointed to the drug addicts, the burned-out buildings, stripped cars, the graffiti, the sidewalks dabbed with spit. "I have nothing to live for. I had a baby out of wedlock. The man I love left me. I feel worthless, and I've been thinking suicide; I'm taking drugs, too."

"Well, have we got some good news for you!" I replied, "Hang around. I'm about to preach."

Her name was Lisa, and she did stay there on the sidewalk. I preached on the love of God, and she accepted Christ. Breaking into a big smile, she gushed out, "I've never felt such peace before. Oh, this is wonderful!"

In that same meeting there were three Christian women that I did not even know, but they had observed everything. They began talking to Lisa, encouraging her, and told her about a drug rehab center that had just opened up two blocks away.

Our close friends Carl and Carolyn Carrigan once again brought up hundreds of New Testaments donated by Milldale International Ministries in Zachary, Louisiana. They drove all the way from Shreveport, Louisiana, in an old school bus that they had converted into a motor home. They called it "Thunder."

Carl, a natural teacher, taught "Sunday school" right there on the street after some of our sidewalk meetings. When people raised their hands indicating that they had accepted Christ, Carl then passed out the marked New Testaments to them. Talking to sometimes twenty-five or thirty people, he would say, "You can use this little Bible to lead a friend to Christ. Turn to page eighty-six…Now turn to page eighty-three…" I was absolutely amazed at how long Carl could hold them there, instructing them with the marked New Testaments!

I talked one afternoon to a man with a sad countenance and drooped shoulders who asked me a question: "I killed at least sixteen men in 'Nam years ago. Sometimes I wake up in a cold sweat. Is there any way God could forgive me?"

Explaining the difference between war and cold-blooded murder, I then told him about the blood of Christ. As we talked, I actually saw relief come on his face and his guilt was assuaged! Thankful and appreciative, he said, "If you never reach anybody else out here, it's been worth it just to reach me."

As I preached on "The New Birth" that afternoon, a slim Chinese gentleman wearing a tie was standing beside his bike and was "amening" me. (A young Chinese student just a few days before, June 4, 1989, had stood defiantly in front of that tank in Tiananmen Square as Chinese troops moved in, extinguishing a prodemocracy movement.) When I finished preaching, he introduced himself to me.

"I'm Pastor Wong of the Healing Stream Deliverance Church on Forty-First and Seventh Avenue. What about coming and training my people?" he asked.

Two weeks later, I met with about one hundred believers at his church. It was murder hauling my rig up three flights of stairs, but I finally made it, out of breath. Teaching them all I could in about two hours, I made plans to take them out on the streets later.

Pastor Wong and a couple of other men helped me take all of my equipment back downstairs and back to my van. Man, was I grateful or what!

Some of Pastor Wong's members were already witnessing and passing out tracts down in the subway, so I believed that this would be a good church to partner with. Looking out of the chalky old window upstairs, I saw Forty-Second Street and bright lights flashing. "God has his people right here in this filth," I said to myself.

Pastor Wong told me about his church's prison ministry and said, "I believe Berkowitz really got saved. You remember him, Son of Sam?" (David Berkowitz is the infamous New York City serial killer of the late 1970s, now serving a life sentence in Sullivan Correctional Facility in Fallsburg, New York.)

"Yes, I remember Son of Sam," I replied, and I hoped that his conversion was genuine.

My friend Burris and I were driving into Brooklyn one morning, and as we turned off Belt Parkway onto Atlantic Avenue, we noticed that there were cops at every intersection, and huge crowds lining the road for miles.

"Mandela! Mandela! Mandela!" shouted the people. Nelson Mandela was in a motorcade directly behind us. (Nelson Mandela, freed after twenty-seven years in a South African prison, was visiting New York City in June 1990.) I guess we were the last vehicle the policeman allowed to pass through, because nobody else was on the road going or coming but us, with the motorcade right behind us.

Then we noticed an athletic black man in his thirties on roller skates. Dressed in a tank top and shorts, he was putting on a show. Laughing and smiling, he had the hordes of people in his hand. Skating in front of us, on the side of us, and behind us, he was circling, jumping, and weaving, and the people were loving it, whistling and applauding. But when the motorcade approached the crowds, once again we heard the roar, "Mandela! Mandela! Mandela!"

CHAPTER 35

GO ON, FOOL

A couple very much in love asked me to officiate at their wedding, and I said I would be glad to do it. But when I drove up and parked at the church, I dropped my car keys on the pavement as I got out of my vehicle. Bending down to pick them up, I split my britches, literally!

I knew immediately that my pants had ripped because I heard the rip, and I felt a lot of air coming through. "Oh, no!" I said out loud. Looking around, I saw two women walking toward me on the sidewalk. Judging by the way they were dressed, I assumed that they were going to the wedding.

"Ladies, I'm the preacher about to do the wedding. Are you headed there?" I asked.

"Yeah, we are," they answered.

"Well, ladies, I'm legit," I said, holding my hands up a little and smiling. "I just tore my pants. I mean I ripped 'em. I need to ask you, can you tell?" I said as I bent over, showing them my backside.

"Yeah, you sure can!" they said, chuckling out loud.

"OK, thank you, ladies. I've got to do something quick," I replied with a worried look, no doubt, and with desperation in my voice. I walked as inconspicuously as I could into the church and went straight to a group of women talking in the foyer. "Ladies," I said, "I need your help. I am supposed to do this wedding in a few minutes. I'm the preacher, and I ripped my pants bad. What should I do?" And I bent over a little bit toward them.

"You sure did!" the women said in unison. Then, one of the women said to me, "Take 'em off. Go in the restroom and take 'em off and give 'em to me. I'll sew 'em up. Hurry!"

So, I stepped inside the men's room, slipped my shoes off, and dropped my pants; and with the door half open, I handed them to her. There I stood, in sock feet, underwear, with a coat and tie on! It seemed like an eternity, but actually it was only about ten minutes before she knocked on the door.

"Here they are, pastor," she said, as she handed me my sewn-up pants.

"Thank you, ma'am. I really, really appreciate it," I said, sighing a big breath of relief. I put my pants on, straightened my tie, and in about two minutes I was standing before a happy couple and a huge congregation and saying, "We are gathered together here in the sight of God and in the face of this company…"

Driving home, I laughed about all that had happened, and I said to myself, 'I have got to lose some weight. I can't believe I split my britches!'

I've always been a little overweight, but I really put on the pounds when we returned to New York. I grew up eating a lot of Southern cooking. My mother, a marvelous cook, constantly fed us fried chicken, fried okra, mashed potatoes and gravy, french fries, cheese and spaghetti, homemade buttered rolls, and cornbread; and she always topped the meal off with dessert, usually a chocolate or coconut pie with the crust made from scratch. That kind of eating will put it on you! So, having a tendency to be fat to begin with, plus good ol' Southern cooking, it was no wonder that I walked around with my shirttail out!

My darling wife, Linda, with her excellent cooking, continued the trend of my eating mouth-watering, delicious meals. Don't misunderstand me. I am not blaming my being overweight on my mother or my wife. I just know that their cooking was so good that it was difficult for me to say no and back away from the table.

Ministering in New York did not make it any easier. Driving in and out of the city, not knowing what might happen in my street meetings, being totally dependent on the support back home—all contributed to a lot of stress. I began to eat even more, not only

Southern cooking at home but all of that Italian food—meatballs and spaghetti and lasagna. I also ate bagels and cream cheese, a lot of pizza, street vendor hot dogs, and other fast food. Year in and year out, I had always weighted between 210 and 220, overweight but not quite obese. But as the months flew by, I got bigger and bigger.

"Dad, you're going to have a heart attack," both Stephen and Stewart said to me from time to time. "You need to lose some weight. You're fat!"

Well, one day I came to my senses and decided to do something about my weight. "Why don't you go to Weight Watchers, Scotty? They'll teach you how and what to eat," Linda suggested.

I followed her advice and signed up. When I weighed in, I was a whopping 254 pounds! I was dumbfounded! I knew that I was overweight, but not that much!

Week after week I went to Weight Watchers and weighed in. I'll never forget the blue ribbon I got when I lost my first ten pounds. Excited and smiling, I couldn't wait to announce the good news to Linda and show off my blue ribbon.

"That's great! Scotty," she said, "I told you that you didn't have to eat salad the rest of your life and that they would teach you how to eat good, healthy food. Keep it up."

Well, I did keep it up, and by learning to eat a variety of foods in smaller portions, coupled with walking and then jogging daily, the pounds came off. In a matter of a few months, I was down to 189. I had lost sixty-five pounds! But I did not tell anybody back home in Louisiana that I had been losing weight, so that summer when we drove into Bossier City, I was lean but not quite skinny.

"Linda," I said, "I'm going to play a joke on Barbara Ann and mother. Making a small sign out of cardboard that read "Deaf Piano Tuner," I knocked on my sister's front door. Marion, her husband, opened the door and even though I had the sign partially covering my face, he recognized me. Then, Barbara Ann saw me, "Oh, my gosh, Scotty, what's wrong with you?" she asked, wide eyed and shocked. "Do you have AIDS or something?"

"No, Babs, I'm OK. I just lost a lot of weight. I want to fool Mother. Don't say anything. Just send her to the door," I said.

Barbara Ann reluctantly called out, "Mother, come here. Someone wants to see you."

As I pulled the cardboard sign up over my face, revealing only my eyes, she said, "Yes?" I pointed to "Deaf Piano Tuner."

"No, we're not interested," she said.

I lowered the sign so that she could see my entire face and asked, "Do you know who I am?"

"Well, your voice sounds familiar," she answered.

"Are you sure you don't know me?" I said. "Mother, I'm Scotty."

"Scotty! No, you're not," she replied.

"Yes, I'm Scotty!" I said again.

"Oh, my Lord, Scotty, what have you done?" Mother said, sighing and putting her hand over her heart.

"I've just lost weight, Mother," I told her.

Well, eventually, we all had a big laugh because my own mother didn't even recognize her own son!

"And mother, think about it—'Deaf Piano Tuner'?" I said, cracking up.

When I preached at Airline Baptist Church, many people were whispering when I walked to the pulpit and said, "Who is that? That's not Scotty, is it?"

Even our very close friend Mrs. Lillian Scott did not recognize me at first. "Have mercy," she hollered out, laughing and hugging me when she saw who I was.

Somebody else came to my mind, my aunt Elizabeth. "I'll have some fun with her," I said. Aunt Elizabeth was always a barrel of laughs, anyway. Smiling, with a glow on her face, she enjoyed anybody's joke.

Placing the sign partially over my face, like I did with my mother, I rang Aunt Elizabeth's doorbell. When she opened the door, once again I pointed to the sign, "Deaf Piano Tuner."

"No, I'm not interested. Thank you, though," she replied and she politely shut the door.

I rang the doorbell again. This time I had the sign at my side so that she could see my face completely. When she opened the door, I looked at her and pointed to the sign.

"No," she replied, obviously irritated, and quickly shut the door.

I waited a few seconds and again rang the doorbell. This time she opened the door fast, stuck her head out and said, "Go on, fool!" and slammed the door!

Laughing out loud, I yelled out, "Aunt Elizabeth, it's me, Scotty. Open the door." Finally, she slowly opened the door.

"Aunt Elizabeth, it's me, Scotty." I said to her.

She was shocked, but then she started laughing and kept on laughing.

"I just didn't recognize you, Scotty. What am I going to do with you?" she exclaimed, still laughing.

"I just lost a whole lotta weight, Aunt Elizabeth."

By the grace of God, I've been able to keep my weight around two hundred pounds for the past twenty-five years, which, I believe, is about my proper weight. But I never shall forget Aunt Elizabeth words: "Go on, fool!"

CHAPTER 36

GOD INTENDED IT FOR GOOD

Christine Pakoz, an extremely mature Christian young lady in our church, Grace Baptist, attended Hofstra University, and she, along with several of her friends at school, accompanied me one Saturday afternoon. My sketch board got blown over by high winds, and as I was setting everything back up, angry Black Israelites began shouting, "You are in our spot. Leave now, you white, blue-eyed devils!"

My reaction? I just felt sorry for them. When hostile individuals unleashed insults, hate, and lies at me, it just made me sad. My heart broke because they were so mistaken, so wrong, so spiritually blind.

The students from Hofstra had never participated in any kind of outdoor evangelism, and this incident unnerved them. I explained that interference of this nature occurred periodically. They relaxed a bit, and, being forced to move by the Black Israelites, we went across the street, and I began preaching over there.

To a very receptive crowd, I exclaimed, "I have a little dachshund named Buster. Sometimes he'll gnaw on a bone for a while in our backyard, and then he'll scratch on our back door, wanting to come in. 'No, Buster, put that bone down. Then I'll let you in.' He'll roll his big brown eyes and, with the bone in his mouth, he'll turn around and either drop it in the backyard or bury it, getting dirt all over his nose. When he gets rid of the bone, I then let him in and clean the dirt off of him. Listen, when we come to Christ, we have to be willing to drop our sins. We must turn away from them. Let them go—like my dog dropping that bone. Be willing to turn from your sin and come to Christ just as you are, and he'll get the dirt off of you and clean you up!"

A number of people expressed interest that day, and the hand of God was evident. The students counseled between meetings, saw the Lord at work, and left on fire for Christ!

One person we met was Lewis Soto, a former drug dealer who had been converted to Christ. He told us that God had recently called him to preach and that he was now taking a Bible correspondence course from Moody Bible Institute. Excited out of his mind when he observed our sidewalk meetings, Lewis said that he wanted to meet with me and learn more about reaching people on the streets. I mentioned that we were consistently at Times Square on Friday nights.

"I'll be there sometimes," he replied.

You know, I probably would not have ever met Louis if that racist gang had not insisted that we move. We would have been on opposite sides of the street. But the sovereign God meant for me to meet Lewis, so he used those Black Israelites to make me move across the street where I would connect with Lewis.

Several weeks later, while some of us were ministering at Times Square on Friday night, Lewis Soto showed up, just like he promised he would. He told us that he had forty-five children in a Bible study in his home recently. Lewis was a very handsome young man who looked sort of like Magnum, P.I., on TV. The people listened to him when he gave his testimony, and I could tell he was impacting many lives. Only God knew what was in store for Lewis Soto.

Pushing my rig to a favorite area, I crossed paths with two Muslims who were selling their wares—perfume, books, garb, incense sticks—everything was spread out on a card table that was set up on the sidewalk.

"Why don't you find a real job?" they said to me as I walked by them.

"Why don't you stop peddling that stuff and preach the truth," I replied.

Later, as I preached on the subject "After Death—What?" I had a very attentive crowd. I reached for my soap bubbles, and as I blew them into the air, I said, "The Bible teaches that our lives are like a vapor—like a bubble. We're here, and then we're gone! Make sure you're ready to face God, because face God you will!"

After the street service, a man approached me and told me he was a schoolteacher. "I don't think you could expect grown-ups to be changed," he said. "You need to get kids when they're young and teach them. Besides, nobody is listening to you."

"You see that crowd?" I said in my defense. "They were listening. And God can change anybody." But before I could say to him that I agreed that we need to reach kids early and teach them, he walked away.

During my next meeting a fierce lesbian gang stormed into my audience. There was no reasoning with them. I had to stop preaching. Speaking to one girl dressed in black leather and chains, I said, "Miss, you're valuable, and Jesus loves you," but she would have none of it; neither would the rest of them. As they defiantly walked on down the sidewalk, my heart filled up with pity and compassion for them.

When I stopped at a red light in the Bowery, a young man, probably in his midtwenties, unshaven and dirty, approached my van.

"You need help, don't you, son," I said to him.

"Yes, sir, I do," he answered, and he said that his dad was a preacher in South Carolina.

As the light changed, I quickly said, "Go home to your dad, son."

A team from England visited our church, and hearing about my street ministry, they just insisted on going with me, which made my day. In the group was a lady in her sixties, a mighty woman of God named Billie, who exhibited great faith. She reminded me very much of Mrs. Lillian Scott, "the War-Horse," our close friend from Louisiana who had worked with me in the carnivals from time to time and had even ministered with me on the streets of New York.

With an energetic personality, Billie just exuded Christ. Smiling and speaking with a characteristic British accent, she said to captivated New Yorkers as they crowded around us under an awning on

Broadway in order to get out of the rain, "We've come all the way from London to share with you the love of God."

A young man who accepted Christ in one of our sidewalk meetings with Billie met with us for dinner a few days later. All of us ate ribs, got barbecue sauce all over our faces, and asked for extra napkins because we had sticky, greasy hands, but we had a blast. The young man shared with us that he now had a job; he seemed like he really was doing terrific. Praise the Lord! The gospel is the power of God unto salvation to everyone that believeth (Romans 1:16).

At Albee Square, a couple who had listened to some of us preach began talking and asking for more Christian literature. "I don't know which one of you it was," the woman said, "but my son used to work with one of you—at Times Square, with somebody. Now he's pastoring a church in New Jersey, doing really well."

"What's his name?" I asked. "I might know him."

"Lewis Soto," she replied.

"Lewis! Hey, I was the guy that trained him in outdoor evangelism. Yeah, he met me at Times Square several Friday nights. I first met him right here in this area," I said. "I've been in his home, met his wife and kids; your son, huh—that was a while back."

The lady continued. "My husband here is Lewis's stepfather. We've all been praying for him, but he's never been saved, have you honey?" she said, looking at him, very concerned. The man sort of nodded no.

Reminding him that John Denver never dreamed when he got into that plane that that would be his last flight, I asked him if he would be willing to give his life to Christ completely right then. I could see that his wife was praying for him. Tears filled the man's eyes, and he repeated the sinner's prayer, calling on the Lord to be his Savior.

How relieved, how grateful he was! His wife, Lewis's mother, was so blessed and happy that she could not be still! She had prayed for her husband a long, long time. Now God had answered her prayers.

Her husband could not thank me enough either. He even came back later and thanked me again.

"Sir," I said, "that's just the grace of God. He's the one to thank."

God's ways are not our ways. Months back, when those Black Israelites forced those Hofstra students and me to move from "their spot," we went across the street, and, conducting several street meetings, we met Lewis Soto. I had trained him to do open-air work, and now God had used me to win his stepdad to Christ!

I thought about Joseph's brothers. They intended to harm Joseph, but God intended it for good (Genesis 50:20). Using those angry Black Israelites, Satan had tried to thwart the work of God, but God had turned the tables on him by leading Lewis Soto by us. Praise God!

Billy Graham held a crusade in Nassau Coliseum (September 1990), and we took Janet Raines, our friend with a myriad of mental problems, to hear him. Linda personally presented the plan of salvation to Janet, and she professed faith in Christ as her Lord and Savior. Only God knew the depth of her commitment, but isn't that true with everybody?

Harry Porthouse, the adult Sunday school teacher at my own church, Grace Baptist in Lake Grove, said to me one day, "Scott, several years ago I stopped and listened to you preach the gospel at Times Square. We didn't even know each other at the time, but God used you that night to turn my life around! I just wanted you to know that." Talk about encouraging words! A guy teaching in my own church tells me that the Lord spoke to him years earlier in one of my street meetings at Times Square!

Another night as we were setting up on Broadway, I heard an annoying voice, and it was loud. Then I saw her—an old woman with freckles, no teeth, stringy hair, and worn, unlaced shoes was singing "La Bamba," slurring the words. Knowing she would interfere with our street meetings, I offered her a dollar if she would move on down the street. Gladly, she took the dollar and left.

Once at Fulton Mall a scrawny little black man was strumming his guitar, creating nothing but worrisome racket. I knew his noise-making would hinder my preaching, so I went over to him and offered him a dollar if he would go away. He gladly took the dollar and left. The next day I was in the same area, and here he came. Once again I gave him a dollar and once again he left. In about a week I was back at Fulton Mall. As I was preparing my sketch board, I heard that awful guitar again. Turning around, I saw him sitting beside the building, cutting his eyes at me. This time I insisted that he leave. "I'm not giving you any more money!" I stated. I never saw him again.

That night at Times Square, I had just finished preaching a sermon emphasizing the love and grace of God when a gentleman in obvious pain walked over to me and said, "My brother fell and broke his neck, and then he drowned! Where was your God when that happened? Your God of love, where was he? I took sixty pills with scotch to end it all, but I lifted my own self up. No God was there!" Disturbing words that I don't think that I'll ever forget. I didn't know what to say to him. As I attempted to communicate to him that incidents like his brother tragically dying bothered me, too, he turned away from me and stumbled down the sidewalk, because he had been drinking. I knew God cared, had all power, and saw the big picture, but we would all have to wait until heaven before we would understand the problem of evil and suffering completely.

Many of us saw her, a very large woman, half dressed, face down, stoned on the pavement. A man in green shorts and high-top boots rolled her over, slapped her face to see if she would wake up, tugged at her purse, which was beneath her stomach, quickly rambled through it, then dashed away.

A distinguished-looking businessman bared his soul to me: "I've started back drinking. My mother has not heard from me in weeks. She doesn't even know if I'm alive," he said with remorse and regret in his voice. I did my best to persuade him to seek professional help. Even though this man prayed to receive Christ and asked God to deliver him from his booze, he inexorably held on to his bottle and refused to throw it into the trash can.

"Come over here," a man said, motioning for me to come over behind the car. When I did, he said, frowning, "Level with me. I won't tell anybody. What's the catch? You're giving Bibles away, and they cost money." I told him that we were Christians and that people had donated these Bibles for us to give away.

"No," he said, "you've got to have an angle. Nobody just gives these away."

"My friend, I'm telling you the truth," I replied. "There is no catch. I'm not after anybody's money. The Lord takes care of me." Leaving, he shook his head, still questioning my words. This was not the first time that someone had questioned me about the New Testaments and Bibles that I gave away. Often, people thought I had a ruse because it seemed that everybody on the street was trying to get their money. For me to be giving away New Testaments and Bibles was inconceivable to many people. But by doing so, it gave me instant credibility.

"Quick, there's one," Burris said to me, as he spotted a parking place at our favorite spot, Forty-Third and Broadway. It was tight, but I managed to squeeze my van in, and we got ready for another night of ministering at Times Square. Then I reached for my steel bar, which was behind my seat, and I pulled up my overhead canopy with it. Flipping on my sketch board lights, a bright aura surrounded me, instantly directing pedestrians' attention our way.

Standing on the van platform, Burris, dressed in a suit and tie, had drawn three crosses on the sketch board. As he talked about eternal life, he said to a nice crowd, "You want it? You can have it. It's free. It's paid for."

"No, you can have it. I don't want it," came a voice from his audience.

"You hear that man? He doesn't want it. He's this man," Burris replied, pointing on the sketch board to one of the thieves crucified with Christ. "I guarantee you he won't get it. He doesn't want it."

Later, when I preached on the subject "What Are You Looking For?" I looked at the faces of many young people—searching faces, curious faces, faces with no purpose or direction—and I declared, "You may be searching for something to fill that void in your life. You may be searching for peace. You're not going to find it in a needle. You're not going to find it in a bottle. I have a good friend (Janet Raines) who has done all kinds of things to herself to get attention because she felt nobody loved her. I want you to know that God loves you. You may be an adulterer. God loves you. You may be in a homosexual. God loves you. God hates sin, but he loves us. God loves you!"

On the way home that night, Burris and I talked about our ministry at Times Square and how the gospel was good news to the people.

"It'll ruin you," I said, laughing. "When I preach in a church, it's like, 'Oh, I've heard all this before.'"

But soon I was to receive some very bad news. Linda and I got a call one Easter Sunday morning (April 1991) from Bob Brooks, pastor of Grace Baptist Church. "Hello," I said, answering the phone.

"Scott, Janet has overdosed. She was found dead in her trailer," he said, with sorrow in his voice. "You know, she broke her leg in that car accident. The doctor prescribed morphine. It looks like she took approximately one hundred morphine tablets. Apparently, it was a suicide."

Linda and I were stunned because we dearly loved Janet Raines, and regardless of what we were told by her doctors and psychiatrists, we always felt that love would pull her through, but we were wrong, obviously. Janet always said that she did not want to live past forty. She was thirty-nine.

One particular night at Times Square, I saw that the sidewalk crowds were walking pretty fast, so I had to get to my point quickly and use brief illustrations and lots of sleight-of-hand tricks and visual aids. I knew they would not stand there very long.

I noticed a lot of couples holding hands, laughing, and strolling arm in arm, so I decided to preach on "The Cart before the Horse." Drawing a cart in front of the horse, I asked a fairly good group, "What's wrong with that?"

"You got it backward, man!" a guy said, pointing at the sketch, then looking at his girl.

"Right," I said, "The horse goes first, and then the cart. Listen up, kids. Hear my heart, OK? Now, don't turn me off. All right? I won't be but a couple of minutes. A lot of you have it backward—you got sex before marriage. You got the cart before the horse. The Bible says that we're supposed to be married first, then have sex. That way, there's no guilt; you're not going to get AIDS. God is for you; he created sex. He says, 'Have a blast, but wait until you're married.' " A lot of my crowd sort of chuckled and looked at each other, but they stayed.

Then I said, "Look, let me ask you a question. Quick, because I know you gotta go. If you knew that somebody had AIDS, would you have sex with them?"

"No, man," I heard someone say.

"Well, what if you had a condom?"

"No—still wouldn't," I heard.

"Well, that's what you're doing," I said. "You're having sex with a condom with somebody who just might have AIDS! Man, that's a risk! Well, that's all. Just think about it."

I could tell that the young people were ready to go, and sure enough they walked off. A girl smiled and thanked me. That was what God wanted me to share with them.

Soon it would be ten o'clock at night, about the time the shows were over. Then large numbers of people would be streaming down Broadway, walking at a pretty good pace, wanting to either take a quick look at Forty-Second Street or head home. But about eleven o'clock, those who were still hanging around slowed down and were more apt to listen. During this period I could take more time while preaching, develop ideas, and use longer illustrations. I didn't have to rush so much.

With the death of Janet on my mind, I preached on the verse "It is appointed unto men once to die; after that the judgment" (Hebrews 9:27). After a couple of sleight-of-hand tricks, I had a massive crowd, and I emphasized that they needed to get in real close where we would not block the sidewalk. And I gave the "Appointment in Samara" illustration: "A merchant sent his servant to downtown Baghdad to get supplies. While he was there, Death startled him. Quickly, the servant returned to his master. 'Lend me your horse,' the servant said. 'I ran into Death in Baghdad, and I want to ride to Samara to escape my fate.' The master was curious and went to Baghdad and asked Death, 'Why did you startle my servant?' Death replied, 'I was surprised to see him in Baghdad, for tonight I have an appointment with him in Samara!'"

I could tell that the Spirit of God had grabbed many in my crowd. How good it was to tell them about "Christ, who was once offered to bear the sins of many, and to those who look for him shall he appear the second time without sin unto salvation."

When God anointed like this, I could not adequately express how I felt. I was just thankful to God that he had called me to the streets. I knew I would not trade places with anybody in the world!

Then I did my rap. "Hey, I'm old to you, probably, but I can rap. Yeah. Listen up," I said. "First the devil is speaking. Then the Lord answers." Moving to the left I said, "Here's the devil—'Who can say what's right or wrong, decide for yourself and sing your song, do it now and have some fun, 'cause life is a party and you are young.'" Moving to the right I said, "Now, Christ—'The rules of God are still the same, and right and wrong, they have not changed, wait till you're married and you will see, it'll be better then, I guarantee, you're not your own, you're bought with a price, so glorify me, the Lord Jesus Christ.'"

I got pretty good applause.

One relatively quiet evening a guy walked into my meeting with a huge python wrapped around his neck, a colorful parrot perched on his arm, and a huge iguana hanging on his shirt. I struggled to retain my crowd, but it was no use. They were captivated by this guy.

"You can take a picture of me for five dollars," he said to everybody, smiling and touching the snake.

I was surprised that a couple took him up on it, giving him a quick five bucks as they snapped the picture. Others just quickly took his picture anyway.

"Hey, that's enough!" he said bluntly.

My crowd long dispersed, I had a conversation with the young man as he showed off his pets. But he was slippery, and I could not pin him down.

"I'm spiritual, but I have my own religion," he said to me as he looked all around, checking to see if anybody was noticing him.

I began explaining that Jesus was the only way to God, but he cut me off, interrupting me and saying, "I don't believe that, man. I'm outta here." And off he went.

Looking into curious faces I said, "Let me give you the best news and the worst news about the Ten Commandments: Thou shalt have no other gods before me. Thou shall not make unto thee any graven image...The Bible teaches that if you break one of the commandments, you are guilty of all...We are all guilty and are under the sentence of death. That's the bad news. But Christ kept every one of the commandments. He went to the cross and bore our guilt on that cross. And the best news I could ever tell you is when you accept him, really come to know him, God sees you just as if you've never broken any of the Ten Commandments!" About that time, a police officer came up and told me I could not preach. I held my ground and reminded him of my First Amendment rights, and folks in my crowd also defended me. The officer huffed and puffed, but he could not blow my house down that night.

I asked a handsome young man who told me that he was Jewish, "What happened to the body of Christ?"

"I don't care. It doesn't matter to me," he replied.

"My friend," I said, "You don't have but three choices. Either his disciples got his body, and they guarded that tomb to prevent that from happening, or his enemies got his body. If they did, what did they do with it? They certainly would not have disposed of it. All they would have to say is, 'Here is your dead Jesus.' And if his disciples didn't get Jesus's body and if his enemies didn't get it, what happened to it; the tomb was empty! The only option you have is that he arose! Think about it. You're a thinking person, right?" The young man nodded his head yes ,and then I asked him another question. "Young man, how do you handle your emptiness?"

"I'm not empty. Do I look empty?" he asked.

"No," I replied," but even in laughter the heart is sorrowful, the Bible says" (Proverbs 14:13).

Then I looked deeply into this young man's eyes and said, "Jesus is the water of life. Until you come to know him, you'll always have something missing in your life." I extended my hand to him, and he shook it and said, "Thank you," and walked away.

As I was finishing up my preliminary drawing on the sketch board, a woman walked up and, out of curiosity, she asked, "What are you doing?"

"Oh, I'm getting ready to preach the gospel. Do you know the Lord?" I asked.

"Oh, I have my own beliefs," she answered.

"Do you mind if I ask what you're basing your beliefs on?" I asked.

"Oh, I don't know. I just sort of pick and choose. It's what I read, see on TV, maybe Oprah, just my opinions. Just all of it together. I mean, who knows?" she replied.

I tried to talk to her about the truth of God's word, but she sort of brushed it all off and slowly walked away.

I said a few words to a photographer about him being empty without Christ. Smug and cocky, he told me that he was not empty, but his face betrayed his words.

That night as I lay in bed, many faces haunted me in the still of the night—the Jewish reporter who works for the *Daily News*—his indifference to the gospel was unsettling; the curious woman whose belief system was tenuous; Liz, a very beautiful girl who resembled Brooke Shields. She told us that all she was interested in was "being bad, sinning, having fun, and partying, doing wrong, period."

As I dropped off to sleep, I saw the freckle-faced runaway who was stoned on drugs.

CHAPTER 37

THE CROSSROADS OF THE WORLD

Friday night meant Times Square to me, period.

As I walk to Forty-Third Street and Broadway, I notice three men trying to break into a parked automobile. The alarm goes off, and they glance up at me. I see my spot beside the steel-structured newsstand. There had been no place for me to park my van, so I plan on having a "walk-in" meeting. The dark green sign pole that I secure my sketch board to with a bungee cord is still there, still bent. The white-capped Muslim sitting at the card table ignores me.

Jimmy and Lee, who hustle sunglasses in the newsstand, wave and smile. We have become friends, and they have been listening week after week as my friends and I preach. The night is perfect, not too loud, rather warm, and thick with people from the four corners of the earth. It is not windy either; wind makes folks restless, like cattle. One time a hard, strong wind blew hot dog tissue paper and newspaper around my face, blocking my vision momentarily as I preached.

On Forty-Second Street, flashing red and yellow lights at the X-rated movies, peep shows, and porno shops seduce people, drawing them in, taking their money, and leaving them jaded. Many in my audience are sex perverts, hookers, drug addicts, and drunks.

Clippity clop, clippity clop goes the sound of horse-drawn carriages with excited tourists looking in all directions as fast as they can, on their way to the latest Broadway show.

Later, under Mayor Giuliani's administration (1994–2001), Times Square will become very family-friendly. The smut and filthy sex shops will move over to Eighth Avenue and be replaced with respectable businesses. But during this period, Times Square is a very seedy, disgraceful place.

Using my rope trick to attract a few pedestrians, I remind my listeners that I do not want anybody's money and that I'm there talking about the Lord. As I demonstrate what I'm saying with another sleight-of-hand trick, I pick up a visual aid, a little wooden man with a hole in it, and I quote Smokey Robinson: "People say I'm the life of the party, 'cause I tell a joke or two. Even though I might be laughing loud and hearty, deep inside I'm blue. So take a good look at my face; you'll see my smile looks out of place. If you look closer, it's easy to trace the tracks of my tears."

But as I speak, the businessman directly in front of me locks up his store for the night, rolling down his steel door with a prolonged, loud, irritating rumble that makes the immediate area darker; but my sketch board lights are working well, so I will be fine.

As the crowd gathers around me, I glance at eyes—curious eyes, lonely eyes, eyes that pity me, eyes of disgust that give me oblique glances, somber, exhausted eyes. And then I see them, eyes that sparkle. These are fellow believers whom I have never met but who are pulling for me because they hear me mention Jesus.

My audience is so close to me that I can hardly gesture, but I am glad because the people will stay together better if they are up close. Besides, I know I cannot block the sidewalk with my crowd. Pedestrians strolling up and down Broadway, looking up, enamored by the bustle and brilliant lights, have to be able to walk on the sidewalk behind my listeners.

Times Square is the crossroads of the world. Chinese are standing there, and sailors, and theatergoers, and women with red caste marks on their foreheads. A wino throws his head back, taking a swig from his brown bag. Tourists stand out with their accents, their cameras, and their clean, well-dressed looks. Three businessmen whisper to each other and point, but they do not walk away. A lady smiles and says faintly "amen" as I mention the cross of Christ.

An extremely well-dressed woman with thin red lips and who is a tad overweight stands directly in front of me. She has on a white dress and jewelry and stands there with a pensive look on her face.

I make it a point to stare into her eyes and I say, "The Hound of Heaven is still after you." Taking a small, brass cup from my sketch board shelf, I quote a Bible verse: "Jesus said, 'Whoever drinks of this water shall thirst again, but whoever drinks of the water that I shall give him shall never thirst but the water that I shall give him shall be in him a well of water, springing up into everlasting life' " (John:4:14). My eyes probe the crowd, looking for the sophisticated woman in the white dress, but she is no longer there.

Explaining to my listeners what it means to put faith in Christ, I grab my old, shoddy, orange canvas-backed director's chair and say, "You see this chair? I believe it will hold me up, but I don't really believe until I actually sit in it." I sit in the chair as people stare at me from all sides. Sitting in the chair, I say, "Now, right now, I'm relying on the chair, trusting it to hold me up. That's what it means to believe in Christ. You rely upon him; you just trust Christ to save you. It's an act of your will. You choose in your heart to believe, rely, trust, put your faith in the Lord Jesus Christ to save you. And when you do that, not just when you say you're doing it, but when you actually start relying upon Christ and what he did for you on that old rugged cross, God saves you, forgives you of all your sins, and gives you everlasting life, fills the void in your life."

When I invite people to put their faith in Christ as their Lord and Savior, hands go up everywhere. I can hardly get materials and Christian literature to everybody.

Victor is standing there—bright, well read, smiling. I see him quite often on Friday nights.

"Victor, my man. You still runnin' from God?" I ask, grinning.

"I'm not running from God," he replies, also smiling.

"You know you are," I answer.

Victor is a man about my age, only his hair is still brown. Tonight he has on a blue and white baseball cap, and, of course, he has on those big, rimmed glasses that he always wears, which match his square face.

Victor has a problem with the concept of hell. "I won't believe in a God who would let somebody burn forever and ever," he had told me more than once.

Many times I have tried to explain to him that God doesn't want anybody to go to hell. "But Victor, if you keep saying no to God, 'God, leave me alone,' one day God will give you what you want. He'll leave you alone forever," I say.

One evening after we have butted heads and minds for well over an hour, I say, "Victor, what's the real reason why you won't come to Christ? It's not an intellectual issue with you, is it? It's a moral problem; am I right?"

"Well, I do enjoy topless dancers," he replies, laughing.

I have tried to win him to the Lord for years, since Elvis died back in 1977. I am still trying.

I am tired and ready to go home, but I feel like I need to preach one more time. In the middle of my message I hear, "Don't listen to him! Don't listen to him!" It's the man with the raspy, guttural voice who has just walked up. I see the homeless every day, the mentally ill, the socially maladjusted. But when I see this man, I instantly think of the demon possessed. He is dirty, has smelly clothes on, and stinks so badly that people clear the sidewalk to get away from him. With a loud, penetrating voice he twists the scripture, lies, scares, and confuses. His throaty, grinding words make you think that someone is channeling through him. He looks mean.

As I pack up to leave, he says to me, "I know you. I've heard you preaching here before."

When I mention the blood of Christ, he shouts, "You know who is in control of this world?"

The Lord Jesus Christ," I answer back.

"Yes, if we let him, but this is Satan's world!" he growls.

Waving good-bye to Jimmy and Lee, the sunglasses salesman, I walk toward my van. Then I feel glass crunching beneath my feet. "Those men broke into that car," I say out loud, seeing the window smashed in and the glove compartment open.

Driving home, I sigh because five lanes merge into one on the Williamsburg Bridge. More construction, and it's after midnight. I think of Linda. She'll be waiting up. She always does. Stewart is graduating in a few days from high school. I can hardly believe it. Stephen is working in Little Rock this summer, far away. I think of the faces on the sidewalks. I think of the people who pray for us and who back us down south.

Gosh, it's nearly two in the morning. I stop at the red light by Spartan Diner. Out of nowhere a guy comes flying by me on a motorcycle, running the red light. "Man, you better slow down," I say out loud. When the light turns green, I drive on down 110, and about a mile further up the road, people are opening their car doors and running to the side of an overpass and looking down. I see a motorcycle on its side, and the wheels are still spinning. Reading *Long Island Newsday* a couple of days later, I see that a man on a motorcycle died that night on that overpass.

CHAPTER 38

ARRESTED!

My good friend Burris Jenkins and I were arrested Friday night, October 25, 1991, at Times Square as we were preaching the gospel.

We were at our usual place at Times Square, Forty-Third and Broadway. We had a couple of pretty good street meetings with a lot of people listening and no distractions, really. A gentleman who apparently had stood in one of our crowds walked over to me and handed me two twenty-dollar bills.

"Sir, we thank you," I said as I tried to give the money back to him, "but we don't take money."

"Well, I want you to have this. Keep up the good work," he replied, closing my hand with the money in it. "Keep it. God bless you," he said.

"Well, how about that!" Burris said, grinning. So I put the money in my billfold. While I was in the middle of my next sermon, a police officer walked into our crowd, saying, "Break it up! Break it up!"

"Officer," I explained, "we're preaching the gospel and giving away Bibles!"

"Do you have a permit?" she asked.

"No, Officer," I said. "We don't need a permit because we don't use a public address system." (I was legally correct.)

"Move!" she demanded.

"No, Officer," I said, "I've been here for many, many years. We're not doing anything wrong." The officer had dispersed most of our audience by this time; she then left, obviously ticked off. We reminded the remaining few listeners to move in close because we did not want to block the sidewalk.

Burris then began to speak, and as he was actually reading John 3:16 from my Bible, several police officers converged on us, demanding that we stop and wanting to know if we had a permit. We explained again that because we did not employ a sound system, no permit was required. The cops then began to say that we were blocking the sidewalk.

"No, Officer, we're not. You can see that people are able to walk in the back," I said, pointing to the people slowly strolling behind our sparse crowd.

"Officer, we have freedom of speech, freedom of religion, freedom of assembly," I said with conviction, but Burris and I were both nervous and upset, not knowing what was going to happen. As the cops ordered us to remove our sketch board and to stop, the crowd was stunned.

"Officer," Burris said, actually very calmly, "we will cease and desist if you would give us something in writing that we can take up in court."

The police then said that they were going to arrest us.

"On what charge? Why are we being arrested? We're not doing anything wrong," we answered. "The law says we have a right to be here. We're giving away Bibles."

Then a cop took the Bible out of Burris' hands. Another cop got in my face and said loudly, "You are under arrest!"

"What for, Officer?" I asked.

"For disorderly conduct!" he replied harshly.

They handcuffed our hands behind our back and confiscated my Bible and all of our equipment, including approximately seventy-five New Testaments given to us by VBS kids of Fillmore Baptist Church and from Belle Park Baptist Church members, two churches in Louisiana.

As they put us in the police car, I told the captain that this was not right and that we were on his side. He responded by saying, "I warned you." Carrying us to Midtown South precinct, they cuffed us to a very low steel bar, close to the latrine. A huge sign in the precinct read "Busiest Precinct in the Nation."

Burris, who spoke impeccable English, looked up at the sign and said, chuckling, "You done real good, Officers; you managed to catch two Baptist preachers!"

The police kept us cuffed to the steel bar for about thirty minutes but held us at the precinct for about an hour. They went through all of our equipment—sketch board, paints, object lessons, literature, Bibles—tagged it all, issued us a summons, and said that we could not get our equipment back until December 4, the date we were to appear in court.

We were then told that we could leave. "God bless you, Officers," we said and began walking back to my van. On our way, we found much of our equipment lying on the edge of the street by the curb.

"Look at this, Burris. That's our director's chair; look at all of this other stuff. It's strewn all over," I said.

Before this night, the policemen normally were friendly to us. Perhaps an officer would ask us what we were doing. When we explained that we were preaching, he understood and left. Periodically, a cop insisted that I move. "Sir," I would say, "I'm preaching the gospel, and I have a right to be here, but if you insist, I'll go somewhere else."

Lately, however, I had been forced to move a lot. Practically every time I started preaching, some officer would disrupt my meeting, scatter my crowd, and make me leave. So Burris and I had agreed that the next time the policeman came down on us we were not going to quit preaching or move. Our constitutional rights were stake!

That was the position we had taken that evening at Times Square. We were trying to send a message to the policeman that we were not going to be pushed around. We had been victims of police intimidation and harassment, and we were tired of it.

I knew that the cops had a very difficult job, especially at Times Square, the crossroads of the world, and I believe in obeying the law; but the law said that we were within our legal rights. We often met fine Christian policeman who encouraged us and who were glad we were on the sidewalk, sharing the love of God. Ironically, the "Cops for Christ" had spoken in our church, Grace Baptist, the Sunday morning before this incident happened. Also, Ricky Walker, a policeman from Shreveport, had even come up and preached with me in New York.

With the drug dealing, theft, murder, crime, and prostitution all around, it was unconscionable that the cops arrested two Baptist ministers who were trying to help the people and who, with the crowd's approval, were doing it without any complaints whatsoever and in a civil way!

When Burris and I returned to our van, he reminded me of the forty dollars that the guy had given us before we were arrested.

"Let's go get a steak, Scotty! I'm hungry, aren't you?" he said.

"Yeah," I answered.

So, we stopped at Tad's Steak House on Thirty-Fourth Street. Burris, as usual, ordered his steak rare, "where it goes 'Moo,' " plus two swimming-pool-size milkshakes. I had my steak cooked medium, as always. But as we ate, we could not help but notice many little mice darting around in the kitchen area. Neither one of us ever ate at Tad's again.

After dropping Burris off at his home, I slipped into bed and, as she usually did, Linda asked me, "How'd it go tonight?"

"Oh, we had a good night," I replied. "I'll tell you about it in the morning," and I did.

Carl Carrigan, my close friend in Shreveport, happened to call me the next morning, and I talked to him about our arrest. Carl told his pastor, Brother Step Martin of Calvary Baptist Church in Shreveport. Brother Step contacted the American Center for Law and Justice, and they provided Burris and me with an attorney.

At our trial, which had been postponed until December 18, the judge asked me what credentials I had. "Your Honor, the authority of the Lord Jesus Christ," I replied.

"Case dismissed," he exclaimed, sounding his gavel. The judge having ruled in our favor, all charges were dropped.

It took some legwork and considerable time, but we finally located and retrieved our Bibles and equipment, which were locked up in a warehouse.

Pat Robertson of the 700 Club sent a TV crew to New York, filming us while we held a street meeting at Times Square, and told our story on national television as they discussed religious liberty.

"Sing unto the Lord; for he hath done excellent things: this is known in all the earth" (Isaiah 12:5).

The American Center for Law and Justice, of their own initiative, filed suit against the New York Police Department and, in order to prevent lengthy litigation, recommended that Burris and I settle out of court, which we did.

Several weeks later Burris and I each received a check for five thousand dollars. Burris, who loved the sea, took a cruise on the *QE2*, and I purchased a state-of-the-art video camera that replaced my other video camera, somewhat obsolete. Using my new camera, I continued videotaping as many street meetings as possible. Praise the Lord!

CHAPTER 39

FLAPPING SHOE SOLE

Christmas 1991 was extra special for us because our son Stephen married Katie shortly thereafter (December 28, 1991). What sheer joy it was for me to officiate their wedding. Everybody felt the presence of the Lord. As Grady, Stephen's cousin and best man, gave a toast at the reception, he said, "I've never seen Stephen so happy." And with rosy cheeks, Katie, bubbling over, said, "I just love Stephen to pieces!"

There were girls in New York who had their eye on Stephen—Lisa, Lila, and Christine were three that I knew of—but he always insisted that he was going to find himself a Southern belle. Linda always laughed and said to him, "Son, you're going to meet somebody, and she's going to be from Chicago or New York or someplace like that, but when the love bug bites, it won't matter where she's from."

Well, the love bug did bite, and Stephen called from college down in Arkansas and said, "Mom, I've met her. Katie is her name, and you're right; she was born in Poughkeepsie, New York, and grew up just south of Chicago!"

Not long after that, Linda and I met Katie, a lovely Christian young lady who loved Jesus as well as Stephen.

Before Stephen and Katie were married, Katie's father, Horst, and I met each other one day in New York City. He was an executive with IBM in Chicago, so I was somewhat nervous about meeting him. But Horst was very cordial, and we had a delicious dinner at Wolfe's Deli, enjoying each other's company.

As we were walking back to the car, the sole on my right shoe came partially lose and began flopping. Extremely embarrassed, I didn't say anything to Horst. I just hoped that he wouldn't notice.

Besides, we would soon be back to the car. Then, Horst exclaimed, "Scott, I forgot those chocolates. I left them in the paper bag in the chair."

So, we turned around and walked back, my shoe sole still lose and bumping the sidewalk. Doing my best to walk normally, I prayed that he would not detect anything out of the ordinary. I didn't think we would ever get back to Wolfe's for those chocolates and then to the car, but we did.

Horst never knew. I told him years later about my loose shoe sole, and I got a huge, hilarious laugh from him.

Now that I knew Horst, I could tell him and not be embarrassed, but I did not know him then.

CHAPTER 40

THE WOMAN ON THE TRASH CAN

Many members of Grace Baptist Church out on Long Island, my home church, donated winter clothing, which my friends and I gave to the cold and needy. Donning the coats, putting on gloves, and wrapping scarves around their neck, the tired and weary men and women were extremely appreciative.

The Royal Ambassadors from First Baptist Church, Bossier, used the proceeds from a car wash to purchase New Testaments for me to distribute on the streets of New York. As I handed them out to people making decisions for Christ in our sidewalk meetings, one man, with tears in his eyes, said, "You mean those kids washed cars so I could have a Bible?" However, on another occasion a guy took one of those New Testaments, tore it up and threw it at my feet. I quickly gathered up the pages scattered around me, wrapped a rubber band around them and for years used that torn up bible as a visual aid in my street meetings.

When the Rodney King verdict was handed down and the Los Angeles riots were occurring (April 29–May 4, 1992), Carl Carrigan, Ray Wilson, Burris Jenkins, and I were ministering at Times Square. We did so with extreme caution, not wanting to incite any trouble ourselves or add to the anger and frustration on the streets of New York. Many businesses were closed, and store windows were protected with sliding iron doors. Broadway was unusually quiet. When we held our sidewalk services, we were the only show in town practically. Large groups listened and many Bibles were given away. Several concrete decisions for Christ were made.

One evening, two men from Grace Baptist, Ronny Best and Manny Scharsmidt, joined me in the city. We had a long conversation with a woman named Jennifer, very attractive and stylishly dressed. But we could not figure her out. She told us that she had lots of people working for her and that she could make large sums of money, fast. Maybe she was a high-class call girl or perhaps she was dealing hard drugs. Maybe she was a plainclothes policewoman. We never did find out for sure.

The Democratic National Convention was showcased nationally from New York City (July 13–16, 1992). Thousands of delegates filled Midtown, but police security was so tight, and there were so many protests and demonstrations, that the area around Madison Square Garden was not conducive for effective open air meetings. While doing one on one witnessing, however, I observed many Christian groups trying to sound a positive note for Christ.

One young man with whom I talked was named Jerry Simons. He invited Christ to come into his life and save him, and by the way he prayed, I believe he was very sincere. Even though his father was a minister, Jerry said that he had been running from God for years and had even ended up in prison. "I can't wait to go home to my dad and tell him what has happened to me!" he exclaimed with pure joy on his face.

One day in the Bronx I was pushing my rig down the sidewalk when I noticed a young woman sitting on a trash can and weeping profusely.

"Miss, I'm a preacher. Can I help you?" I asked, as I stopped, leaning over toward her.

"My mother is dying, and I don't know what to do," she lamented.

"I'm Scott. What's your name?" I asked.

"Leisha," she said, wiping her tears and sobbing.

Looking at her, I saw a swollen-eyed drug addict, probably about thirty, but who looked much, much older. We talked awhile, and I had prayer with her. Giving her a marked New Testament, I said, "Leisha, take this Bible to your mother, and read these verses to her, the ones that are underlined. Be sure and do that, OK?"

She said she would.

About a week later when I was back in the area, she came hurrying up to me and exclaimed with an enormous smile, "You know that Bible you signed? It's buried with my mother. I did what you told me to do."

"Great! She's in the hands of the Lord now," I replied.

A number of times after that incident, Leisha stood and listened as I preached the gospel, and one day she accepted Christ. From then on, Leisha's life slowly began changing, so much so that she hardly looked like the same woman I first saw crying her heart out on that trash can.

As the famous hymn "I Know Whom I Have Believed" says so beautifully:

"I know not how the Spirit moves,
Convincing men of sin,
Revealing Jesus thro' the Word,
Creating faith in Him."

One morning as I walked to where I was going to preach that day, a guy pushed some literature in my face. "Jesus is coming October 28! Jesus is coming October 28!" he declared, with kamikaze conviction. The man was a middle-aged Korean who was announcing the exact date when Christ would return. (A Korean cult had predicted the return of Christ on October 28, 1992.)

"Yes, Christ is coming!" I said back to him. "But nobody knows when!" Without even pausing, he ignored me and continued announcing his prediction.

It was a cloudy day with rain threatening, and I was ministering not far from a street vendor, a small, tanned Hispanic man who was selling sherbet. Preaching on "Attitudes," I said, "Some people deny the existence of God. Some doubt he exists. Others run from God. Some ignore God. Some blame God. Others search for God. Some know about God, but there are some people who actually know God. Do you know the Lord?"

A while later, the little Hispanic fellow came over and in a very quiet, humble manner said to me, "I'm waiting for his return, too. We're in the last days. I'm a believer."

He then gave my friend Richard McDermott and me some sherbet. "Coconut! It's good! Thank you!" I said, offering him some money.

"Oh, no, that's for you guys," he said, smiling.

"Well, Rich, we better get. Looks like the rain is coming," I replied.

We gave the vendor's son, who had been playing around his cart, some "Little Red Bibles." Saying bye to Rich, who was heading back to Jersey on the subway, I pulled away and, glancing in my mirror, I saw his son giving the Bibles to his dad's customers.

I was glad to have made friends with that street vendor because it was very important to maintain good public relations with everybody who was working around me on the sidewalks, as well as the store owners, meter maids, and police officers. They could make you or break you. We often assisted each other. Sometimes a vendor would watch my rig when I had to go to the bathroom or I had to put a quarter my meter; and I would do the same for him.

I talked to Ronald again, the thirty-three-year-old Puerto Rican from the Bronx who was a drug addict. I had preached to, reasoned with, listened to, pleaded with, and prayed for him for three years. The last time I saw him, he said that he had just been released from prison. I didn't think he had ever seriously considered repentance.

Drawing an imaginary line on the sidewalk, I said, "Ronald, on this side of the line you're relying on your good works, your religion, whatever, but in order to get saved, you must step to this side of the line, trusting and relying upon Christ alone to save you. Will you do that?" Once again, Ronald said, "No, I'm not ready." I felt he wasn't willing.

But we went and got a hamburger and Pedro, a man with a hurt foot, went with us. Pedro had just accepted Christ. I was hoping that his decision would influence Ronald.

Later, I preached on "Choices"—"You're tied up on the train tracks, and the train is coming. Somebody tells you to get up. Help yourself. But you're tied up; you can't! Somebody needs to untie you. Hear me, please. You're in bondage. Somebody tells you to give it up. Quit the drugs. But you can't. You're bound. Somebody needs to set you free. Christ can set you free. He's the only one who can."

At that moment Ronald said he was ready to accept Christ. We prayed together, and he called on the Lord to save him. I was skeptical, but I encouraged him to attend Manhattan Bible Church.

Then, to my delight, a few weeks later Ronald approached me, just beaming with the love of God. He thanked me for not giving up on him and seemed to be on top of the world. Praise God!

One day as I chatted with a committed Roman Catholic who worshiped the Virgin Mary, two other men stopped and listened to our conversation, then joined in, each with foreign accents. This happened quite often—while I am counseling with one person, others overhear, stop, and participate in the conversation.

These three men were from three different countries, and all three had a name which began with the letter A—Albert, Abby, and Andy. Lo and behold, all three men trusted Christ to be their Lord and Savior!

I was preaching on "The Only Sin God Will Not Forgive." Using a metal heart and a magnet, I said, "The Spirit of God draws you to Christ. Every time you say no, your heart gets a little harder…"

As I declared the gospel, I noticed a girl paying close attention, but her friend, wearing a large gold ring in her nose, tugged on her arm to leave, and the girl pulled away a few seconds, but then left with her friend. Based on Jesus's parable in Matthew 13, I knew that

I was a seed scatterer. Some gospel seed fell by the wayside, some on stony ground, some among thorns; and some fell onto good ground. I saw this scenario being played out constantly in my street meetings. In this case, with one girl being pulled out of the meeting by her friend, I could see Jesus's words being fulfilled: "Then cometh the wicked one, and catcheth away that which was sown in his heart. This is he that received seed by the wayside" (Matthew 13:19).

One day I attempted, using Old Testament scriptures, to prove to an old Jewish gentleman that Jesus was the Messiah. He shook his head no, so I left him alone. But as I preached on the topic "How Do You Stand Before God?" he walked up to me and in front of everybody said, "I would rather go to hell than except Jesus as Messiah! What are you getting out of this anyway? Nothing! See what I mean?" After hearing his words, it was difficult for me to continue preaching, but somehow I did.

My friends and I had some good conversations with a number of people. George led Jose Torres to Christ and referred him to Brooklyn Tabernacle. David shared with us about a guy who worked at Channel Seven. "He was contemplating suicide," David exclaimed, "but he accepted Christ, hallelujah."

I had a conversation with a young Asian, dressed in a loose-fitting orange tunic and wearing white, high-top leather shoes. A large rice-paddy hat shaded his slanted eyes as he carried a vase and a bell.

"Jesus is just another spiritual leader," he said nonchalantly and walked down the sidewalk without looking back.

Going to Courtney's restaurant, we noticed a tan, skinny man with long, hairy legs. Dressed in a dingy, sweaty track outfit, he was throwing dice and talking to himself. Then he grabbed a bottle of Windex and sprayed it on the windshield of a Rolls-Royce that had stopped at the red light, hoping for a little change.

We talked to him quickly about the Lord when the light turned green, and he replied, "What did Jesus ever do for me?"

"Christ died for you!" we answered.

"That's his problem!" he barked back; then he looked at his face in the shine of another car that had now stopped at the light.

Packing up, I heard Frankie across the street, blaring on the microphone, and I cringed. His shouting turned many people off. I knew he meant well, and he was my brother in Christ. I had talked with him about his approach, but he was determined to bombard others with this method. Open air preaching falls into disrepute when someone slams others with the Bible. I saw a monk, dressed in a gray hoodie. standing on the sidewalk between 141st and Third Ave. in the Bronx. He had three large banners, two of the Virgin Mary and one of Jesus. Strolling up next to him, I asked him who was more important, Mary or Jesus.

"Well, Mary is the mother of God," he answered. We had a lengthy conversation, and he told me that he had given up his true love and marriage for his church. I admired his sacrifice, but I tried to explain to him that if he really came to know Christ, the Lord would probably allow him to marry—if he had the desire to. But I don't think I altered his thinking one iota.

Looking out of the window one Saturday afternoon, I saw Linda working in her garden. She always had a beautiful garden, and this year was no exception. Her tomatoes were huge. I thought of John Denver's song "Homegrown Tomatoes": "Only two things that money can't buy, that's true love and homegrown tomatoes." The rest of her garden—peas, squash, cucumbers, and green beans—seemed to be doing well, too. I tilled the garden, stuck her beans and tomatoes, and mended the fence from time to time; but Linda worked the garden, hoeing, pulling out grass and weeds, and keeping it watered "so everything won't croak," as she always said. Hard work, but she enjoyed it immensely.

I cleaned up the kitchen and started the dishwasher. Then I sat down and began reading the paper. In a few minutes, Buster, our dachshund, began growling really low, grrrrrrr. Glancing up from the newspaper, I said, "What's wrong, Buster?" He didn't look my way; he just stared into the kitchen, and he continued growling softly. Finally, he walked over to me and lay down beside me, growling louder and still staring at the kitchen.

"What are you growling at, Buster?" I said as I leaned over in my chair and looked toward the kitchen. Then I saw what had stressed him out. Soapsuds were knee deep in the kitchen! I jumped up and saw that the dishwasher was running over, pouring suds everywhere. Our kitchen was small and was closed in, so the suds were contained and rising higher by the second—clear, white, sparkling bubbles, glistening in the sunshine that was beaming through the kitchen window.

I turned the dishwasher off and said, "Man, what am I going to do?" I quickly looked out the window. Yes, Linda was still in the garden. I thought, "Garbage bags!" Opening the cabinet under the sink, I pushed gobs of sparkling white soapsuds away with my arms and grabbed several big, black plastic bags. Then I began stuffing armloads of suds into the bags. It was like trying to corral moonlight! Scooping up armloads at a time, I pushed the suds off of my arms, sliding them into the bag. Glancing out the window, I saw Linda was still in the garden.

What was that? I heard dripping. "Oh, no—the basement." I ran downstairs and into the basement. The suds were dripping down all over our basement floor. "Well, I'll take care of that later," I said to myself. Hurrying back upstairs to the kitchen, I took a quick peek out the window—yes, she was still out there. I continued trying to fill up the plastic bags with suds, but the suds were so light that I felt like I was putting a mist into the bags.

Oh, no. I heard Linda walking up the deck steps. "Scotty, what's going on?" she asked as she came through the back door. "Linda, the dishwasher ran over. I'll take care of it."

"What did you do?" she asked. Holding the bottle of dishwashing soap, she said, "Did you use this?"

"Yeah," I replied.

"That's not the right soap. I can't believe you did that!" she exclaimed, but she was beginning to laugh. So I was in the clear!

"Linda, go sit down. I'll clean it up. I was trying to help you," I said.

"Yeah, well, you should have known better than to use that soap. Use this—dishwasher powder!" she replied.

We finally got rid of all the soapsuds, and I mopped up the basement. Trying to explain, I said, "I was reading the paper, and Buster started growling. Then I saw 'em—soap bubbles everywhere! Where is Buster? Buster!" I called. He was hiding out somewhere. I felt like I should have done the same! "How's your garden?" I asked.

Giving me a look that said "How can you mention my garden now?" Linda looked up at me, paused, and then said, smiling, "I can't believe you, Scotty. I would be ashamed to tell anybody I did that." We've laughed many a day about that incident!

CHAPTER 41

THAT THE POWER OF GOD MIGHT BE PRESENT

I have had friends, family, and churches ask me, "What should I pray for concerning your ministry?"

"More than anything else," I've said, "pray that the power of God will be so present in the sidewalk meetings that people will be genuinely converted to Christ, made right with God, and have their lives changed." I cannot alter the nature, habits, behavior, or the hearts of anybody. Only Almighty God is able to do that. God alone grants repentance unto life and brings lasting transformation.

It does happen. I recall a lesbian, very depressed, who accepted Christ. She said that for the first time in her life she had self-worth. No doubt the Holy Spirit touched her way down deep inside and performed a miracle in her soul. Mentioning the gay lifestyle, the Bible says, "But such were some of you: but ye are washed, but ye are sanctified, but ye are justified in the name of the Lord Jesus, and by the Spirit of our God" (1 Corinthians 6:9–11).

What great news we heard on Long Island. Katie Beers, a ten-year-old girl, had been found alive (January 1993). A man by the name of John Esposito had kidnapped her, chained her in a dungeon beneath his house, and held her captive for seventeen days. Finally, Esposito himself revealed the bunker to the police, and Katie was rescued. What surprised Linda and me was that the house where Katie was held was located almost directly behind our house in Bay Shore. In fact, with a strong bow I could have shot an arrow into Esposito's backyard. That's how close his house was!

Not long after Katie Beers was rescued, my good friend Price Harris from Shreveport ministered with me in the city. One morning

I waited in the van for Price. As he stepped up into the seat, I said, "Price, I don't mean to rush you."

"Oh, no, you're just sitting here with your seatbelt on and the motor running," he replied, laughing.

During this time in our lives, Linda and and I still had our little dachshund named Buster. We dearly loved him and tried to take good care of him, feeding him well—too much, really—and playing with him a lot. I told everybody that Buster was family and that he was smarter than most of my friends. Price more than once had said jokingly, "If there was such a thing as reincarnation, I'd want to come back as Scotty's dog, ol' Buster."

Arriving in the city, Price and I hardly saw anybody outside on the streets because of the frigid, blustery weather. I had bragged about how many people there were on the sidewalks of New York, so Price asked, "Where is everybody?"

"It's cold, Price. They're downstairs," I answered. And sure enough, going down into the subway, we could hardly move on the platform because of the hordes of people. As we shared the gospel, many trains were delayed, causing huge crowds to extend far down the platform. Price, a fantastic singer, began singing "Amazing Grace." Many people joined in. Hearing those melodious words of that famous hymn echo down the subway tunnels was inspiring and heartwarming to tired New Yorkers trying to get home. We all sensed the power of God working, reminding folks of God's great love and mercy and grace.

Very much aware of the Waco siege (February 28–April 19, 1993) when federal agents had stormed the compound in Waco, Texas, killing cult leader David Koresh and many others, I worked with twenty-five college students from Virginia Beach. Nobody in our crowds seemed to associate us with cults, however. And I was thankful for that!

One bright day in Spanish Harlem, I said to a very attentive audience, "I find that many people are lonely on the streets. Ever feel just plain alone? With people everywhere? You know, Diana Ross said in her book *Secrets of a Sparrow* that with all her success, her family, and everything, 'that aloneness has never left me.' " When I invited people to accept Christ, the power of God fell and many people, I believe, were genuinely saved. Praise God!

Later, while observing those students share Jesus and lead others to Christ, I was privileged to be a part of what God was doing. God was the one shooting the bow. We were just arrows in his quiver.

One young lady named Wendy stood out above all the other students. With long, brown hair, straight teeth, a beautiful smile, and an energetic personality, she was very attractive, glowing with Christ- likeness. Extremely articulate, Wendy told me that her sister was in Atlanta; her father was in Somalia; her mother was in North Carolina; and here she was in Harlem, New York, witnessing for Christ.

Wendy greatly encouraged me with her kind words. She quoted Jim Elliott, the missionary who was killed attempting to evangelize Indians in Ecuador (January 8, 1956): "He is no fool who gives what he cannot keep to gain that which he cannot lose."

Patti Cohen, staff writer for *New York Newsday*, did a story about my street ministry—"Preacher on a Mission" (Tuesday, July 6, 1993). I think her article helped me gain a little credibility, which you can never get enough of if you're preaching on the sidewalks. Patti was Jewish, but I reminded her that Jesus was Jewish, and I shared with her that the gospel was for the Jew first.

"For I am not ashamed of the gospel of Christ: for it is the power of God unto salvation to everyone that believeth; to the Jew first, and also to the Greek" (Romans 1:16). Patti was open to what I said, and I thanked God that I was able to witness to her. I ached for the Jewish population in New York.

A gunman from Brooklyn, Colin Ferguson, opened fire on a Long Island train (December 7, 1993). Six people were killed, and nineteen others were wounded before he was stopped. I happened to be on several trains that particular day, but not on the 5:33 to Hicksville!

One afternoon a sickly man in a navy coat bumped through the people who were standing on the platform in the subway. Obviously suffering from some devastating illness, he was spitting and slobbering everywhere. People were raising their arms to protect themselves from the saliva going in all directions. One woman was extremely offended. Upset and losing her patience, she pointed her umbrella at him and threatened, "If you don't quit spitting all over me, I'm going to ram this umbrella up your filthy ass!" The poor guy winced, then stumbled on down the platform, trying to control himself but unable to do so.

Walking down the subway platform to catch the F train to Queens Plaza, I heard beautiful clarinet music. The musician was panhandling, but he was good, as many New York street musicians are. I threw a little change in his case and asked, "Would you play 'Happy Birthday' to Jesus? It's his birthday, Christmas, you know." He smiled and played to the Lord.

It gets bleak down in the subway. Emptiness and hopelessness seem to hang in the air. Tired commuters wait. Puddles of dirty water stand between the tracks. Thin, white tissue paper covered with mustard is lying all around. But as the light from the engine reflected off the tunnel and the rumbling, squeaking train approached, those sweet, clarinet notes of "Happy Birthday" to Christ resounded throughout the subway corridors and brought peace, light, joy, and hope.

The Open Air Campaigners invited me to attend a conference in Ottawa, Canada, in February 1994. Asked to share the various object lessons, visual aids, and props that I used on the streets, I deemed it an honor, and I sensed the power of the Holy Spirit as I spoke; there were scores of evangelists from countries all over the world, and to be able to impart what the Lord had taught me on the sidewalks of New York city was very satisfying.

A sharp, very well-educated Hindu in a nice, expensive suit listened to me as I preached about Jesus being the only way to God.

He later opened up a conversation with me. As I illustrated my position on the sketch board, he was very concerned about a speck of paint I got on his suit.

"What's this?" he asked, somewhat upset.

"Blue paint. It's tempera; it'll come off," I replied.

We talked about the resurrection of Jesus and Gandhi. "God is the hub, and all religions are the spokes. They all lead to the same God," he declared, lecturing me.

"I know what you're saying, but Jesus said that he was the way, the truth, and the life. Nobody comes to the Father except through him," I answered. He flatly rejected that and walked away, sporting his new suit A little later, a cop told me to leave because the store manager said that I was blocking his door and people could not enter his store. "You'll have to move," he said.

"Sir," I replied, "I've been at this very spot for years. The manager has never said a word. The security guards watch us through the window. Let's go talk to the manager."

The officer said, "No, if we do, he will just deny that he called the cops."

I felt that the policeman was out of line, but I did what he said to do, and I went further down the block.

With my black paint brush I drew a cross as I talked about the Son of God dying for our sins; then I let red paint drip down the cross, depicting Christ's blood.

Then, a man began to verbally assault me, lashing out with venomous hatred. Trying to return good for evil, I replied, "My friend, I love you, and Jesus loves you." Many in my crowd began walking away, not wanting to be a part of this.

"F*&^   you…f*&^ Jesus," he angrily shouted, almost foaming at the mouth. I didn't know what I had said that triggered his acrimony, but I suspected something had happened in his past that caused him to explode on me; perhaps my mentioning the cross and the blood of Christ had offended him.

I had experienced interference numerous times, but I sensed this man was volatile. I didn't even know him, but he loathed me. Very concerned, I didn't know what to do. I could not quell his rage.

"I could skin you like a hog!" he said, with revulsion.

Well, I knew you boil a hog, rather than skin it, but I wasn't about to correct him. Practically all of my crowd had left by now, so I slowly began to put my equipment away, folding up my sketch board and putting the lids on my paints. About that time another man walked over to me and said softly, "You better watch out for that guy. Be careful. He's dangerous."

"Yeah, I know. Thank you," I said, nervously.

I had parked a long distance away, at least eight blocks, and I was by myself, which compounded my fear. "Lord, I'm trusting you to take care of me," I prayed to myself as I slowly pushed my rig toward my vehicle, determined not to look back or act scared. I didn't know if he was behind me are not. I thought perhaps he was. As I made my way down the sidewalk, many people were around me, but soon I was alone, far from anybody else, and everything got very quiet.

Knowing that around the next corner I would be completely out of everybody's sight, I felt that would be an ideal place for him to jump me. As I turned the corner, I looked back, my heart beating fast. He wasn't there! I was in the clear. Quickly, I loaded everything and drove away. Very few times in my life have I been as afraid as I was that day. Thank God he protected me; no doubt the Lord was answering people's prayers for me.

I thought of the words of the Master: "Blessed are ye, when men shall revile you, and persecute you, and shall say all manner of evil against you falsely, for my sake. Rejoice, and be exceeding glad: for great is your reward in heaven: for so persecuted they the prophets which were before you" (Matthew 5:11–12). In a parallel passage Luke says that when we're hated for Christ's sake, we should leap for joy (Luke 6:23).

Well, I didn't leap for joy because I was persecuted, but I sure enough did leap into my van to get the heck out of there!

CHAPTER 42

IT'S BETTER TO DO SOMETHING THAN NOTHING

As I declared the good news of Jesus Christ, there was a ministry going on at that very moment, in the now, the present. At the exact time that I was preaching the gospel, the Holy Spirit was zeroing in on individuals, reminding them that they needed to get right with God, communicating that they could be set free from their addictions, their fears, their gnawing guilt, and that they could have peace with God. The Lord was at work, actively reaching out to people and saving them, right then, at that very second, and certainly that fact should not ever be minimized.

However, the drawback of sidewalk evangelism was that it was very difficult to follow up those who made decisions for Christ; I knew that they needed to be connected to a local church where other believers could help them grow in their knowledge of Christ. I did what I could to follow up, but, ultimately I trusted God, the Holy Spirit, to continue his work in people's lives.

"Being confident of this very thing, that he which hath begun a good work in you will perform it until the day of Jesus Christ" (Philippians 1:6).

Following up those professing Christ was of the utmost importance; but, first of all, I sought to present a solid gospel and a clear invitation, emphasizing repentance and the Lordship of Christ.

Secondly, I tried to go over the plan of salvation in depth with those whom I counseled, reminding them of the cost of discipleship.

Thirdly I gave out much Christian literature—New Testaments, "Steps to Peace with God," "The Four Spiritual Laws," "Smiles,"

"Little Red Bibles," and also a list of churches to as many people as I could who had indicated that they had just accepted Christ. Later, in my ministry on the streets, I began distributing business reply cards so that I could be contacted. When I received a card, I paid the postage and sent the inquirer a follow-up letter and enrolled him in a Bible correspondence course, similar to the Mail Box Club used by the Open Air Campaigners.

Fourthly, I phoned or even visited key people who made decisions for Christ and who seemed extremely impacted by the Spirit of God.

But it was not easy locating people in New York City. I spent hours searching for a specific apartment. Often people were not home. Some neighborhoods were extremely unsafe, and parking was invariably a problem. Trying to visit someone to do follow-up was difficult, stressful, and time consuming.

I thought about follow-up in this way: If I witnessed a terrible car wreck on the Long Island Expressway, hopefully I would pull over and try to help, dialing 911, breaking the car window, pulling someone from a burning vehicle. The ambulance would then carry the injured person to the hospital; the doctor would perform surgery; the nurse in rehab might work with the guy awhile. All parties involved were important, each having a specific job to do.

On the other hand, after seeing an awful wreck on the LIE, I would never say, "Well, because I cannot take the injured person to the emergency room and operate on him and nurture him back to health, I'm not going to do anything! No, I would do what I could by calling 911 and yanking him from the flames. Other people would have to be involved so that the man could fully recover.

In the exact same way, I would never say, "Well, I know many of those people on the sidewalk are lost, but since I won't be able to baptize them and grow them in my church, I'm not going to even give them the gospel." No, I would do what I could, counting upon others to do what I was unable to do. Better to do something than nothing.

One day in the subway a gentleman by the name of Samuel Williams accepted Christ. He lived close to Manhattan Bible Church, but I did not have my list of churches with me, and we could not think of the exact address of the church. Someone in our group spoke up, "Hey, that man on the train back there was a member of that church, and he gave me a tract. It's got the address on it." We gave Samuel the address, and naturally he was thrilled.

About an hour later a student from Word of Life Bible College came by and recognized us because we had trained him in open air evangelism. The student shared with us that he was now attending Manhattan Bible Church. When we told him about Samuel, he replied, "Give me that card. I'll personally follow him up."

This incident reminded me that salvation was of the Lord and God was very much involved when the gospel was preached in the power the Holy Spirit. And he continued being involved in people's lives long after I was gone, using any number of people to do so.

Once a pastor friend from down south chastised me in a letter, accusing me of being anti-local church. Knowing almost nothing about my sidewalk ministry, he insinuated that I did not follow up anybody. Not long after that, I was at Times Square, and I talked to a young sailor from Mississippi who had been saved under that very pastor's preaching.

"I've really backslidden," the sailor told me. After talking with him for over an hour and going over several Bible verses with him, we had prayer, and the young sailor left rejoicing.

I wrote a letter to my pastor friend and told him that I spent half my time on the street encouraging believers, challenging them to be faithful to their local church—doing follow-up! Then I shared with him that I had recently done some follow-up on one of his converts! My pastor friend wrote back, apologized for his previous words scolding me, and has exhibited a wonderful Christian spirit toward me ever since.

In this kind of ministry on the street I had to believe in the power of the gospel, the power of the Word of God, and the power of the

Holy Spirit. If I hadn't, I would not have lasted six months on the sidewalk. God's Word did not return unto him void (Isaiah 55:11). The gospel was the very power (dynamite) of God (Romans 1:16). The Word of God was the Sword of the Spirit (Ephesians 6:17). The Word of God was sharper than a two-edged sword (Hebrews 4:12). Faith came by hearing the Word of God (Romans 10:17). Some people might not believe those verses, but I did—with all my heart!

The Great Commission involved much more than just preaching the gospel to the lost, but, as an evangelist, I was called to do just that. I had a specific, limited task. The apostle Paul said, "Christ sent me not to baptize but to preach the gospel (1 Corinthians 1:17). Others also were to be involved in discipling, growing, baptizing, and teaching the new converts.

Outdoor evangelism was like a radio or television ministry in some respects. The evangelist on the radio or TV preached the gospel, believing that others were listening, being blessed, encouraged, even being saved even though he neither saw nor heard from most of them.

Referring to the people I had preached to on the streets, an adversary, posing as a Christian friend, once said, "Scott, I don't believe in leaving them. You are leaving them."

My spirit rose up like the hair on the back of a razorback hog!

In response I said, "No, I'm not leaving them; you are. There are thousands upon thousands of people walking on these sidewalks, and you've not even tried to evangelize them. You've left them. I haven't. You've left them without even giving them the gospel. I think it's better to go to the people and give them the gospel and do what you can to follow up on them, than not to go to them at all and not even give them the gospel. No, I have not left them; you have!"

It's better to do something than nothing!

CHAPTER 43

TWO HATS

In January 1995, the Lord dropped something right in my lap. For years I had prayed for a center to house, teach, and train others in open air evangelism. Many individuals and groups had stayed in our home, but always I had prayed for a centrally located facility out of which to work. God answered that prayer.

Farmingdale Baptist Church asked me to be their pastor. After meeting with the church membership, which was down to approximately two dozen, I explained that I would not and could not give up my street ministry. They said that they understood and would work with me, provide housing, and even help support my outdoor evangelistic ministry. The church had excellent facilities, was twelve miles closer to the city than where we now lived in Bay Shore, included a parsonage, and was accessible by train. In return, I would preach, teach, and endeavor to grow the church. Believing this was God's will, I said yes.

This meant that I would be wearing two hats: evangelist and pastor. Relying on the strength and grace of God, I prayed that I would wear both hats well and that the Lord would be glorified. I explained my decision to those back home who supported us, and the vast majority continued to stand behind us. Putting our home up for sale in Bay Shore, we moved into the parsonage.

Soon I was back on the streets, but now I had to prepare sermons for Sunday morning and evening, plus I taught the Bible at Wednesday night prayer meeting. In addition, the normal pastoral duties of counseling, visiting, and administration often kept me up late at night.

The congregation at Farmingdale Baptist was small, but there were some mighty men and women of God who attended. Bob and Judy Campbell, along with Fi Fi Goubran, Fred and Marlene Zwikelmeir, and Pete and Jewel Mavromatis had kept the church doors open with their faithfulness, having been members for years. Cheryl and Buteau Joseph and scores of others became special friends.

Then there were Roy and Barbara Roberts, two more wonderful people. Roy, the music director, was a black man about my age. Always smiling, he was easy to work with and was an excellent singer. But he had no rhythm whatsoever! Waving his hand, he would lead a song with 4/4 time using 3/4 motion.

"Roy," I said one day, "you are the only black man I have ever met who has no rhythm." Was he offended? No way. "I know, but I'm all you've got!" he replied, chuckling like he always did.

One day Roy, who called me "Rev," referred to Linda as "Rev Mother"!

Our close friends, Burris and Jana Jenkins, became members at Farmingdale, and one day the three of us went to downtown Brooklyn to preach the gospel like I had done countless times before. But this was no ordinary day. This was the day the O. J. Simpson verdict was going to be given (October 3, 1995).

As we set up our sketch board on Fulton Street, there was a buzz in the air.

"He'll get off," some were saying. "Guilty, I believe he did it," others mumbled. "Naw! He didn't do it!" was heard over and over.

Preaching on the cross, I proclaimed, "When Christ died, God the Father placed all our sins on him. Jesus bore your death, your judgment, your hell on that cross. He was buried and arose again. The wonderful, thrilling good news is that when we put our faith in Christ as our Lord and Savior, God pronounces us not guilty! You stand before God just as though you have never committed a sin."

As I was speaking about being pronounced not guilty before God, my crowd all turned their heads to the right at the same time, toward a noise, a rumbling. We all heard it. The noise was like "the wave" at a college football game. It came toward us and got louder and louder. "Not guilty! Not guilty! Not guilty!" Then the sound of "not guilty" reverberated past us and went on down the sidewalk.

The people on the street, predominately black, began hugging each other. Men and women embraced; total strangers high-fived each other, thanking God and shouting and clapping.

I felt that O. J. Simpson was guilty. Still do. And later it was clearly proven that he was guilty. But I was not about to voice my opinion at that time. I would have been asking for trouble. To declare in that environment that O. J. Simpson was guilty would have been incendiary language.

Even though we were white and very much in the minority, my friends and I were not scared. There were other whites around. But we felt uncomfortable. Were we in danger? I did not think so. I did know that if the verdict had been "guilty," I would not have wanted to be in downtown Brooklyn!

We slowly got our equipment together and casually walked back to my van. We all breathed a sigh of relief when we were out of the area.

One morning as I drove across the Williamsburg Bridge, I looked at the huge buildings in the financial district, and I thought about the bombing of the federal building in Oklahoma City. What a dastardly act, killing 168 people and injuring many others. "What would prevent somebody from blowing up some of these big buildings?" I thought to myself.

Not long after that, I was ministering in the financial district, and a young woman walked up to me after I had just preached. She introduced herself as Julie, and she was excited about my being close to the World Trade Center. Asking me several questions, she promised me that she would be at my church in Farmingdale Sunday.

Telling Linda about Julie, I didn't know if I would ever see her again. But I was wrong. She and her husband Tim, along with their son, Nicholas, showed up. They lived near the Verrazano Bridge miles away, so they had ridden trains for nearly two hours. All of us at the church were elated. To see connections between the street meetings and the church was uplifting.

Sunday after Sunday Tim, Julie, and Nicholas came to Farmingdale, various ones of us picking them up at the train station. Most of the time Linda prepared Sunday dinner for all of us, and we all got to know each other very well. I came to think of Tim like a son, really. Before long I had the privilege of baptizing both Tim and Julie. Several months later Julie gave birth to Sophia, a precious baby girl.

Tim met me in the South Bronx one afternoon in order to minister with me. Knowing that he had drug issues in his past, I said to him, "Tim, I've been in this area for years. These people know that I have nothing to do with drugs. It would ruin my reputation and credibility if you ever tried anything around here! You know what I mean."

Tim assured me that he was clean and intended to stay that way and that he wanted to try his hand at preaching, using the sketch board and object lessons. He was incredible on the street! Without question, he did the best job of anybody I had ever seen preaching on the street for the very first time.

Tim, in his late thirties, had overcome some major hurdles in his life—drug addiction, feeling unloved, having to make his own way. But with his winning personality and his ability to relate to those on the street, God, no doubt, had awesome plans for Tim.

Farmingdale Baptist Church began to grow, but it was slow growth. Surrounded by Catholics that were deeply embedded in cultural Catholicism, we met families and neighbors who were mostly all Catholics. Going to christenings, being confirmed, attending Catholic school, being married and buried in the Catholic Church, playing bingo and being involved with Catholic charities—that was their way of life; it had been that way for generations. Even when our church won a Catholic on Long Island to Christ, it was extremely difficult to pull him away from the Catholic Church.

In spite of the Roman Catholic doctrine concerning the sacraments, which was incorrect and unbiblical, I knew there were many

Roman Catholics who were saved. But so many more were not. They just had religion and not a relationship with the Lord Jesus Christ.

It was not easy switching hats, going from a pastor at the church to an evangelist on the streets. Juggling both ministries was very challenging.

The businessmen and women in the financial district were the most difficult to reach with the message of Christ. The affluent, self-made movers and shakers were hard to penetrate with the gospel.

One afternoon directly in front of the New York Stock Exchange on the corner of Wall and Broad, a small but attentive crowd listened as I talked about the Bible verse "What does it profit a man if he shall gain the whole world and lose his own soul?" Then, as I was putting up another sheet of newsprint on my sketch board, a sharply dressed gentleman asked me, "Are you going to be here awhile?"

"Yes sir," I replied, "I'll be here for about another hour."

"I'll be back," he said, "I've got a friend I've been talking to. I want him to hear you."

A half hour later as I was addressing about twenty people, I saw that gentleman walk up with another guy, apparently his friend that he had told me about. They stood in the back of the crowd up against the side of the Stock Exchange. They didn't stay long, perhaps five minutes; then, the gentleman nodded at me, and they both walked away, talking to each other. I was blessed, however, because that man, obviously, had been sowing the gospel seed to his business associate. I had watered it. And in due time God would give the increase.

One day when I got home from the city, Linda was totally frustrated. "I've lost my car keys. I've looked everywhere," she said, throwing her hands up.

"I'll help you, honey," I said. "We'll find them."

Well, we looked first in her purse, then all through her car, all around the car, on top of the car, then the house, the church, the church grounds. Still no keys. So I gave her my set of keys to her car.

A couple of days later as Linda was shopping at Waldbaum's, she heard over the loudspeaker, "Will the owner of the car with the license plate YR249 please come to the office?"

"That's me!" Linda said, out loud. "Has somebody run into my car?" and she headed straight to the office. The manager was standing there shaking the car keys in his hand as she walked up. "Are these yours?" he asked.

"Yes, where in the world did you find them? I've been looking everywhere for them," she replied.

About that time a lady spoke up, "I turned them in. I knew you would drive yourself crazy wondering where they were, so I wanted to tell you that I saw them protruding out of the passenger side of the car, in the door. I took them out and turned them in."

"I've searched everywhere for them. Thank you so much," Linda said, laughing. "You mean I've been driving around for two or three days with them in the passenger side?"

When I got home, Linda met me, smiling, with the car keys in her hand. "You won't believe where they were," she said. "I left them in the passenger door. A lady spotted them and turned them in at Waldbaum's!"

"In the passenger door?" I asked.

"Yeah," Linda said, "I don't normally open that door, but it was raining that day, so I ran around to that side, and unlocked that door and quickly put the new insurance card in the glove compartment. I guess I just slammed the door and left them sticking out. I can't believe we overlooked them there."

Grace Fellowship Baptist Church of Andrews, North Carolina, sent their pastor, Mark Chase, and fourteen team members of the church to work with me on the streets. Oh, how I enjoyed seeing all of them laughing and eating around the table in our fellowship hall!

One day they all piled into my van. Talk about being packed in like sardines! I gave them a quick tour of Manhattan, letting them out uptown and meeting them at the Statue of Liberty downtown; we had party-time fun, but I will never attempt that feat again.

God anointed, protected, and blessed our adults' and children's meetings in marvelous ways. And I will always be grateful because it was a huge responsibility transporting that group in and out of the city.

Pastor Loman from the African Congo happened to visit Farmingville Baptist Church, and, learning of my street ministry, he joined me on the streets one evening. How excited he was when he saw the sketch board and the numerous props that I used to attract and hold a street crowd.

"You must teach me this method! Thousands in my country can hear the gospel this way!" he exclaimed with unbounded energy. For the next two weeks I spent hours with him, making him a sketch board and supplying him with many visual aids. I taught him as best I could before he returned to Africa.

"Thank you, my brother," he said. "I know the Lord will use all of this to win many souls in my country to Christ."

A large group, this time from Kentucky, including our friends John and Anita Moore, whom we had met at Grace Baptist Church when we first came up to New York, conducted vacation Bible school at our church in Farmingdale. They did a super job. One afternoon all fifteen of them accompanied me to the streets, and, I believe, caught a glimpse of the "biggest foreign mission field in the world" as they participated in open air meetings on the sidewalks of the Big Apple.

Some mornings before I left for the city, Linda and I had breakfast at the Spartan Diner, both enjoying hot bagels with our coffee. At the diner we met Mohammed, a devout Muslim, whom I came to know rather well. We both were trying to convert each other.

One day Mohammed and his wife, Zenna, also a very devout Muslim, invited me to their home to discuss Christianity, Islam, Jesus, Mohammed, the Bible, and the Koran. I jumped at the opportunity, and all of us shared our views over cake and coffee.

"If you'll come to Farmingville Baptist Church, I'll attend your mosque," I said one day to Mohammed. He agreed. So one

Friday I went with them to the mosque in Westbury, out on Long Island. I was required to wash my hands and take off my shoes before I entered. The mosque was cold, spiritually dead. There was no singing. The women sat in the back; everybody bowed and chanted in unison. Then a cleric delivered a sermon praising Allah, "the only true God, and Mohammed, his Prophet, peace be upon him." I was served refreshments afterward and I felt extremely welcomed.

Mohammed and Zenna never came to church with me, however.

Linda had another fantastic garden with huge tomatoes that she shared with our congregation at Farmingdale. I can't believe that we celebrated another anniversary—our thirty-fourth. My, how the years roll by when you're having fun.

Once, when Bill Britt, my evangelistic friend from Louisiana, was visiting us, I forgot my anniversary, which I had never done before. But we had been so busy that it had slipped my mind. "Scott, do something! Buy Linda some roses or chocolates or something—a card," advised Bill, laughing, but I knew that he was serious. Well, I did purchase a card, and I bought Linda a red and silver aluminum foil balloon on a stick that said "Happy Anniversary." That balloon stayed up twelve years! Much longer than many marriages.

Our younger son, Stewart, who had recently earned his master's degree at Louisiana Tech, told us about a girl from San Diego named Sharon. "She is a ballerina with the Houston Ballet," he said, "and I want y'all to meet her." In a few weeks Linda and I were in Houston for Christmas, and Stewart introduced her to us. Sharon, a lovely, Christian young lady, adored Stewart, and we could tell the feeling was mutual.

A couple of months later, Linda and I hopped on a train out of Grand Central Station in New York and met up with Sharon, on tour in DC. We actually got to see her perform in the ballet, which was quite a treat! In July 2000, Stewart and Sharon flew up from

Houston to New York to be married. Linda and I drove to Kennedy to pick them up. Stewart getting married! Hard to believe.

It seemed like yesterday that he was playing with a caterpillar in a jar as Linda watered flowers in our backyard.

"Stewart, it's time to let him go," said Linda. "He wants to go see his mama."

"No, he don't. He don't have a mama. I threw her over the fence!" answered Stewart as he continued looking at the caterpillar crawling up the grass inside the jar.

Where had the years gone? I remembered when Stew accepted Christ and when I baptized him at Grace Baptist in Lake Grove. Now he was getting married!

Picking them up at the airport, we learned that Sharon's wedding gown did not arrive with the rest of her luggage. What were we going to do? I had no choice but to drive to Kennedy airport at five o'clock the next morning, the morning of the wedding, and pick up her dress. Everybody, especially Sharon, breathed a sigh of relief when I showed up with her gown.

They were married at Farmingdale Baptist Church, and I had the privilege of performing the wedding ceremony (July 20, 2000), as I had done at Stephen and Katie's wedding. Lots of family and friends were present; it was a simple yet beautiful wedding with all of us sensing the very presence of God. As they cut the wedding cake, Sharon smeared cake icing on Stewart's face, to the sheer delight of everybody watching! Stewart's birthday was the next day. What a birthday present—a gorgeous bride!

Several months after they were married, they shared with Linda and me that when Stewart first met Sharon, he was a bit reluctant to tell her about my ministry on the streets, not knowing how she would accept it due to the stigma attached to street preachers. But he eventually told her about my ministry on the sidewalks of New York, and Sharon was thrilled about it. After they told us this, Sharon was quick to add that Stewart was proud of what I did, which was good to know! "I might even perform a 'Christian ballet dance' in one of your meetings," Sharon replied.

One evening at Times Square, Neil Patrick Harris, the actor, walked into my street meeting as I was preaching about being justified before God. I recognized him instantly. Then, a guy in the crowd starting disagreeing with me. "No, that's not right," he said. "You've got to live right, too!" he interjected.

Answering him, I said, "Don't misunderstand me. I'm not saying it's not important to do right, but you do right because you are saved, not in order to be saved."

The man persisted. "Hey, I'm a Christian, and you are not correct," he argued. (I thought, "You are as Christian as Osama bin Laden!")

"Listen, let me talk to you after the meeting, OK?" I replied.

Sensing friction and disharmony, Neil Patrick Harris walked away. Finishing up, I asked my listeners to receive Christ and several people responded, but not Neil Patrick Harris. He was long gone.

Having lost my patience and being extremely disgruntled, I said to the guy who had rudely disagreed with me, "Hey, why couldn't you wait?"

"But you are not correct," he answered.

"Well, there was a well-known actor in the crowd. You made him leave!" I answered, disgusted. "We could have talked later."

The guy, I guess, was a brother in Christ, but his behavior was indefensible, in my opinion.

On another occasion, beneath the flashing lights of Broadway, I had a very interesting conversation with a handsome young man aspiring to be an actor. He reminded me very much of James Stewart, Talking about the cost of discipleship, I said to the young man, "It won't be easy, in fact, it will be extremely hard to stand up and live for Christ in the Broadway play environment." He agreed, but he went ahead and committed his life to Christ.

"Carry the torch high," I said, challenging him.

After we prayed, I said, "You are now my brother in Christ, young man."

My good friend Price Harris of Calvary Baptist Church in Shreveport, Louisiana, invited me to join him and his team in Jamaica. It was a privilege to work with Price, so I gladly went. The trip was refreshing. The bluish-green waters of the Caribbean and the brilliant sun were such a contrast from the frigid weather of New York much of the year. Price and I talked about the time he sang "Amazing Grace" one cold day in the subway.

We had fun at the beach, to be sure, but we worked day and night, preaching in churches, the marketplace in Montego Bay, and in several public schools. After singing their Jamaica National Anthem, hundreds of students, dressed in their clean uniforms, listened to gospel singing and preaching. Only God in heaven knew how many young people got saved. I do know that we always ran out of literature wherever we went.

Soon, however, the pressure of being a pastor hit me right between the eyes. Returning to Farmingdale, I got a late night phone call. "Hello," I said.

"Are you the pastor?" a voice said to me.

"Yes, may I help you?" I answered.

It was the police. "Would you come to this address (a home in the Farmingdale area)? A young man has committed suicide," an officer replied. His father has asked for you."

I went, but I hope I never have to do that again. How tragic. The kid had not given his parents any indication that anything was wrong, so I could only imagine what they were going through. Asked to help officiate at his funeral, I felt so inadequate. His mother and father were devastated, and so was I.

CHAPTER 44

THE OLYMPICS

Howard Greer of Prince Avenue Baptist Church in Athens, Georgia, invited me down to share the gospel at the 1996 Summer Olympics in Georgia. Excited and honored that he thought of me, I said yes, of course. Most of the events were in Atlanta, but some of them were in Athens, so that's where I ministered.

Strolling among the crowds, I declared the gospel with visual aids and object lessons that I used on the streets of New York. One afternoon I spoke to more than fifty German athletes as they sat around waiting for a soccer game. Understanding English remarkably well, they were very open to what I had to say.

One evening in a large outdoor restaurant area, literally hundreds of people were sitting at tables, dining, relaxing, and discussing the events of the day. Wanting to preach to them, I was not sure how to go about it. So I waited. And I prayed. And I waited some more. Then the soccer team from Brazil, dressed out in their colorful yellow T-shirts and bluish-green shorts, put on a soccer exhibition in the center of the area, completely surrounded by people. That was my chance.

When the soccer team finished and the people were cheering, I seized the moment. Stepping into the plaza, I said, "Folks, I'd like to tear this newspaper up and make it come back." I had them. Then, using my set of weigh scales, a dirty rag, and a red cloth, I proclaimed the good news of the Lord Jesus Christ. When I was done, I received a huge ovation. Many Christians shouted, "God bless you, Brother!" I thanked God for giving me that opportunity and enabling me to present Christ.

Of all the experiences I had at the Olympics, one took precedence over the others. A group of teens, dressed in chains and leather, like many in Greenwich Village in New York, at first resented me when I attempted to share the gospel with them. Some were openly hostile. But for several days, I went to where they hung out. I began listening to them, and I sought to build relationships with them. God broke down many barriers, and some of them counted me their friend before the week was over. A young man named Putty told me that he had no father, no brothers or sisters, and that his mother had died, an obvious suicide. Talking with him extensively about the love of God, I saw a change taking place in his life before my very eyes. God's love touched that young man's heart, and I felt that he was a key reason why God had me at the Olympics.

Returning to New York, I found Farmingdale Baptist Church doing quite well. The congregation was increasing in numbers, and I felt that the people were growing in their love for each other. I knew that I needed the strength of the Lord to pastor the church and preach on the streets also.

It was very encouraging to me to have members of Farmingdale minister with me on the streets of New York. But one night something happened that really shook me to the core. Several of us had parked on Thirty-Eighth Street and were walking to meet my friend Al Terhune. Looking forward to preaching at Times Square, I was pushing my rig across Thirty-Ninth Street when a New Testament fell out of my bag onto the pavement. Jana, one of our group, bent down to pick it up, but a cab came speeding by and struck her, knocking her down. And the cab didn't stop. All of us were terrified, not knowing how badly Jana was hurt.

"I'm OK. I'm OK, but I can't get up," Jana said, touching her back; immediately we thought she was paralyzed.

"It's my back, my back," Jana said, groaning.

"Jana, why didn't you get out of the way?" I asked.

"I didn't realize the taxi was coming so fast," she replied.

We gently helped her to her feet, but she couldn't stand up on her own without excruciating pain. Angela and Tom, a young couple from our church, stayed with her while I went to get the van.

"Oh, Lord, please let Jana be OK," I prayed, quickly returning. We carefully put her in the front seat of my vehicle and carried her to Bellevue Hospital. X-rays were taken, revealing a cracked vertebra, but Jana would be OK with rest, we were told. We thanked God that she was not injured more seriously. Soon, Jana was herself, walking like she was lost, laughing, and talking noisily like always.

One afternoon .in the Bronx as I was putting words on my sketch board, some paint dripped on a guy's sneaker. "You gone pay me for my shoes," the young man ordered. "I paid good money for 'em."

"It's just tempera paint. It'll wash off," I replied, as I continued on the sketch board, not really that concerned.

Then, he got louder. "You ruined my shoes," he angrily said, pointing down at his shoe.

"Listen, young man, that little dab of paint didn't hurt your shoe," I retorted. "Wash it off. I'm sorry, but you were standing too close."

He then reached into my rig and started pulling out my heavy chain. "No, put that back," I said, forcefully.

About that time two guys said to the young man, "You heard him. Put it back. Get on back to Brooklyn." (They obviously recognized his Brooklyn accent there in the Bronx.).

"Everything's OK, fellas; thank you, though," I said to them, trying to avoid a fracas.

The young man whose shoe had a little paint on it, then let go of the chain and mumbled, "F*#+ you!" and left. And the two other guys followed.

I preached to a smattering of people, and about a half an hour later, the two guys came back, bragging, "We took care of that guy. We broke his leg in the subway. They took him to Lincoln. We told him to stay the f+*^ out of the Bronx!"

"Man, did you hurt him? I didn't want you to do that," I replied.

"He had no business botherin' your stuff," they said.

I don't know if those guys broke the young man's leg or not. They told me they did, and I don't think they were jivin' me.

Later, I shared the incident with Carl Carrigan, my good friend from Shreveport.

"Well, glory!" he said, smiling and puffing out his chest, "that'll teach 'em to leave the prophet of God alone!"

CHAPTER 45

"ZIP-A-DEE-DOO-DAH DAYS"

Zip-a-dee-doo-dah, Zip-a-dee-ay
My, oh, my, what a wonderful day
Plenty of sunshine heading my way
Zip-a-dee-doo-dah, Zip-a-dee-ay

There were days when everything was going my way. I had beautiful weather, good listening crowds, no hassles with the cops, and there were many professions of faith. I knew people were praying for me, and I could actually feel their prayers. Christians encouraged me. My sermons were unusually anointed by God. I called these "Zip-a-dee-doo-dah days." One of my favorite props was a crystal and one day after I got people's attention with the rope trick, I quickly began throwing the crystal into the air.

As I threw the crystal higher and higher, I told about a man gambling with his entire inheritance, a huge diamond: " 'Throw it up over the water,' somebody shouted. As he threw the diamond high in the air, the ship moved and the diamond bounced off his fingers into the water. Don't gamble with your soul. Jesus said, 'For what does it profit a man if he shall gain the whole world and lose his own soul?' (Matthew 16:26),"

I couldn't believe the number of people that had gathered all around me. Heaven came down and glory filled my soul! Then, a young man raised his hand in the crowd and asked if he could give his testimony. I had to be careful about who I allowed to say a few words because there were shaky individuals out there who would bring reproach upon this ministry by the way they acted and talked. But in this instance, I answered, "Yeah, go ahead."

Stepping up and facing the crowd, he said, "My name is Leonard Richardson. Christ saved me in prison. I went to prison for armed robbery, but now I wear a beeper and work for a bank."

Man, did that validate my preaching, and I thanked God for Leonard's words.

One day the Lord was very gracious by bringing a guy to me who had accepted Christ in one of my meetings months earlier. With a big smile, he exclaimed, "I'm attending Brooklyn Tabernacle, and I'm going to college, too. Oh, yeah, I'm reading through the Bible." How excited he was, and I was "pumped" after he shared his story.

Having little success while conducting several meetings in the cold shade, I moved across the street to the warm sunshine. Using a numbers game, "The 111 Puzzle," as I called it, I was able to draw a huge crowd that instantly gathered around me up close. Then I preached on "The Four Spiritual Laws."

Looking into many Christless eyes, I invited my listeners to give their hearts to Christ. The people responded immediately, and at least fifty people made decisions for Christ.

Jose was one of them. He was very teachable and hung on my every word as I talked with him, emphasizing that he needed to become involved in a good church. I gave him a list of churches, and a Christian woman, who had been in my meeting, then began to share her testimony with Jose. Inviting him to her church, she assured me that Jose would be visited and followed up.

A few minutes later, I began preaching on the topic "What Are You Looking For?" While I was speaking, a man standing in my crowd answered a phone. Glancing at him, I said, "That's a first. A guy making a phone call in a street meeting. That is a first. That is great. You know what I'm saying? It's a different world, isn't it?" (Of course, cell phones soon became so available that everybody carried one.)

That day in the Bronx I had guys and gals piling up all around me. As I painted on the sketch board, there was construction with big heavy equipment working in the background. Out of the corner of my eye, I saw her watching me, a black woman in her twenties, short in stature.

"What's your name?" I asked.

"Lorraine," she replied, and she began opening up to me. Total strangers often shared their secret thoughts and hidden pain. Sometimes after hearing me preach and as we talked privately, they started unloading their burdens. They would not dare do this with their priest, minister, or rabbi, but I was totally anonymous, someone they would never see again, so they held nothing back. All walls came down; all pretense faded, and masks came off. Some vented their anger on me; bitterness erupted at they spewed vitriol and caustic remarks. Some people confided in me about intimate personal problems; addictions were confessed. Affairs, tax evasion, unscrupulous principles in their business, and other secret sins were brought out in the open, often to soothe their consciences.

As Lorraine became transparent, I could tell she was hurting deeply. "You're pregnant and you are on drugs," I said.

"I'm in a program, methadone," she answered.

"Yeah, but that's bad for your kid," I replied.

"I know, but I need help. It's not easy in the streets where I come from. It's not easy. There's drugs all around me and you gotta be strong," she said.

"It must be terrible, but the Lord can change that," I said.

"I give up sometimes. I say, 'Lord, why can't you help me? You help everybody else. Why can't you help me?' " she said sadly.

"Well, you stick around, Lorraine. The Lord will help you," I told her.

As I declared the gospel, I used a number of visual aids, one after another. Then I hung the big coat hanger hook on my lip and dropped the yellow plastic disc that said "Later" on it. "Bite that hook, and Satan will pull you into hell!" I said.

Looking into curious, anxious faces, I said, "Robert Harris, you remember him? In San Quentin? He was killed. Capital punishment.

He said, 'You can be a king or a street sweeper, but everybody dances with the grim reaper.'"

Picking up an hourglass and turning it upside down, I continued, "One of these days, life is going to run out on me. It's going to run out on you. Don't bite that hook. The devil will tell you, 'You have plenty of time.' You don't have plenty of time. Life is going by; it's going by. 'Time, old gypsy man, will you not stay? Put up your caravan just for one day? Time says no, gotta go, gotta go.'"

Many men and women made decisions for Christ and stood around and talked with my friends and me. I really sensed that the Spirit of God was working. I did not know for certain, but I felt the Spirit of God touched Lorraine. She was not there by accident. God had led her there.

Several days later in that same area, a gang leader told a couple of my friends and me, "I like youse guys' courage. As long as youse guys want to come back here, nobody will bother you. I'll see to that!" He took a Bible that we offered him, and then a long, black, stretch limousine picked him up and drove away.

Once again I had a wonderful opportunity to help train several future ministers in open air evangelism. All were foreign students. One man was from Nigeria and spoke five languages. Another was from France; one was from China, and he shared with me about his recent visit in a Chinese prison with a man who had been jailed twenty-five years for daring to preach the gospel out of doors. After hearing about that Chinese brother in prison, I was ashamed of myself for complaining about my problems on the streets of New York!

Another student was from England; still another was from Japan. What was so encouraging to me was the fact that all of these preachers would return to their own countries and possibly put into practice what they learned one windy spring in Brooklyn. The Bible says, "And the things that thou hast heard of me among many witnesses, the same commit thou to faithful men, who shall be able to teach others also" (II Timothy 2:2).

I went to the Fort Green projects, where, the day before, a four-year-old little boy was hit in the head by a stray bullet during a drug war. Pieces of metal shattered in his brain. As I passed out "Smiles," the children, men, women, and long-legged teens that were playing basketball were very receptive. I met a man named Joel Porter. As we chatted, I mentioned that I was from Louisiana. "Buddy Roemer, ever heard of him?" he asked.

"Buddy Roemer? Yeah, we graduated from Bossier High School together!" I replied. Later, I preached on three questions: Is God there? Does he care? Is life fair?

One day in the Bronx, a man named Lewis told me that he had seen me preaching several days earlier in Manhattan. Always, I was amazed when this happened. As large as New York City was, with millions of people, from time to time someone would tell me that he had been in one of my street meetings way across town, perhaps a day or two earlier.

"I'm Roman Catholic," Lewis said when I asked him if he knew the Lord.

"Are you sure you're going to heaven?" I asked.

"I've got it stacked in my favor," he replied.

I presented the gospel to Lewis, explaining that we are not saved by our good deeds. "Would you accept Christ, relying upon just him and what he did for you on the cross?" I asked.

"Yes," Lewis said, and he began to cry. "Why am I crying?" he asked.

"Because you just found the Lord!" I told him. I gave Lewis a marked New Testament, and he couldn't thank me enough. A "Zip-a-dee-doo-dah" day!

Standing in front of Furniture King, I said to an elderly black gentleman with an orange cap, "Let me show you something. We have little Bibles that we give away, and I'm talking about the Lord. You see these three little ropes? I want to make them all the same size. What's your name? My name is Scott."

Shaking my hand, he replied, "George."

Soon others stopped and began listening. It was a gorgeous day, sunny, with a nip in the air, but not really cold. Well into the message, I said, "Now when God looks at us, he doesn't look at the color of our skin, what we have on. He doesn't care what the name of our cat is, who we are; he looks at our heart, and when he looks at our heart, we're just pretty much all the same. Nobody is any better than anybody else. We're all sinners. Christ died for all of us. We all have to be born again to go to heaven. Let me do this newspaper trick. There's nothing magic about what I do. It's just sleight-of-hand, and we're Christians talking about Jesus, and you're valuable, and I hope you have a good day; it's a beautiful day, isn't it?"

I heard somebody say, "It sure is."

"You know, do you thank the Lord for your health?" I asked while I did the newspaper illusion. "I've been on these streets since 1977. I'm from Louisiana originally, but I'm still stuck with my accent. Can't get rid of it, you know. One thing I have learned is that a lot of us have lots of problems, isn't that right?"

I heard someone say, "That's right."

"Sometimes you may look at somebody, and he may not look like he's got any problems, but way down deep inside, he's got some problems. You may be like this." I picked up a compact. "On the outside everything is cool. Nobody knows. See, we have to project an image. Know what I mean? But on the inside we're broken." (I opened up the compact, and it was cracked and shattered.) "We're empty; feel like nobody cares; don't have a sense of why we're on this earth; all messed up inside. Folks, the devil hates you. He's your enemy, not the Lord. The Lord loves you. Jesus said, 'I didn't come to condemn the world but to save the world.' He said, 'I came that you might have life and have it more abundantly.' The devil will do all he can to turn your mind from God. He doesn't want you to take Jesus seriously." As I concluded, I invited people to accept Christ, and George, the old gray-haired, black gentleman, prayed to receive Christ and took a Bible. I held up business reply cards and said, "If you would like to enroll in a Bible correspondence course, just fill this card out and send it to me. You don't even need a stamp." Many hands reached and took them from me.

The sun reflected off the newsprint, making me squint. I heard, "Check it out. Check it out," from guys barking at pedestrians walking down the sidewalk, attempting to pull them into their stores. After putting my message outline on my sketch board, I turned and people were everywhere, standing, waiting. Sometimes it was like that. But while using my red macrame twine, I cut my finger with the scissors, blood dripping on the pavement. A man in the crowd gave me a napkin, but I didn't think I would ever stop bleeding! Talking to people standing there, straining to hear, I said, "You may be like that prodigal son. But God is waiting on you with open arms. He has been chasing you a long time with a big bucket of love." The response was so great that I knew that the Holy Spirit was mightily at work!

After I had finished preaching and had talked with a number of people, a girl named Snowy walked up to me. A black woman in her forties, she had a round face and melancholy eyes. But she began to sing with just a sprinkling of people still hanging around—"He's got the whole world in his hands." Nobody listened much; but it didn't seem to matter to her. Snowy then told me that God cared for me and loved me and that I was obeying him.

"Your song touched me," I said, clasping her hand and kissing her on the cheek.

"God will bless you," she replied.

Later, holding the arrow in my hand, I described it. "This arrow is aluminum. It has three feathers; it has a certain stiffness; that's called the 'spine.' It was made for my bow, a forty-pound pull. The bow and the arrow go together. My friend, you are made for God. You and God go together." As I declared the good news, the noise around me was unusually loud. Airplanes roared overhead, and at the same time, a fire truck, with its siren blaring, struggled to squeeze through the thick traffic. But my crowd stayed with me. I don't believe anybody walked out of the meeting!

Despite the deafening racket and pandemonium, one of the people who called on the name of the Lord was a man named Oscar. As he prayed, two people were standing on the corner, waiting to cross the street. When Oscar looked up, one of those waiting was a minister who had been witnessing to Oscar. They recognized each other. The preacher said to me, "I've been trying to win this man to Christ." That was absolutely incredible to me! The other person who had been waiting for the light to change was a Christian woman who smiled and quoted scripture, saying, "One sows; another waters; but God gives the increase."

One breezy April afternoon I talked with a huge guy in a blue T-shirt, named Sal. "I'm a drug addict," he shared with me. "All my friends are either dead, married, in jail, or like me, hanging out and getting high. I'm no longer on heroin. I'm on pills. I went to the hospital on a detox program. I'm back out on pills. I even give pills to my friends."

"Why do you take drugs? Ever thought about it, Sal?" I asked.

"To get high," he replied, "I'm beginning to think I need a miracle."

Giving him the address of Teen Challenge, I urged him to check it out.

Walking by a small park, I saw a whole string of junkies, both men and women, sitting on a bench. "Hey, y'all. Let me show you a newspaper trick," I said.

"You're white with blue eyes and a Southern accent," one man said to me.

"Oh, God don't care if I'm white," I answered. Then, using my set of weigh scales, I shared with them the good news of the Lord Jesus Christ. Oh, how they thanked me, their prejudice erased!

I was honored one day to work with sixteen Mennonites. Having come from Pennsylvania to start a church in New York City, they exemplified purity and decency. The men, with their thick, black beards, and the ladies, with their beanie caps, radiated warmth and sincere, Christian love; they were shining as lights in a spiritually dark and morally loose city.

Yes, sometimes I went for weeks without any real problems whatsoever—"Zip-a-dee-doo-dah days"! Many people stopped and listened. Store owners were unusually friendly; the policemen were kind and considerate, and they complimented me. The weather was neither too hot nor too cold. I could tell that scores of people were praying for me, really and seriously praying for me. My heart swelled with satisfaction because God engulfed all that I attempted to do. Like Burris's boat, *Ararat,* that was made to sail, I felt that I was made to do exactly what I was doing—sharing the riches of God's grace to spiritually bankrupt recipients who were walking down worn-out sidewalks.

CHAPTER 46

EVERYDAY OCCURRENCES

I see many headsets today. It's like everybody is trying to escape. One lady walking down Second Avenue has a headset and a green T-shirt that says "Leave Me Alone." An old man goes through the trash, but the one legged beggar who shakes his tin cup constantly in front of the drugstore is not there. He looked so bad the last time I saw him, unshaven, with sunken eyes. The other day as I preached, he would not make eye contact with me, not for long, anyway. His rattling tin cup bothered me a little, but I raised my voice over the noise.

A black woman comes out of the Social Service building on Fourteenth Street. Wearing a green sweater, she pulls it down over her shoulders and begins to scream with a very high-pitched, shrill voice. Turning around and around, the woman hollers, "Nobody will listen to me! Nobody cares! Nobody will listen to me! Nobody cares!" Everybody mostly ignores her.

Extremely intelligent and articulate and able to argue his case exceptionally well, the Muslim says to me after we discussed the concept of the trinity, "You really are insane! You need to be committed. God cannot be three yet one!" Gloating and convinced that he's correct, he leaves, shaking his head. I chuckle, remembering that some of Jesus's religious contemporaries said that he was beside himself!

"Let me illustrate it with this rope," I said to a nice group that had gathered around me at Albee Square. "Miss, if you'll hold this end, and sir, if you'll hold this end—hold it tight. Now, let's say that on this end is God, and over here is man…"

"OK, break it up! Break it up!" I heard somebody say.

I turned and, seeing a cop, I said, "Officer, I'm preaching the gospel."

"No, you're not!" he replied.

"Yes, sir, I am," I said, trying to explain. "I use visual aids and object lessons to tell people about Christ."

"Well, you're not going to do it here. If you don't stop, I'll arrest you!" he said, bullylike.

"Sir, I have a right," I replied, noticing that practically everybody had walked away from my meeting; they had really been into what I was saying, and this cop ruined it.

"If you're here in half hour, I'll arrest you," he answered and walked on down the sidewalk in a cocky sort of way.

This was becoming more and more commonplace, getting threats from the policemen. Standing there, I didn't know what to do. A black guy who obviously had seen everything said, "That's just the devil. He hates when we preach the gospel." We talked a little bit, and he tried to encourage me. Then he began walking around and preaching at people and quoting the Bible, but nobody was stopping. This was the normal way people preached on the sidewalks all over the city. They meant well, but mostly they were ignored.

He came over and prayed for me and reminded me again that Satan was using that cop to derail me. I thanked him, and he melted into the crowd.

Nervous, I made sure that I waited at least an hour, but the officer who had rudely interrupted me never returned. The young black guy was correct. This was just an attempt by Satan to prevent me from sharing the gospel. I knew that I was involved in spiritual warfare. The NYPD was not my enemy. The devil was! "For we wrestle not against flesh and blood, but against principalities, against powers, against the rulers of the darkness of this world, against spiritual wickedness in high places" (Ephesians 6:12).

One evening at Times Square, Burris and I were talking to a limo driver who seemed to have a real problem with adultery. While our conversation was taking place, a drunk began to dance and put on a show. He said to the limo driver, "Don't listen to them! Don't listen to them!"

Trying to get rid of the drunkard, I bought him a hot dog, but he did not leave. I prayed with him. He still did not leave.

"Beat it! Or I'm going to call the cops!" I ordered. But that tactic didn't work either. Finally, I led him down the sidewalk away from Burris and the limo driver. Getting confused, he wandered off. Walking back to where Burris was, he told me that the limo driver sloughed off everything he said.

Later, Burris and I talked to a fine Christian couple from Longview, Texas. "Hey, I'm from Shreveport!" I told them. "Not far from you."

"We know; we're in Shreveport a lot," they replied. They assured us that they would keep us in prayer.

A thin black guy walked up and asked for some money. I reached for my wallet, but then I changed my mind. Instead, we took the guy to Wendy's and bought him a bowl of chili. We shared Christ with him and gave him the address of the Salvation Army and Grace and Hope Mission.

Two godly women ran Grace and Hope Mission, located on Fourteenth Street and Third Avenue. Living above the mission, they showed a gospel film and served hot meals every Friday night. One day at noon I saw them playing the trumpet and the accordion on the street corner. Nobody was stopping, but they were out there trying. I admired their zeal.

One day a very distinguished gentleman in advertising who was about ready to retire talked to me. He had gone his entire life without the Lord, and he did not see anything wrong with chasing girls, which was comical, given his age. I challenged him to attend Calvary Baptist Church on Fifty-Seventh Street, but I was not optimistic that he would ever show up.

After talking with this man I thought about a guy that I had met on the train years ago when I first visited George in Hicksville.

His name was Hal. He also was in advertising. He told me he was responsible for the "Parade" supplement in the newspaper.

"Hal," I asked, "what's your life all about, my friend?"

"All I do is ride this train in and out of the city, day after day after day," he answered. "That's all I do—work, work, work."

I shared the gospel with Hal, but I don't think he heard me.

A man one day stood in my crowd, and he had a can of beer hidden in a newspaper. After I had finished preaching the gospel, I talked with him a few minutes, and he accepted Christ. I noticed the can of beer, but I never mentioned it. But he immediately began to ask me questions about drinking, and he also expressed a concern for his parents. I think God was ridding him of his old habits and placing a desire in him to reach out to others, which is exactly what happens when a person comes to know Christ.

"Therefore if any man be in Christ, he is a new creature: old things are passed away; behold, all things are become new" (2 Corinthians 5:17).

Al Terhune was a short guy from Jersey. He wasn't fat, but he was stocky. In his fifties, fair skinned, with a dark beard and red cheeks, he was losing a little hair, but it didn't bother him a bit. Married with three daughters, Al was a talented sidewalk preacher, constantly charming his listeners. We worked together quite often. Al was funny, full of jokes, and with his humor he had instant rapport with his street crowds. Proficient with "magic," Al was always learning some new tricks. I usually did maybe two sleight-of-hand tricks, but then I quickly got into the gospel, using my sketch board and visual aids. But Al would use four or five sleight-of-hand tricks. That's what he liked to do, and he was good at it.

One cloudy afternoon Al did the rope trick and said, "I've got another one, folks. What I'm going to need is for everybody to take one step forward. You're going to love this one. I took a shower before I came here, OK?" Smiling, the people stepped forward.

Then Al did the coin trick. Then the newspaper trick. Then a new sleight-of-hand trick.

When he asked a young woman, "Will you hold my skissors? I can't say scissors," everybody laughed.

Al preached on justification and quoted Romans 5:1, Ephesians 2:8, and Romans 5:8. Hitting a spike with a rock, he quoted John 3:16. "Christ died for the ungodly," he said. "They don't come as ungodly as me, and here I am preaching the gospel of Jesus Christ. I know I'm a sinner. I'm from Jersey City. I lived in the projects all my life. I remember being a teenager and taking a baseball bat to somebody's head because he was in a different gang than I was." When Al invited people to put their faith in Christ as their Lord and Savior, it looked like his entire crowd raised their hands. Praise the Lord!

Al and I ministered in the Financial District one bright fall day. Businessmen played chess behind us on their lunch hour in Liberty Park. Addressing a white-collar crowd when it was my turn to preach, I said, "Jesse Ventura said, 'My wife goes to church every Sunday 'cause she needs to, and that's a weakness'…The question before us this afternoon is, do you really think it's weakness to need God?" After I preached, a number of businessmen and women took Christian literature from us. Then I walked up to a young man who had been listening. Tanned, with thick, black hair and wearing a brown leather jacket, and with a camera hanging around his neck, he seemed very interested in what I had just said.

"My friend," I said, "there will always be an emptiness," but before I could complete my sentence he replied, "Yeah."

"Until you connect with Jesus," I said. "He is the water of life. You're not here by accident. God led you here."

We had a meaningful conversation, and then the young man left. Stepping back, I noticed a man carrying a sack lunch and several women in sneakers. Then a Sikh, wearing a black turban, black suit, and tie, and having a neatly trimmed black beard, walked past Al and me like he was late for an appointment.

One evening as some friends of mine and I were packing up and leaving Midtown, I noticed a thin little man in blue khakis working with some buckets of water and ropes on the sidewalk. Chatting with him, I learned that he was a window washer who cleaned the windows of the tall skyscrapers in Manhattan.

"Man, don't you get scared when you're like fifty floors up?" I asked. "I've seen you guys way up there."

Looking straight up and seemingly undaunted, he replied, "Well, after about five stories up, it doesn't matter how high up you are."

"Make sure you are right with God," I said to him as my friends and I began walking back to my van.

Even with the threat of rain and heavy clouds rolling in, I had a wonderful crowd. "Hear me, please," I said, projecting my voice so everybody could hear. "What I'm about to say is very narrow minded, very intolerant. Not politically correct at all, but hear me please; here me out, OK? Jesus said, 'I am the way, the truth, and the life; no man comes to the father except by me' (John 14:6). You say, 'That's so narrow minded!' My friends, don't turn me off. Let me explain." As I spoke, I turned and drew a house on the sketch board. "My wife is a great cook. Let's just say that we invite all of you for breakfast—Linda makes homemade biscuits, bacon, eggs, pancakes—the works. All of you are invited." I then drew a road to the house and scribbled "Delaware Avenue." "But in order to get to our house, you gotta go down Delaware Avenue."

Somebody said, "That's not fair. I don't want to go down Delaware Avenue. I want to take sixth Avenue or Broadway."

"You can if you want to," I said, "but you won't get to my house. Now, here's the point. God wants all of us to go to heaven; everybody is invited. You're all invited. But the way to him is through Jesus Christ. He's the way. Somebody says, 'Well, I don't want to go that way. I want to go another way. I have my own religion.' Well, you can if you want to, but the Bible says you won't get to heaven. You see, God loves all of us the same. God is no respecter of persons. He's not partial. God doesn't have one way for the Jew, another way for the Muslim, another way for the Hindus, still another way for the Christian. No. God says I love all of you the same. My son died for all of you and rose again, and all of you must come to me the same way—through him!"

Considering the controversial nature of my sermon in our society today, I felt that my message was well received, and I thanked God.

Several of us—Carl, Al, Ellis, and I—were sharing the gospel with group after group at Fulton Mall. When it was my turn to preach, I wrote on the sketch board in block lettering, "Who Is Jesus?"

In the middle of my message a man bellowed out, "He was just a prophet, like Moses and Abraham, and he's dead."

Trying not to sound argumentative, I answered him, "The Bible says that he arose from the dead, proving that he was the Son of God."

"Where does it say that in the Bible?" he asked, sarcastically.

"If I show it to you, will you believe it?" I said.

"I doubt it; the Bible was tampered with," he replied.

"Well, if you won't believe it, why should I show it to you?" I asked. (I used this strategy quite often, saying, "Why should I show it to you if you won't believe it?")

Our Brooklyn crowd, hearing us, began increasing in size. Then, a small, slender black man with loose, shaggy pants, interjected, "What difference does it make if he died for us? That was two thousand years ago!"

"My friend," I replied, "does it make any difference what Abraham Lincoln did? What he did many years ago affects us today."

Then the small, slender black guy brought up the race problem.

"I can give you the answer," I said, as I turned to a woman in my crowd. "You see this lady? She's a black lady, but I don't even know her, and she doesn't even know me. But she's a Christian and loves me, and I'm a Christian and love her. Christ is the answer."

The woman smiled and said quietly, "That's right."

Then Ellis took over. Another one of my preaching buddies, Ellis Beresford was a light-skinned black with a Jamaican accent. Because he prayed with such fervor and power, we often asked him to pray before and after our street meetings—off to the side, unnoticed, where people would not think we were Pharisees or hypocrites praying on the corner to be "seen of men" (Matthew 6:5).

Ellis had a big smile, was friendly, and yet was very serious minded. When I was threatened by hostile blacks from time to time, I was glad to have Ellis by my side. He loved the Lord Jesus Christ, was not afraid to stand up for Jesus, and was always ready to defend my preaching and me.

Taking a few steps into the crowd, Ellis began speaking with authority. "What this man is saying is true. I used to doubt that Christ was God. But I began to study my Bible, and I discovered he is God. I gave my heart to him, and when I did, I began to shake like I was hit by an electric current, and now I'm out here on the streets preaching about him."

The two men who had caused a disturbance were disarmed completely. Ellis continued and preached an anointed message, with lots of people thanking us and agreeing with us, most of them being black.

A teacher at Christ for the Nations Bible College in Stony Brook asked me to take dozens of students to the streets for training in open air evangelism. I told him that I would deem it an honor to do so, but I was uptight just thinking about it. People back home must have been praying for me because I sensed the hand of God at every turn, from finding a convenient parking place quickly to not having any interference. We had many successful sidewalk meetings. A few of the students gave testimonies, and many had the opportunity to share Christ one on one. I knew they would never be the same after ministering on the front lines.

Speaking to a man one day on the corner of Fourteenth Street and Second Avenue, I said, "I saw you standing here, and you look kind of lonely."

"It shows, uh?" he answered, a little embarrassed. He told me his name was Tom O'Brien.

He and I talked a little bit, and then Tom said, "I hope Jesus can help me get over my loneliness."

Giving him a banana, a cup of coffee, fifty cents, and a "Smile," I told him, "Jesus is the water of life, and he can help you get over your loneliness. I guarantee it, Tom."

A taxi driver in Fairlawn, New Jersey, named Richard McDermott, was a committed Christian who sometimes met me in the city in order to evangelize. He usually passed out tracts, "Smiles," and other Christian literature, although he did preach occasionally.

"A guy pulled a knife on me in the taxi, but I got away," he told a crowd one afternoon in lower Manhattan. "But I knew I was prepared to meet the Lord. Are you prepared? Jesus said, 'You must be born again or you won't go to heaven' (John 3:3). Have you been born again?"

Richard was a young man in his late thirties who was very quiet natured, organized, and deliberate in everything he did. Extremely faithful, he sometimes stood in the subways for hours by himself, passing out tracts. Average size, he went bald at an early age, and for a while he wore a toupee. He was unmarried, and after our street meetings, sometimes girls hung around him and whispered about his "gorgeous green eyes."

"Rich, did you get that girl's phone number?" I would ask, laughing, "She sure seemed interested."

"The Lord will lead me to the right one if he wants me to get married," he would softly answer.

Driving across Brooklyn on Atlantic Avenue, I saw a LIRR train pass above me on my left and then go underground like a giant whale going underwater. Looking everywhere, I drove around for well over an hour, but I finally found a parking place. But I still was at least five long New York City blocks away from where I wanted to preach. Feeding my parking meter, I set my sketch board up not far from Brooklyn Tabernacle. After struggling for several minutes to get somebody to stop, I finally asked a kid who was walking by if he would stop and help me get a crowd. "I'm preaching the gospel, young man," I said. He consented, and in a few minutes several more shoppers started listening. Preaching on "The Rich Fool" (Luke 12:13–21), I had three points: At the Top, Life of the Party, and Eat, Drink, and Be Merry.

"Now, folks, I don't want anybody's money." (I pulled from my rig some huge five-, ten-, and twenty-dollar bills.) "But it would be nice to have some of that, wouldn't it! I heard Ted Turner say on *Larry King Live*, 'Money won't make you happy, but only those of us who have it know that!' Jesus said, 'A man's life consists not in the abundance of the things which he possesseth' (Luke 12:15)."

Afterward, I had an interesting conversation with a distinguished man in a brown suit. From Peru, he had a PhD in linguistics. Seemingly unaware of his need for Christ, he walked away without realizing that in his present condition he was already condemned for not believing and under the wrath of God at that very moment.

Later that day, as I was preaching, three blacks wanted me to say that Jesus was black.

"Jesus was a Jew," I exclaimed. "He probably was pretty dark, but he was a Jew, not a black man. He was a carpenter, you know, and worked outside in that hot, Galilean sun, but he really wasn't black; he was a Jew."

While I continued speaking, a teenager, when I wasn't looking, tried to steal the rope ladder that I used for an illustration, but people in my crowd scolded him. "Can you believe that? He's trying to preach to us, to do us good, and some guy's trying to take his things," one woman said.

I hurried back to my van because I knew my meter was running out of time. I sure didn't want to get a parking ticket; in this area a parking ticket was fifty-five dollars.

Two buddies joined me one evening at Times Square—Sal Costanza and Mark Hurd, both fine young men of God. Sal, my mechanic, was also studying to be a pastor. Steeped in the knowledge of the Bible, Sal preached for me at Farmingdale sometimes when I was out of town. Mark was an astute businessman. He ran his own company and was a natural at anything he tried. Sensing a call to preach, he also filled the pulpit for me when I was away.

During one of our meetings that I felt was composed of many believers, I preached on the second coming of Christ. "One day Jesus will return with power and great glory," I declared. When I was finished, a jovial black guy with a big chest and a broad smile approached me. "Can I ask you a question? I'm a Christian, too," he said.

"Sure, brother, go ahead," I replied.

"You said that when Christ returns, he'll bring back those believers who have died with him. Why do you say that?" he asked. "They are in the grave. They'll be resurrected when Jesus returns. I don't understand."

"My friend, yes, their bodies will be resurrected. But their spirits are with Christ, and he'll bring them back with him when he returns. Let me show you," I answered. I turned to 1 Thessalonians 4:14 and read, "So them also which sleep in Jesus will God bring with him."

"No," the young man emphatically said to me, "they are in the grave!"

"Their bodies are in the grave, but their spirits are with Christ, and when he returns, he will bring them with him," I said.

Sal and Mark were listening as this guy and I debated for about twenty minutes. "What does this mean?" I asked.

"Let me finish," he said. "You keep interrupting me. Let me finish."

Our dialogue was very friendly, and both of us were smiling; but neither of us could convince the other.

"Well, my friend, we've reached an impasse. But you are my brother, and I love you, man," I replied.

Grinning and chuckling, he answered, "I love you, too." Then he gave me a huge bear hug.

Both Sal and Mark were very teachable, and they had minis-tered with me on the streets before; so, they understood that this kind of conversation took place from time to time.

On the sidewalks of New York City, I never knew what somebody might ask me. "Be ready always to give an answer to every man that asketh you a reason of the hope that is in you with meekness and fear" (1 Peter 3:15). I constantly prayed for wisdom as I counseled with people, and I tried to be prepared for anything!

CHAPTER 47

BORING? NO WAY!

Preaching the gospel on the sidewalks of New York City was anything but dull. I never knew what was around the corner, literally. Sometimes I was shocked, stunned by what I saw and heard. Other times I was saddened, perplexed, and I was entertained, constantly. No two days were ever the same, and certainly no two street meetings were alike. When I was on the sidewalk, I didn't know what might happen. Yes, I got bone tired, but never bored. I lived in suspense, never knowing what to expect.

One afternoon, not far from Soho, several of us were conducting street meetings—David Braun, Burris and Jana Jenkins, Richard Solomon, and I.

After preaching on the subject "Ever Feel Empty?" I walked over to a very attractive young woman who had been listening. Wearing a blue low-cut blouse and light blue shorts and showcasing big gold earrings with her hair pulled back in a bob, she was a knockout! We began talking about God, the holiness of God, and God's love. I kept trying to find out if she was a Christian by asking her several questions, but she quickly changed the subject. Using my red cloth and dirty rag, I illustrated that Christ's blood covers all our sins. Then she revealed to me something that caught me completely off guard. Pulling me off to the side, she said that she was born a little boy. "I've had the sex change," she told me, meaning, of course, that she had had all the surgeries and treatments and was now a woman.

Trying not to reveal my surprise, I told her that God loved her no matter what. "If I accept Christ, what gender do I have sex with?" she asked sincerely.

"Miss," I replied, "you must accept Christ as your Lord and Savior. Do that first. Get that issue settled. Then get into a good church; read your Bible. I don't have all the answers. God the Holy Spirit will reveal to you what you should do and what you should not do."

"Can that blood actually cover everything?" she asked, questioning its sufficiency.

"Yes, it avails for everything," I said, knowing that I was telling her the truth.

"I'll think about it," she said. After I had a brief prayer with her, she slowly walked away.

Often, I was confounded on the streets, but bored? No way!

One day after setting up my equipment in front of McCrory's, I wrote on my sketch board "Who Is Jesus?" I had four points: a Man, God, the Son of God, and Lord. After I had explained the best that I could that Jesus was a man and yet also God, I began talking about Jesus being the Son of God. Then a man interrupted me, saying, "If you show me in red where Jesus in his own words said that he was the Son of God, I'll eat it!"

A large crowd was already around me, but it got bigger, wanting to see what was going to happen. "Show me in red where Jesus said in his own words that he was the Son of God, and I'll eat those words!" the man reiterated arrogantly.

A young lady who had been listening to me preach and who had been "amening" me was standing in the front of the crowd. Facing the guy who had challenged me, she exclaimed, "If you'll be quiet, he'll show you!" As she looked at me, I could tell that she was depending on me to come through. I turned to John chapter 10 and showed him, in red letters, Jesus's own words, where he said he was the Son of God.

"OK, let's see you eat it!" I said as I put the Bible up to his face. "Come on, you said you would eat it!" Everybody began to laugh, including the lady that had looked to me to prove him wrong. Several people pointed their fingers at him and said, "Come on, now. Come on, now. Eat it. Eat it."

The guy was still staring at John chapter 10 when another man began shaking his hand over the Bible. I did not know what he was doing, and I said, "No, that's the word of God!" He then said, "I was just pouring salt on the words!"

"Oh," I said, laughing.

Then the guy shoved the Bible away and said, "No, that's not true. Jesus is not the Son of God. The Bible's been tampered with." Then he stormed off amid jeers and catcalls.

Challenged? Yes, but never bored!

My friend George Naggy looked like Carroll O'Connor, so much so that from time to time in our street meetings I would introduce him to the crowd by saying, "Well, we've got Archie Bunker up next. Give him a hand."

The people instantly noticed the remarkable resemblance to "Archie," and usually clapped and smiled. You could hear, "He does look like Archie, doesn't he?"

Laughing, George retaliated by referring to me as Andy Griffith.

One day "Archie" was preaching and a pigeon flew over him, leaving a glob of white pigeon droppings running down his forehead.

"We all know what God thinks of your sermon, George!" we said, joking. I had fun on the sidewalks of New York. It was never a dull day.

Often, huge eighteen wheelers lined the side streets. Camera crews were busy filming. Microphones, heavy black electrical cords, and lighting equipment that were scattered all around made it difficult to drive through. One day in Brooklyn, not far from Junior's, known for its famous cheesecake, I saw a number of black men— extraordinarily black—milling around in front of the bank. Learning they were Aborigines from Australia that were in town for that very reason—to make a movie—I grabbed my bag of tricks and object lessons and quickly shared the gospel with them, surprised that they understood English so well. They appeared to be extremely interested. Only God knows what was accomplished, but I felt that just as the Lord guided the arrow to Jehu's heel, he directed those indigenous Australians to me so that I might share the good news of Christ with them.

A few minutes later I found myself eating a delicious piece of fresh strawberry cheesecake at Junior's, with a hot cup of coffee, of course. As I briefly shared a word with the waiter, he interrupted me. "I don't know what you're talking about. I've never heard of him [Jesus]. The cross, what do you mean?" he asked, with a puzzled face. I left him a "Smile" along with my tip, but I never had an opportunity to say anything else to him, and I never saw him again; and I ate cheesecake at Junior's every chance I got.

Most people that I met in New York had a smattering of gospel truth; the vast majority of which just did not have a correct understanding of how to be made right with God according to the Bible. However, I did bump into a person from time to time who had never even heard the name "Jesus."

One evening at Times Square I had an interesting conversation with a gentleman from China. Dressed in a sharp business suit, he told me he had never heard about Jesus Christ. "Who was he?" he asked. Attempting to start a conversation with him, I said, "What is life about?"

"Money! What else?" he said rather loudly, and walked across Broadway into the masses of people.

Preaching on the sidewalks was never humdrum. More than a few times I had an individual in my audience holding a python around his neck. One day a guy was listening while gently petting the feathered head of a big auburn rooster, soon to be engaged in a cockfight, no doubt. At certain times and places drug deals were going down; pills were exchanged for cash; lesbians kissed; homosexual men held hands and carried on as I shared the good news.

Late one evening a guy walked into my crowd and said, "Women don't really care what size a man's d ^*# is! It don't matter to them, I tell ya."

Jack Kreidler, my OAC evangelist friend from Rome, was giving his testimony, and a hooker walked up, grabbed him in the crotch, and said, "From Italy, huh!" Laughing, she strutted on down Broadway in her high heels.

Bill Britt, whom I had known for years, was an anointed preacher if ever there was one; and, man, was he comical and entertaining, always telling funny jokes. One hot day in the South Bronx after Bill had led many people to Christ, he handed out business reply cards. "Fill this card out, folks, and we will send you some aides" (many in his crowd thought he meant AIDS). There we were in the South Bronx, where a large percentage of our crowd, without doubt, was infected with HIV, and Bill was talking about sending them some "aides." Perhaps we were being callous about that terrifying disease, but later we had fun with Bill over that comment. "That was real smart, Bill," we said, in jest, "as if there is not enough AIDS around here!"

Ray Wilson, another friend from Louisiana, was fired up one night as he preached. Somebody in his crowd began refuting him, shouting out, "That's not true!" Ray barked back with great intensity, "I rebuke you in the name of the devil!" (He meant, of course, to say in the name of Jesus.) You think my buddies and I didn't rub it in—that slip of the tongue?

It was Fleet Week, and hundreds of sailors decked out in their all-white, creased uniforms walked up and down Broadway, looking at the bright lights, talking to each other, and enjoying themselves. As I began drawing up a crowd, a black Muslim who had set up a card table not far from me walked over and arrogantly proclaimed in front of everybody that Allah was the true God, and Mohammed was his prophet. Of course, this scattered my crowd, like blackbirds fly off when you get too close to them.

"You're not going to preach tonight," he boasted. "Every time you start, I'll run 'em off!"

Over and over the Muslim did this, and he prevented me from preaching effectively because he was so annoying and disruptive.

I was chapped, but what could I do? Being frustrated, I said, "Lord, I'm going to try one more time. If you don't intervene, I'm leaving."

Using a sleight-of-hand trick in an effort to gather another group of people, I glanced at the Muslim and saw that he was watching. But when I did the newspaper trick, sailors gathered around me, coming from all directions. Boom!

They were there, perhaps forty of them. Other people soon followed, and I had a massive audience.

"Get in close, folks, I can't block the back," I said.

The power of God fell on me. I had a supernatural anointing from the Holy Spirit. With all of those sailors in their white uniforms teaming around me as well as other people, I looked at the Muslim, and I could tell that he was fuming by the expression on his face. I felt like saying to him, "Come on. Come on. Go ahead and try to interfere!"

A young man who was soon to be a missionary in the Middle East worked with me one day in the city. When we ate lunch at Wendy's, there was an extremely attractive young lady sitting a few feet from us. Dressed provocatively, she was indeed a beautiful girl.

"Should I witness to her?" this young man asked. He was obviously wanting to have a conversation with her.

"Go ahead. You're single," I said, laughing a little bit.

Well, he began talking with her, and soon I joined in. We learned that the young lady had been a prostitute for about a month and was the daughter of a preacher. After emphasizing that she was valuable and reminding her of the consequences of her actions, we had prayer with the girl.

When she left, this young man earnestly said to me, "You know, I always wondered if I could marry somebody who was a prostitute, and believe me, I could definitely marry that girl, prostitute or not!"

Stuck in traffic on Thirty-Fourth Street, I had my window rolled down. A cab driver going the other direction pulled up beside me.

As we looked at each other eye to eye, he shook a fistful of dollars in my face. "Don't you wish you had that?" he said, bragging.

"I've got something better—Jesus, the Water of Life!" I replied. Handing him a "Smile," I said, "Here, this is more valuable than money." The cab driver's smile disappeared, and his face fell as he sped away.

One crisp, early spring day when Troy Terrel was preaching, fire trucks, with sirens blaring, came from all directions. Firemen jumped off trucks and started pulling hoses just a few feet from the street meeting. Troy's crowd didn't think much about it. They looked at the smoke across the street and then fastened their eyes once again on Troy. In the middle of all of that confusion, with firemen walking around, working, pointing at the smoke, and yelling, Troy shared the good news. To our amazement his audience stayed.

A half hour later, Carl, with his white baseball cap on, had his listeners eating out of his hand. He was having fun with the big rat trap he held; his wife, Carolyn, had colorfully decorated it, and we called a "Sin Trap." Carl said, jokingly, "I'm quick, very, very quick. My hands are so quick I can almost catch two flies leaving in different directions." Many people had gathered around him, wide eyed, anxious to see what was about to happen. About that time a large furniture truck started backing in behind the crowd, pushing the people in tighter. Spotting a lovely young lady with a beautiful smile and who was wearing a green windbreaker, Carl, undaunted, said, "This looks like a nice lady," as he took her hand.

"Are you right handed or left handed?" he asked.

"Right," she replied, grinning.

Holding her right hand, Carl asked, "This is the hand you write with and eat with?"

The woman nodded yes.

Carl then dropped her right hand and grabbed her left hand. "Then let me use this hand," he replied. The woman laughed out loud, and so did everyone else.

Carl, full of energy and passion, then emphasized that you can flirt with sin, but sooner or later you'll get caught, like you'll get caught if you play around with a rat trap.

"Be sure your sin will find you out!" he warned.

A few minutes later, Carl preached his classic sermon titled "The Empty-Heart Question." Oh, how the Spirit of God moved that afternoon. All sorts of people came to know the Lord. Neither the fire nor the furniture truck prevented the gospel from being effectively proclaimed.

One evening Carl, Troy, and I were working Times Square. The weather was pleasant, the sidewalks overflowing with pedestrians—relaxed, taking in the sights and sounds of Broadway.

Troy, a handsome, athletic young man in his late twenties from Shreveport, was terrific on the streets. He and Carl had been with me on many occasions, from the Bronx to the Bowery. With Troy's charm, charisma, and Southern accent, he had attracted a huge crowd, like a magnet attracted paperclips. I was afraid the cops would come down on us because people were having difficulty moving down the sidewalk. I knew that was irritating to folks, and we were not supposed to do that. But we got by with it; I was greatly relieved when Troy finished. The cops didn't show then.

While I was preaching a few minutes later, once again we had a fantastic listening audience. Very conscious about allowing people to walk behind our crowd, I repeatedly reminded everybody to step in close because we "can't block the back."

Many people were into what I was saying—"God has two sets of books. One is called the Books; the other is called the Lamb's Book of Life…"

A female officer touched my arm. "I'm preaching the gospel, Officer," I said to her. She nodded and pointed me to several other policemen, standing to the back of my sketch board.

Walking over to them, I said, "Yes, sir."

"How much longer you gonna be?" one of them asked.

"Oh, probably about fifteen or twenty minutes," I answered.

"I don't think that's gonna happen. You're blocking the entire sidewalk," he said, but in a calm, polite manner.

"No, sir," I said, "they can walk in the back, back there."

"There's too many people," he said.

"Officer, these people want to hear about Jesus!" I pleaded. About that time Troy pointed the video camera in their direction; instantly they quit insisting that I stop. (I tried to videotape as many meetings as possible.)

"Go ahead, finish up," the officer said.

"Thank you, Officers," I replied.

Most of my crowd had stayed. Walking back to my sketch board, I said, "Folks, hear me, please. Could all of you come forward? We have a right, but we can't block the sidewalk. The officers have a hard job, and they're trying to keep everybody free back there."

I continued speaking, but I began slurring my speech. Explaining to the crowd, I said, "My mouth has gotten dry like cotton because those officers are watching me, and I don't want to block the back."

I finished my message, and, thank the Lord, many decisions for Christ were made, and we gave away a number of New Testaments.

"Carl," I said, "did they want us to leave now?"

"No, no," said Carl. "The big guy with all that stuff [brass] said, 'It's OK if you'll keep 'em in.'"

"Praise the Lord; the police intimidate me more than anything," I answered.

Carl, a godly man, but always the clown when there was fun to be had, bent over to Troy and me and said, while laughing and turning round and round with his Bear Bryant-looking hat on, "Here's the thing. If you had all the experience with the cops, doing wrong as I did, then when you're doing right, it's kind of fun!"

Then, on a serious note, Carl said, "I was glad when the big guns came in and they were understanding; they weren't mad. Heck, let the cops come in there and tell those people, 'You're going to have to open this up.'"

"Technically, that's what they are supposed to do," I said. "They don't have a right to move us."

The officers had assigned a cop to make sure pedestrians could walk behind our meeting. Before we left I told her, "I know you have a hard job. We're on the same team. God bless you."

"You, too," she replied.

One day in Brooklyn as David Braun painted block lettering, policemen busted some guys who were hustling stolen merchandise such as CDs, watches, and clothes; they cuffed them and put them in the back of the police car. This took place within a few feet of us. Later, when I was preaching, my entire crowd started looking behind me, across the street. So I stopped speaking and looked also. Two teenage girls were fighting and cussing, walking in a circle, flipping each other off! A big-boobed girl with a green handkerchief on her head kept saying, "You can't do s*#+*!" The smaller girl, dressed in black and yellow, kept repeating the *F* word. No two sailors ever used filthier language. The crowd, who had encircled them, urged them on.

In a few minutes, the brawl was over, and my crowd turned their heads back around, and I started proclaiming the gospel again. Preaching on the sidewalks of New York City—boring? No way!

CHAPTER 48

ANGELS?

"Are they not all ministering spirits, sent forth to minister for them who shall be heirs of salvation?" (Hebrews 1:14).

Glancing down the street, I saw the intimidating, racist Black Israelite preachers of hate. With bandannas on their heads and dressed in Hebrew garb, several of them had long shepherd staffs as they stood guard. Their spokesmen, one reading scripture, another interpreting, angrily bombarded passersby with their volatile words and hostility. The Lord reminded me that his angels were encamped around me and were much more protective and reliable than those Black Israelite sentries!

Many times I felt the sheltering, providential presence of God as I preached on the sidewalks of New York City. Unusual incidents caused me to ask, "Could this have been an angel of God?"

When I was working alone one day, a young man whom I had never seen appeared. I could not help but notice his eyes; he had the bluest eyes I had ever seen. Possessing a quiet demeanor, he began assisting me. When I tore away the newsprint from my sketch board, he crumpled it up and put it in the trash can; then he helped me tighten the next sheet of paper, smoothing it out and clipping it down with bulldog clamps. With his own quarters he fed my meter, preventing me from, perhaps, getting a parking ticket. Aiding me as I passed out "Smiles," he didn't say very much. But there was a presence about him. Thanking him, I kept observing his blue, peaceful eyes staring back at me. I felt like he was serving me. After staying with me a couple of hours, he was gone. When I got home that afternoon, I said to Linda, "Honey, do you think angels have blue eyes?" And I related to her my experience.

"Talk about a bargain," I said to fifteen or twenty shoppers gathered around me, "Accept Christ, and he'll give you everlasting life. It's free..." Then the verbal onslaught began.

"That's not true! Don't believe him. He's a f+*^ liar!" said several guys who were shouting at me, all at the same time. When preaching on the street, I projected my voice in order to be heard because I did not employ a PA system; but I did not scream. So I was struggling, trying desperately to hold my listeners, but I was determined not to get into a shouting match with those guys.

Standing directly in front of me was a tall black man wearing glasses. With his arms crossed, he said to me, "Preach it; I'm with you."

Getting my second wind, I felt the power of God take over. I spoke with great authority and passion, with unction that came only from the Holy Spirit. The crowd swelled, and many decisions for Christ were made. Those berating me left, and the tall black guy with glasses disappeared, too. As I distributed "Little Red Bibles," I looked for him, but he was nowhere to be found.

"Babe, I think a black angel came to my rescue today at Albee Square!" I said to Linda when I returned home.

One day a man shoved me and adamantly declared, "God does not love me. God does not love anybody. God hates me. God hates everybody!" The man's thinking was twisted, distorted, and confused. He was livid! What made him feel this way? Did some tragedy take place in his life? I wondered.

But another man stepped up and exclaimed, forcefully, "Don't lay a hand on this guy. Leave him alone. You hear me?" Reluctantly, the first man walked away. But who was this one defending me?

"I saw you here in 1977. Some of us are God's warriors, you know. God sent me here to protect you," he said. Before I knew it, he had slipped away into the masses of people. Could this have been an angel of God?

John Wesley, in his *Journals*, page 124, told about a man who struck at him several times with "a large oaken stick, but every time the blow was turned aside; I know not how; I could not move to the right hand or left."

I certainly was no Wesley, but one night at Times Square a man fiercely disputed what I said and angrily threw a canned Coke at me, but missed. How, I didn't know, because he was no more than three feet from me. Did an angel swat it away?

One Friday night when Jerry, Darlene, and I were ministering at Times Square, I observed a young, dark-skinned man that was standing off to the side in one of our street meetings. He was dressed rather weird, wearing sandals, a white robe, and a white turban, but he seemed to be listening to my every word.

When I finished preaching, I said to him, "My friend, I saw you standing there; have you ever accepted Christ?" He answered, "He's the only way." Then he said, "Nobody may know what you do, but God knows." I felt like he was looking into my soul. Was he talking about some sin in my life? Was he referring to the ministry? What did he mean by those words, "Nobody may know what you do, but God knows?"

I was caught off guard. Then I heard him say softly, "It's not by might nor by power but by my Spirit, says the Lord." Quietly excusing himself, he walked into the gobs of people moving down the sidewalk.

"Scotty, you look like you've seen a ghost!" said Jerry.

"I believe God sent that man to me. He could have been an angel," I answered.

"I took two pictures of him," Jerry replied.

Talking about what had transpired that night, we walked back to the van. But I could not find my car keys. We all fumbled through our clothes, and I discovered a hole in my pocket. We looked everywhere for the keys—beside the van, in the trunk, under the van, on top of the van—but the keys were lost. We had had a walk-in meeting, so I quickly shoved my sketch board and paints up under my van. We backtracked several times, walking to where we had preached, but the keys were nowhere to be found. Coming back to my van, we saw a man running off with my sketch board.

"Hey, man, bring that back!" I shouted. "You believe that? What's next? At least he didn't get my paints," I said to Jerry and Darlene.

There we were, at Times Square, at one o'clock in the morning, locked out of my vehicle, and we were worn out! We knew we couldn't leave the van overnight because it would not be there when we came back; so we *were* thinking about trying to get into the van with a coat hanger and, perhaps, hotwiring it. Jerry knew how to do it; I sure didn't!

But looking again around the windshield wipers, I spotted the keys. "Hallelujah! There they are, y'all!" I exclaimed loudly. Somebody had obviously found them and placed them there. But who? The man with the turban came to mind.

I don't know how the keys got there, but as I was sharing this experience with a friend a couple of days later, he said, "Your guardian angel may have put them there."

I am not saying the guy was an angel, but it was interesting to note that when Jerry developed the pictures that he took of the man, only one picture turned out, and only the man's clothes could be seen. No flesh was in the picture.

Carl and I were preaching at Times Square, or at least we were trying to, because, once again, a black Muslim was interfering. Dressed in his white cap and white outfit, and seated at a card table adjacent to us selling his wares, he got up constantly and walked into our crowd and spitefully accused us of preaching lies and promoting a white man's religion. "Allah is the true God. Jesus was just a prophet. Don't listen to these liars," he said, snarling. I had heard all of that before, a number of times.

This made people nervous, and they slowly, two or three at a time, walked away.

Waiting until we built up another crowd, he did the same thing, dispersing people over and over. (This was a common tactic of this group, waiting until we got a good audience and then barreling in and causing everybody to leave.)

Standing beside our sketch board, Carl and I were frustrated, to say the least, and were about to call it a night.

Then, something almost eerie happened A very distinguished black gentleman in in his forties, well dressed in a light brown suit, walked up to us and said, "God told me to be here at Times Square tonight at this time. He had an assignment for me." He opened a small notebook, and in precise, carefully written print, he showed us a list of places, dates, times—what he called his "assignments."

He pointed to Times Square, August 31, 9:30 p.m. There we were at Times Square, August 31, and it was precisely 9:30 p.m.

Carl and I were puzzled. We didn't know if we were talking to a weirdo or some kind of nut. But the man seemed very normal and sensible, not somebody from *One Flew Over the Cuckoo's Nest*! Without saying anything else to us, he walked over to the card table and said something to the Muslim. We could not hear what he said because of the street noise, but we saw the Muslim fold up his card table, grab his bag, and leave.

The man walked back over to us and said, "I must be going; I have another assignment." Confounded but very glad that the Muslim had left, Carl and I were talking, but when we turned back toward this guy, he was gone. It was like he vanished into thin air!

"Where did he go?" I asked. "He was standing right there."

"I didn't see him walking away or into the subway, did you?" asked Carl.

"No, I didn't either. Did you see that notebook? I replied. "He was here at 9:30, just like what was written in that book."

"And he took care of that Muslim," said Carl.

We could not explain what happened. Was the distinguished man an angel? Who was he? And the notebook, with all of those assignments; how strange.

Carl and I preached a couple of more times without any interference from anybody and had some marvelous results, with many people accepting Christ. And we talked about what happened all the way home, and still talk about it.

These were just a few of many unusual, inexplicable incidents that prompted me to think, "Could this have been an angel?"

I didn't know for sure, but as Colin Raye sings, "That's my story and I'm sticking to it."

CHAPTER 49

THE LONE RANGER

Driving on the Long Island Expressway, I was not looking forward to standing alone on the street corner and trying to preach the gospel. I dreaded getting out on those sidewalks. Working by myself, I sometimes felt that way; not very often, but sometimes I did, to be perfectly honest. Often I could not gather a decent audience, and it was humiliating. I was paralyzed by fear—fear of failure, fear of the cops harassing me, fear of faces staring at me. I imagined what they must be thinking, and it made me even more afraid. One day, I actually turned around and went home. I didn't tell anybody that I had gone back home, not even Linda, and I always shared my soul with her.

As I entered Queens, I was worn to a frazzle. Traffic had been extra heavy that day. Then I found myself stuck directly under a bridge in the curve of the road that led me onto the Brooklyn Queens Expressway. Ahead of me was an oil spill from an eighteen wheeler. I came to a complete stop, muttering a few choice words to myself.

Looking out of my van window, I saw all kinds of debris beside the road—beer cans, paper, broken glass, trash, even some old clothes that somebody had discarded, months ago probably. Shaking my head and complaining, I turned on the radio, and, so help me, Merle Haggard was singing "Big City!" I sat there, listening:

I'm tired of this dirty old city
Entirely too much work,
And never enough play.
And I'm tired of these dirty old sidewalks,
I think I'll walk off my steady job today.

"Yeah, Lord, that's how I feel," I exclaimed. God understood; he put up with me all the time.

Often I preached on the streets by myself, and that wasn't easy. My friends could not make it, so I went on alone. I knew God was with me, but it got lonely out there.

It was much easier to minister on the sidewalks when other evangelists and fellow workers were with me. Does not the Bible teach that one can chase a thousand and two, ten thousand (Deuteronomy 32:30)? Having two or three friends stand directly in front of me caused others to stop, to check out what was happening. A crowd drew a crowd. Also, when I worked with a team, I had people who helped me unload and carry my equipment to my preaching location and who counseled at the street meetings. In addition, when several of us preachers worked together, we loosened each other up by laughing and joking with one another.

"The same old rope trick! Haven't you learned anything else, George?" I might say, causing George to grin.

Al, looking at me, might say, "Well, I've heard this sermon before, and it's not any good. That's why you're not on TV, Scott."

This would make me smile and chuckle. "Your brain is as loose as BBs in a Red Rider," somebody else might say. Jesting with one-liners made all of us relax and helped put us at ease, sort of like Marines in the movies clowning around with each other before they hit the beach.

It was extremely stressful trying to present Christ on the sidewalks, with some locations being more difficult than others, so being loose made it easier and more fun, actually. Being uptight made it much more difficult. And, like it or not, our attitude and mood were communicated to those we were trying to reach. So I always preferred to have friends with me instead of being by myself. Even the Lone Ranger had Tonto!

There was an upside to preaching by myself, however. I relied on God more, I think; and, when alone, I always had an unusual sense of the presence of God, like he was standing next to me.

One afternoon while sitting in my van by myself and contemplating what message I should preach, I saw the man who had threatened to kill my friend Burris a few days earlier. The guy was dangerous looking, with his ragged, torn clothes and loud, profane speech. He was leaning up against the side of a building, and I was afraid to get out of my vehicle because of the guy. Flipping through God's word, I read, "The Lord will fight for you." I felt the Holy Spirit speaking to me and saying, "Well, what are you waiting for?" When I stepped out of my van, the guy left, and with confidence and peace that comes only from God, I had a marvelous day preaching the gospel.

Preaching alone taught me how to get a crowd from scratch, how to get people to stop and listen when I had absolutely nobody in front of me to attract others. I learned that smiling and being friendly and amiable really drew folks in. I discovered that I needed to be very entertaining with my "magic tricks" in order to grab listeners and to gain rapport with them. Without a doubt, ministering by myself made me a better, more effective street preacher. So I thank God to this day for the many, many times I was alone.

Having said all of that, I still preferred having others to work with.

That day, after I had listened to Merle Haggard's song "Big City" and the traffic began moving again, I decided to take the Williamsburg Bridge. Glancing at the Manhattan skyline to my right, beyond the graveyard, I felt helpless. "Who am I to think I can make a dent in that huge city?" I said to myself.

After observing a gay rights demonstration, I went to a favorite spot. Looking up, I saw David Braun of OAC waving at me, and he had a bunch of young people with him.

"Will you work with me today?" he asked. "I've got about twenty students from a college in Ohio who need some experience in the open air."

"You better believe I will," I answered enthusiastically, and silently I thanked God that I would not have to be by myself that day.

David was a great person to work with. Totally unselfish, humble, steadfast—just a super guy! And he was a great soul winner, listening to people and applying the gospel to their needs. With his short hair, he looked like a fit Marine, tall and straight.

What an afternoon we had! Hundreds heard the gospel. The students caught on quickly, and it was a glorious sight to watch them sharing their faith and leading people to Christ. That old, cracked, worn-out sidewalk, with "rap" jarring our minds from loud boom boxes, was turned into holy ground!

During one of the meetings we conducted that day, one couple in my crowd stood out. They were Puerto Rican and in their late thirties. Their eyes were more than sad. Depression engulfed them. Dressed in a light gray coat, the woman had her hair pulled back and parted down the middle, and long, crystal earrings dangled from her ears.

The young man had a dark beard and shaggy-dog, black hair, uncombed. Looking groggy, both had glassy eyes. I could easily tell that they were on something. When I invited people to accept Christ, they were the first to raise their hands. David, an excellent counselor, spent extra time with them; and, later, as I conversed with them, I learned that their names were Mary and Arcadio Sanchez. They told me they had always wanted to come to Christ, but never had the courage before today.

Later, I visited them. Both had cleaned up and were glowing with the light of Christ! What a marked contrast from the way they looked at the street meeting on the lower East Side! Two totally different people, they were.

Mary had been carrying a New Testament with her everywhere and had been reading the Gospel of John. Her hair was combed out long, and she had peace all over her face. "I feel great! My heart feels fulfilled. I've never felt better," she exclaimed.

Arcadio said they had been listening to Billy Graham the last couple of nights. "Some people might think we would be back on the street in a couple of weeks," he said, "but we're following through."

"We're in a good church, and I'm starting to feed myself a little of the word of God every day," added Mary.

As I left, I hugged them and prayed for them and their small son, David. The Lord reminded me that I might not be able to reach everybody, but by his grace I could reach some!

In October 1999, the New York Yankees won the World Series, their twenty-fifth. They were dubbed the team of the century, and graffiti fell thick during their celebration parade in the canyons of lower Manhattan. The Yankees parade, the New York City Marathon, the Ku Klux Klan rally on the courthouse steps, the new ABC broadcast center at Times Square, the excitement at Rockefeller Center—whew! Sometimes all of it was overwhelming! I often felt extremely insignificant amid all the hoopla, demonstrations, partying, big-spending tycoons, and fashion.

But God had called me to New York, and I strived to be faithful.

One day I received a warm letter from Emmanuel Fokuo of Ghana, West Africa. He had accepted Christ in New York a while back, and he wrote me expressing how thrilled he was and requesting literature so that he could learn more. Oh, how his words blessed me, because they authenticated my ministry. To God be the glory!

At one of our meetings, a young man named David made a definite decision to accept Christ. Then, one evening several weeks later, he showed up out of the blue and gave his testimony to the crowd.

"I want you to know that what these men are telling you is true. I came to know Christ at this very spot. Now I'm in a church. My life is already different." he said. Once again God was gracious by allowing me to see some of the "fruit of our labor." This buoyed me, like saying "Sic 'em" to a dog!

CHAPTER 50

THE GAMBLER

You've got to know when to hold 'em,
Know when to fold 'em,
Know when to walk away,
Know when to run.
—"The Gambler," sung by Kenny Rogers

The philosophy of how to play poker that Kenny Rogers sang about in his catchy song "The Gambler," I adopted when it came to dealing with the policemen.

Times Square was changing in many respects, on the surface at least. The X-rated flicks, kinky, peep shows, and porno shops were no longer on Forty-Second Street. Mayor Giuliani's administration (1994–2001) had replaced them with restaurants, thriving new businesses, and freshly renovated buildings. The NASDAQ building now stood where Nathan's hot dogs were sold years ago! The "Crossroads of the World" was definitely becoming more family friendly.

Now, Broadway and Seventh Avenue were crowded with tourists, strolling couples with children, and businessmen and -women. Times Square still had its share of perverts, but there was a totally different atmosphere than in previous years. Even the lights were brighter!

But as my friends and I ministered at Times Square, we were still confronted by false ideologies, hedonistic, carefree, pleasure-mad men and women who were steeped in relativism. I sensed that the darkness of atheism was engulfing the city. More than once, I had some student laugh in my face when I mentioned that God created everything. There seemed to be a dogmatic worship of Darwinian evolution.

One evening my friend Ellis and I talked at length to a slender, blond young man named Robin who was from England, actually. An extremely bright individual, he had read extensively the writings of Richard Dawkins, the famous atheist.

"Robin," I said, "if there is no God, then there is no such thing as absolute right and wrong; life has no meaning whatsoever."

"That's just the point. Life has no meaning at all, and of course there are no absolutes!" he replied.

Ellis shared his heart with him and attempted to reason with him. Robin listened, was polite, but he still held on to the idea that man was no more than the product of chance, in a universe that came into being by sheer accident.

Under Mayor Giuliani's administration, more and more restrictions were put on peddlers, street vendors, artists, and musicians. Although my friends and I didn't fall into any of those categories, but rather were sharing the gospel and distributing New Testaments, we were often treated as if we were one of those groups. City officials' attempts to "clean up the city" actually beleaguered those of us who preached the gospel in a soft, nonthreatening way, which was legal, I might add. In recent months the cops had been interfering with my street meetings more and more. Attempts to shut my friends and me down were escalating. What was I to do? I believed in obeying the law, and I really tried to do that. I also knew that, as an American citizen, I had a constitutional right "to exercise freely my religion." I looked at the Bible for the answers.

The apostle Peter said, "Submit yourself to every ordinance of man" (1 Peter 2:13). But when told by the authorities to stop preaching and teaching, Peter replied, "We ought to obey God rather than men" (Acts 5:29).

"Lord, show me what to do in each situation," I prayed.

On the side of the NYPD's squad cars were the letters "CPR," which stood for courtesy, professionalism, respect. Through the years I had met scores of policemen who exhibited all these traits. Their job was to serve and protect, and that's what they were doing. Many of "New York's Finest" were dedicated and did an extremely difficult job, often being misunderstood. I did my dead level best to respect the police and obey the law. I prayed for the cops, and on a number of occasions I told them so.

Bob Campbell, a retired New York police officer, was a member of my church. Manny Rodriguez, another New York cop, who was stationed at Midtown South, was also a member at Farmingdale Baptist Church. My friends and I got to know many policemen by face. And they recognized us. We tried to witness to them, offering them New Testaments. Some took them; others didn't.

I talked to captains and sergeants, endeavoring to have a good relationship with the policemen. I wanted them to understand that I was an ordained Baptist minister, pastor of Farmingdale Baptist Church, and that I preached innocuously and was not some "loose cannon" shouting at decent, law-abiding citizens. I understood that they had a job to do, but so did I.

Policemen for years had pulled drunks out of my street meetings and stood to the back, making sure I was not disturbed. Several had commended my team and me for preaching. "Keep up the good work!" they said. Many policemen knew that by law they could not legally make us stop preaching.

But I had met dozens of New York City policemen who either did not know the legal rights of the average citizen or abused those rights, so they used other tactics to shut us down. Some used intimidation, pushing their authority around. "Do you have a permit?" an officer might ask.

"Sir, I don't need a permit because I'm not using a PA system. I'm preaching and giving away Bibles," I would say.

Then he would say, "You're blocking the sidewalk."

"Sir, I'm legal as long as people can walk behind my crowd, and you can see that they are clearly passing," I would reply. (Broadway show crowds really did block the sidewalk. Bands and street entertainers did, too. I never saw one cop ever make any of them stop.)

Then he might say, "You can't use a stand."

"Sir, I'm not selling anything. My sketch board is not a hot dog or a vegetable stand. I've used this equipment for years," I would answer.

One evening a very rude, abrasive cop told me that I could not use my small briefcase which held my object lessons. "What about the shoulder bag?" I asked.

"That's OK," he added. But when I continued having access even with the shoulder bag, he told me that I had to stop because a woman had complained. I did not believe him. Nobody was complaining. People wanted to hear what I had to say! With the crowd standing, waiting for me to continue, I replied, "But all of these people want me here!"

"Stop, now," he ordered. Louis and Jessica Rivera, a fine Christian couple from our church, were with me, so I certainly did not want to get into trouble with the authorities.

"American men and women have died for my right to be here, Officer. This is not right, but I'll do what you say," I replied, acquiescing to his bullying.

I moved many, many times, but when the cops made me move or forced me to quit preaching, the people in the crowd took up for me. "Go catch the crooks, Officer, leave these men alone," they would say. "I'll give you a summons if you don't move," I was told repeatedly. I was sometimes threatened with an arrest. "What for, Officer?" He would not reply.

The French writer and philosopher Voltaire (1694–1778) said, "I do not agree with what you have to say, but I'll defend to the death your right to say it."

I felt our society was becoming so concerned about being politically correct and so obsessed about not offending anyone that we had forgotten Voltaire's inspirational words, and we were in danger of losing our freedom of speech because of it.

"Officer, I've been at this place for twenty-two years," I said to a short Italian sergeant who had been using every tactic imaginable to shut me down.

"I've never seen you here," he replied.

A gentleman who owned a business came to my defense and told the cop, "Officer, this man has been here for years. I'm not with him. I'm Jewish. But I believe that what he's saying is true."

"Sir, we're on your side. We're telling people about Jesus. Somebody might be changed and not shoot you in the back," I said to the officer, but that did not faze him.

I looked at this sergeant directly in the eyes and said, "Officer, I'm willing to die for what I do." Upon hearing those words, the sergeant became strangely solicitous. I felt like he started showing concern for what I was trying to do, which he certainly had not exhibited when he first walked up.

There were some absurd means used to try to scare me off. One night a cop, pointing at my sketch board, said, "You cannot display."

"Can't display? Look around, Officer. This is Times Square," I said, chuckling. "What do you mean I can't display?"

Cops have said words like this to me: "You can't do this until eleven o'clock. You can't use visual aids and sleight-of-hand tricks. Your camera tripod must have wheels. You can't use a High-Eight video camera."

I told two different officers, "This is Times Square, not Tiananmen Square!"

One day I said, "Linda, I'm tired of these cops harassing me. They used to bother us a little—just at Times Square. Now they're busting us in Brooklyn, in the Bronx, everywhere!"

"Well, be careful. Don't get in any trouble," she replied.

I had been blindsided years ago by the cops, and my friend Burris and I had already been arrested, cuffed, carried to jail, and our Bibles and equipment confiscated back in 1991. The charge was disorderly conduct. The charges were dropped; reparation was paid to us when theAmerican Center for Law and Justicefiled suit against the City of New York. But that was a distressing experience, awful to go through, and I didn't ever want to be arrested again.

But my friends and I were tired of being pushed around by the police. The time was coming when we were no longer going to "fold 'em and walk away," as the song "The Gambler" said. We were going to "hold 'em."

Maybe we were rolling the dice, gambling that the police would either leave us alone or back down if we refused to stop preaching the gospel. But we were going to stand our ground!

CHAPTER 51

ARRESTED AGAIN!

I was arrested again for preaching the gospel at Times Square, along with my friend Al Terhune, on May 26, 2000.

My team and I were preaching at the corner of Forty-Third and Seventh Avenue in the heart of Times Square. It was a beautiful night in June. George Naggy preached first, and then I prepared my sketch board and turned to the crowd, a very relaxed crowd, multicultural, with a few businessmen sprinkled throughout.

"How are you tonight, ladies and gentlemen? Having a good time in New York?" I asked. After I had preached for about fifteen minutes, many people responded favorably and took Christian literature. Several of us began talking to various individuals.

Al Terhune wrote on the sketch board "The King Is Coming," which drew a nice sidewalk audience. Just as he began his message, cops came down on us. Driving up in an NYPD van, they quickly surrounded us.

"You are going to have to move. I want you on the side streets," the officer in charge demanded in a very harsh, rude manner. Tall, with a reddish mustache, he reminded me of George Custer of the old West, only his hair was not as long.

"Come on, people, move on. It's over!" he shouted and motioned to everybody to leave.

"We have a right," I said.

"They never chase those black guys away" (referring to the Black Israelites), someone said. "Why aren't you chasin' them?"

"Don't worry about the black guys; move it," the officer ordered.

"We have a right. I'm in charge here, sir, and we're not leaving," I said, trying to hold our ground.

"All right. Arrest these guys. Put handcuffs on them," he said arrogantly, with a total disregard for our First Amendment rights.

I reminded the crowd of what we were doing. "We're preaching the gospel. We're preaching the gospel," I said, as another cop handcuffed my hands behind my back.

George warned the officer, "You're going to get into trouble, Sergeant."

"Come on, come on," the officer ordered.

"This is wrong. This is wrong," somebody said.

"Let's go. Move on, people!" the sergeant shouted to people who had slowed down and were observing what was taking place, many of them open-mouthed, stunned.

"We have a right to be here," I said in defense.

Referring to me, he said, "He's under arrest—disorderly conduct. Anybody else?" said the sergeant.

"Folks, we're preaching the gospel. We're not selling anything. We're giving away Bibles," I said to those looking at what was happening.

Al said, "I'm with him."

"He's under arrest, too, disorderly conduct," said the sergeant, referring to Al. "Come on, people. Let's go. You gotta keep going," he shouted to those hanging around on the sidewalk.

Jana, one of our team members and our camera lady, said to the officer, "You know, there are quite a few of us."

I was taken by the arm and put in the van, in the back. George said to the sergeant, "You're going to stand before God. You're going against God. You're going to give an account." Another team member said, "You better believe you're going to give an account."

Apparently, the officer did not care what was being said to him, and he shouted again, "Let's go. Move out, people," and pedestrians moved on down the sidewalk.

"You're trampling the Constitution also," someone said.

I was observing everything from inside the van, and I still had my lapel mic on. Al was put in cuffs, his hands behind him. Then he was escorted to the van and joined me in the back of the van.

"Why don't you lock up all of us?" Jana asked. "Why don't you do that?"

"No, once I take this down," nodding at our sketch board, "you'll leave also," the sergeant replied.

George said to the sergeant, "There were just about thirty-five people here. We weren't stopping traffic."

Instantly, it looked like the idea clicked in the sergeant's mind, giving him, perhaps, a legitimate reason to arrest us. "Yes, you were!" he argued.

Jana reminded him by saying, "There is such a thing as freedom of speech." (Jana had grown up in Czechoslovakia under communism, where they certainly did not have freedom of speech.)

"I'm the police out here, and it's my opinion," said the sergeant.

"Why not stop these other guys?" George asked.

"We're stopping you first," answered the sergeant.

Jana was still videotaping everything, and she said, "Freedom of speech."

Addressing her, the sergeant said, bullying, "Someday you sit down and talk to me about it. Right now—disorderly conduct!"

"God gives us that right to preach the gospel and the Constitution as well," another team member said.

Looking at the sketch board, the officer ordered, "Take it down, take it down."

Referring to Al and me, Jana asked, "Where are you taking them?"

"To the precinct," the sergeant answered. "Let's go. Pack it up!" he ordered again.

Jana said, "Would you get the keys from Scott for the van?" Then, addressing the sergeant, she added, "How many robbers did you lock up tonight?"

"Oh, a robber here and a robber there," the sergeant replied sarcastically.

"Or drug addicts?" asked Jana.

"Let's go, pack it up," he demanded.

A lot of people were slowing down and viewing everything. Looking out of the police van window, I could tell the people were shocked.

Jana asked, "Where is the precinct?" The sergeant at this point realized he was on camera and began to soften up a bit and said, "West Thirty-Fifth Street, between Eighth and Ninth Avenue."

George told the sergeant, "Well, looks like the city is going to be fined again."

"Turn the light off." (George reached up and switched off the sketch board lights.) "Gotta whole Die-Hard battery," said the sergeant to two or three other officers as he looked at our equipment.

My team members got my car keys and lapel mic and told the sergeant that both Al and I had IDs. As all the cops looked at my rig, George said, "I'll take it to the vehicle," meaning my van.

The sergeant hesitated and then conceded and said in an insolent way, "If they set it up again, we'll take it down again."

George, addressing other team members, said, nodding at the sketch board, "He wanted to take this. I wouldn't let him. I told him I'd take this back to the vehicle."

Al and I will were then driven away to Midtown South Precinct and kept in cuffs for a while. Then we were set loose. We filled out paperwork and were released about a half an hour later. In a few minutes George, Jana, and other team members showed up. We walked over to the desk and prayed for the NYPD and left.

Both Al and I were given summonses for disorderly conduct and were to appear in court at a later date.

Our court date was weeks away, and even though I was confident the ridiculous charge of disorderly conduct would be dropped, waiting and pondering the outcome bothered me immensely.

After we were arrested I was extremely nervous and uptight about what might take place on the street the next time out. A group was coming up, and I was concerned that the cops would interfere and ruin our ministry at Times Square.

So when Wake Cross Roads Baptist Church in Raleigh, North Carolina, sent seven young adults, most of them seminary students, to work with me, I did not mention to them that I had recently been arrested.

Later, as all of us preached and witnessed at Times Square one night, I was really praying that we would not be bothered by the police. Our entire church was praying and several members went in with us for moral support. But all was quiet on the Times Square front!

The next morning I showed the team from Wake Cross Roads Baptist Church the videotape of our arrest, and they understood and actually were laughing and joking about it.

"You mean, Brother Scotty, you knew the cops might have busted us, and you didn't warn us?" they said, scolding me, with smiles.

God really used that group from Wake Cross Roads Baptist. After our street meetings the students made friends with those hanging around and took extra time discussing with them what it meant to be followers of Christ. Sitting on the curb and leaning up against buildings, they gave their testimonies to those of a far different culture than that in North Carolina. We also spent hours in the subway, sharing Christ with hundreds on the platforms.

One evening I noticed a large motorcycle gang on St. Marks Place in Greenwich Village. After doing a newspaper trick and talking a little about the Lord to the guys sitting around and leaning up against their bikes, I called on Ben, who was one of the seminary students from Wake Cross Roads Baptist Church who, I could tell, was very capable and full of the Spirit of God.

"Ben, step up here and tell these guys how you came to know the Lord," I said.

Ben, with a surprised look on his face, did what I asked him to do and gave a marvelous testimony to that motorcycle gang. They listened, and they thanked him.

Later, Ben said to me, "I was scared to death, Brother Scott!"

Finally, the date when Al and I were to appear before the judge to answer the charge of disorderly conduct arrived. We stood before the judge on June 27 (my wedding anniversary, of all dates!). Explaining that we were preaching the gospel, the judge immediately dismissed the charge of disorderly conduct.

We took no action against the NYPD, although we probably had a pretty good case. We just wanted the police harassment to stop.

But it didn't. On the Fourth of July weekend as I was preaching, a number of officers ordered me to stop preaching, accusing me, once again, of blocking the sidewalk. (The videotape clearly showed that the foot traffic had ample space to walk behind my street meeting.) I complied, but my crowd stood up for me and refused to be dispersed. Then another sergeant approached the scene after being called by the officers who had forced me to stop preaching.

When the sergeant arrived, I told him that I was a Baptist preacher and that we were preaching the gospel. He understood completely and told me to go ahead. The crowd roared, cheered, and clapped on my behalf and voiced their support. What an encouragement they were!

All of the police officers then left.

CHAPTER 52

FUN IN EUROPE

I was blessed with the opportunity to attend the Billy Graham Conference for Itinerant Evangelists in Amsterdam in August 2000. Al Bohl and I had attended this conference back in 1983. Then, most Third World evangelists carried their belongings in plastic bags, wore sandals, and generally looked very poor. But now in 2000, the vast majority of Third World evangelists wore nice suits, carried computers, pulled carry-on luggage. What a change!

There were ten thousand evangelists from over two hundred countries present at this conference. I heard many touching testimonies. One man from Africa said that due to tribal warfare he was the only one left in his immediate family. At great peril, many were sacrificing everything for Christ. I had given up nothing in comparison.

The program was loaded with outstanding speakers: John R. Scott, William Franklin Graham, J. I. Packer, Josh McDowell, just to mention a few.

Anne Graham Lotz, the daughter of Billy Graham, moved my heart the most! Truly, she was anointed and gifted by God. To be a part of this great army of evangelists was humbling.

After the conference, I traveled in Europe—a lifelong dream. I "po-boy'ed" it from country to country, staying in cheap hotels, hostels, and church camp facilities and renting out small, economical rooms. I had always heard that everywhere you go, people speak English. I do not believe that now; many places, perhaps, but not everywhere! So it was not easy trying to decipher which train to board as I quickly left one country and entered another. Also, I had always heard that many Europeans could speak a number of languages. I discovered that was indeed true. One afternoon on a train, while all of us were eating our lunch at straight up noon, I had a very interesting conversation with a gentleman who could speak seven languages fluently.

But I had myself a time! Leaving Amsterdam, I toured London and enjoyed all the sights—Buckingham Palace, Westminster Abbey, Big Ben, London Bridge, Trafalgar Square, the British Museum. I was captivated by Speaker's Corner in Hyde Park. A person would mount a soapbox, literally, wait for others to gather, then deliver his speech. Sometimes the guy was a communist, spreading socialist propaganda. Often the speaker was a real crackpot; other times, the person was a Christian preacher.

Speeding through the tunnel under the English Channel, I quickly arrived in Paris. Walking around under the glowing lights at night with the Eiffel Tower in the background was when I really missed my darling wife, Linda, the most. I never want to go back to Paris without Linda. How she would love the Champs Elysees! Visiting the Louvre, I was not particularly impressed with the *Mona Lisa*, but I wasn't the only one.

On to Rome, and the first place I visited was the Coliseum, only imagining all that had taken place there. I toured the Vatican and walked through the Sistine Chapel, astounded at the monumental work of Michelangelo. I'll never forget soaking my tired feet in the famous Tritone Fountain. How cool and refreshing! Nor will I ever forget the gypsy who swiped my glasses' case, thinking that it was my wallet. When I gave her a couple of bucks, she returned it and fled!

In Zurich, Switzerland, as I was about to enter a famous cathedral, I asked a formal, prim woman, "Is the gospel preached here?" Appalled that I dare ask such a question, she responded, by saying, "Good Lord, no, but the architecture is breathtaking!"

In Berlin I saw "Checkpoint Charlie" and some remains of the Berlin Wall. On the streets of New York City, I had used the Berlin Wall as an illustration of the wall of sin between God and man. Now I was at that wall—the very place where so many families had been cut off from each other for years.

In Prague, Czech Republic, I took pictures of the statue of John Huss, who was burned at the stake in 1415 for bucking the Vatican, adhering to the teachings of John Wickliffe, and preaching out of doors. Walking over the Charles Bridge with its numerous statues and sculptures, viewing the magnificent Prague Castle, and standing among the tourists and watching the twelve apostles appear in the Old Town Clock were memories forever etched in my mind.

Throughout Europe I saw with my own eyes the vacuum in people's lives, the empty churches, the irrelevance and unimportance of God in society. Perhaps it was like this before World War II when Hitler was able to capture and control the minds of the public.

Returning to New York, I felt revitalized, ready to take on the world. The Billy Graham Conference had energized me, and traveling in Europe was a good break from New York City. But now, it was back to work. There were people to be reached with the glorious gospel of Christ.

CHAPTER 53

GONE!

Several months later, Brother Bowyer, pastor of Wake Cross Roads Baptist Church in Raleigh, invited me to preach to his church, and he arranged for me to speak at Southeastern Seminary in Wake Forest, North Carolina, on street evangelism.

Many members of Wake Cross Roads had worked with me on the sidewalks in New York, so I was not among strangers. As I preached in the church, I felt totally accepted and appreciated. However, the famous NASCAR driver Dale Earnhardt had just been killed at Daytona Beach (February 18, 2001), and hearts were heavy because of his untimely demise.

While speaking at Southeastern, I was so warmly received by the students and faculty that I was pleasantly surprised. This was my first time to address a seminary audience, and I was nervous. I felt much more at home talking to shoppers in Brooklyn than I did in the chapel service! But I believe the Lord God fulfilled his purpose in me that day.

My prayer to God was that he would use me to inspire some of those students to attempt sidewalk evangelism, perhaps even call a few of them to engage in a street ministry full time. I knew that a person had to be called of God to preach on the streets because there was no prestige or money in it. Besides, this was the twenty-first century, with mass communication at our fingertips. By means of TV, the radio, the Internet, and social media, we could reach millions. So why preach to small crowds on the sidewalk?

Then, of course, there was the stigma that was attached to street preaching. More than once I had stood around in a circle conversing with fellow ministers on various occasions. "I'm pastor of Second Baptist, and we're on TV. We run about eighteen hundred in Sunday school," someone might say. Another would add, "Well, we're building a new educational building, so we're not on TV, just radio." Then, someone might ask, "Scotty, where are you pastoring?"

"Oh, I'm not pastoring now," I would reply. Then I would say, almost apologizing as I said it, "I'm a street evangelist. But it's not what you might think. We have standing, listening crowds."

"Oh, that's nice. Hey, let's go check out the buffet," someone would say. Without being paranoid, often after I mentioned my street ministry, I was left standing alone.

But in my mind those ministers could preach to church-oriented, biblical, world-view congregations, who had heard the gospel hundreds of times, until the cows came home!

On the street corner, I was getting to preach the gospel live, face to face, to Moonies, Muslims, misfits, masters of the universe, movie stars, murderers, perverts, pedophiles, prostitutes, pimps, Hindus, hillbillies, communists, Catholic priests, nuns, Orthodox Jews, junkies, thieves, atheists, drug dealers, the demon possessed, and countless others who would never step foot in the church and who would quickly change channels with their remote if they came across some preacher on TV.

Yes, those ministers could fish in the bathtub till Jesus comes. Give me Toledo Bend!

Wake Cross Roads Church in Raleigh, North Carolina, continued to send young people to New York to minister with me on the sidewalks. A young man by the name of Marcus Allen, who, along with Dr. Cky Carrigan, had worked with me on the streets of New York before, was their leader. Marcus, a slim young man, who probably never had a weight problem, and who probably never would have a weight problem in his entire life, was gifted with great leadership ability; his wife, Stacy, complemented him very well, too.

Marcus and Stacy brought with them a group of seventeen teenagers, many of whom were still in high school. He rented a van so that he could help transport everybody in and out of the city. It was not easy in all of that New York traffic to follow me, but Marcus did a super job.

One bright, sunny afternoon in Brooklyn, Marcus preached the gospel using the acronym FAITH, and the people were thick around him, anxious to hear. When he asked listeners to accept Christ, dozens of people called on Christ to be there Lord and Savior. My heart overflowed with joy when I saw all of those teenagers sharing their faith, talking one on one, and distributing New Testaments. Marcus also preached for me at the Sunday morning service at Farmingdale Baptist, delivering a solid message edifying the people of God.

When that bunch of kids left New York, they were totally different teenagers having ministered on the sidewalks of New York City.

In August 2001, seven Southeastern Seminary students worked with me on the streets. Some of them were going into missions. Hopefully, they picked up a few pointers in outdoor evangelism that they could use all over the world.

Dr. Cky Carrigan, the son of Carl and Carolyn, was their leader. He was a very learned man, a professor who mixed and mingled with all classes of people. His expertise was dealing with cults, so he had plenty of opportunities on the sidewalks, sharing Christ and using his apologetic skills with various cult members and followers of weird religions that were so prevalent in New York.

After ministering on the streets for several days, we toured the Twin Towers, and we all were amazed at the spectacular view! While standing on the solid glass observation floor, I looked straight down. I didn't like heights, and, boy, was I glad to step back off the glass onto the main flooring! I always felt privileged to minister with Cky and the students he brought with him, and I once again was sad when they left to return to North Carolina.

A few days later, Linda answered the phone and heard my sister frantically ask, "Has Scotty left for the city?"

"No, he's right here," answered Linda as she handed me the phone.

"Scotty, thank God you're still home," Barbara Ann replied in a panic mode.

"What's the matter, Barbara Ann?" I asked, sensing something bad had happened.

"Turn the TV on. Quick! New York has been hit by terrorists!" she exclaimed, her voice shaking.

Flipping on the remote, I saw one tower on fire, and, like everybody else in the world, I couldn't believe it.

"Thank God, Scotty, you're not in the city," Babs said, breathing hard.

"Well, I was headed to the Bronx today. I had not planned on being in the financial district," I said.

Linda by now was watching, and all of us saw the pictures coming in—the plane exploding in the tower, then the other tower, and the towers crumbling with smoke and rubble. What a terrible sight!

Assuring my sister that we were all OK, I hung up the phone but was glued to the TV. Everybody's lives changed on 9/11. I thought about those Southeastern Seminary students that had just visited us. We all had been in the Twin Towers just a few days earlier!

Soon, all of the roads and bridges heading off of Long Island were closed, and nobody could leave the island. Like everybody else, our hearts broke for all of those lives that were lost and for their families and loved ones. I thought about the courageous firemen, policemen, and emergency workers.

Many times I had preached the gospel practically in the shadow of the Twin Towers, on Wall Street, and at Liberty Park. I felt like I had probably shared Christ with some of the people who were killed that day. Only God knew.

How strange it was for me to view lower Manhattan without the Twin Towers. For years and years as I drove into the city, I had stared at them, beaming a bright silver on a sunny day. Now, they were no more. Gone!

Many times in my street meetings I had used the Twin Towers to illustrate the meaning of sin: "Sin means falling short of God's standards. Look, if you try to jump from the World Trade Center to the Empire State building, you'll fall short. I might jump five feet. You might jump ten feet. Carl Lewis might jump twenty feet. But we will all fall short. The Bible says, 'All have sinned and come short of the glory of God' (Romans 3:23). We all fall short of God's requirements. We're all sinners!"

Would I ever use the Twin Towers as an illustration again?

For many weeks after 9/11 people on the streets were unusually receptive to the gospel. One afternoon a very tall Hasidic Jew, dressed in his black suit and cap, stood and listened a long time as I shared the good news. Often the Hasidic Jews, upon hearing the name of Jesus, walked away with their head down. But as I quoted passages from Isaiah and Jeremiah, he remained until I was finished, took Christian literature, and talked with my friends and me about his relationship with God. Without doubt, 9/11 had much to do with his heart being prepared.

My friend Price Harris visited us, and one day we walked around lower Manhattan, appalled at the devastation. We saw the huge cross that the workers had erected out of steel beams that they found in the debris.

In the weeks and months following the terrorist attacks on 9/11, I had a little anxiety from time to time as I took the subway or crossed the Brooklyn Bridge or drove through the Midtown Tunnel. But I knew God was in control, and I was in his hands.

CHAPTER 54

STAY THE COURSE

One Sunday morning a fine Christian gentleman at First Baptist Church of Cotton Valley, Louisiana, told me to "stay the course." That's exactly what I intended to do.

One afternoon not far from Brooklyn Tabernacle, as the people pressed around me, I lifted my heavy chain and asked for a volunteer. A muscular black man without a shirt on, probably in his thirties, stepped forward. I wrapped the chain around him and began to ask him about sin. "Do you ever lie?" I asked.

"Twenty-four/seven," he answered.

"Ever steal? Cheat?" I asked.

"Yeah, man," he replied, bragging, knowing that everybody around us was looking.

Then, with people encircling us, I talked about how sin enslaved us. "We can't break free! But when you come to know Christ, he sets us free! Jesus said, 'You shall know the truth, and the truth shall set you free' (John 8:32)."

As I said those words, I pulled the chain off of the guy and dropped it in a pile on the sidewalk, with a ringing clang. I talked to the young man, thanking him for volunteering. I then prayed with him and gave him some literature.

Months later, as I reasoned with my crowd, I said, "Just because you believe something doesn't make it true. I could believe I'm in Chicago, but I'm not in Chicago; I'm in New York! You may have your own religion, your own belief—but that doesn't make it true... I might believe I can fly; but I can't fly!"

Out of my peripheral vision, I noticed a young black man who was kneeling down in front of me, listening. When I was through preaching, he stood up, smiling, and asked, "Do you remember me? I'm different. I was the guy without a shirt. You put a chain on me to make an illustration. Remember?"

Looking at him a little closer, I replied, "Yeah, I do. You volunteered. But I hardly recognized you!"

"I know. The Lord has turned me around. Man, it's working; it's working!" he exclaimed, almost shouting.

When somebody came around and shared words like that with me, I could not contain my exultant joy!

The city looked like a war movie. The streets of Manhattan were lined with armed soldiers, policemen, and the National Guard. Because of the war with Iraq and the threat of terrorism, all of the major attractions of New York were closely watched in the interest of national security—the Statue of Liberty, the Empire State Building, Times Square. There were huge concrete barriers in the financial district preventing cars from moving up and down Wall and Broad. Also, war protesters were blocking traffic in Midtown and causing chaos during rush hours. But by God's grace, I was still preaching the gospel on the sidewalks and still pastoring Farmingdale Baptist Church.

We had cookouts, volleyball, softball, and all sorts of fun and games in an attempt to draw people from the neighborhood to our church. Often many of them came to our parties, but we seldom ever saw them step foot inside our church. From time to time, however, we were able to win somebody to the Lord and baptize him, which energized our fellowship!

Many times when groups came up to New York to work with me in the city, they also helped canvas the area around Farmingdale Baptist Church, leaving flyers, circulars, and other Christian literature advertising our church. Our members were very faithful and dedicated, and a number of them even went to the streets with me—Jerry Hoffmann, Mark Hurd, Lonnie McLaughlin.

Betty Miserndino was seriously ill and often had to spend time in bed. (One Saturday when I visited her in Mount Sinai Hospital, I noticed that the elevator automatically stopped at every floor. I learned that the elevator floor buttons had been disengaged because it would be considered work by many to push them on Saturday!) But Betty joined us when she could. Luis and Jessica Rivera, Becky Halligan, Richard Ries, and several others also accompanied me. Burris and Jana Jenkins were mainstays, although Burris was rapidly losing his health. I did not know how much longer he would be able to work with me on the streets.

Tim Wilbanks continued to astound me with his ability in the open air. I poured my life into him, believing that God had called him into the ministry and that he would one day serve the Lord all around the world.

A preacher friend of mine said to me one day, "Scotty, I couldn't stand being rejected. How do you take that day in and day out? My members might be half asleep, oblivious to what I'm saying, or even adamantly opposed to my words, but, as a rule, they remain seated and stay silent. But where you are—anything could happen. At any time!"

I understood what Bob was saying. Most ministers never had to deal with the snobbishness that I encountered while on the streets, to be perfectly honest. Even when a minister on television or the radio was delivering his message, he did not see people switching stations or turning him off or changing to another channel. Rejection was transpiring, but the minister didn't actually see it taking place.

But when I preached on the sidewalks, I sometimes saw, heard, and felt complete repulsion from certain individuals. One evening I was sharing my heart to a Times Square crowd—businessmen and -women, tourists, out of towners, students, a few children, the lonely, the empty, the ordinary. While I was describing the agony of Christ shedding his blood on the cross for our sins, a young man standing two feet in front of me said to his buddies, out loud, "Come on, let's go. We don't have to listen to this shit!" Then four young men just turned their back on me and walked away, leaving a gaping hole in the front of my crowd. It was blatant, open, cold-blooded, in-your-face rejection, not only of me but of my Savior. That was not easy to absorb, a total disregard, disdain, and disrespect for the blood of our Lord Jesus Christ.

In January 2002 I was part of Price Harris's team to Jamaica. We held three revivals, conducted street meetings, spoke to a Bible college, and preached the gospel in sixteen schools, some having as many as eight hundred students. We praised God for the wonderful opportunity to share Christ. However, while in Jamaica, I got some bad news. Linda called me and said sorrowfully, "Scotty, Burris died."

Burris had been in bad health for a long time, his physical condition slowly deteriorating. Having lost sufficient weight, he was noticeably shorter and bent over and could not straighten up his head. No longer could he drink from a glass. My heart ached.

In spite of not feeling well, Burris had been faithful to share the gospel. We had gone through everything together on the sidewalk. The four of us—Burris, Jana, Linda, and I—had spent many happy times together. One day as we sat in traffic, Burris said, "Scott, I have the answers to all the world's problems, but nobody ever asks me."

"Man, Burris," I replied, laughing, "You think you know so much. That's the New Yorker in you!" Burris just smiled. I would really miss him.

One dreary afternoon as I shared the gospel, a man walked up to me and said, "Ten years ago I saw you guys with the sketch board, and I stopped and listened. I knew the Lord, but I was very much backslidden, about to leave my family. Thank God you were out there that day!"

Then the man showed me some Bible verses on little cards. "I'm involved with Evangelism Explosion. Ever heard of it?" he asked.

"Yeah, Dr. Kennedy of Coral Ridge Presbyterian Church—that's the program he started. That's super. Keep it up!" I replied. I tell you no lie. Jawing with that guy made me soar like an eagle!

I was privileged to work with Eric Brisco of the Open Air Campaigners in Boston. He had that Boston accent, and, of course, I have that thick, Southern accent, but we somehow understood each other. I loved the way he said "hat" for "heart."

Eric, a slim, tanned guy, was a fine-looking man who was capable of preaching in any pulpit in America. About ten years younger than I was, he was an incredible sidewalk preacher. A master on the sketch board, his sketches were a work of art, really.

We had a noon-hour meeting in Boston directly across from Old South Town Hall, which used to be a church. Our forefathers met there to plan the Boston Tea Party. Eric was concerned that a guy named Jack would interfere, and sure enough he did. Jack had a vendetta against Christians and did all he could to wreck our meeting.

One of our team members whose name was Gordon was a very mature young man and a godly man, a super preacher as well. But having grown up on the mean streets of Philadelphia, Gordon had a way of defending himself. When Jack, this acrimonious troublemaker, got so close to Gordon that Gordon could smell his breath, Gordon yelled, "Get outta my face!" Jack, still being obnoxious, did not move; so Gordon shoved him, yelling again, "I said get outta my face!"

Jack continued falsely accusing us, however, and attempted to run off our audience, composed mainly of businessmen on their lunch hour. We had some pretty good meetings, however. Eric had had heart surgery and, holding two x-rays in his hands, he said, "This one on my left is before the surgery, and the one on the right is after the surgery. Now, it's like I have a brand-new 'hat'! Did you know that when you come to Christ, God will give you a new 'hat'?"

At Harvard Square we detected a bit of smugness, to say the least. After one small, anemic meeting, I talked to a man with a large, white beard who reminded me of William Booth of the Salvation Army. He had listened to us for a few minutes, however.

"My friend," I asked, "do you ever think much about the Lord?"

"Not if I can help it. I don't believe in God. I'm an atheist," he replied.

He thought he would shock me with his answer, but he didn't. I had been on the streets of New York too long. I reminded him that he was getting older and that he would face God, whether he believed in him or not.

We had a street meeting with some students who attended Boston University. I talked about grits and Cream of Wheat. Some of the students thought they were the same. "Come on! You're supposed to be the bright minds of the future," I said, poking fun at them. They smiled and loosened up. Reasoning with them, I said, "Now, if God says that in order for you to go to heaven, you must eat grits, the devil will give you cream of wheat!" They got my point. All of us felt that the Lord was moving, trying to get their attention. We prayed that they would take God seriously.

Dr. Cky Carrigan, a professor at Southeastern Seminary, visited us again in New York, and as usual he brought some of his students along. I relished working with them because I knew that what they learned on the streets of New York could be transmitted to others, which I believe is true discipleship.

We were all ministering one afternoon in the South Bronx at one of my favorite locations. A few minutes after I had finished preaching, I looked up and saw Cky, smiling big, obviously very excited.

"Scotty, let me tell you what just happened. Did you notice that guy that rolled up in the wheelchair?" he asked.

"Yeah, I saw him," I replied.

"Well," Cky said, still in high spirits "I tried to talk to him about Christ, but he didn't know English, only Spanish. There was a Hispanic woman standing there, and I didn't even think she knew the Lord; but anyway, I asked her if she would interpret for me. She said that she would. I went through the gospel with the guy. She interpreted, and the man—he was saved! He began to cry and said, 'Gracias, gracias.' He couldn't thank me enough. That woman—she saw what happened, too. I thanked her, and she walked away; but

I believe God was speaking to her, too. But that guy was so happy. I believe that was a divine appointment if ever there was one."

All of us were thrilled and were glad to be a part of what the Lord was doing in people's hearts.

At Washington Regional Hospital in Fayetteville, Arkansas, on July 15, 2003, Linda and I waited anxiously. Then, out through the double doors came Stephen with a contented grin on his face. "I present to you Matthew Joseph Teague!" he exclaimed, as he invited us into the room. Soon, cradling his firstborn son in his arms and still grinning, he said, "Katie's fine, too." And we could see that she was glowing!

Holding our first grandbaby, Linda and I thanked God that he was healthy. Stephen and Katie were thrilled, and, of course, I was soon bragging about how Matt already had been contacted by both Harvard and Yale! Sharon, Stewart's wife, was present and shed many tears of joy. She was determined to hold that baby and almost missed her plane because of it!

No little baby was ever hugged and kissed and loved on any more than Matthew Joseph Teague, but before we knew it, our time was up with Stephen, Katie, and Matthew; and it was back to New York.

Late one evening at Times Square a young man, proud of his pigtail, it appeared to me, and possessing a know-it-all attitude, blamed Christians of committing more atrocities than any other religion. Vehemently arguing, he said to me, "Christians condoned slavery. Look at the Crusades, the Spanish Inquisition!"

"There is a difference between professing Christians and real Christians. Christ taught that we are to love our enemies. The evil that many have committed in his name is not a true picture of Christianity," I replied just as strongly. "Think for yourself, young man, instead of letting some professor think for you. Do your homework!"

A few minutes later, I listened to a very self-assured and independent woman who arrogantly rejected the Bible, claiming that it was "sexist and full of errors." Speaking like an expert on God's word, she refused to listen to me. Quickly, however, I slipped in a question. "Can you give me five teachings of Jesus?" I asked. This stumped her. Confounded and embarrassed because she couldn't do it, she stepped away defiantly, her high heels clicking.

One afternoon I spoke with five soldiers from Pakistan, and I asked them this question: "If you found out that everything you have been taught about Mohammed, Islam, and the Koran was not true, would you give it up?"

"No, we are Muslims!" they proudly answered.

Thinking maybe I was misunderstood, I reiterated the question. "Just suppose, now" I said. "Just suppose you discovered that all you have been taught was false. Just suppose now, a hypothetical case, just an illustration. Just suppose you found out that all you have been taught was not true, would you turn from it?"

"No, no, no," they all answered, "we are Muslims!"

"Even if you found out it's not true?" I asked.

"No, we would never give it up. We are Muslims!" they replied.

Their answer bordered on insanity! Talk about spiritual blindness! Totally and completely brainwashed—that's what those Pakistani soldiers were.

CHAPTER 55

A BUCKET OF WATER IN GHANA

At the Billy Graham Conference for Itinerant Evangelists in 2000, I met a man named Reverend Justice, who had invited me to come to his country, Ghana, West Africa, to conduct open air meetings and to train his people in this kind of evangelism. In November 2003, I was privileged to go to Ghana.

Arriving in Accra, the capital, I stepped off the plane at midnight into the most stifling heat I had ever felt, and I grew up in Louisiana, which can be terribly hot and humid. Then three men drove me on rough dirt roads, full of deep potholes, through the blackest night I had ever seen. I had read about Africa being "the dark continent," and, believe me, it was dark! Finally, we reached our destination, Akeem Oda, and I fell into bed, exhausted.

A short four hours later, I was handed a bucket of water with which to bathe, and fifteen minutes after that, I was singing in a tin-roofed church with two hundred smiling, dancing fellow believers. Drums sounded like a Tarzan movie. Soon I was dancing with the believers in a circle, and later I preached to many curious eyes and expectant faces.

Using interpreters, I had the opportunity to declare the good news to hundreds and hundreds of people in huge open air meetings in and around Accra. Without doubt, I had the biggest crowds of my entire ministry. At one place there were over a thousand people. Reverend Justice, describing this massive outdoor meeting, said, "They were thick!"

For several days after that meeting, I was hoarse and had a difficult time being heard, but there were untold numbers who made commitments to the Lord Jesus Christ. Praise the Lord!

There were three villages that no white man had ever entered, according to Reverend Justice. He took me to meet the chief. With tribal markings on his cheeks, the chief sat in a big chair and listened as I presented the gospel to him. Reverend Justice interpreted. After getting permission from the chief, I was able to preach "Christ and him crucified" well into the night to Africans in all three villages. Under a very dim light, I explained, as I struck my large railroad spike with a stone, "Jesus was nailed to that cross. He took your sins and my sins on that cross, but he didn't stay dead. Christ is alive today."

As many bowed their heads to receive Christ, tiny fires burned at a distance throughout the villages.

The people in Ghana loved the visual aids that I used to illustrate the gospel. Three pastors took a keen interest in this method of evangelism. Hopefully, they will use what I tried to teach them in a mere two weeks in order to reach their own people for Christ.

We drove to Elmina Slave Castle on the coast, where, years earlier, slaves were held before they were shipped far away, never to see their beloved country, family, or friends again. Our guide told us that men called "freedom fighters" often tried to slip behind the castle walls and free their countrymen who had been captured. But if the freedom fighters were caught, they were thrown into a dark dungeon and the door was not opened until all of them had died. Then, their corpses were dragged out.

I stood in that dark dungeon and the heavy, steel-framed door with skeleton bones painted on it was slammed shut. For a split second I experienced the horror those freedom fighters must have felt, only in my case I was released. Walking all through Elmina Slave Castle, I was ashamed of being a white man.

In Ghana the people worked very hard, especially the women, who rose early in the morning and gathered wood for their ovens and swapped eggs for bread and bananas for dried fish. Surviving was what life was about.

One afternoon as I rested in a mud hut, I felt something move under my pillow. Startled, I raised up and saw a tiny mouse dart into a hole. I thought about how blessed we were in America compared to the people in Ghana, West Africa.

However, the Christians I met were extremely happy and contented, and they treated me royally. Leaving Ghana, I had memories of cocoa beans laid out to dry, mothers toting wrapped-up babies on their backs, snails for dinner, and hands pounding "fu fu."

CHAPTER 56

THE GOOD OL' USA

Even though I missed my Christian friends in Ghana, it was good to be back in America—with fast food, air conditioning, Walmarts, shopping centers, and enough electricity!

Soon I was declaring the good news to a lively New York City street crowd, up close, eye to eye. There was an electricity in the air, and I experienced feedback from my listeners. I had heard movie stars talk about the difference between the stage and screen. They all said that there was something special about being "live" on stage, receiving vibes from their audience, over against just acting in front of a camera for a motion picture. I knew where they were coming from. There was really nothing quite like "live" onstage preaching in the existential moment!

Standing in front of the NASDAQ building with the people actually pushing a little to get closer, I quickly reached for my small white board and markers. As I drew lines, I explained, "When you come to Christ, God forgives you of your past sins (I erased some of the lines). He forgives you of your present sins (I erased some more lines). He forgives you of your future sins (I then erased the remaining lines). God wipes the slate clean. You stand acquitted in his sight, absolved of all charges. That's the fantastic gospel of Christ!"

Several of us were sharing Christ with people from Samoa, Yemen, Korea, China, and Iraq. New York City—what a pond to fish in! As I counseled a couple from Hong Kong who had some very difficult and serious questions that I struggled to answer—about the innocent suffering and the problem of evil—five Muslim women, veiled and dressed in black, stood behind us, waiting to talk to me.

When the Chinese couple moved on down the sidewalk, hopefully with some of their questions answered, I gave the Muslim women some "Little Red Bibles," then we talked several minutes about Christ and the resurrection. I believe the movie *The Passion of the Christ* made an impact on them, based on what they told me.

Many of us have a difficult time witnessing about Christ because we don't know how to begin talking to people about him. We find that it's difficult to go from talking about the ballgame, the weather, your job, and what's going on in the world to the subject of Jesus. Making the transition from talking about everyday life to talking about the Lord is not always easy to do.

But the beauty of a good street meeting is that it's so conducive for talking to people about spiritual things. The transition has already been made. You've shared the word of God, and a number of people have stopped and heard a little of it, and so it's easy to start a conversation up about Jesus because the subject of Jesus has already been brought up in the street meeting.

It gets hot in New York City, too! Standing in unbearable heat one day, dripping with sweat, I looked up and a young lady was walking toward me with a cold bottle of water. "Here, I think you could use this," she said, smiling. "God bless you, miss; man, that looks great! Thank you. Thank you!" I replied. No doubt, that girl was a Christian, and God would not forget what she had just done for me.

I had prayed for clarity that day, because communication is the name of the game. I believe the Holy Spirit is the Great Communicator of the gospel; and I believe he got through to this old gentleman because the man slowly walked up to me and said, "I accepted Jesus as my Lord and Savior. They have found a spot on my lung, and if it's cancer, I want to be prepared to meet God." After I prayed with him, he thanked me and walked away, knowing that he was now right with God—because of the love, mercy, and grace that God demonstrated to all of us by sending his Son, the Lord Jesus Christ, to die on the cross for our sins.

Over the weekend Reverend Justice called me and said that he felt like a revival was breaking out in his area in Ghana. "Some Muslims have been saved, and the churches are growing," he said with excitement. Hallelujah!

One day as I stirred my tempera color paints and prepared to preach, a gentleman asked, "Do you remember me? I talked with you a while back. I'm the Hindu."

"Yes, I remember your face," I replied. And I did. "Have you been thinking any more about Jesus?" I asked. He nodded his head yes and then asked for another business reply card. When I gave it to him, he said, "I'll be back." But I never saw him again.

About that time a young man, part of a student TV crew, asked me about the recent presidential debate. When I gave him my opinion, he had no more to say and quickly began talking to someone else. I moved on down the street because they would be an unnecessary distraction.

As I was about to begin, I noticed a young man who had been observing my sketch board work. "What's this?" he asked. "You an artist?"

"Oh, no. I'm not much of an artist. I use paints to illustrate a little bit. I'm preaching the gospel," I replied.

"I see," he said, and started to leave.

"My friend, do you ever think much about the Lord?" I asked.

"No, not really. I'm Jewish," he answered.

"Hey, Jesus was Jewish," I said in a light manner, smiling.

Several of his friends walked up while we were conversing, and I could tell that he was somewhat embarrassed, but I asked him anyway, "Young man, what happened to Jesus's body? You know, they buried him."

"I don't know, maybe the ants got it," he said, laughing, looking at his friends.

"Look," I replied, "I know you have to go, but if you're a thinking person, you'll ask the central question of history—Jesus's body was not there on the third day, so what happened to it? Think about it, OK?"

He looked at me straight in the eyes and said, "I will," and he and his buddies strolled on down the sidewalk.

After I had preached on the topic "Mind Boggling," in which I emphasized the incarnation, a blind man insisted that I move. "You're in my spot!" he exclaimed. So I left.

But later I saw Joan. Joan was really a black man dressed up in women's clothes. Always wearing big, dark sunglasses, he obviously was messed up and had a low self-image. I saw him periodically and was grateful to God that he had listened to me preach again. Once I told him that he was valuable and Jesus loved him, as I handed him a "Smile." He seemed to appreciate it.

I talked with a young guy who was hung up over the color of Jesus. I detected that his mind had been poisoned by Black Israelite propaganda, but he prayed to invite Christ into his life.

"Listen, if you came to know the Christ that I know, he'll replace that hate with love," I said to him.

With the remark that I made, he threw the Bible down that I had given him and told me to keep my false prophecy. Stubbornly, he stomped away. Then I realized that he was mocking God and just playing with me and was not genuine. There was nothing I could do but pray for him.

One beautiful, autumn day, I looked up and saw the Fulton Mall Security Guard who had wanted a New Testament a week earlier. The women's group from our church had ministered with me the previous week, and we had run out of Bibles. Totally depleted of Bibles, I told the security guard that I would give him one the next time I was back in the area. "Be sure and give that security guard a New Testament," Linda reminded me that morning when I left Farmingdale.

"Hey, my man, here's that Bible for you, remember?" I asked.

"Oh, yeah, thank you, man. God bless you," he said.

Driving home, I wondered whose life had been touched by God. As I got on Southern State, the traffic really began to slow down. "What is this?" I said out loud, "Oh, Belmont! I knew I should have taken the Long Island Expressway!"

CHAPTER 57

REFLECTION IN THE WINDOW

As the subway slowly creaked away, I saw a reflection of myself in the window of the train. "Man," I said to myself, "you look old. Where did all that gray hair come from?" I felt like I was sixteen, but I was over sixty! Our days are "swifter than a weaver's shuttle" (Job 7:6). I knew I had to be about the Master's business because my life, like the hourglass that I used on the sidewalks, was running out. Fast.

A team from First Baptist, Bossier, flew up to minister on the streets. The group was composed of several very mature Christians: Sonny and Jackie Deprang, Jennifer Foster and her daughter Katie, and Patti Robertson (formerly Patti Sherrod).

One bright, sunny day on 149th Street and Third Avenue in the Bronx, with the group from First Baptist, Bossier, forming my initial crowd, I was able to attract many more people around me. They were mostly Hispanic, lower middle class, and they were ripe for evangelism.

Drawing a line on my sketch board, separating God from man, I said, "You remember that Berlin Wall that separated communist East Berlin from free West Berlin? I got to visit that wall, what was left of it. Well, the Bible teaches that there is a wall between sinful man and a holy God. We are separated from God because of our sin—a wall of sin. On that cross, Christ broke through that wall—the barrier of sin (I then made a cross with my paintbrush, connecting God and man.). Listen up. Hear my heart. This is so important. When you come to know Christ—really come to know him—you're connected to God, reconciled to God, no longer cut off from God because of your sin. You're made right with God!"

Many people prayed out loud to receive Christ. What a beautiful sound, hearing lost sinners calling upon the Lord to save them.

What music for God to hear! Standing there, I thought about the Brooklyn Tabernacle Choir singing "His Favorite Song of All"—"when lost sinners now made clean lift their voices loud and strong."

One of the women in the group from First Baptist, Bossier, was, of course, Patti. Along with Al and Doris Bohl and Mrs. Lillian Scott, she used to accompany me at the carnivals and fairs, which seemed like a lifetime ago. Patti, a marvelous singer, was a fantastic soul winner who had a heart of pure compassion. After the meeting, Patti began to talk to a young woman who had been intently listening. Patti presented the gospel to her, and the woman wanted to be saved, but, mentioning a large window in the building across the street, the woman said to Patti, "Don't look now. My boyfriend might be watching me. We're Muslims, and if I turn to Jesus, no telling what he would do."

I had been listening to the conversation, and, while looking down the sidewalk, I pretended that I was carrying on a conversation, but actually I was praying for the young woman. Patti managed to give her a New Testament, which the woman quickly slipped into her purse, but the young woman was shaking, gripped with fear—paralyzing fear. On the way home, all of us talked about how tragic that woman's situation was, and we prayed for her again.

Waller Baptist Church, my home church in Bossier City, Louisiana, sent a large group of Acteens and their chaperones to share Christ on the sidewalks. What a challenging experience that was, working with two carloads of teenage girls!

One evening at Times Square I told them to walk down Broadway, but "be back in five minutes and melt in as part of my audience." Five minutes came, then ten, then fifteen, and they were nowhere to be seen. They were with the adults, so I figured they were all right.

I conducted my street meeting, and when I finished, here they all came, laughing, eating pretzels with mustard and hot dogs—not the least bit concerned, oblivious to everything but the bright lights of Broadway! Well, what could I say? They were just kids.

"We kept trying to round everybody up, Brother Scott," one of the chaperones said, "but they went in all directions." Hey, everybody was OK; that was what was important.

We had a couple of more sidewalk services, and all the girls were very useful, passing out tracts and talking with others on the streets. One day those young ladies will make great women of God, without question, but they were appalled by the decadence and immorality in New York. As they left, I thanked God for safety, ideal weather, and grace with the authorities.

Billy Graham had what was to be his final crusade in Queens in May 2005. I knew the city was ready for a great harvest. I could not attend, however, because our second grandbaby was due. So we were with Stephen and Katie in Arkansas.

Linda and I stayed with Matt while Stephen took Katie to the hospital. They barely made it. But they did, and on June 29, 2005, Anna Grace was born. Having two sons ourselves and then a grandson, at last we had that little girl. God was so good, granting all of us a healthy baby, and we got on our knees and thanked him for our precious little granddaughter.

Linda and I rode the train into Manhattan at Christmastime. We thoroughly enjoyed ourselves as we walked around Rockefeller Center, looking up at the star atop the huge Christmas tree and watching the ice skaters skating joyfully around, with "Silver Bells" playing in the background. Staying close together, we walked around arm in arm to keep warm.

New York City, it has often been said, can be the loneliest place in the world. In the middle of the glitter and glamour on Fifth Avenue, Linda and I observed sad faces and "lonely voices, crying in the city, lonely voices, sounding like a child."

CHAPTER 58

"GIVE MY REGARDS TO BROADWAY"

"I don't know how much longer I can do this," I said to Linda one day after I had driven in from the city.

"Well, you're not as young as you used to be, Scotty," she replied. "Don't overdo it."

Was it time for me to hang it up? The Big Apple had grabbed my heart and held it for years. Could I walk away from New York? And could I do it now?

I had been going "lickety-split" for twenty-six years in New York. They had been glorious, self-fulfilling years, but fighting the traffic, hassling with the cops, conducting street meetings which always contained an element of suspense, hosting groups who came up to minister with me, pastoring Farmingdale Baptist Church—all of it together had been very stressful and had taken its toll on me.

Linda and I sought the Lord's will about this matter, and it was like the Lord said to me, "Go. You can return and minister from time to time."

I thought about Farmingdale Baptist Church. I had been their pastor for over twelve years. We loved everybody very much ("all except one," I always said, which, of course, was a joke), and they loved us. How would they feel? What about our New York friends? My preaching buddies? The people on the street who needed the "gospel truth" so desperately? I saw their faces on the sidewalk. How would I manage without sharing the gospel in New York?

I knew my calling to be an evangelist had not changed. I identified somewhat with the apostle Paul who said, "I consider my life worth nothing to me, if only I may finish the race and complete the task the Lord Jesus has given me—the task of testifying to the gospel of God's grace" (Acts 20:24).

I think the Lord was telling me that he had other places for me to go, and that I needed to trust him.

Telling our church family that we were leaving was extremely difficult, because all of us had become very close.

"We understand," many people said, "but we love you and will miss you. Be sure and come back to see us."

"Hey, we're leaving, but this is not good-bye. We'll be back. You know me. I'll have to come back and preach on the streets from time to time," I said, with my heart breaking.

Just as Julius Caesar crossed the Rubicon in 49 BC, an event that launched the Roman Empire, in February 2006, Linda and I crossed the Hudson, taking the George Washington Bridge out of New York City, and drove south to Dixie. The New York skyline was in my rearview mirror.

The swallows of Capistrano returned each year from Argentina, six thousand miles away, to the mission in the village of San Juan, Capistrano, in California, amid ringing bells and cheering crowds. I would not hear ringing bells and cheering crowds when I returned, but, the Lord willing, I knew in my heart that I would be back to New York City.

> Give my regards to Broadway
> Remember me to Herald Square
> Tell all the gang at Forty-Second Street
> That I will soon be there
> Whisper of how I'm yearning
> To mingle with the old-time throng
> Give my regards to old Broadway
> And say that I'll be there e'er long.
> —George M. Cohan, "Give My Regards to Broadway"

Linda and I were amazed; astounded, actually, at how God had provided. We had lived our lives on miracles. Yes, we had struggled at times, but we had never been without. We always had enough. When funds came in slowly, we prayed. Then I went to the city and preached the gospel, believing that God would provide some way, somehow. He always did.

Our mailing list had never had more than approximately two hundred names on it, but only about fifty families and six churches had consistently contributed to this ministry on a monthly basis. That was not very many. Some people had given a one-time offering, which we greatly appreciated. Others had given periodically. All some people could do was pray for us, and we never took them for granted. It had been phenomenal, absolutely incredible, the way many people had stood behind us all of those years. We referred to them as "the faithful few."

Month after month, year after year, they had sent checks, cards, and notes of encouragement, reminding us that they were praying for us and backing us. From time to time someone would even apologize for being late with his or her support! And it was very humbling to receive a check that had been written out by "shaky hands" because the giver was aging. The faithful few had provided for our health insurance, which was an unbelievable act of generosity on their part. There was no way we could have afforded health insurance if our friends, our faithful Christian friends, had not come to our aid. Phone calls had been made, parties had been given, and money had been raised in order for us to have "brand spankin' new" vans—several of them over the years! The faithful few had backed us and prayed for us and stood behind us in good times and bad times. When the economy was bad, they had still given. When they had sickness, they had still given. When they moved, they had still given. When they lost loved ones, they had still given. When they really couldn't afford it, they had still given.

I often thought of the verse that said, "For unto whomsoever much is given, of him shall be much required" (Luke 12:48). I knew that my Lord had expected me to be wise and trustworthy with all that he had given me. Linda and I both had tried to be faithful with all that the Lord had entrusted us with, as God was our witness.

Vacation Bible schools and Sunday school classes had sent love offerings. RAs had washed cars in order to raise money to purchase New Testaments for me to give away. Thousands of New Testaments had been donated. Friends had made it possible for us to fly home on standby with minimum cost. Others had worked hard on the streets with me. By God's grace we had been able to put our sons in Christian schools for several years in New York.

I had tried to communicate in my newsletters how much we appreciated people's sacrificial giving, but did they really hear my heart? "Oh, God bless the faithful few. You know who they are!"—I had prayed that prayer many, many times. How could I ever express my thanks? No words were adequate.

Yes, Linda and I had been "blown away" at how the faithful few had supported us. What would they think about our moving back home? Most of them, I felt, would understand, and God was our source, ultimately. He had always provided. Would he not continue to do so?

We settled in Chester, Arkansas, between Fort Smith and Fayetteville—forty minutes from our grandkids. The Lord led us to an old home, but one we could afford. Built in the seventies, the house had a lot of character, with stone floors and wooden shutters.

The main part of the house was connected to a dog trot, two log cabins with a breezeway between them, and each with a fireplace. The log cabins were erected in 1863, when Abraham Lincoln was president. They had been restored, of course, but the logs were hewn out by hand many years ago.

Chester had ninety-nine people. What a change from New York City! Instead of being crowded with houses and apartments everywhere, we were in a pleasant valley, surrounded by the beautiful Ozark Mountains. Elbow room!

Yellow honeysuckles and wild pink roses blended together naturally on our fence, and in our front yard there was a magnificent magnolia tree covered with huge, white, sweet-smelling blossoms, enhanced by dark green leaves. Linda soon had gorgeous red roses, as well as other colorful flowers, sprouting up everywhere.

I quickly hung a swing on a grand old oak tree in the backyard for our grandkids to play on—although I realized it would be a while before they would be big enough to swing!

Chester had a Norman Rockwell-looking post office, a grocery store with a gas station, an antique hotel, plus a couple of churches. That was it! But we were fifteen minutes from town, with a Walmart, of course. A crystal-clear picturesque creek with a waterfall ran through Chester.

Before long our entire family was "creekin' "—swimming, paddling around in large inner tubes, and throwing tennis balls into the water and watching Blackie, our Lab, retrieve them.

On frosty mornings, Linda and I, each with a hot cup of coffee, sat in an old porch swing and gazed at our neighbor's cattle and horses in the pasture beside us.

One day Ronney, my brother-in-law, gave me a call. "What you doin', Scotty?" he asked.

"Oh, Linda and I are just a-swangin'," I replied.

"Swangin'? Swangin'? I can tell you are in Arkansas!" he said, laughing.

We didn't just sit in that old porch swing, however. Having taken video footage for over twenty-five years of my street meetings in New York City, I continued working on my training video. Finally, after toiling with it off and on for more than four years, I completed it in Chester. It had been a monumental task. Over twenty hours in length, the training video covered many aspects of outdoor evangelism—how to gather a crowd, dealing with hecklers, using the sketch board, working with the police, conducting children's, teen, and adult meetings, using visual aids and sleight-of-hand tricks, ministering in the subway, and many other areas of outdoor preaching. My prayer was that the Lord would use my experience on the street to help others in the future whom God called to this type of ministry.

As we became familiar with the area, I realized that there were many lost and unchurched people living in close proximity to us. One day I said to myself, "You know, Scotty, it makes no sense to go around the globe telling people about the Lord and not even to try and evangelize those living in your own neighborhood!"

So I began going door to door. I met many "good ol' boys" who only went to church for a funeral. One young man who lived relatively close to us was stoned on meth half the time and walked the roads. Unwed mothers with babies but no husbands and who lived on food stamps and who felt forsaken were sitting in old, worn-out mobile homes not far from us. When I asked people questions about how to go to heaven, their answers were just what I had heard on the streets of New York City—"Just believe in God and be a good person; do your best." I discovered quickly that I needed to be a fisher of men in and around Chester.

Down south in the spring of the year I saw patches of white webs in various trees. Each web was full of worms that were literally eating away the life of the tree. If not removed, the worms would completely destroy the tree, and it would die.

For years in New York City, I had talked with numerous people who had rejected a biblical world view and had replaced it with secular humanism, which was eating away at American society, destroying us.

Now, living in Arkansas, I learned that the same man-centered philosophy had taken hold here in the Bible Belt, and, like in New York, there was a falling away from the faith, and our Southern heritage, steeped in Bible knowledge, was being destroyed like those trees that were being decimated by those worms. If we as a nation did not repent and turn back to the true and living God, I felt we were in danger of God's hand of blessing being removed from America and of judgment falling, if it was not happening already.

However, one morning I received unexpected but surprising good news! A lady who had been trying to locate me for several years came across a "Smile" tract which had the phone number of Farmingdale Baptist Church on it. Getting my number from the church, she gave me a call. " You don't remember me, but I was in your street meeting in the financial district in August, 2001, just before 9/11," she said. " I've often thought about all of those people in that crowd because just a few days later, the Twin Towers fell, but I want you to know that God used you to get me into seminary and into full-time Christian service." Wow! Praise the Lord! What an indescribable feeling I had that day. But I, too, had often thought about those in our street meetings in the financial district before that awful day on 9/11.

In 2007, Linda and I went with Price and Ann Harris to Jamaica as part of their team. I had been to Jamaica several times, but this was the first time for Linda to go. We had braved cold winters for years in New York, so we both were looking forward to the warm weather and were anticipating swimming in the blue-green waters of the Caribbean.

We ministered in the streets, held several revivals in churches, and preached at several schools. Seven hundred high school students stood very still in a schoolyard one hot, sunny day as I preached the good news of Christ. With their brown uniforms on, they listened closely. When I talked about salvation being a gift of God—something we could never earn by doing good deeds—many said yes to Christ!

We visited the School for the Deaf in Mandaville, which I had been to several times. Price and I had seen a number of those students grow up. One girl named Latasha always captured everybody's heart with her smiles, beauty, and sweetness. Now she was a lovely young lady. I was so glad that Linda got to meet her.

Using my props and visual aids, I preached the gospel to the deaf students with an interpreter communicating my message in sign language. As always, they were very receptive, but I had to be extra careful with my sleight-of-hand tricks, or they would have detected how I did them with their exceptional eyesight!

As we visited an orphanage, Linda's heart nearly collapsed. Holding those tiny babies in her arms and kissing them was almost more than she could bear.

"They don't have a mama or a daddy to love them, Scotty," Linda said, crying on my shoulder. Trying to console her, I put my arm around her and replied, "Honey, those nurses do a fantastic job, and God has not forgotten those babies."

Neither Linda nor I will ever forget those tiny faces with sweet, dark eyes staring back at us and languishing in despair. At the end of our stay in Jamaica, we were all drained, but we felt God had anointed our efforts, and, as always, it was a joy to work alongside Price and Ann. Oh, yeah, we did manage to go swimming in the Caribbean, and our entire group visited Ocho Rios and had a fun, slippery time climbing up those Dunn's River Falls!

One day I got a call from First Baptist Church of Winslow, a small church twenty minutes from Chester, up winding, steep Highway 71. After meeting with the church, I was asked if I would consider being their pastor. I shared with the congregation that I would be traveling quite often back to New York and to other countries and that both Linda and I would be gone a lot, helping to take care of our mothers.

"I'll give it a try, but I don't know how long I'll be able to do this," I said. The people understood, and before I could blink, I was a pastor again. The folks at Winslow treated us like family; the church grew a little, and we baptized a few people, but, as I figured, I could not continue to pastor, given all that was on our agenda. After about a year I resigned, but I knew that God had me there to help the church through difficult times. First Baptist Church, Winslow, will always have a special place in our hearts. Soon after we left, the church called a fine young man to be their pastor, and they're doing great.

PART THREE:
OTHER COUNTRIES

CHAPTER 59

FARAWAY PLACES

When I was contemplating leaving New York, I believe the Lord spoke to my heart and said, "Trust me." I felt that there were other places besides New York City that he now wanted me to share the gospel of Christ. Doors began to open.

The Philippines

Dr. Bill Bailey of Bossier City, Louisiana, invited me to be a part of his team to minister in the Philippines. I was delighted to go and went with him for several years straight (2006–2013).

Dr. Bailey usually took doctors, nurses, pharmacists, preachers, and other Christian men and women with him. The physical needs of the people were addressed, and the gospel was preached. Harrell Shelton, associate pastor of Airline Baptist Church in Bossier City, and I presented the good news of Christ, using a large Evangecube and several visual aids.

Pastor Alan Guevarra was our Filipino leader who arranged for us to work with local churches and pastors. Short, like most Filipinos, Alan was a natural leader. No doubt, young Filipino soldiers like Alan had served bravely alongside the Americans in World War II. I noticed immediately that the Filipino pastors helped each other, and there seemed to be no jealousy among them. All were willing to do menial tasks, and all listened to Alan.

Medical clinics were set up at various locations. Each clinic had several stations: a pharmacy, a dental chair, an eyeglasses station, a place for general practice, and a spiritual station.

Sometimes we ministered in a small church building, but often we were outside under a mango tree or a brush arbor. At each place we went, people waited in long lines to receive medical attention. Groups ranging from ten to fifty registered and then sat down and listened to the gospel. Always, we had interpreters, but many people could understand a little English. Harrell and I took turns preaching the gospel, from morning till night, and the Filipino people, mostly nominal Catholics, were extremely receptive to the message of Christ. Each year that I went to the Philippines over a thousand people accepted Jesus as their Lord and Savior.

One afternoon a very old, toothless woman in an out-of-the-way village received the Lord. She began hugging and kissing me, saying, "Jesus, Jesus, Jesus," as she pointed to her heart. Tanned and very wrinkled, she smiled and gave me a string of beads that she had made herself for me to take back to Linda. As we drove away from that tiny village, which was very ignorant of the pure gospel, I saw three little indigenous boys, completely naked, playing with a tiny bird. Having captured it, they had tied a string to one of its legs, preventing it from flying away.

Mount Pinatubo had erupted in 1991 and, along with a massive typhoon, had spread ash deposits for miles and miles. One afternoon we visited an old Catholic church which had been covered in ash so much that the entire first floor was beneath the surface.

In Sta Rita, I got to preach the gospel inside a huge Roman Catholic church filled with people waiting for medical treatment. Normally, as Dr. Bailey's medical team examined patients, prescribed medicine, gave shots, performed minor surgeries, pulled teeth, and fitted glasses, we preachers had a corner outside, hopefully in the shade, and there we preached to group after group.

As I was setting up outside on a basketball court, Alan asked me if we wanted to preach inside the church.

"Inside that big Roman Catholic church? Why, yes!" I exclaimed.

"The priest is away," Alan replied. "It'll be OK."

The church began filling up. I was given a microphone and a fantastic interpreter, Pastor Serrano. More and more people filed in and were seated, with idols, icons, crucifixes, and statues of the Virgin Mary everywhere.

Often I had preached to Catholics on the sidewalks in New York, particularly in the Bronx, but never inside a Roman Catholic church! For the next half hour from the pulpit, I proclaimed the glorious good news of Jesus Christ.

"We worship a living Savior...eternal life is a free gift...give your heart to

Christ...he will clothe you in his righteousness," I declared, praying that God the Holy Spirit would communicate the truth to the people. Explaining how to accept Jesus, I saw heads bowed and heard people repeating the sinner's prayer. Hands went up from all directions, indicating that they were relying just on Christ, not the sacraments, to be their Savior and Lord. Probably 150 people professed faith in Christ in that one meeting. Later, Harrell had a similar experience. To God be the glory!

I spent the late afternoon riding around with Rio my favorite interpreter in the side car of his motor bike. Whew! What a ride! Long taxis, called jeepneys, decorated with multicolored designs came at us from all sides, filled with occupants. The jeepneys open in the back where riders can quickly climb in, and slide down benches against the wall. Many have names such as "Ramblin' Rose" or "Mercy of God."

Rio and his wife, Gemma, recently married, are a wonderful Christian couple who minister in that area, Sta Rita, Pampanga. I shared many object lessons and visual aids with Rio, and he is the kind of faithful preacher who will use them.

A major denomination in Pampanga is called "the Church of No Christ." As we drove around, we spotted these churches everywhere. Beautifully built, they look like cathedrals.

Rio and Gemma live in a one-room, garage-looking church building where Rio is the pastor. No, they don't have an expensive, ornate church like the churches in that Christ-less denomination, but they certainly have the Lord Jesus Christ!

Bernadette, a very lovely, kind Christian woman in the Philippines, is the sister of Pastor Alan. She always is extremely helpful, bringing cold ice water to all of us on Dr. Bailey's team, and assisting us any way she can.

I learned that during the monsoon season, Bernadette has to walk to work every day in water up to her waist. She changes into dry clothes, earns a few pesos, and then returns home.

We ministered one year in Coron, in the beautiful Palawan Islands, known for their crystal-clear water. Coron is the scuba-diving capital of the Pacific, and divers explore sunken Japanese ships from World War II and swim among the spectacular coral reefs teeming with marine life.

Some of us just had to go swimming in that blue water, which, like the sirens of Greek mythology, seemed to be calling out to us. How refreshing it was, but Dr. Bailey cut his foot on a coral while climbing back into the boat. But he is a doctor. He knew what to do!

I kept noticing a few people in small boats. "They are guarding the bird nests," Alan explained. Swiftlet nests are in the rocky crevices on the islands. How do they make their nests? The birds excrete their saliva, and when exposed to the air the saliva jells. The birds then make nests out of it. The nests are collected, sold for hundreds of dollars each, and then a soup is made from the nests that, to many, is a real delicacy. Bird nest soup! I cannot imagine eating soup made from the saliva of a stupid bird!

As I preached the gospel under a make-shift bamboo and banana leaf arbor to protect us from the scorching sun, several men eased their way through the people, helping a man who had an injured foot swollen twice its normal size. How relieved he was when he got medical attention and when a piece of bamboo, which had caused the infection, was removed. Then he was given priceless antibiotics. Looking around, I could not help but notice a little girl who had a horribly deformed face. Standing close to her daddy, she tried to hide. Glancing at her, I cried in my soul.

SCOTT AND ALAN

Libby Horton, one of our team members, fitted hundreds of people with glasses, and they were very proud of them, tucking them away in their new glasses cases. Then Libby passed out balloons to the children.

Dr. Bailey had extracted so many teeth that as we left the islands and I looked out of the plane window, I joked, "People are walking around everywhere with gauze in their mouths, Dr. Bailey!"

On our way back home we stopped in Tokyo and toured the city for an entire day. I was surprised to see thousands of people wearing masks to protect themselves from germs.

One afternoon as we visited the beautiful, glittering Buddhist and Shinto temples, scores of people prayed and chanted before gold idols, seeking forgiveness. Many lit incense sticks and blew smoke into their faces, hoping for better health and a brighter future. I felt sorry for them, and I thanked God for the truth of God's word.

Our Japanese tour guide was extremely friendly and could speak five languages fluently. Several of us witnessed to her, and she promised to read the New Testament and *Mere Christianity*, by C. S. Lewis, which one of our doctors, Dr. Rao, gave to her. I truly believe that the Holy Spirit was convicting her and that eventually she will be saved.

One year we ministered in Baguio City, a beautiful, mountainous area known for its colorful flowers and vacationing tourists. We drove up steep, winding roads, with trucks and cars constantly passing each other. It was downright scary, and I was glad when we arrived!

With cashew trees blowing in the hot wind, we went to work immediately, laboring from early in the morning until late in the afternoon, day after day. Bent over for hours and with his back killing him, Dr. Bailey pulled tooth after tooth and dropped them, clinking, into a metal pan as roosters crowed and little baby chicks pecked in and around his feet.

Dr. Kirk Cofran, not in the best of health himself, gently removed a growth from a baby's forehead as a nervous mother held her baby's head still. The pharmacist, Don Salyer, and his wife, Lorene, talked, made friends, met needs, filled prescriptions, and never complained.

Harrell, standing tall and huge in his light green scrubs, was unbelievably flexible and adept at doing whatever was necessary— labeling medicine, offering advice, pulling teeth, preaching.

Glenn Carter, proudly wearing his purple and gold LSU cap, was always working extremely hard, sweating and laughing, wanting to make his life count for the Lord.

Billy Weatherall, a young, handsome soldier who had served in Africa, Iraq, and Afghanistan, was constantly bragging on people as they tried on glasses. "You look great!" he said, smiling, knowing he was exaggerating.

Many in this area worshiped rocks, animals, and ancestors, but upon hearing about the true and living God, over a thousand, once again, put their faith in the Lord Jesus Christ.

While we were in Baguio City, I was very concerned about my new little granddaughter, Jenny, who had been born just before I left for the Philippines. The date was February 7, 2009, a day that my family and I will never forget. My son Stewart and his wife, Sharon, had their first baby, a darling little girl named Jenny Lou Teague. But there were major complications at her birth. Her diaphragm had not fully formed, which often allowed organs to enter the chest cavity, preventing lung growth. We had prayed for days, pleading with the Lord to make her well. He answered our prayers! Doctors at Texas Children's Hospital corrected the defect laparoscopically for the first time in hospital history. For a month, Jenny lay in critical condition. When I flew to the Philippines, we felt that she would be OK, but still there was a question mark in my mind. While in Baguio City, I prayed constantly for her. When I returned, however, I learned that she had fully recovered! Today, Jenny is a perfectly normal child in every way. Praise God, from whom all blessings flow!

A number of times while in the Philippines, we took a boat ride to Corregidor, where so much fierce fighting had taken place during World War II. Viewing the caves that were dug out on high cliffs and had been used as strongholds, I thought about the heroic efforts of American and Filipino troops as they fought side by side against the Japanese, shooting and being shot at.

Pastor Alan's church was located on the Bataan Highway upon which the Bataan death march took place in 1942. I was born December 21, 1942, several months after that brutal march, during which thousands of Filipino and hundreds of American prisoners had died. Our group toured the huge, white Bataan Memorial Cross on Mount Samat.

I thought about the many lives that were lost at both Bataan and Corregidor in order to preserve our freedom. Without those soldiers' ultimate sacrifice, I would not have been able to preach the gospel, years later, outside the walls of the church in America or anywhere else, for that matter.

"Alan, come quick! There's a snake in the kids' bedroom," screamed Elnora. Having heard his wife's desperate cry, Alan rushed in and killed not one but two cobras! Although this happened just before we arrived one year in the Philippines, Alan told me all about how he killed those snakes with a knife. We held a medical clinic in the very building where this took place, and I found myself constantly on the lookout for a snake!

"Did you eat the cobra?" I asked Alan.

"No, we eat pythons but not cobras," he replied, smiling like he was hungry!

One afternoon as we took a break and did some souvenir shopping, I talked to a Buddhist from Japan. The Lord opened his heart, and he joyously received Christ as his Lord and Savior; but he wanted more information about Jesus. Dr. Twilley, our dentist, searched his luggage and found a copy of "Four Spiritual Laws," which the now ex-Buddhist gladly took, nodding and graciously thanking us.

Close by was a young man with a mask covering his face to protect him from the dust as he drove around on his motorbike. He had a sad story, feeling very insignificant and forgotten; but, praise God, he, too, came to the Lord, and Dr. Twilley's assistant, Delaine, gave him her own Bible, a very expensive one, because the young man promised us he would read it. We all knew the Holy Spirit was at work!

One year I came back from the Philippines with an acute sinus infection. I had the worst headache of my entire life. Then Linda got bitten by a brown recluse spider in Chester and ended up in the emergency room. Even though she was treated with medication, her arm was red and swollen for days. It took a while, but eventually we both recovered, thank God.

In May 2011, my dear, sweet mother went home to be with the Lord. For months we had been trying to help take care of her, making many trips to Bossier.

Finally, at age ninety-seven, she was escorted by the angels into the arms of her Savior. My sister, Barbara Ann, who was with her when she breathed her last breath, said, "Scotty, Mother had a big smile and great joy on her face."

I knew I would always miss my mother. But I also knew that by God's grace we would see each other again in glory!

But God is good all the time, and soon we were blessed with another grandbaby. Stewart and Sharon had a beautiful baby girl, Clementine Rose Teague, born on November 3, 2011. Oh, how we thanked God for her, as we did for all of our grandchildren. Soon we would be holding her gently on the red-maned, wooden rocking horse that we had purchased years earlier in Pennsylvania.

Linda's mother was still hanging on, but, seemingly, going down every day. Having made numerous trips to Southaven, Mississippi, to see her, we were worn out. Memee was in and out of the hospital and rehab, but she wanted to remain at home, so we had a care-taker with her most of the time.

Year after year as I was part of Dr. Bailey's team to the Philip-pines, I was constantly blessed. One afternoon as we were packing up and getting ready to leave the medical clinic, a woman named May was very excited about her new glasses. When I gave her a Bible, she hugged me real big and exclaimed, "Now, I've got my own Bible, and with my new glasses, I can read it!" May then gave me a set of earrings to take back home to Linda. They were made from cheap red glass, but she gave them from her heart, and they were priceless.

Having just returned from the Philippines one year, I learned that Linda's mother had just passed away, March , 2012. She had been in hospice in Fayetteville, and the nurses were wonderful to her, keeping her as free from pain as possible. Oh, how Linda will miss Memee, but, glory to God, she is in the very presence of God! Soon and very soon we are all going to see the King together.

In 2013, once again the flight to Manila was brutal, but to be able to hug my Filipino friends was worth the long hours in the air. One day a pretty teenage girl with a bright yellow shirt on kept hanging around, needing some dental care. Dr. Bailey decided against pulling one of her teeth; instead, he urged her to brush better. When the girl sat down beside some of us, I began to share the gospel with her, and May, the woman who had given me a set of earrings for Linda the previous year, was my interpreter! Patricia was the girl's name, and she received Jesus as her personal Lord and Savior. "My mother is a voodoo witch doctor," she told us.

"Read the book of John," I said, as I gave her a small Gideons New Testament.

"My mother will not allow that, but I'll do it anyway," she replied, smiling. May God bless that young lady! It was an honor to be a part of Dr. Bailey"s team and to minister in the Philippines for a number of years. God alone knew how many people came to know Christ as their Lord and Savior, but thousands professed faith in him. The Christian men and women on his team –and I have mentioned just a few of them- are friends of mine to this day.

At the end of each trip to the Philippines, Dr. Bailey liked to take all of us out to eat authentic Filipino food. He would eat anything! Not me. Many of my interpreters told me that the Filipino people ate rats, so I learned quickly to find me some pizza!

(DR. BILL BAILEY AND HIS WIFE, VICKIE)

India (May 2006)

A fine, Christian gentlemen, Pastor Chacho, of Huntington, New York, had shared with Farmingdale Baptist Church, when I was their pastor, about the great need for the gospel in his homeland of India. I had been deeply moved and told him that one day I would love to preach the gospel in India. Not long after that, Pastor Chacho contacted a close friend of his, Pastor Abraham, head of Ebenezer Bible College, in Kerala, India, and told him I would like to come and minister with him in his native country. Soon I was on my way. My legs cramped badly during the long flight, over thirty hours, but I made it finally.

Pastor Abraham picked me up in Kochi and carried me to Ebenezer Bible College, where I was to stay. The campus was immaculate and well kept, with rubber trees everywhere and gorgeous, eye-catching flowers—orange, yellow, and red.

The next day I began instructing approximately seventy-five male students in outdoor evangelism, using the props, visual aids, and object lessons that I had employed on the streets of New York City. How excited the men were! "More, more," they exclaimed, "teach us everything!" They assured me that this method would be very useful for them to reach the villages with the message of Christ.

I felt my main reason for going to India was to train students at the Bible college in open air evangelism, but I was able to preach the gospel also. When I preached out of doors, however, Pastor Abraham was nervous and insisted that I not do it much. "It's dangerous!" he explained, "You're American. The radical Hindus might harm you, even kill you. Our men don't fear persecution; but often it's life threatening for even us to preach." He showed me a picture of one of his former students who had been killed and pictures of two other students who had been hacked by machetes for their faith in Christ.

Kerala is a communist state with the hammer and sickle on posters everywhere, but the communists do not oppose the gospel like the Hindus. Christianity is considered a foreign religion, and many Hindus connect it to the British oppression in India during the last century.

Even though I was unable to preach out of doors very much, I did get to preach to hundreds of children and adults indoors. At a kids' camp, many Hindu women with dots on their foreheads, surrounded by numerous children, sat quietly and listened as I proclaimed, "There is one God. He created the sun, the moon, the stars. He created you and me. The breath you breathe, God gave to you. You and I are created in his image. God is not like a rock or a piece of wood. God is Spirit…he has a Son. His name is the Lord Jesus Christ. He died on a cross for your sins and my sins. But he came back alive!"

There were countless decisions for Christ! After the evangelistic service, everybody was served cake and green tea, which was greatly appreciated.

India has fifteen official languages and over three hundred dialects, so I had an interpreter at every place I preached. At one location I had three different interpreters who spoke different dialects. I would say, "God loves you," and one interpreter would translate "God loves you" to the second interpreter; then the second interpreter would translate "God loves you" to the third interpreter. Finally, the third interpreter would translate "God loves you" to my listeners.

While we drove across steep, rugged mountains, I saw thousands of rows of plants, luscious and symmetrically terraced. "That's green tea," Pastor Abraham said. The mountain roads were paved but very treacherous, with winding curves and drop-offs thousands of feet below.

Gandhi once said, "India lives in her villages," and I understood what he meant. Masses of people were everywhere in horrible living conditions with very little electricity, fly-infested meat hanging in open air markets, and impure water. My heart wept as I saw dusty grass huts filled with skinny, dark-skinned people, staring out at us with hopeless eyes.

The paganism was appalling. Hindu shrines, places of worship, temples, idols, as well as elaborately constructed wooden totem poles with angry-looking carved gods, brightly painted, were everywhere! Driving carefully around Brahma bulls, which are worshiped, Pastor Abraham said, "Better to hit a child than a cow." I had never seen such spiritual darkness. Pastor Abraham told me that "the Hindu religion has 330 million gods."

One afternoon I rode an elephant, and later Pastor Abraham and his family gave me a boat ride on a spectacular lake. As we talked and laughed, I was told by his two beautiful daughters that their parents would select the men who would be their future husbands. "You've got to be kidding!" I replied, as I ate very spicy food.

"No, they will," the girls said, "but we trust God that he will direct them to the right guy."

"But what if you don't love him?" I asked.

"We will learn to love him," they answered.

423

"Do you ever have any input, any say-so?" I asked with concern.

Laughing and glancing at their parents, they answered, "Oh, maybe a little."

The men at the Bible College sang with strong joy in their hearts. I could hear in their voices their unyielding commitment to Christ and their desire to evangelize India. They reminded me of the singing at Victory Temple in San Antonio years earlier, and of the singing at the Billy Graham conferences, only the singing was more moving—which I did not think was possible.

As I left, the students presented me with a big sign: "Please Come Back!" Many of them were already using the visual aids I had given them and were sharing Christ with other Indians. As you can imagine, this was a great encouragement to me! One student then told with me that when he accepted Christ, his parents disowned him, and as he told me his story, he wept for his family. The guys at the school were "losing their lives for Christ," content to evangelize and plant churches, laboring in total obscurity.

Brazil (July 2006)

In the summer of 2006, I had the privilege of ministering in Brazil with Dr. Wayne Jenkins and a large contingent of preachers, physicians, and carpenters from Louisiana. Flying into Sao Paulo, an enormous city of twenty million people, our group conducted vacation Bible schools, repaired an orphanage, and met many medical needs. When food was distributed and Bibles were handed out, the people were overwhelmed, extremely grateful. The native language of Sao Paulo is Portuguese, so we always had interpreters with us, regardless of what we did.

The street team of which I was a part preached in city squares, parks, the streets, and in the favellas (slums), with human waste in the crooked, hilly, stony paths leading into the tiny, crumbling little houses. We walked around the neighborhoods and went door to door on the narrow streets and presented the gospel. As they did when Jesus walked the earth, the common people "heard us gladly."

One evening, several of us visited a high-security women's prison. Depressed, distraught, and demoralized women were seated all around the huge room. My good friend Carl Carrigan from Shreveport, who had worked with me in New York City many times, did a rope trick, which they enjoyed very much. Then, after I did the newspaper trick, I took my set of weigh scales, my dirty rag, and my red cloth and presented the gospel. The women paid very close attention to what we said.

But when our singer, a very sweet, humble young woman, began to sing, God's power fell! It was an awesome moment. The Spirit of God filled that place. Many of the imprisoned women wept openly, cried out to God to be delivered from drugs, and called on Christ to save them. What happened was inexplicable, because the supernatural work of God saturated that prison after that young woman sang. I believe many of those women were truly converted by the Lord that night.

Before our team left, we visited the magnificent Iguazu Falls in Argentina. Much larger than Niagara Falls, they were spectacular. I pray that the Lord will allow me to return to Brazil one day.

Ukraine (July 2007)

As I stood to preach in the small church, I'll never forget the exuberant, joyful singing of the Ukrainian Christians, who just a few years ago were under the steel hand of the Soviet Union. Oh, how the music resonated throughout the building! I knew that no political system, no form of government, no difference in language or culture could divide us. We were all just brothers and sisters in Christ.

Kiev, the capital of Ukraine, is a very modern city with its own subway, heavy traffic, and gold-domed Orthodox churches. A huge titanium statue of Mother Russia, with a drawn sword in her right hand and a hammer and sickle in her left, overlooks the entire city.

Some of our group ministered in Kiev, but my party was composed of a medical and evangelistic team, and we worked in the villages a short distance from Chernobyl, where the people lived just like they did immediately after World War II. Everything was old and falling apart, with lawns that needed mowing. Uncut grass was very noticeable everywhere. Outdoor toilets with no paper and rusty-looking wells dotted the landscape. There was no air conditioning, and the temperature each day was over one hundred degrees. Driving through the neighborhoods, we spotted huge storks nesting, and as we entered homes, we saw pictures of Stalin and statues of Lenin as well as icons of saints and the Virgin Mary— many times on the same wall!

I presented the gospel as clearly as I could to those who came each day to the makeshift medical clinics. There were not any huge crowds, just a sprinkling of people—three or four at a time, maybe nine or ten later, then six or seven. They were all very, very old. I'm talking eighty years of age up into the nineties.

As I looked into the eyes of the old Ukrainian and Russian women with their head scarves on and as I looked into the hollow faces of the old, worn-out men, I realized that they were the reason God had sent me to Ukraine. Having grown up under atheistic communism and having only a touch of Orthodox religion, which had confused and misled them, they had no hope whatsoever. When I shared the love of Christ and how they could know God and have a personal relationship with Jesus, how they could have their sins forgiven and have the assurance of heaven, their eyes began to shine and their minds began opening up and receiving the good news. It was heartwarming for me when I heard them repeat after the interpreter the sinner's prayer to receive Jesus into their heart. Many came to a saving knowledge of Christ. Praise the Lord!

Pastor Alexander, with whom we were working, was the kind of man who took seriously those who accepted Christ and no doubt will be faithful to follow up.

A number of gypsies came by the clinics, and one afternoon I realized that as I preached to them, I was standing in a huge ant bed! But as I slapped my ankles and legs and cleared the ants from my socks, the gypsies continued to stand there and listen to the gospel.

Later, several of us went to their pitiful-looking homes and shared the word of God to a few of them, as outdoor fires softly burned and as tiny ducks ran around our feet. I carefully presented the gospel to one middle-aged gypsy woman who, I believe, really did come to know Christ. When we drove away, she was smiling and joyfully waving good-bye, her hand high in the air. Only God really knows people's hearts, but I believe a number of gypsies were truly converted. I saw the peace of God move into their faces.

One afternoon, I accompanied my friend Dr. Bailey as he made visits to the elderly who were sick. As he examined the cramping legs of a very old woman, her husband showed me a picture of their son, a fine-looking soldier who had been in the Russian army. "He left and never came back," the old man said, sobbing and wiping his eyes. Talk about aching inside for somebody—I sure did.

Mexico (2007)

In the past, I had preached the gospel along the border in Mexico, but on this trip I was part of a team of twelve who traveled into the interior. Flying into Mexico City, we then took a bus to the town of Cordoba and began ministering to approximately one hundred students at the Mexican Indian Bible College.

We had to be up, dressed, and seated for breakfast in the dining hall at six thirty—that's in the morning, of course! Before we ate a typical Mexican meal of beans, tortillas, and fruit, the students, both men and women, sang very memorable, melodious songs in

Spanish, expressing great joy around the tables. Their music was worth getting up early for and prepared me for the day!

In our group, the men poured concrete, which I was not good at, and helped with the general overall construction on the campus, while the women taught sewing. One of the main reasons why I went to Cordoba was to teach the national pastors a different way to do outdoor evangelism, but I really did not have much opportunity to do so. However, I did preach the gospel in a number of small churches, and I held several children's meetings. With a spectacular view of mountains far off and red, orange, and white flowers up close, we conducted one of the meetings at an orphanage, very well attended with many young people and adults present.

They seemed to like my visuals, especially the Russian dolls. Several wooden dolls are inside each other. Starting with the largest to the smallest, I said, "When people look at us, we don't let them see the real us, do we? We put walls up. We hide behind masks. Do you ever feel invisible, like nobody cares? We have to fit in, project an image. But you know, God sees through all those barriers." As I held up the last doll, which is extremely small, I said, "Do you know what God says when he sees the real you? He says, 'I love you, and I sent my Son, the Lord Jesus Christ, to die for you.'"

One day at a soccer field, the college students spread out a round, multicolored parachute which the children quickly sat down on, pushing the air out of the parachute and laughing and playing. The students had built a good relationship with many of these children, and they sang songs with the kids, did skits, and performed a puppet show. Using my props, I presented the gospel. The children were glad that we came and wanted us to come back.

One very talented young man told us that he had moved from America to Mexico to protect his kids from drugs, which was a sad commentary on our country. Having been raised a Catholic, he knew only "good works religion." When he accepted Christ, he realized that Christ's righteousness had been imputed to him, and he was beside himself. Oh, what a great God we serve!

Before leaving, we all went swimming in a huge, outdoor pool built with solid rock and fed by an underground spring. The blue-green water was very, very deep. I finally got up enough nerve to jump off the high diving board. I didn't think I would ever surface!

As we looked out of the window on the bus ride back to Mexico City, we were all amazed at the huge, active volcano.

Uganda (September 2008)

The smiling, laughing children waved vigorously at us as we drove into the villages, composed of nothing more than mud huts with thatched roofs, having no electricity, no indoor plumbing, no running water. Seeing women carrying back-breaking loads of sticks was a common sight. We were working in the area where Idi Amin, "the Butcher of Uganda," had massacred over three hundred thousand people in the seventies.

I was privileged to minister with a group from Macedonia Baptist Church outside of Atlanta, Georgia. We stayed with Tommy and Teresa Harris in Jinja. What faithful servants they are! The medical team that I was a part of, which included Dr. Bill Bailey of Bossier City, Louisiana, was superb! They treated hundreds of people. Many of the children had lice and fungal issues. To see them receive medicine that would cure them was thrilling.

My responsibility was to preach the gospel. Pouring out my heart to Africans in small churches and schools, I was blessed big time! Big-eyed children sat crammed together on wooden desks and listened as I declared, "God loves you. He knows how many hairs are on your head. You're valuable. God knows your name."

I conducted an open air meeting in a fishing village beside Lake Victoria, one of the sources of the Nile River. Many days we saw crocodiles, large and small, sunning on the muddy banks of the Nile. As I captured attention by doing several sleight-of-hand tricks, the fisherman, both men and women, gathered up real close around me, some eating sugar cane as I spoke. There were Muslims in attendance, and the wife of a very powerful and influential Muslim wanted to accept Christ, but she refused to do so because of fear of her husband. I had talked with him earlier, and he wanted nothing to do with Jesus. Dr. Bailey, however, led an entire Muslim family to the Lord one day as we walked around a wretched place that they called a hospital, praying for the sick and afflicted.

My interpreter, Malcolm, began using some of my object lessons and visuals and was amazed at how they attracted large crowds. Malcolm spoke seven dialects and was a gifted evangelist. Can you imagine how God could use him to teach others and to spread the gospel to his fellow Africans? He was saving up money to be married. He had to purchase three cows in order to obtain his wife. Laughing and joking, I made a small contribution. "Be sure and use this money to get that bride!" I said, being certain that he would.

We entered a prison one afternoon that had deplorable living conditions. The men slept on stone floors, crowded together on blankets. There were no beds. They caught rainwater in order to bathe. In the courtyard more than two hundred prisoners, dressed in orange shirts and yellow shorts, crowded under a tin roof to get out of the sun. Others watched and listened from their cells.

They were anxious to hear about the Lord. Several of the prisoners were Christians, and they had already been witnessing to other inmates. "I would rather preach to you than preach to the largest church in America," I exclaimed, and the guys clapped and cheered. Using many visuals and then the large Evangecube, I said, "Christ took the rap for you on that cross. And he arose! When you accept him as your Lord and Savior, God drops all charges against you. He pardons you. He sets you free from the penalty, the power, and, one day, the very presence of sin." I deemed it an honor to preach to them. Many received the Lord and thanked us over and over for being there.

One afternoon, while several shirtless men banged on drums and whistled, performing for tourists, we marveled at beautiful Lake Victoria. We began taking pictures of roaring white rapids; then we saw a man holding onto a plastic gasoline container, swimming in the rushing, swirling water. Again and again, he went over the treacherous rapids, trying to earn money from onlookers. I could not believe the risk he was taking because beneath the surface of the water were giant rocks and boulders. We were told that a swimmer had recently died while attempting this feat.

Leaving Uganda was sad because we felt such love from everybody. Part of the time we had worked in a small mud church with a huge stump root right outside the front door. Driving away, we noticed several eight- and nine-year-old boys jostling for our plastic water bottles that we had thrown away in a garbage bag, beside that old stump root. They would use them for toys.

Rwanda (2009)

This was my third trip to Africa, having previously visited Ghana and Uganda. Several groups partnered together to try to help meet the physical and spiritual needs of the people—Africa New Life Ministries, Compassion Connect, and Whitesburg Baptist Church in Huntsville, Alabama. Dr. Bailey and I were asked to join them.

"Allah! Allah! Allah!"—I woke up every morning to the Muslim call to prayer, long before the roosters crowed. In fact, the Muslim chant and the roosters sounded the same all over the world, only I would much rather hear the roosters!

As in other countries of Africa, the needs of Rwanda were overwhelming. One doctor reported that every child in a village that he visited had worms. Hundreds of children were treated for lice and skin diseases and were given antibiotics, and how happy the people were to get glasses and to be able to see clearly at last.

I preached the gospel daily, most of the time under a huge tent. Using the large Evangecube and a number of my object lessons, I was able to present Christ to hundreds of people, about fifty at a time. There was an openness to the gospel that was very apparent, and many people were saved. To God be the glory!

One day I heard an agonizing cry. As I opened the door in the medical clinic, a woman was on the floor screaming and pulling her hair in anguish. The nurse standing there told me that the woman had just learned that she tested positive for HIV.

Children bathed under a shower in the open air, scrubbing themselves and washing their clothes, simultaneously, while others played on a makeshift car, seated on a flat board and rolling it on two logs. The teens made their soccer balls out of rolled up banana peelings wrapped with strings; but when someone in our group presented a kid with a brand-new soccer ball from America, he could not keep his eyes off of it and, obviously, could not wait for us to leave so that he and his buddies could kick it around!

Traveling through the bush, we saw huge ant hills, zebras, deer, wild hogs, giraffes, hippos, wildebeests, monkeys, impalas, and baboons. While taking pictures of the baboons, I lost my glasses. "If anybody sees a *National Geographic Special* that shows a baboon wearing glasses, they're mine!" I said, with everybody laughing.

As you know, Rwanda had experienced war between the Hutus and the Tutsis in 1994. The genocide was targeted mainly at the minority Tutsi population. The French government and the United Nations were also politically involved. Thousands upon thousands of Rwandans were killed—many shot, others hacked to death with machetes. The movie *Hotel Rwanda* depicted this war. Driving down many of the roads where, years ago, bodies had been left in the ditches, we visited the actual hotel where numerous people hid for their lives, and we later toured the memorial, which showed pictures of the atrocities committed. I never want to see that again.

Romania (2010)

Accompanying Price Harris of Calvary Baptist Church in Shreveport, Louisiana, and a group of twenty from Sardis Baptist Church in Boaz, Alabama, my trip to Romania was very moving and thought provoking.

The Romanian countryside, with its rolling hills and herds of sheep, was soothing to my mind. Each herd of sheep had a shepherd close by, sometimes in a small hut. Sprinkled along the way were fields of red poppies and haystacks. Strong horses and strong farmers plowed together. We ministered in several churches in Cluj-Napoca and Timisoara. Oh, what praying people the Romanians were. One after another they stood and prayed, long and hard. As they sang, I felt their great love for God and country.

Romania did not gain its freedom until about twenty years ago. Back in December 1989, a Hungarian Reformed minister, Pastor Tokes, was being evicted from his church by the police because he was speaking out against the communist regime and the brutal dictator Ceausescu. Pastor Tokes's congregation gathered around him and would not let him be taken. This incident spread like wildfire and sparked a revolution throughout Romania. Over one hundred thousand people gathered in Liberty Square in Timisoara; they prayed and sang hymns. Soldiers and tanks came down upon the people, and a terrible bloodbath ensued, with many people dying. Still, they would not stop praying. Within one week, Ceausescu was overthrown and Romania was free!

Price asked me to accompany him to see the museum depicting all of the carnage. With Romanian songs being sung and actual footage of the revolution being shown, it was heartbreaking. Above us were two flags: On the left was the red communist flag with the yellow hammer and sickle in the middle. On the right was the red, yellow, and blue Romanian flag, but there was a big hole in the center of the Romanian flag where the communist hammer and sickle had been cut out! I developed a deep respect for the Romanian people. What strength and resilience they displayed throughout those hard years of persecution.

We visited the very Reformed church where the revolution began, and we walked around Liberty Square, where the people had prayed. Later, I talked to the daughter-in-law of Brother Andrew, the courageous Christian who had smuggled Bibles into Romania before the revolution. She told me he slipped in over five hundred thousand Bibles!

One morning we visited an elderly pastor who was now paralyzed. Under communism, he was forced to quit preaching and ordered to pick up garbage. Having prayer with him, we sang, "How Great Thou Art," and a team member played on his trumpet "What a Friend We Have in Jesus." The old pastor, who had suffered so many indignities, cried tears of gratitude. That scene is etched in my mind forever.

Visiting an orphanage for unwed mothers, Price held many little babies, including a beautiful little girl dressed in pink, with a pink ribbon around her head. A number of the women in our group gave very encouraging testimonies. Both they and the mothers were strengthened.

Romania is known for its gypsy population, and we went into some gypsy villages and conducted a few small street meetings. The gypsy children grabbed our hearts with their big brown eyes, gorgeous skin color, captivating smiles, and memorable giggles. We ministered at a church that feeds the gypsy children twice a week. The pastor invited us to share the gospel, and scores of kids accepted Christ. Given the gypsy lifestyle, Jesus is their only hope.

We preached in two different prisons, one high security. The warden showed us poems written on prison walls by political dissidents, poems that expressed prayers for their persecutors, and poems praising God. One of our interpreters was a close friend of Richard Wurmbrand, who wrote *Tortured for Christ.* All of us sensed the mighty work of God as we ministered in the prisons. We gave testimonies, sang, and preached the gospel. Many prisoners called on the name of the Lord to save them. At the high-security prison, each member of our team was given a letter opener made by the prisoners. Fashioned from steel with a sharp blade and a bone handle, each letter opener was ornate yet very deadly. That was ironic, because the guards were careful not to allow us to take anything dangerous inside the prison walls, not even a camera. Yet we each walked out of the prison with quite a weapon!

After a Sunday morning service, a well-dressed Romanian woman approached me; she was obviously upset and under conviction. "I should have come forward. I wanted to," she explained. We talked a couple of minutes, and then, through her tears, this woman committed her life to Christ. Happy and excited, she laughed and cried simultaneously. "I just received the Lord," she told the pastor and her nephew, who had brought her to church.

During our closing service, Price led the congregation in "I've Got a Mansion Just Over the Hill Top," and Cheri Taylor sang "I Bowed on My Knees and Cried 'Holy.' " I thought I would rapture!

Even though I was ministering mainly overseas in a number of foreign countries, I continued traveling to New York periodically. Watching the NBC *Nightly News* and seeing the skyline of New York City made me yearn to declare the truth of God's word on those hard, concrete sidewalks.

But it wasn't the same. Many of my co-laborers had gone on to be with the Lord, including George Naggy, Phil Foglia, Jerry Langston, and Burris Jenkins. Others were no longer around. Al Terhune was preaching in Europe. Ellis had a thriving ministry in Africa. Getting older like I was, Art Williams was not in New York very often.

But Richard McDermott was still driving that taxi in Jersey, was still single, and was still passing out tracts by the hundreds of thousands. I did manage to meet up with him and Ken Fisher one day, and we all took turns preaching and later enjoyed some New York pizza just like the good old times.

I began to recruit other friends to work with me. One hot, humid, summer day, Greg Karris, a man I had known for years at Grace Baptist Church, accompanied me to the Bronx. After holding a couple of interesting street meetings, I began to talk to a guy who had been listening to me preach. As I attempted to share a few verses of scripture with him, I realized I couldn't see! Duh—I had forgotten my glasses! Well, Greg began to read the Bible for me. Thumbing through verse after verse and reading them to the guy, Greg and I both led that man to Christ. Praise the Lord!

One afternoon my friends Jill and David Lance went with me to downtown Brooklyn. Jill, wearing thick glasses, was a brain! And David, her husband, was the music director at Grace Baptist Church. Both had a desire to win people to Christ and were very concerned about the direction our nation seemed to be heading. They loved animals and had kept our dachshund, Buster, on several occasions.

As I was preaching hard and gesturing, I knocked my glasses off with my left hand. Both lenses went skidding onto the pavement into my crowd. Yes, I was embarrassed! But my audience stayed with me, perhaps feeling sorry for "that old man"!

Driving home later, we all laughed at my clumsiness. Then, we all began to sing "You Are My Sunshine," which made stopping and starting in that heavy traffic seem easier. "Jill," I asked, "do you remember when you and Ron King were with George and me, and the cops made us move away from the subway entrance? We rolled my rig right down the middle of the sidewalk with my sketch board wide open. That thing was four feet wide; all the paints were open. People must have thought we were nuts! Remember?"

"I remember," replied Jill, laughing out loud as she slapped her knees!

Preaching the gospel in other countries had become my focus, but I constantly thought about New York, and ever since I left New York, there had not been one Friday night that I had not thought about Times Square. I guess I always would.

CHAPTER 60

PERHAPS, MAYBE

When I first started preaching, my pastor at Waller Baptist Church, Brother Stogner, said to me, "Remember, Scotty, ministry is not buildings, budgets, or baptisms. It's people." Well, after proclaiming the gospel for years and years, my ministry certainly had not been buildings. Even though I had worked to build up the kingdom of God, I had not erected any steepled edifices of brick and mortar. My ministry had not been budgets. Our budget had never been large; our finances had been recorded the old-fashioned way, by hand. My ministry had not been baptisms. I had baptized some folks, but, like the apostle Paul, I had always felt "Christ sent me not to baptize but to preach the gospel" (1 Corinthians 1:17). My ministry had been delivering the basic evangelistic message to relatively small groups of people, live, face to face, who were difficult to reach by any other means.

As I had looked into various faces and declared the good news, I had sensed that the Holy Spirit was speaking to people in that very moment. I had asked God to let me preach to tons of unconverted people, and the Lord had granted that request, giving me the opportunity to spread the gospel from little mud huts in Uganda to Manhattan skyscrapers. The Lord knew that I had endeavored to pour my life into others so that my ministry would have a ripple effect and touch lives in the future. But God also knew my faults, my weaknesses, my regrets, my sins. Yes, God knew my heart, and we both knew that at best I was "an unprofitable servant" (Luke 17:10).

What did I have to show for my ministry? Not much. Sure, I had preached to thousands of lost people, but where were the converts? I had seen countless "decisions for Christ," but could I put my hand on any of them? A few, maybe, but not very many. Had I wasted my life? Had my ministry been disappearing smoke?

Sometimes these thoughts haunted me. But I always came back to the fact that God's word "would not return void." That's what the Lord said, and God knew that I had preached his word. I had not watered it down or changed it to make it more palatable; I had, with the ability God had given me, tried to be faithful to the message of the gospel and to declare it, like it is. That I knew. Because I had complete confidence in the power of the gospel and the word of God, I knew, without any doubt in my mind, that some people had been saved. Just how many, only God knew. Through the years, however, the Lord had led many people back to me who had told me that they had been converted through my preaching, and I was thankful to God for confirming his word.

Every once in a while somebody would say to me, "Well, Scotty, there will be a lot of people in heaven because of your ministry." Perhaps, maybe.

Dr. Martin Luther King Jr.'s famous words were "I have a dream." Well, I too have a dream, or maybe I should use the word "hope." Now I don't just *hope* that I'm saved. I *know* that I'm saved, by the grace of God. I know that one glorious morning when I cross over Jordan and step on those streets of gold, the first person I'll see will be Jesus. I cannot wait to see him smiling, and I cannot wait to look into those kind eyes of his. Will I hear him say, "Well done, thou good and faithful servant"? Perhaps, maybe.

Then I hope someone will come running up to me and say, "Scotty, I got saved one day on Fordham Road in the Bronx. You never knew about me. You assumed that your meeting was a bummer." I hope to hear someone say, "Glory to God! I came to know the Lord Jesus Christ at one of your street meetings at Times Square." Perhaps, maybe.

I hope to see all of those who had supported us with their prayer and finances. I hope to see rewards, huge rewards, hung around their necks. And, if I could, I'd like to be able to carry each one around on my shoulders and shout to all of heaven that these were the ones who made it possible, humanly speaking, for me to preach the gospel. Perhaps, maybe, I'll be able to do that.

I hope to see Madsu, the Muslim, clothed in Christ's righteousness instead of in that white robe and cap that he always wore around. Wouldn't it be great to look up in heaven and see that gypsy woman from Ukraine, the one waving at me with the ducks around her feet the last time I saw her? I hope to see that little girl with the deformed face in the Philippines. Only now in heaven, she would probably be a grown, beautiful woman with a new, glorious face! Perhaps, maybe. Wouldn't it be awesome to have someone say, "You know, I was in the World Trade Center on 9/11, but I had been saved at one of your sidewalk meetings earlier, so thank you for being in the financial district that day." I hope to see the guy who had AIDS who was straddling his bike on Fourteenth Street, only now he wouldn't have that dreaded disease but would have a nice, new body, perfect like Jesus's glorious body. Perhaps, maybe.

I hope to see the kid that was in the wheelchair at the Fort Worth Stock Show, the one whose mother, year after year, pushed him up close in order for him to see me shoot the bow; only now he would be smiling, standing beside his loving mother, and the wheelchair would not be seen anywhere and would never be needed anymore, ever. It would make my first day in heaven to see those two Catholic nuns who stood in that loud noise at the Houston Stock Show, helping me get a crowd.

Perhaps, maybe, our Japanese tour guide will be there. And that African chief in Ghana, sitting in his big chair, the one who gave me permission to enter his villages and who listened to me closely when I told him about Christ dying on the cross for him—perhaps he will be praising the King of Kings around his throne. Worthy is the Lamb!

Then, perhaps, I'll turn and hear that laugh—"Hey, hey! I made it!" That could only be one person—Janet Raines. Oh, I hope to see her smiling in heaven. She might even be driving a golden chariot, only better than she did that Hyundai stick shift! What a hug she would get from Linda and me.

Only God knows who will be in heaven, because only he knows people's hearts. He knows if someone truly repents and believes in the Lord Jesus Christ. Our records, membership rolls, and statistics mean nothing. Only God knows whose names are written in the Lamb's book of life. I don't know the people who were truly converted to Christ as a result of my ministry. Will there be many? Perhaps, maybe.

I do know that whatever was done, God did it.

APPENDIX

A Brief History of Open Air Preaching

Open air preaching has been an effective method of evangelism throughout history. In the Old Testament there are many instances of outdoor preaching. Beneath the "unpillared arch of heaven" Noah warned of coming doom. Joshua gathered all the tribes of Israel to Shechem and cried, "Choose you this day whom ye will serve" (Joshua 24:15). Samuel preached in the thunder and rain at Gilgal (1 Samuel 12:18). Elijah stood at Mount Carmel and shouted, "How long halt ye between two opinions?" (1 Kings 18:21). Ezra, Nehemiah, and Jonah all preached the message of God in the great out of doors. Charles Spurgeon said, "Indeed, we find examples of open air preaching everywhere around us in the records of the Old Testament" (C. H. Spurgeon, *Lectures to My Students*, volume 2, page 92).

In New Testament times, most of the preaching was done out of doors. John the Baptist declared, "Repent, for the kingdom of heaven is at hand" (Matthew 3:2). He preached to massive crowds in the wilderness of Judea. "Jesus was to all intents and purposes an open air preacher. His great Sermon on the Mount was delivered under the blue canopy of heaven. The hillside, the fisherman's boat, the Galilean Road, the slopes of Olivet, and in many other places outside the walls of the synagogue our Lord preached the good news of the kingdom of God" (Spurgeon, *Lectures*, volume 2, page 92). The apostle Peter preached his magnificent sermon at Pentecost in the large, outdoor Court of the Gentiles. The church at Jerusalem, having suffered a great persecution, was scattered, and Luke says, "They that were scattered abroad went everywhere preaching the word" (Acts 9:4). Paul preached anywhere he could gain a crowd—in the streets, at Mars Hill, and at the marketplace (Acts 17).

In the early Christian centuries (AD 100–400), from Clement of Rome to Chrysostom, open air preaching was powerful and influential. However, church buildings developed in the fourth century (Edwin Charles Dargan, *A History of Preaching,* volume 1, page 67), and many of the church fathers delivered their messages indoors.

During the Middle Ages (AD 400–1500) there are few traces of open air preaching. Rome was in control, and the church gradually declined. But when Saint Francis of Assisi (1182–1226) began preaching in the streets, no longer was the gospel of Christ to be imprisoned within stone walls (James Burns, *Revivals: Their Laws and Leaders,* pages 93–94). Dominicas of Spain (1170–1221) gathered crowds in the marketplace by raising the cross, and then he proclaimed the gospel.

During the fourteenth century, outdoor preaching prepared the way for the Protestant Reformation. John Wycliffe (1324–1384) and his "poor preachers," who came to be known as Lollards, preached everywhere in the open air.

During the Protestant Reformation (the sixteenth century), we read of Martin Luther (1483–1546), Savonarola, and John Knox declaring in the great out of doors the glorious good news. It's interesting that the English Baptist preacher John Bunyan (1628–1688) was arrested and imprisoned for preaching out of doors and for holding religious meetings without the permission of the state church. While Bunyan was a prisoner for preaching outside, he wrote his immortal book, *The Pilgrim's Progress.*

During the eighteenth century, open air preaching reached its peak in both England and America. In England, George Whitefield (1714–1770) and John Wesley (1703–1791) spearheaded the evangelical awakening in Britain (1738–1791). Their main method of evangelism was "field (open air) preaching." When Whitefield first mentioned outdoor preaching to some of his friends, they thought it was a "mad notion" (George Whitefield: Field Preacher, James Paterson Gledstone, page 71). F. R. Webber, in *A History of Preaching in Britain and America,* says, "When George Whitefield took his stand in the open air on February 17, 1739, the first note of the great evangelical awakening was sounded" (volume 1, page 341). John Wesley preached for half a century in the open air. "To this day field preaching is a cross to me. But I know my commission and see no other way of preaching the gospel to every creature" (*The Journal of John Wesley*, page 331).

In the First Great Awakening in America (1726–1750), outdoor preaching was done everywhere. Gilbert Tennent (1703–1764) preached out of doors throughout the colonies. Even though Jonathan Edwards (1703–1758) preached his famous sermon "Sinners in the Hands of an Angry God" indoors, his writings talk about the great movement of God in the out of doors. The churches could not accommodate the crowds that came to hear George Whitefield, so he preached in the open air in America, just as he had done in England.

In nineteenth-century Britain, preaching out of doors was rampant in the Grassroots Revival of 1859–1860. "The reports of revival activity are so replete with accounts of open air work that to attempt to sketch the development of open-air evangelism seems futile" (J. Edwin Orr, *The Second Evangelical Awakening in Britain*, pages 214–15). William Booth (1829–1912) and the Salvation Army zealously carried forward the Grassroots Revival of 1858–59. He and the army held open air services all over London. Charles Spurgeon (1834–1892) preached to thousands on the London Commons (Mendell Taylor, *Exploring Evangelism,* page 322).

In nineteenth-century America, there were numerous preachers on the frontier who journeyed from place to place preaching the gospel of Christ. These "circuit riders" preached much of the time in the open air. The circuit rider system gave rise to the innovation of the camp meetings, of which outdoor preaching was a main feature. This led to the Second Great Awakening in America (1795–1842). We read of Barton Stone, Bishop Francis Asbury, and Peter Cartwright all preaching in the out of doors.

During the first part of the twentieth century, outdoor preaching was very prevalent in both Britain and America. Parties of eight to ten pushed and pulled carts, carrying the basic minimum requirements of life. They lived simply and slept where they could, holding open air meetings on the village green, the town square, the beach, the racetrack, the fairgrounds.

Hundreds of street preachers carried the gospel throughout the land. In America, R. A. Torrey (1856–1928) often preached in the open air, as well as Gypsy Smith (1860–1947) and Henry Ironside (1876–1951). Billy Sunday (1862–1935) was converted as a result of a street meeting conducted by the Pacific Garden Mission in Chicago.

The "gospel wagon" was also employed. This was a horse-drawn wagon covered with Bible verses. Several Christians could ride in the gospel wagon. Some were singers; others gave their testimonies. Preachers took turns sharing the gospel in parks, on city streets, at rodeos, and at fairs. Sometimes Bibles were sold for financial support. Many rescue missions had gospel wagons. Melvin Trotter, who conducted open air meetings with gospel wagons that were connected to rescue missions, once said, "We can trace hundreds of conversions to our work in the street" (Melvin Trotter, *These Forty Years*, page 57).

Bible Institutes across the country required students to do open air work. In rural communities "brush arbor" meetings drew the unchurched to hear the gospel. But as giant strides were made in transportation and communication during the latter part of the twentieth century, outdoor preaching waned. Many ministers who formally preached on the streets began preaching on the radio and then on television.

Still, there were some who continued to preach the gospel in the out of doors. The Open Air Campaigners and the Pocket Testament League were two organizations dedicated to taking the gospel to the lost and unchurched.

The ministry of Billy Graham (1918–) is saturated with open air preaching—in giant outdoor stadiums, in parks, on beaches, and on downtown streets. Graham filled Trafalgar Square during his

1954 Greater London Crusade, and then forty thousand crowded into Hyde Park to hear him preach (Cott Flint, *The Quotable Billy Graham*, page 244). In New York in 1957, Billy Graham preached in the open air at Times Square under the lights of Broadway. "The people stretched from shoulder to shoulder as far as the eye could see" (John Pollock, *Billy Graham: The Authorized Biography*, page 184).

Stephen Olford (1918–2004), the pastor of the prestigious Calvary Baptist Church in Manhattan, often preached the gospel in the open air at Columbus Circle. Author Blessitt, who has carried a wooden cross literally around the world, constantly preaches in the open air.

Donald Soper (1903–1998), the prominent Methodist minister in London, preached at Speakers Corner in Hyde Park for years on Sunday afternoon. Today, there are many other Christian preachers who preach out of doors in Hyde Park.

Through the centuries there have been untold numbers of dedicated ministers who have dared to preach the gospel out of doors in an attempt to evangelize those who were not in church. Many of them have labored under extremely difficult circumstances, often being misunderstood and viewed with contempt. Still, they have been faithful in declaring the gospel of the Lord Jesus Christ. Their names and faces are known only to God. May their reward be great in heaven!

The incomparable Charles Spurgeon once said, "What the world would have been if there had not been preaching outside of walls, and beneath a more glorious roof then these rafters of fir, I am sure I cannot guess" (Spurgeon, *Lectures*, volume 11, page 108).

About the Author

Scott Teague of Chester, Arkansas, has pastored, ministered at carnivals and fairs, and preached the gospel on the streets of New Your City for more than twenty-six years, as well as in numerous countries around the world. He holds a bachelor of arts degree from Louisiana Tech University, a bachelor of divinity degree (equivalent to the master of divinity) and a master's degree in theology from Southwestern Baptist Theological Seminary. He and his wife, Linda, have two grown, married sons and four grandchildren.